AF333602

NEW YEAR 2018,
FOR LUCY AND DERRICK
COLLEAGUES FRIENDS AND
FAMILY,

FROM
LAURIN RAIKEN
STUDENT AND
FRIEND OF
LÉO BRONSTEIN

# Romantic Homage

*My*

# to Greece and Spain

*Fable. Their Art*

*By*

Léo Bronstein

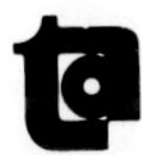

Transaction Publishers
New Brunswick (U.S.A.) and London (U.K.)

Library of Congress Catalog Number: 93–9949
ISBN: 1–56000–117–8
Printed in the United States of America

Library of Congress Cataloging-in-Publications Data

Bronstein, Léo.
Romantic Homage to Greece and Spain / My Fable. Their Art / Léo Bronstein.
p. cm.
Includes bibliographical references.
ISBN 1–56000–117–8
1. Art—Mediterranean Region. 2. Art, Spanish. 3. Art, Greek.
I. Title.
N7258.B76 1993
709—dc20

93–9949
CIP
r93

# *Publications of Léo Bronstein*

*Lutte et réconciliation: Essai sur la manifestation du réel dans l'art,* Paris, Felix Alcan, 1927

*Altichiero: L'Homme et son oeuvre,* Paris, J. Vrin, 1932

*El Greco,* New York, Harry N. Abrams, 1950

*Fragments of Life, Metaphysics and Art,* New York, Bond Wheelwright, 1953

*Five Variations on the Theme of Japanese Painting,* Freeport, Maine, Bond Wheelwright, 1969

*Kabbalah and Art,* Waltham, Mass., Brandeis University Press, Distributed by the University Press of New England, 1979

*Romantic Homage to Greece and Spain/My Fable. Their Art.* Transaction Publishers, New Brunswick (U.S.A.) London (U.K.), 1993.

The chapters "Decorative Woodwork of the Islamic Period" and "Enamel," in *A Survey of Persian Art,* ed. Arthur Upham Pope–Phyllis Ackerman (London and New York, Oxford University Press) Vol. III, 1937

"Research Program of the Institute—The Documentary Survey," *Bulletin of the American Institute for Persian Art and Archaeology,* Vol. I, no. 6 (1934), 16–17; IV, 3 (1936), 153–58; V, I (1937), 42–46

"Space Forms in Persian Miniature Composition," *Bulletin of the American Institute for Persian Art and Archaeology,* Vol. IV, no. I (1935), 15–28

"Some Historical Problems Raised by a Group of Iranian Islamic Potteries," *Bulletin of the American Institute for Persian Art and Archaeology,* Vol. V, no. 3 (1938), 225–35

# Contents

Dedicated to my daughter Ariana
in memory of my brother Léo

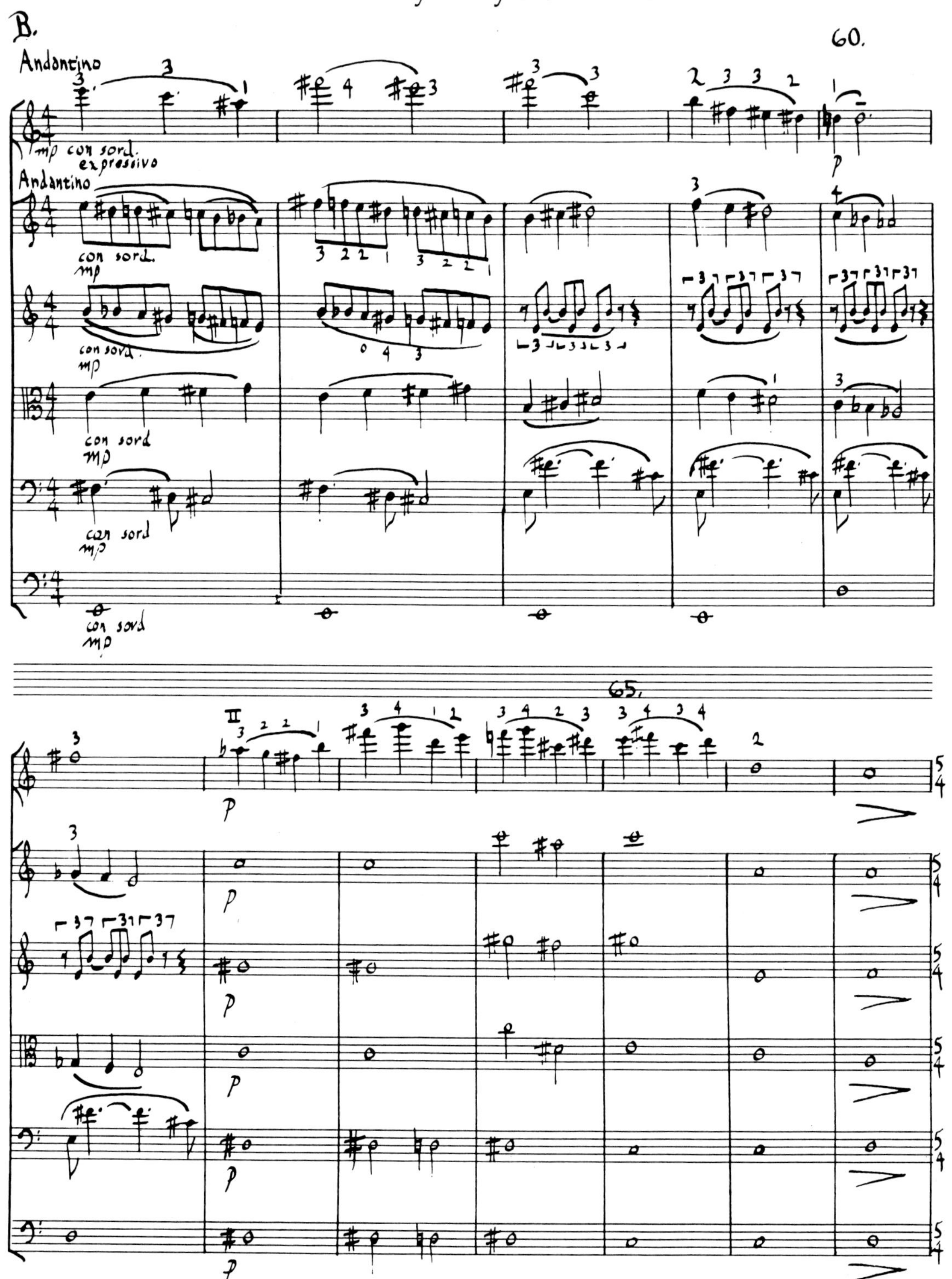

# *Acknowledgments*

"THEIR LIVING ART." The last words of this book. Words written in the knowledge that the art would go on and he would not. But Léo Bronstein does go on, in his own art of seeing, letting us see, the life of their art, making it more ours than it could ever have been without him. And so, of these acknowledgments, the first must be made to him.

Second only to these, the reader's thanks as well as the editor's must go to Raphael Bronstein and his daughter Ariana Bronne. Raphael, an inspiration in his field, the violin, was better known than his brother Léo in his; he added another beautiful dimension to the book with his music; quietly, patiently, he and Ariana helped pay the expenses of preparing for publication. Helping them to help, tireless in the tiresome tasks of liaison, accounting and all the detail involved, was Jean Matin, Raphael's friend and Léo's for a lifetime; there is no way she could be thanked as she deserves.

Assistance in checking references, obtaining illustrations and permissions to quote, editing text—every bit of it was indispensable. It seems best then that the rest of these thanks, fervent all, be in alphabetical order.

Annika Barbarigos and Bro Uttal were with Léo on the last of his journeys in preparation for *Homage.* The bond of friendship made smooth the ways; the bond of understanding gave Anika's photographs their special relevance. Without the boxfuls of slides and documentation gathered for Léo in New York as well as abroad, and the hours given me to identify it all, it would have been impossible after Léo's death to turn his ms. into this book.

Dr. Ted Feder had much admired earlier work of Léo's; when we turned to his Art Resource for visual material he was more than generous in supplying not only that but his firm's research facilities as well; of great help in this was the friendly interest of Lisa Polenberg, Dr. Feder's then research assistant.

We are grateful to Valentine de France for her permission to reproduce photos by her late father, Georges de Miré, from Pierre de la Coste-Messelière's *The Treasures of Delphi.*

Bertrand Michel was similarly kind in allowing us to quote from *The Frescoes of Tavant* by his father, Paul-Henri Michel.

Lucas Myers, editor by profession, gave essential guidance in the preparation of copy; he made a style sheet masterly in reconciling authorial idiosyncrasies with publishing practice; he did a massive job of checking quotes; above all else was his sympathetic loyality to the text.

Robert Pomerance has from the first given warm and benevolent legal guidance.

Professor Laurin Raiken, once a student of Léo's and now Director, the Arts and Society Program of New York University's Gallatin Division, has each year introduced his students to Léo's work; he has over the years brought together those who wished to promote Léo's books and those who could; it was he who proposed—and Gallatin's first Dean Herbert I. London who in his perspicacity brought to being at Gallatin—the *Léo Bronstein Homage Fund* of which Laurin is administrator.

Raymond Schrag for many months was cheerfully supportive in exercising his attorney's art to help establish the fund at New York University.

Kathryn Soman, checking sources and procuring illustrations, continued and completed the work of her predecessors; in this as well as copy editing and vast correspondence her help has been inestimable, her dedication a tribute in itself to Léo's work.

Ever pleasant and unflaggingly helpful has been the staff of the New York Public Library, especially in its Arts Division.

Thea Wheelwright has published two previous books of Léo's; for *Homage*, as for those, it was she who determined the format. Helping her to ready the book for the printer was Marvin McKay of

Pine Tree Composition; even more than for his professional expertise we are grateful for his friendly caring attitude. Without Thea Wheelwright of the Kennebec River Press *Homage* in its present form would not exist: in overall design as in typographical detail she has embodied Léo's thought. Here, as from the first, she has shown a love, a devotion, an understanding to be found nowhere else.

Eleanor L. Wolff, editor

# *Foreword*

There have always been strong ties between Spain and Greece. They consist of historical coincidences, emotional and temperamental affinities and even the similarities of the cadences and rhythms of the Greek and Spanish languages. They are two countries situated at the extreme outer limits of Europe—Janus-faced nations in a sense, with one eye on the continent of which they are physically a part and another on a more exotic and alluring continent. In the case of Spain there is much of the African in the blood and the collective subconscious of its citizens. In the case of Greece, Asian attitudes, Asian mysticism and, indeed, Asiatic mystery lurk just below the skin—just below the surface of the Greek earth.

Both of these countries have experienced "Golden Ages" of incredible wealth and splendor. The Classical and Hellenistic periods for Greece and the age of the Baroque—the seventeenth century in the case of Spain—witnessed these respective nations as virtual masters of the known world, setting the standards for culture, as well as ruling with an authority and toughness thought unchallengeable until certain tragic flaws began to make themselves known and eventually caused a weakening and final *Dämmerung*, after which the fortunes of these two great lands fell precipitately into a state of lassitude and malaise.

It is easy to understand the cultural comprehension that some Greeks have had of Spain and some Spaniards of Greece. In the early 1930s the great Greek novelist and poet Nikos Kazantzakis travelled throughout the Iberian peninsula recording his impressions of the country in a diary, later published under the title *Spain.* It is a unique testimony to the innate affinity of an artist for a culture foreign to his own yet related in an inextricable way to his sensibilities. One of the most moving passages in this book is Kazantzakis' description of women in a darkened church kneeling in prayer. It is worth reproducing in this context as it seems to capture the essence of Spain and the Spanish "soul" better than do descriptions in all the travel accounts of Iberia by many writers—from Mme. d'Aulnoy in the seventeenth century to James Michener in the twentieth:

> In the shadowy light of the Cathedral, I contemplated the women kneeling and praying for hours on end, their wrists crossed, like crucified figures themselves. Other women came in from the market with their shopping in their hands: vegetables, a melon, a fishtail sticking out of their baskets. They held them tightly, like their own child, and stared at the Christ on bended knees, overcome by feeling. Surely in a moment all women are transformed to mothers mourning their child. This is the oldest, deepest aspect, most truly their own. But here in Spain the expression on their faces is more primitive, more bitter. The face of the Spanish woman seems to have captured its genuine hypersensual essence: suffering and death. How God becomes man inside the womb of woman, this simplest of mysteries, one sees here in Spain with a shudder of awe.

One of the friends of Kazantzakis in Spain was the extraordinary novelist and philosopher Miguel de Unamuno. Unamuno was Professor of Greek at the University of Salamanca. In his own writings his intimate knowledge of Greece, Greek culture and Greek language is often present. His homage to Greece was paid in a long poem in which he borrowed verses from the writings of one of his favorite contemporary writers, Kostis Palamas.

* * *

Léo Bronstein was neither Greek nor Spanish. Nonetheless, he immersed himself deeply in the cultural and emotional roots of both these nations. Although much of his intellectual effort was directed toward deciphering the mysteries of Persian art, his affinities for Spanish and Greek painting (and the cultures that produced them) were obviously of passionate importance to him. As a historian of Spanish art, I was first introduced to Bronstein through his book on El Greco (1950). It is not art historical writing in the conventional sense, but something quite different and intriguing. Bronstein's book on this most complex of Mannerist painters is actually an emotional biography / autobiography of both the artist and the writer. Its analyses of Greco's cultural roots and the transformations brought about by his move to Spain are masterful. At the same time, the author is able to evoke the atmosphere of these two places in a most moving way. A brief quotation from Bronstein's description of one of El Greco's most extraordinary paintings, the *View of Toledo* (c. 1610), at the Metropolitan Museum of Art, New York, will suffice to evoke the descriptive powers of this author:

> Never has such a landscape been painted. And yet all the simplest and usual elements of a landscape painting are there: sky, hills, a city, the deep gorge of a river, trees, meadows, roads. But the main thing is missing: the feeling of space, of distance. Dominant, instead, is what in painting is usually conveyed by the human figure only: the feeling of activity, of drama. The sky is rent catastrophically in a chaotic rush of its clouds: while the earth dashes to meet it in an upward surge. The movement of the hilly roads, now crossing each other, now separating, form a curious ornamental and active pattern of interlaced triangles. There is a strange rearrangement of the topography of Toledo . . . The city is presented both full face . . . and in profile . . . Did El Greco tell us here, in this reconstructed image of Toledo, his own myth and his own judgment of the nearest-to-heaven powers of earth? Is this a mysterious portrait

of the inner man's crime of power, with punishment—and redemption—in it?

Bronstein has been able to give full vent to his passion for Greece and Spain in the present volume. The reader must be warned. It is not an easy book to read. It is sometimes dense and opaque—an interior monologue on a theme of passionate obsession. Bronstein's imagination and fantasy are given a wide-open stage. However, for the reader whose passions and obsessions—or whose intellectual interests—encompass the theme of this volume, reading *Romantic Homage to Greece and Spain* can be an extraordinary experience.

Professor Edward J. Sullivan
Chairman
Department of Fine Arts
New York University

Glossary. Castilian equivalents of Catalan forms:

| | |
|---|---|
| Carrer del Comtes | Calle de los Condes |
| Consellers | Consejeros |
| llotje | lonja |
| Priorat | Priorato |
| Sant Climent de Taüll | San Clemente de Tahúll |
| Sant Iu | San Ivo |
| Santa Maria de Taüll | Santa María de Tahúll |
| Santa Maria del Mar | Santa María del Mar |
| Santa Maria del Pí | Santa María del Pino |
| Sant Pau del Camp | San Pablo del Campo |
| Sant Pere de Galligans | San Pedro de Galligans |
| Thessaloniki | Salonica |

# *Prologue*

*One more tale, the last one,*
*And this chronicle of mine is finished.*
*Fulfilled the task ordained me by God,*
*Me, a sinner . . .*

Pimen, in Pushkin's *Boris Godunov,*
Scene 5 (Translation Léo Bronstein)

INDEED: One more tale to tell and my Chronicle shall be finished. Old Pimen, the monk of a new age—yours—I am. Old, very old now, writing at the edge of night's and day's light in my silent cell, loving its stillness, loving its silence and the silenced memory of what lives in it.

For, once, long ago, when young and walking along life's ways of tumult and noise, I met great, important and strange beings and great, important and strange events.

And now I am telling their story, a true and great and strange story. Not of kings and princes and of their ministers, their armies, their ancestors and progenitures, or of their strifes, murders, repentances and loves; not of the comedy of life, but of the tragedy of life and the glory of God in it. I, the eyewitness and the new monk of a new age, I am telling you the tale of lordly beings, of their deeds in mind's body.

And:

*God guard me from those thoughts men think*
*In the mind alone*
*He that sings a lasting song*
*Thinks in a marrow-bone.*[1]

Yeats's last prayer. And mine too—for the souls of all people-thoughts, ancient and young, my contemporaries all known to me in my mind's hand, my mind's eye, ear, taste, smell and thought.

And thus I enter into the last tale—the last intrigue—of my chronicle, the tale of beings-ideas, beings-monuments, beings-people at once: the tale of Art.

And who, I wonder, will read or listen to this tale of metaphysics, of life and of art told anew? I wonder. Young people, I suppose.

For youth is what cannot—does not want to—separate. Ideas and bodies are one for them. Two are as one. Presence of adhesion. Immediate. *Touch.*

Mature age cannot but separate. The one is as two. Presence of cohesion. Mediate.

Listen, young people: The song in marrow-bone.

# I

*Córdoba.*
*Lejana y sola.*

*Jaca negra, luna grande,*
*y aceitunas en mi alforja.*
*Aunque sepa los caminos*
*y nunca llegare a Córdoba.*

*Por el llano, por el viento,*
*jaca negra, luna roja,*
*La muerte me está mirando*
*desde las torres de Córdoba.*

*¡Ay que camino tan largo!*
*¡Ay mi jaca valerosa!*
*¡Ay que la muerte me espera,*
*antes de llegar a Córdoba!*

*Córdoba,*
*Lejana y sola.*[2]

Death. Looking at me. From the towers of Cordoba: *my* living, future tale looking at death up there, up on the towers of Cordoba. Looking at another's death: at death not as if at life and thought and expectation, inevitable, impossible, yet to be reborn; not as if at some unachieved agonies of death, nameless, faceless, mindless and graceless; but at death one with fear and desire and pride and yearning and knowledge (right conduct: *¡Ay que camino tan largo!/¡Ay mi jaca valerosa!*)—the heraldic death, I say: body's *pride,* soul's *pudeur,* mind's *play. ¡Ay que la muerte me espera,/antes de llegar a Córdoba!*

Heraldic: the deadly fear of dying anonymous—me, a part of my clan, thus not me any more—nothing, anything!—at the bloody battlefield; the pride then and the plenty, at dying assured, heraldically: individuated, signaled—I, Me.

With no explanations from me, thank God: my fame as a Chronicler came, it is true, late to me in my life, but came finally. My explanations are known now and easily to be found by all those who wish it—in my other, older tales. Tales of the Heraldic man and his secret deeds and monuments in us, of the Apocalyptic man in us, the punishing and rewarding lord, and his inevitable deeds and monuments; of the free, or Psychomachic man, the evil-fighting knight in us—of his deeds and monuments, impossible yet freely chosen and built. And more: of how, grieving over the fallen bodies of so many feal and blood-related warriors, the two great lords of the medieval—heraldic—mind, often rivals, the youthful *Accident* and the venerable old *Essence* became—enlightened there—blood brothers and allies; and how, the same memorable day, at the same battlefield the haughty leader of all of us, Lord *Substance,* was deadly wounded, and how his humble and honest vassal, the knight *Structure,* was chosen the Leader of all . . . Now, all of them—Presences only. Beings = Presences.

And so, this last tale of mine becomes and remains simply the why and where I have met each and all of them—my own looking and my own witnessing:

*Córdoba.*
*Lejana y sola.*

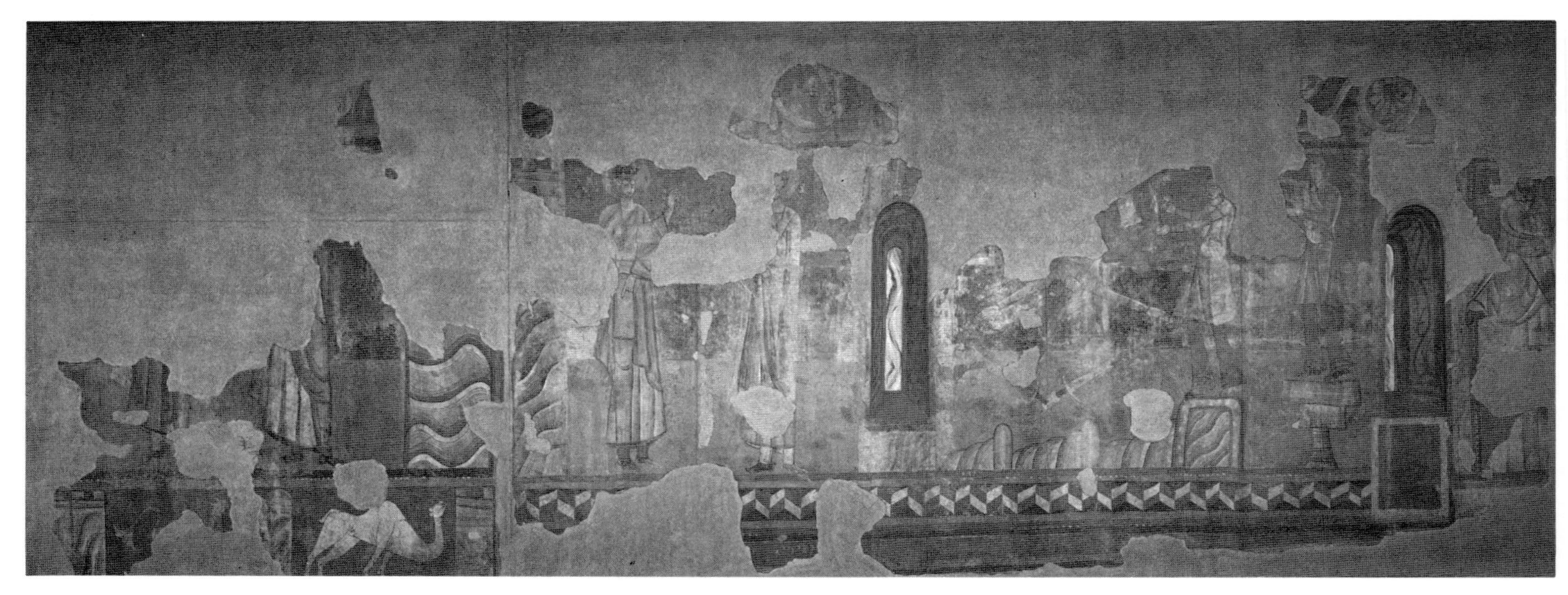

1. Acrobats, or *Jongleurs,* wall painting from San Juan de Bohí

# Part I

# Eros, the Ancestor

IT ALL STARTED with the *Jongleurs,* the Catalan fresco, now in Barcelona (*Plate 1*). *It:* my tale's intrigue of dissent, contacts, unions between my questions and no-answering, my answers and no-questions, between Presences and my witnessing. But the Ancestor—the Ancestress—of the *It,* the Ancient one, I met much earlier in life. I vividly recall that distant day. A hot July afternoon in Avignon. At the Papal palace. Close to my eye was the heat and the fatigue of the river below, and the tall hills of Provence beyond. I looked, leaning on the long wall of the ample terrace. And saw the mountain in closed distance: it was sick, very sick, with heat and fatigue, feverish, gasping. Above it I saw the descending day's sky placing on the feverish summit its cool promise of relief—the ardor of blue, slowly muted, now pale gold, now pale blue and very light purple.

In all the earnestness of youth, I saw a friend's hand on a sick and burning forehead. I saw unmistakably there the *solitude* of that mountain summit and the *solitude* of the sky too, total, absolute. And I saw their *solidarity,* total, absolute. Not solitude *and* solidarity. Not solitude *or* solidarity. But Solitude-Solidarity: the new adventure chanted by new poets.

That is how, that is where, I saw—and recognized at once—the Ancestor. Of all presences and events and of my witnessing.

Solitude-Solidarity in the high lands: in the world of the Prime Mover of stars, planets, Milky Ways, of all Ways still to be found.

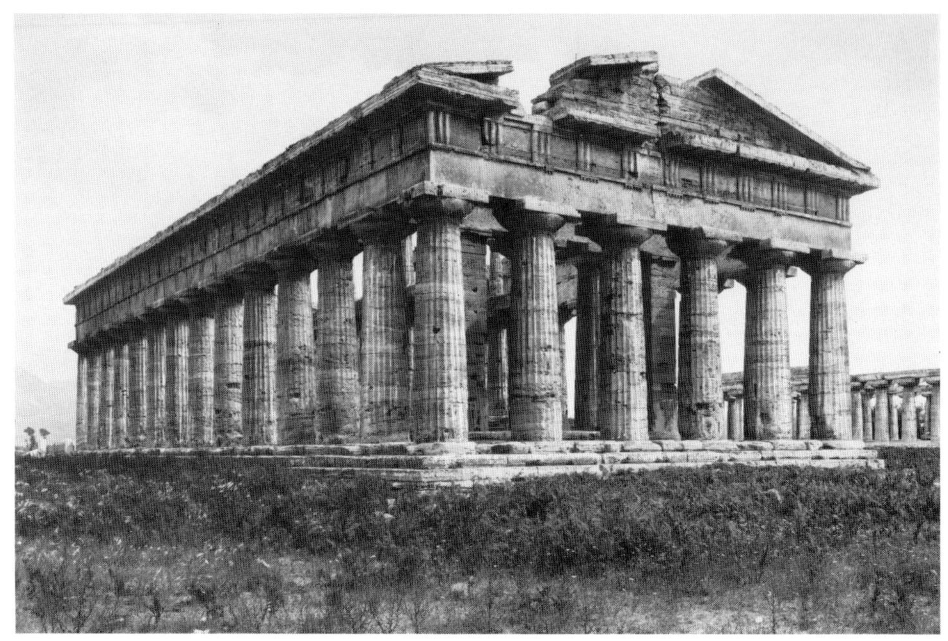

2. Temple of Poseidon, Paestum

Solitude-Solidarity in the low lands: the acts of thought (substances and structures or forms; accidents or the transient, and essences, or the permanent); the acts of body (pleasure-pain in all its explosions: sex, viruses, light). Not love. For love is still Solitude-and-or-Solidarity of love-hatred. But *Tendresse.* To be Solitude-Solidarity is to be *Tendresse.*

*

At the beginning was *Tendresse:* the Ancient Ancestor of the Intrigue among beings=ideas, beings=monuments, my no-questioning no-answering, my being-witnessing.

For *Tendresse,* the Solitude-Solidarity of man-in-the-world is itself this very Intrigue. Indeed, how could a feeling, a transient accident of *Tendresse,* even as young and assertive as mine in Avignon, become a conviction, a permanence, a proof? I still question this—still today.

How could Solitude-Solidarity be two separated entities (which they are ''in mind's thought only'') and be at once (as they are in the ''marrow-bone'' thought) their equation?

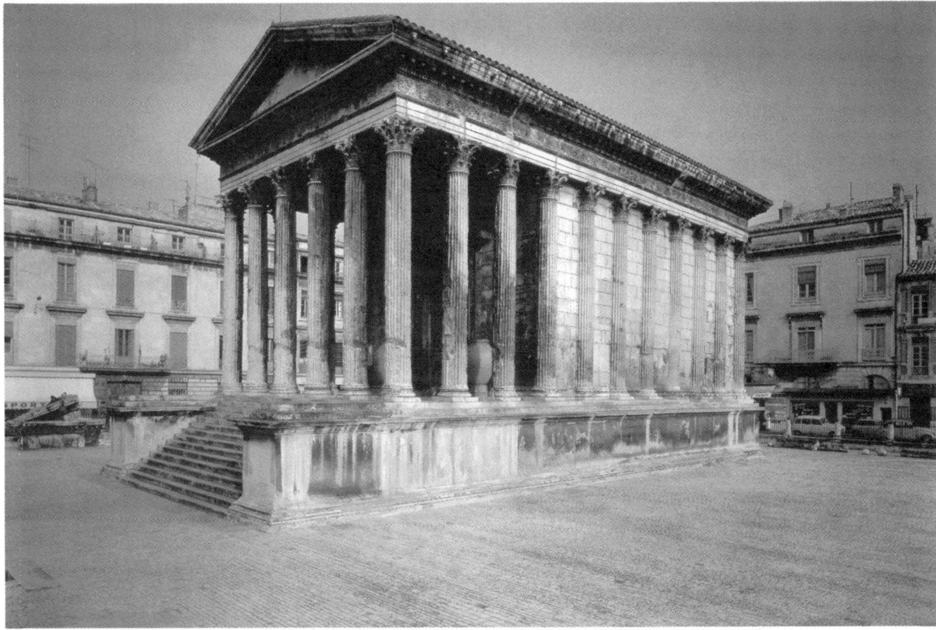

3. Maison Carrée, Nîmes

And how could the Ancient's Intrigue be inherited by all his children and children's children?

Here is what his youngest child and my acquaintance of later years, Dame Architecture, once told me of her own destiny, her history. "See," she said, "my Doric Temple—Doric Greece!—the proud, not haughty, columnar gait-and-support of its own incurved world and sensitivity; its columnar envelope allowing penetration anywhere on all of its four sides, a finite, self-enveloped, thus isolated entity (*Plate* 2). Solitude of the Greek temple, solitude of a Greek figure—the inexorable finity of Greek meditation, of Greek exaltation also: 'Good is what is finite, Evil is what is infinite.'!

"And, facing it, the solidarity in ancient Rome's creations: the Roman-Etruscan temple—Greece's young relative—its guiding frontal access, stepped and exclusive, continued into the open columnar porch, to be further continued into the in-walled, half-hidden columnar envelope of its sanctuary (*Plate* 3)!

"And this Roman continuity of one architectural element into another (including Rome's great urban compounds)—how structurally homonymous with that of the Near East, Rome's oldest realtive! Solitude of Classical Greek 'stability,' or the living permanence of a total, finished being; solidarity of Roman-Oriental 'mobility,' or the living continuity of becoming—are they two opposite actors on the stage of your Intrigue? Yes, if comprehended as two independent and related facts, as *links* of a chain of facts-and-influences: the Greek temple, the Roman temple. No, if seized in vision's and mind's dual truth, as one and the same historical attitude; as one dominant historical cycle—the bunching of facts-and-influences into one global cycle-attitude, built here, and evolved, around an historically chosen engineering-aesthetical device: Antiquity's post-and-lintel and its primacy.

"And the same with the next—not isolated from the former, but cotangent with it—architectural cycle-attitude, the dramatic 'intrigue' of the restless arch, the (overlapping later Roman antiquity) medieval cycle, *par excellence:* the *central,* metaphysical, stability of the all-encompassing cupola—Solitude!—the *centered,* metaphysical mobility of the continuous vault—the slow emergence and the final culmination of the interlocking groined, pointed vaults, the complete, subtle, and so liberating energies of the young Gothic: Solidarity!"

And, after having seen how good were her creations, Dame Architecture sat herself down, she told me, rested and meditated. A new column-and-arch encompassing rhythm of stability-mobility, a new cycle-attitude—still in the midst of the polyphonic audacities of late Gothic—was the result of this intense recollection and meditation: the centered-"stabile" Renaissance, the expanded "mobile" Baroque. "Then," she said, "I arose again. And my new work began. From the depth of the architectural past I evoked and brought to prominence the humblest and darkest function of a reborn device (as my sister Dame History told me so often: the humblest upon yesterday's background is the proudest on today's foreground): the help-needing and so help-giving cantilever. Around this reinvented engineering-aesthetical device a new architectural cycle-attitude came to be born—still unachieved.

"In unison with the growth of the democratic-folk exigencies of the present age, the nineteenth and twentieth centuries, there came to this new 'folk' device the help of all the other 'folk' materials, reinforced concrete, glass, and, in growing complexity and subtlety of alloys, the light metals. A lofty and daring weight-liberated—thus a most-spiritual (= weight-free) within the most-material (= weight-bound)—architecture was born. And here too, exactly, the meaning of a total Solitude-Solidarity, the Ancient's *Tendresse,* embraced in one gesture, the apparent aloofness of a skyscraper, the *I* of Sullivan's and his descendants' creations, and the factual solidarity of I-in-the-world in a Wright, Le Corbusier, Neutra. And,'' added here, smiling, Dame Architecture, ''how similar to the present age appeared to me, sometimes, the age of later Rome, Rome's symbiosis of imperial, all-devouring tyranny and greed with the hidden, democratic-folk structure of her moral-juridical thought, a combination that gave us the vertiginous and arrogant vaults of Rome, all built, however, with the help of the cheapest 'folk' materials, 'vulgar' rubble held together by the stubborn elasticity of 'vulgar' cement: Abbot Suger's *'mens hebes ad verum per materialia surgit.'* ''[3]

*

The story I heard from Dame Architecture, she heard in her childhood from the Ancestor. Does she still believe in it today? I did not ask. It did not matter. What mattered was what I have learned: that all communication between all beings, children and grandchildren of his, is possible only in the universe of beings-attitudes. Not in the universe of facts. The *and* and the *or* in a being-fact—the ''evil-and-or-the-good''—make of it a stranger to him, stranger to *Tendresse,* until the loss of these in-and conjunctions recreates of it a new child of his.

But—such is my feeling now—I learned this much earlier, the very day I met and recognized the Ancestor. And was recognized by him. And I followed Solitude-Solidarity wherever the quest took us: from Hesiod's descent into Okeanos and the Seasons—the beginnings, oh face of Greece!—made one with the descent into the soul, to our ascent onto poetry—the Endings, oh mask tragic, comic mask of Greece!—made one with the Fool's cry: ''People, People, People! Not Money!''

Long before my monkhood, I became the Ancestor's shadow—separated, for all others, from *Tendresse*—but for him and for the light around him, he: the traveling Shadow-Ancestor-I. This is how it all started, I have said: *it,* our tale. It started with

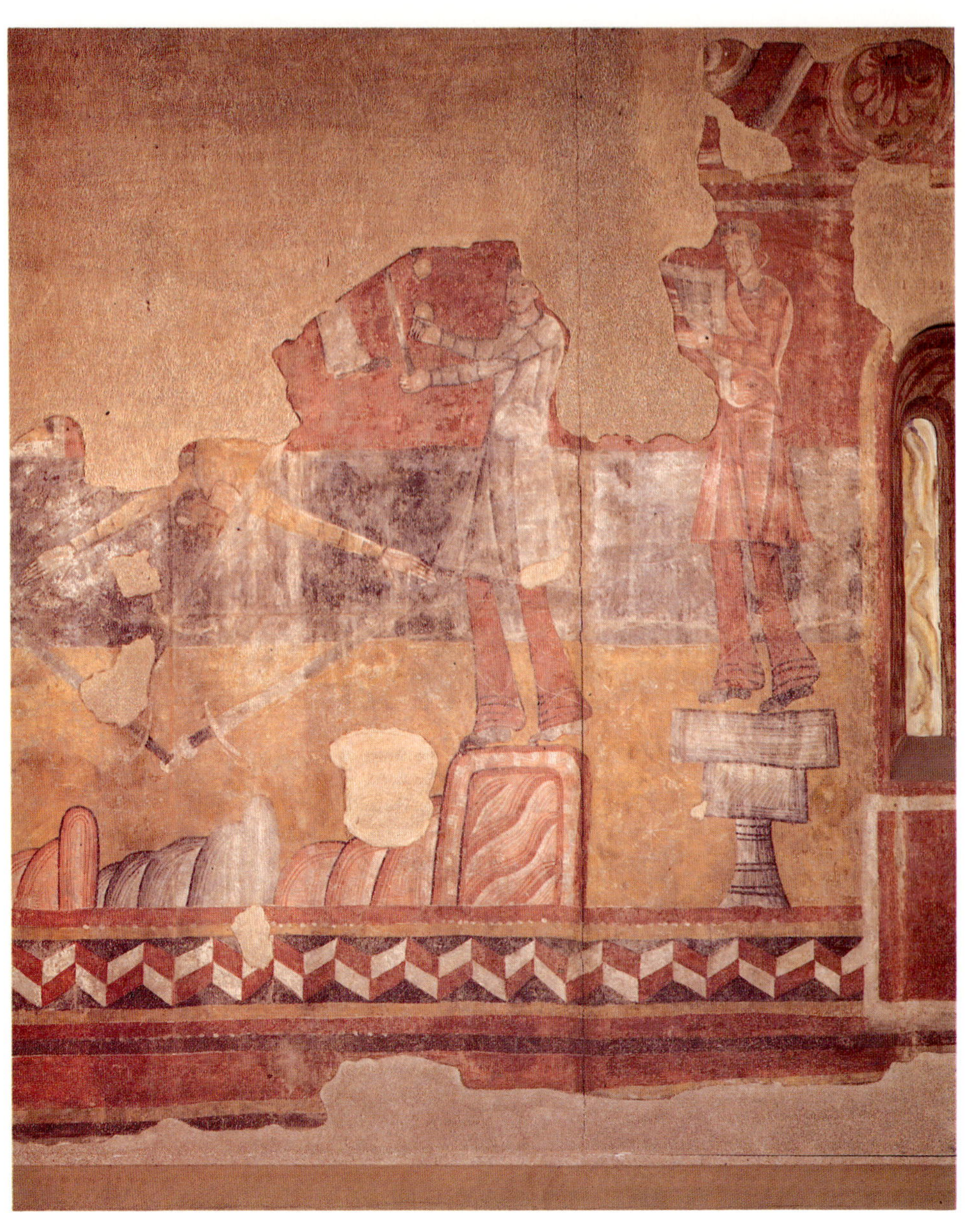

4. Acrobats, or *Jongleurs,* detail of Plate 1

the Romanesque Catalan fresco, the *Jongleurs*—an astonishing new being facing us *(See Plate 1).*

On a large wall of a Pyrenean early twelfth-century church[4] was painted—in hues of light grey, brown, lilac and other each-other-supporting hues (a typically Romanesque prowess: the very poverty—economy, rather—of chromatic means achieving there the greatest possible psycho-chromatic wealth, inherited, it is true, from the pre-Romanesque past, Merovingian-Visigothic-Irish and Carolingian-Ottonian)—an episode *supposedly* belonging to the prophet Daniel's dream vision (Daniel 3:5). One half of the wall is almost entirely—except for its inner and upper friezes of animals-and-monsters—occupied by two hierarchic and formidable figures standing upon erect rock-as-if-architecture pedestals in front of an as-if-suddenly-immobilized rock-tower structure; the other half of the wall shows a scene full of noisy commotion: two performing acrobats, a musician playing a harp, all supported by similar rock-like structures, but, in obvious contrast to what happens in the other scene, these are restless structures, yielding, each in a different stage of submission and expressive accompaniment, to the weight and the seesaw equilibrium of the animated bodies; these simple rock-pedestals are animated by their adhesion to, their sympathy, as it were, with the meaning of the half-floating, unstable, living bodies above them (*Plate 4*).

The meaning of all this—what could be the meaning of it, its *real* subject matter? Why was such primacy given—almost an entire wall of a small church's nave!—to an episode theologically or liturgically without primacy? And why was equal size—equal importance—given to the acrobats, a transparent paraphrase of what could at that time be conceived close-to-vice, as to the two majestic figures on the left, paragons of what could have been conceived then as highest power, perhaps highest virtue (power of Evil? Nebuchadnezzar and his mountebanks, as is generally assumed?[5] But who knows really? For how could such serene dignity be given to such an evil power? Good power then? Saints? Highest virtue? Why not?) What secret and perhaps daring thought of a medieval man, the understander of the beautiful = ugly (daring, because defying or fulfilling theological *musts*) was revealed here: the equation of the awe-inspiring power-or-virtue-holders and the ''low'' acrobats? But above all, this question: how did the medieval Chris-

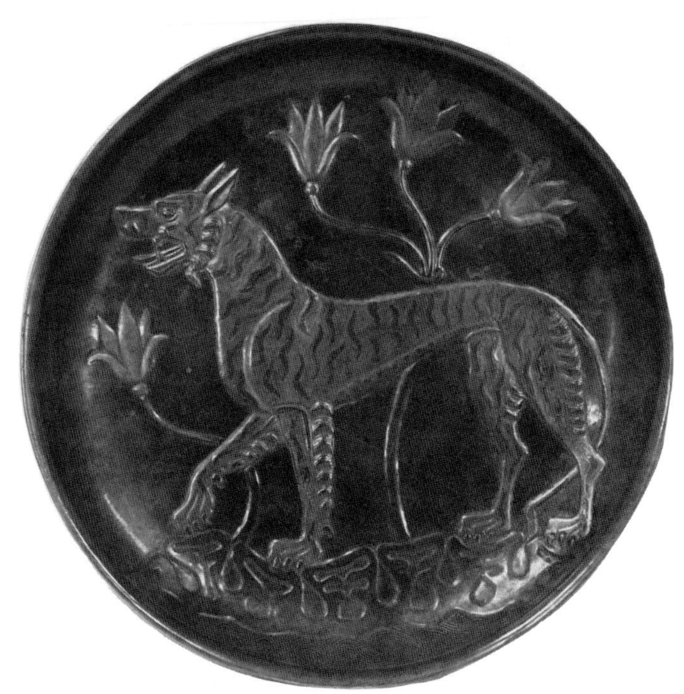

5. Sassanian silver plate

tian artist come to his courage of *free* and creative choice, and his will to animate with dramatic significance (the good-evil's unavoidable drama, as I saw it there) the inanimate objects, such as the rocklike foundations supporting human figures or animals and monsters—a decorative ''device'' known already in the old Orient (*Plate* 5), accepted often, without change, by Christians (*Plate* 6) and here, at San Juan de Bohí, a live, significant device-being?

How did the medieval Christian artist come to the *free* choice of a *significant ornament,* ornament not only ''decorative'' or even structural-compositional but a vehicle of expression, of human emotion, *motion's e-motion?*

Much more typical, more truly medieval, it appeared to me, was this freedom of a *significant* choice than all the formidable, solemn pictorial-biogrammatic ''schemata'' accepted from Late Antiquity—all the complex, calculated and secretive grouping of sacred images in ingenious didactic ensembles, the irrevocable signalizations of man's appurtenance to the divinely and theologically ordained cosmos!

The *Jongleurs* was much more than this. That is why I have said: It all started with the *Jongleurs* in Barcelona.

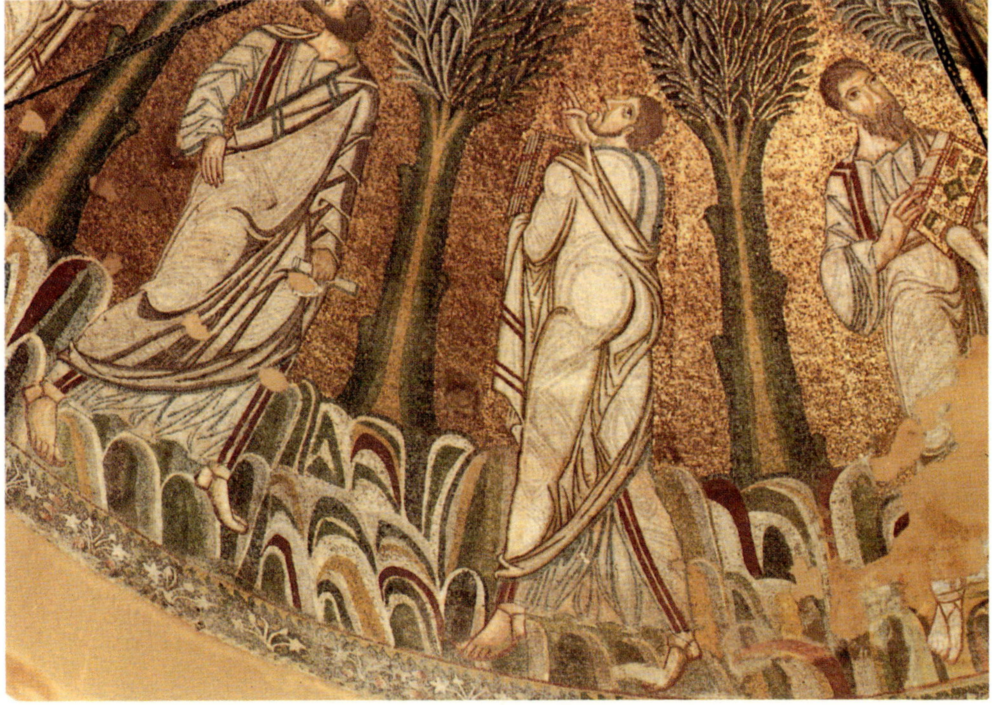

6. Rocks under the feet of the Apostles, detail of cupola, Saint Sophia, Thessaloniki

*

And the Ancestor spoke:

''Somewhere at the bottom of any human attitude, collective-individual, there is present a dual being . . .''.

But what the Ancient went on to tell me then, I shall include later in this tale of mine. For, at that very moment, I-shadow-he found myself on the balcony of a tall stone house, leaning over the narrow moonlit Mediterranean street. It was, indeed, the very beginning of Hans Christian Andersen's old and cherished story, *The Shadow.* The story of a young northerner in search—a hunger? a thirst? the ''marrow-bone'' song of a bygone romantic age?—of warmth, health, and of the friendly unknown.

It was a northerner's unquenched yearning for the friendship of the south: a powerful, forlorn sentimentality. A nocturne. And who, in the presence of the Ancestor, would dare or wish to laugh at it?

*

Across the street, a balcony opposite mine, its sharp and adventure-full iron lacery coming impetuously towards mine, sent me a message: I, Ancient-Shadow was invited to enter the brightly illuminated window door into the unknown home of unknown people. My own shadow then grew (the moon shone brighter and brighter, so Hans Christian Andersen tells us), lengthening across the street, climbed the opposite wall, crossed the other balcony and through the now opened window entered the stranger's friendly home. And left me. What a scented and touching music—red and green garland of tenderness in the full moon's light—bridged the void between the two balconies: Beethoven's last sonorities, the last and fullest solitude of man, the last, the fullest solidarity in man!

Nothing else, suddenly.

My shadow's new life started then, auspicious and always mine, in this unchanged—transferred now into mind's sameness with what had been mine a moment ago.

Even as in Ancient Greece, where body's death, abhorred, lonely, bored and lost land of shadow, became honored, accepted, when transferred into mind's life, oh Okeanos!—so also my humble shadow was honored and accepted—adopted—by the unknown people behind the lighted balcony door opposite mine.

My shadow entered mind's home—Okeanos!—thence mind's city and its streets, gardens, views, its event-full monuments and people and their trans-lucid meanings. A totally transferred and same life—the mind's life-in-death.

*

On the city's outskirts along the warm and restful shore, wave after wave came to greet me: all the stories, small and great, of mind's (man's) history still on earth.

''Who would believe—but we believe!'' said one of the white-crested waves, a swift-legged, small one, ''that man's expansion of interest and of knowledge in mind-and-body's happenings could come from a totally different expansion of man's interests and knowledge? That (we little, swift-legged waves, we love to be precise) the Renaissance and post-Renaissance geographic expansion in *width* into new, unknown continents and cultures, could be transferred *in toto,* as a newly acquired intensity or dimension of mind, into his narrowest extension *in depth:* psychology's rapid—deeper and deeper—descent of scrutiny?''

''Yes,'' said another, much grander wave. ''And who would believe—but we here believe it!—that in man's (we mean our contemporary man's) creative demands, the origins, the attitude, the meaning of our contemporary art (we pagan Oceanids have our art!), its strongest demand, the epic permission to deform, could come, transferred there from a demand equally intense but totally divorced from art, from an attitude political-social in its origin: man's demand and man's struggle for the rights of the exploited on earth, the oppressed?''

'' . . . all the oppressed,'' repeated, murmur-within-murmur, the surrounding sister Oceanids, so that much became lost or fragmented in the shimmering noise of Ocean's story: ''—all the struggles for the underdog . . . Babeuf's tragic failure . . . a forgotten episode of the French Revolution[6] . . . Babeuf's fight for the *vingt-quatre millions d'opprimés*[7] . . . this end-product of all the previous 'underdog' revolts, peasant, artisan, during the long feudal centuries . . . Babeuf, the French revolutionary condemned to death by the French Revolution's Establishment . . . Revolt of the underdog smashed then . . . Smashed? . . . Babeuf's failure did not fail . . . it was *transferred in toto* . . . into the modern world of all fights for the underdog *on all levels of life* . . . ever deeper and deeper levels, ever narrower and narrower channels . . . from the social-political-economic levels, external, discernible, vast, to the levels and channels, darker, narrower, cryptic, of poetry-philosophy's fights for the underdog: the priority of perception, of body, of the *uomo qualunque* in us . . . for the rights of each being-conduct, each discipline of mind or of hand, to rely on its own, independent, intrinsic resources . . . *Solitude* thus, *Solidarity* thus in poetry, philosophy, science, politics, art . . . .

'' . . . Merleau-Ponty's 'It has seemed to us that matter, life, mind could not be defined as three orders of reality or three kinds of being, but as three levels of meanings or three forms of unity.'[8] . . . And the narrowest of all, the humble level of man's thinking with the hand-and-eye, art . . . the struggles there for the exploited

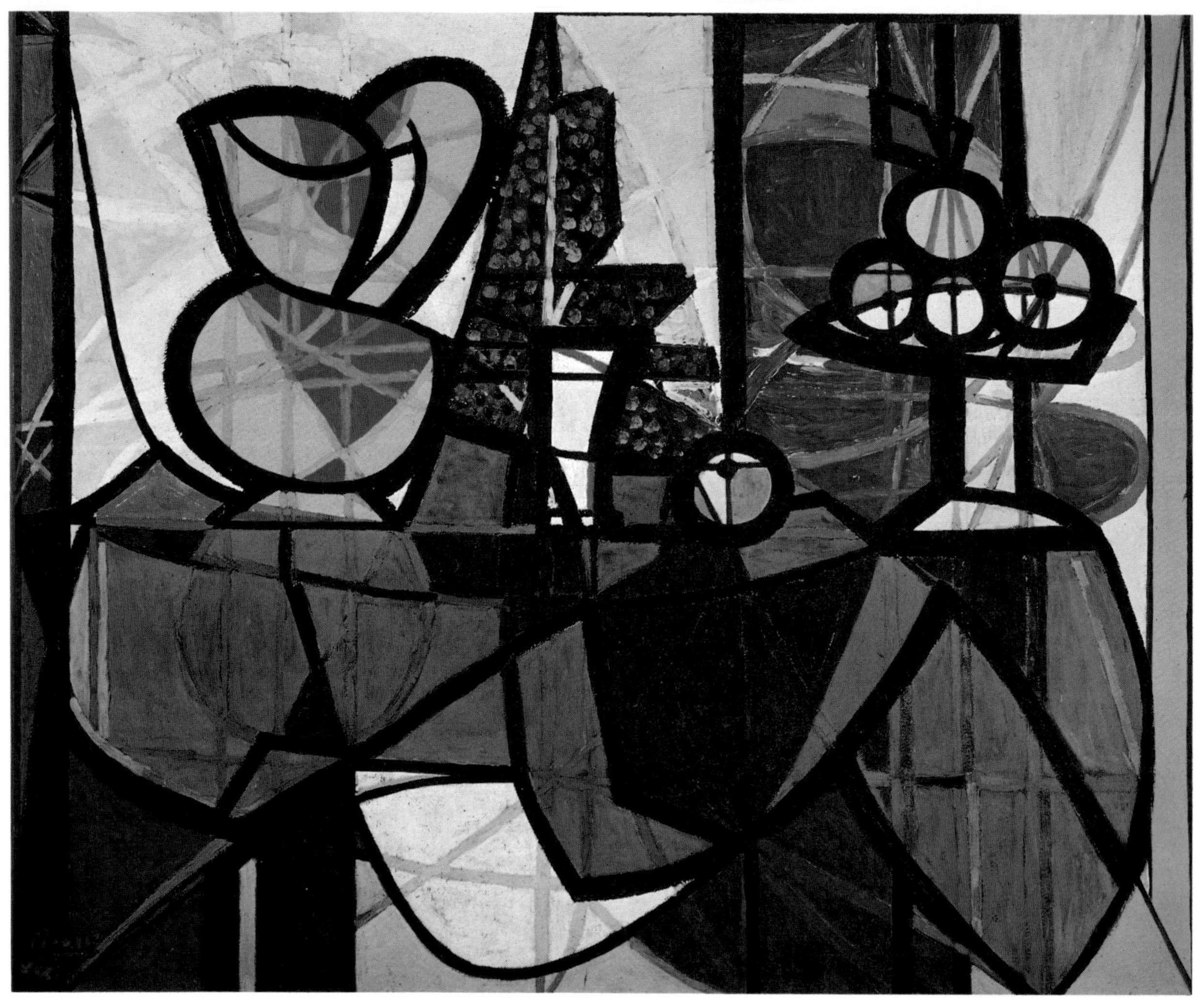

7. Picasso, still life

underdog in painting . . . nineteenth and twentieth centuries' travail of emancipation from the oppressive lordship of optic illusion and consistency . . . the struggles of the pictorial serf, the pictorial *shadow* . . . Courbet's exaltation of shadow as an independent—independent of light—creative, free being of the future; Manet's fraternal exaltation of light-with-no-shadow, of light as a different, hidden or translucid new shadow-structure . . . a new world of solitude, of mutual solidarity . . . shadow-light . . . deliverance . . .

" . . . then Cézanne preparing Picasso's final, if not total *deliverance* of the 'underdog' . . . Picasso's (all twentieth-century painting's!) . . . shadow becoming a living, free, independent, fully creative being, a new emancipated builder of a new consistency-meaning (*Plate 7*) . . . a Being . . . . Justice-attitude of a particular fact (Babeuf) transferred globally—significance, structure, behavior, all at once—into the same Justice-attitude but of a totally different fact: very simply, the creator-creature's *function* of the shadow in the art of painting . . .

" . . . the meaning of Transfer . . . of History . . . in Art . . . Justice transferred . . . Solitude-Solidarity, transferred into extension, into proportions and massing, into light and color. . . .

"Justice within the very significance—the direction, the act—of a line, of a significant intense curve, of an ornament. . . . "

The murmuring chant of the Oceanids stood suddenly still, anxious and expectant. Covering the trembling horizon came from Ocean's somewhere a very great, oblique wave, an immense concave mass-curve of dark jade green water-and-thunder, sweeping away, silencing all other sister-waves:

"Shadow, who left the moonlit street and the body of the Ancestor's Shadow, shadow left alone, go now. You have learned. Now go back. And listen to the scent of the dark green Ocean curve."

And the frail, long shadow of a young northerner in search of warmth—a thirst? a hunger? the lonely heart's "marrow-bone" song?—left the beyond-another-balcony's shore and city and started his wandering back.

Up and through the great mountains, valleys and waters I started wandering back.

It was Greece! The taste, the smell, of the honey of metamorphoses!

Melissa, the Bee, and her gift to the spirit of Greece; Melissa, the Cretan nurse of the child Zeus, she, the goat Amalthea also, her gifts of mime and future tragedy to Greece's body, her nursing the child Zeus when, saved by Rhea's motherly trick from his fath-

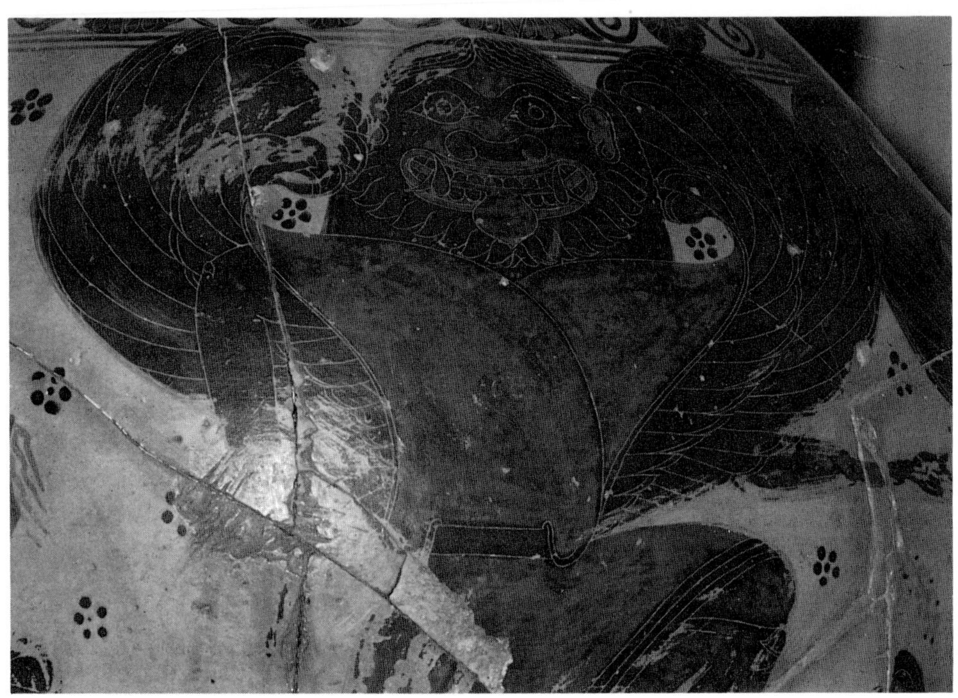

8. Harpy, proto-Attic grave vase

er's fear, terror and greed, he was swiftly brought to Ida's grotto by the strong-limbed *curetes,* the young priest-artisans of the future, of dance, of metals, and of statues; she, the Cretan Goddess, serpent and dove and column, later Helena, Pasiphaë, still later Medusa, terror, irony, and Protectress of Beasts; finally Athena, formidable in her beauty and hovering meaning of bird and serpent up there on the face of the old Hecatompedon; she, *La Femme Civilisatrice,*[9] Mother-Daughter, Demeter-Persephone, the Virgin-and-Mother, to her, in sameness of myth, the young Zeus-Dionysos-Triptolemos, the young corn, is sacrificial son-lover.

*Greece!* The scent, the taste, the Honey of metamorphoses, all Greece; serpent and dove, rude and gentle, secluded and open, all at once (even as on the other edge of their Middle Sea, the sister of Hellas, Spain, is rude and gentle, secluded and open too: such, from the high-pitched terrace leading to her castle, is Segovia's Spain-defining deep view—and what a view!—of her two opposite, innermost landscapes: to the right, the rude, vast, monotonous, naked and proud solitude of the burnished Meseta, Spain's Catholic essence; to the left, the gentle, exuberant plenitude of a richly attired greenery wedded to the not very distant fires of Segovia's cathedral; solidarity released, Spain's theology of accident-within-essence; Spain's hungry yet generous contrasts and harmonies, all there!).

Shadow, wandering through ancient Hellas, wait there now a while! Wait: monsters first, the penumbral threshold to Greece's ''classic'' home! Monsters—the Orient's sun-and-moon-and-stars devouring, devoured, fighting, protecting Beasts, Lion, Bull, Serpent-Dragon, Bird—when transferred into Greece, monsters in man's soul: memories incarnate of evil, of evil fighting the good, of good fighting the evil (*Plate 8*). Then—the opening of dark grottoes: *Delphi!* The honey of Greece—Melissa!—of mind's culture, the honey of highest abstraction: man-without-monsters: Delphi's exquisite frieze from the Treasure House of the Siphnians (*Plates 9a & b*).[10]

Beyond these mythic narrations—the social pride of the prosperous and grateful island of Siphnos—exquisitely told by two Ionian artists working there independently yet harmoniously together (so accomplished was their skill, talent and vision!), beyond these myths, there is, always waiting for you, shadow wandering alone!, a much more ancient, incessantly revived myth: Goethe's myth, never told to the end by the poet, of Faust's descent into the dark abyss, abode of the ''Mothers.'' Great, yet not secret myth, soul's and mind's descent and return, known by all men of all ages and all ways: such the world of animals' activity—Beasts, Monsters!—at the bottom of sculpted temple walls or stupas in ancient India becoming gradually an ascending series—level upon level—of human, then more-than-human, then more than more-than-human worlds; and such the same ascension from the low bottom of animal activity to the vicissitudes of human and finally super-human activity and sovereignty of saints and Christ on, say, the façade of the twelfth century (1160–68) Romanesque church of Ripoll, at the foot of the Catalan Pyrenees (*Plate 10*).

For never—at any stage of visual creation—never could there be only the *what* or the *how* of the subject represented, but, underneath them, identified with them, a new, *another,* subject, a sec-

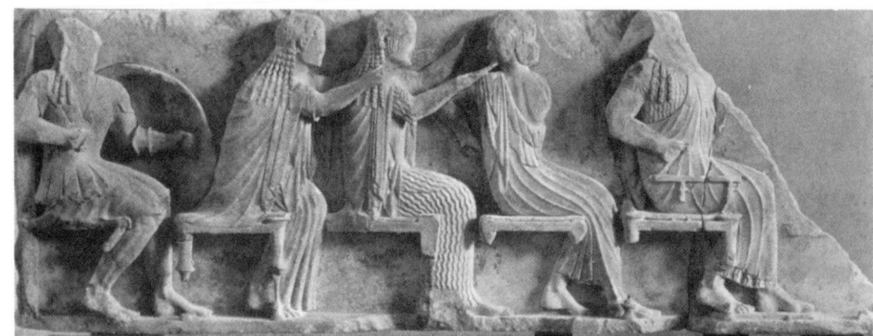

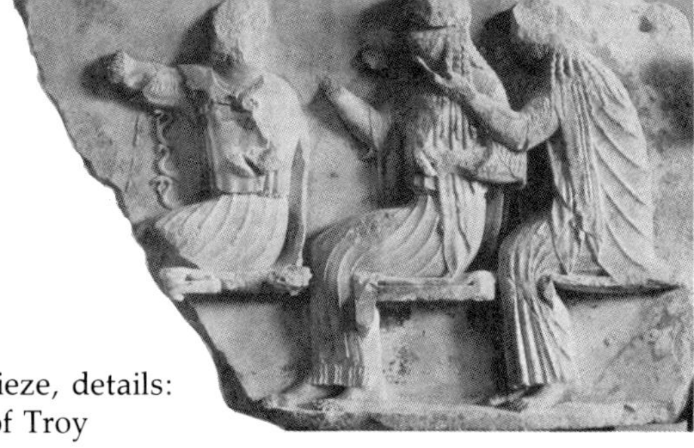

9. Treasure House of the Siphnians, Delphi, east frieze, details:
   a. Gods and goddesses looking on at the battle of Troy

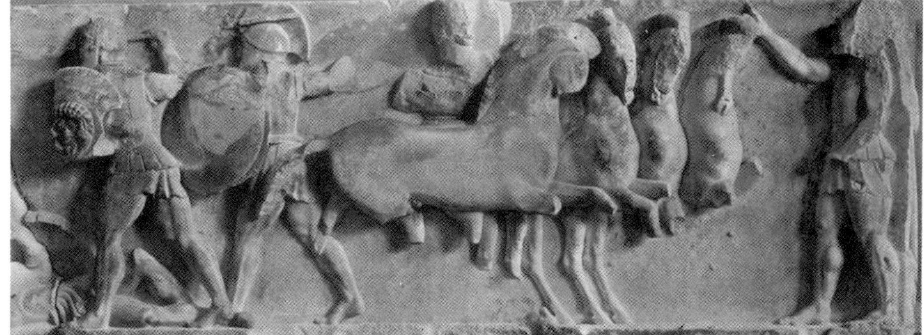

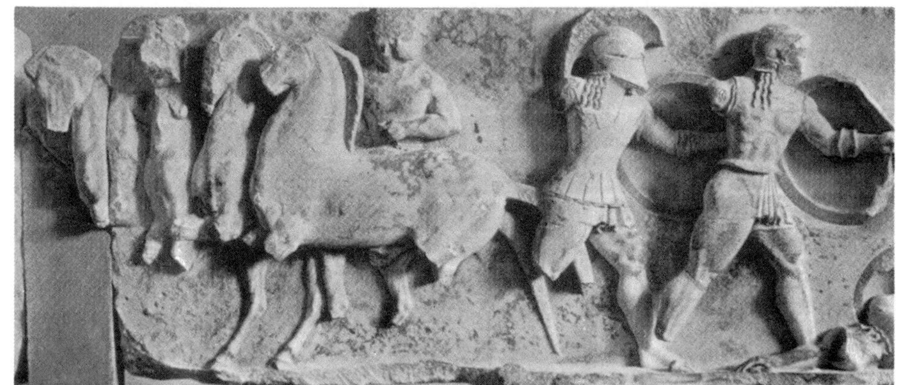

9. b. The battle of Troy

ond, sub-subject, a *what-of-the-how* subject-fable. The honey of Siphnos: touch, hear, smell, taste and abstract its subject-fable narrated in marble and in depth!

Surrounding the dissonance and struggle between the humanized Beasts—the Titans—and the Gods—scene of enmity, dominion, astute will! (*Plate 11*)—is the fable of the other scenes: the harmony of friendship, Faust's return to light and action; the friendship, the harmony of two radiant creatures of beauty, the horse and the *kouros*—a closest alliance of swiftness and will's ability, of space tamed (the horse) and of time taming (*kouros*)—this most earnest gift of Greece, the gift of art's Bee.

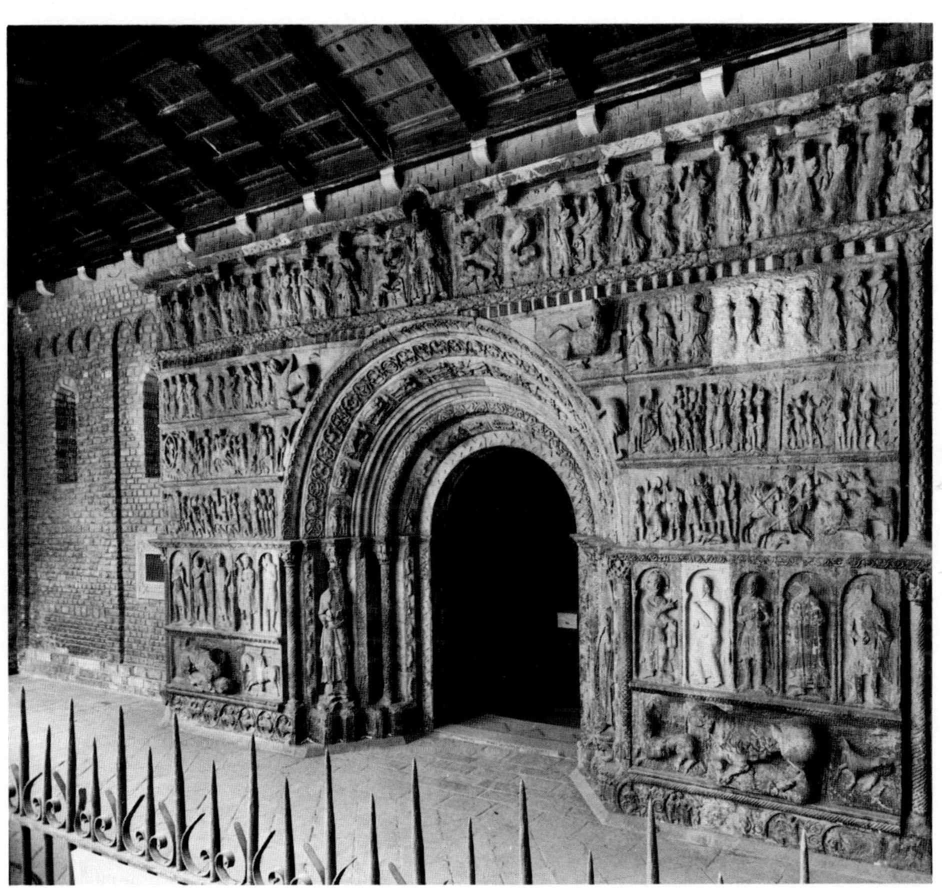

10. Façade, Ripoll monastery, Gerona

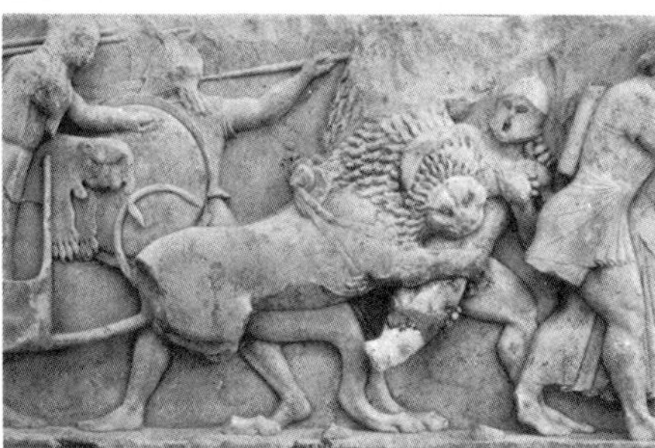

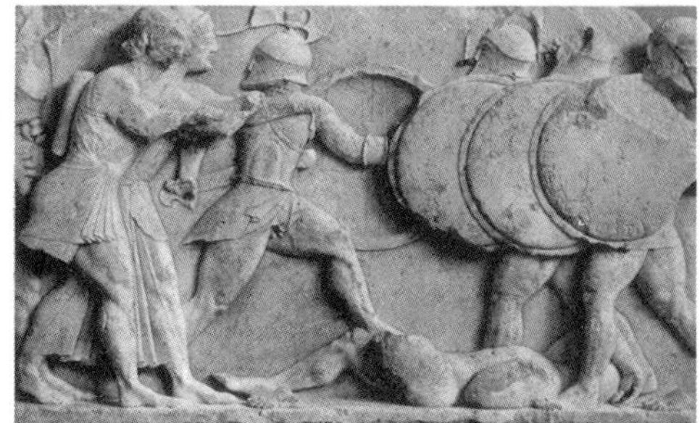

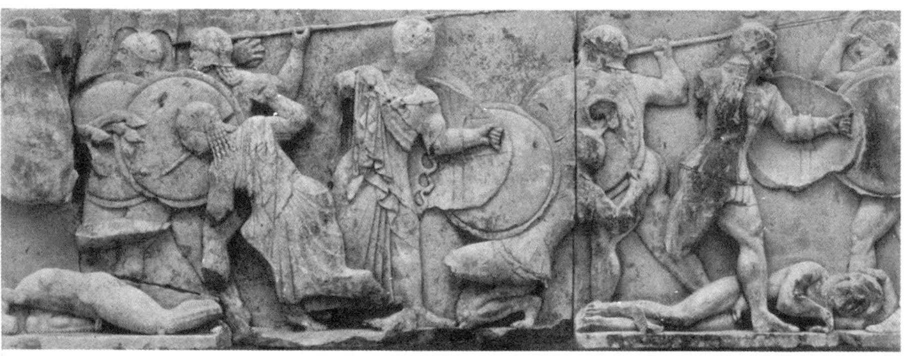

11. Treasure House of the Siphnians, Delphi, north frieze, detail: battle of giants and gods

There it is, the Greek gift of total transfer: from the universe of metaphysical alliance—the three-oneness of beauty, goodness and truth, to the universe of Bodies' alliance, the Beauty, the goodness, the truth of a perfect—irreplaceable—bodily line and curve! And the Fable is told lucidly in depth on the Siphnian four-sided frieze.

At first youth and his steed are both still allied to the distance, however small, that separates them (*Plate 12*). Then, after plunging, invisibly, beneath the two great battles (the battle of Troy—between the jealous, not yet truly human humans, in the presence of the Olympians—and the battle of giants-monsters and gods themselves) they re-emerge on the opposite side of the marmoreal frieze, their own alliance now finally achieved, total (*Plate 13*): *kouros* and horse becoming one harmonious self—two different independent beings, united by the sole virtue of their human choice and their moving perfection (the *centaur,* man and

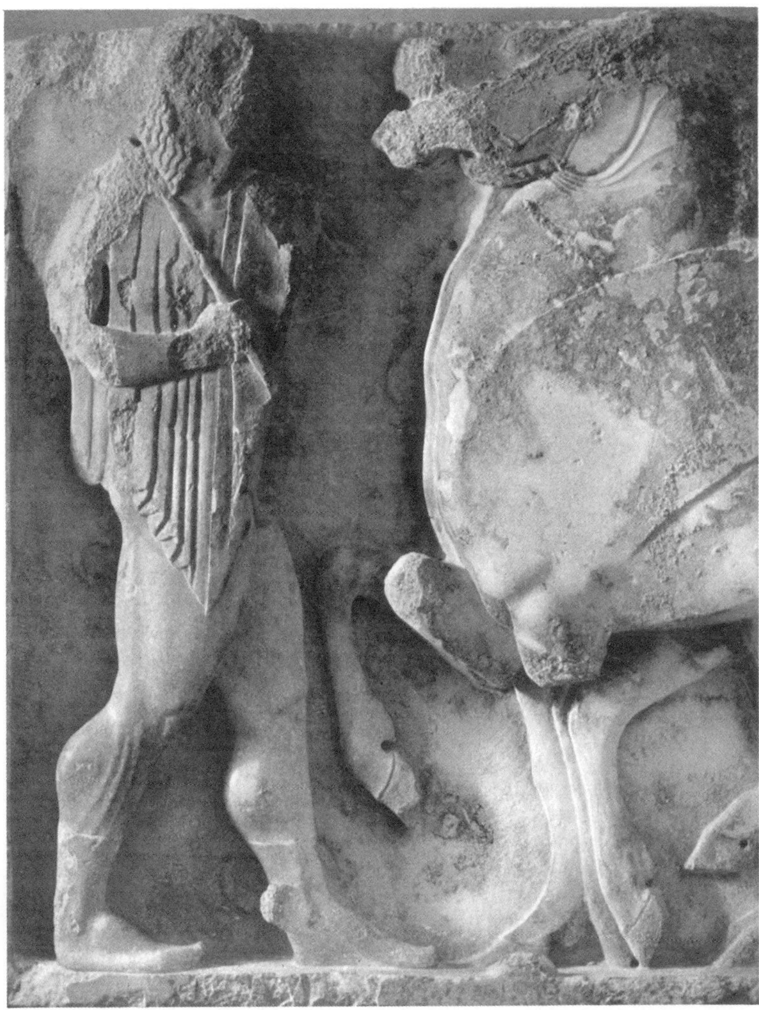

12. Treasure House of the Siphnians, Delphi, west frieze, detail: Hermes and horse

horse fused together by a not-human choice and will, is a monster still, problematic victim of the evil: hence the morbid, yet invention-full fascination the centaur and his world had for the Christian Italians, when, many centuries later, pagan Greece came back to their Renaissance).

And the Siphnian fable spread throughout all Greek lands. The beautiful friendship of the most beautiful animal being, the Greek horse, with the most beautiful human being, the Greek nude, in closest alliance now, is thus the first *persona* of Metamorphoses met by me, the returning Shadow. In Greek thought, in

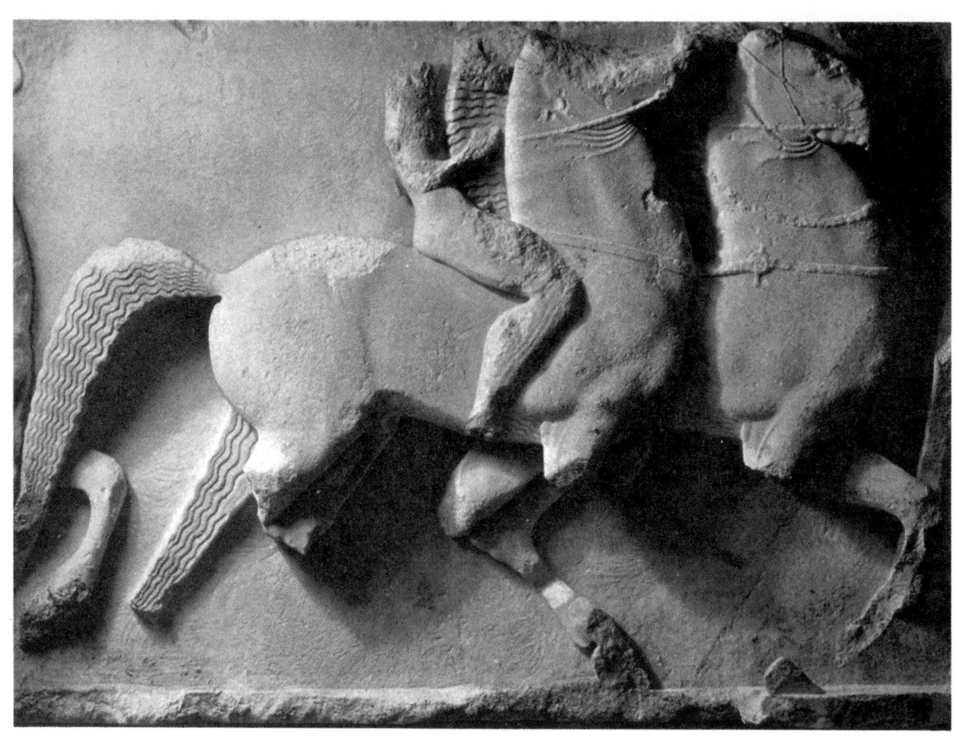

13. Treasure House of the Siphnians, Delphi, south frieze, detail: horseman

Greek verse, song, building and every other art, it was for me the love-supporting curve, the line of that alliance and friendship, tenderly curving towards the fullness of the circle. The terror or the inexorability of this fullness, the circle's self-continuance and at the same time stillness, the *Aeternitas* of the Present, and the Presence, the terror of perfection, Medusa's petrifying face, is changed into liberation's joy by the very loveliness of that curve!

All fables being one Fable, this is also the fable of Perseus severing Medusa's head—liberating man from the Beast's close reality by attacking her body as reflection only in his shiny and protecting shield-mirror.

And the hidden shadow-story of the Greek *kouros*-horse's curve is mirrored in the entire history—sub-history—of the sovereign Greek human figure, the only sovereignty Hellas accepted without battling it: the sovereign curve of youthful bodies—*kouroi* and *korai*—in the pre-''archaic'' and ''archaic'' era, when the impetuous ''order of nature'' and the meditative ''order of mind'' had not yet been equated (hence this era's ''activism'' or detailed ''realism'') (*Plates 14a & b*), has retained the dominant oblong roundness, not fully circular in intention, of the horse's silhouette (*Plate 15a*).



And slowly, during the most creative—the ''transitional'' and early ''classical'' eras—eras of abstract ''naturalism'' and exalted meditation, when the ''order of mind'' and the ''order of nature'' became equated, the curve of the human and equine silhouettes (the *back* of the Greek statue would be the greatest and ''purest'' Greek invention!) became also equated with the fullness of a perfect circularity (*Plate 15b*).

*

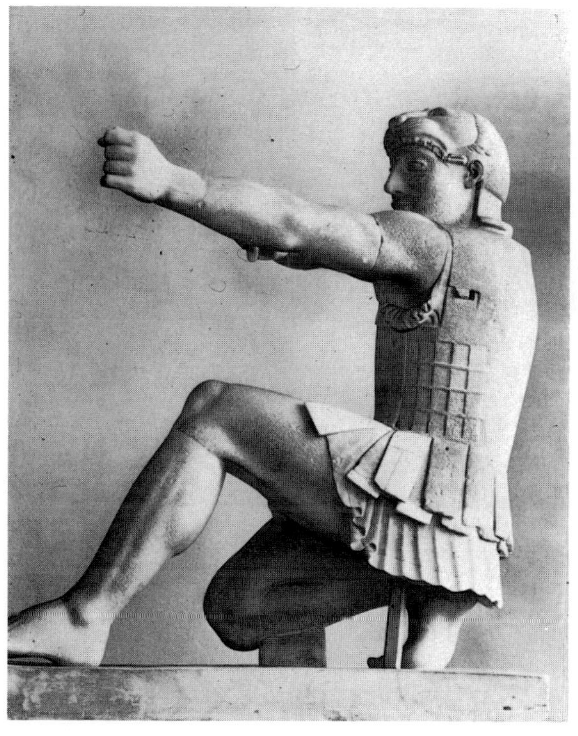

14a. Kneeling archer from Aegina

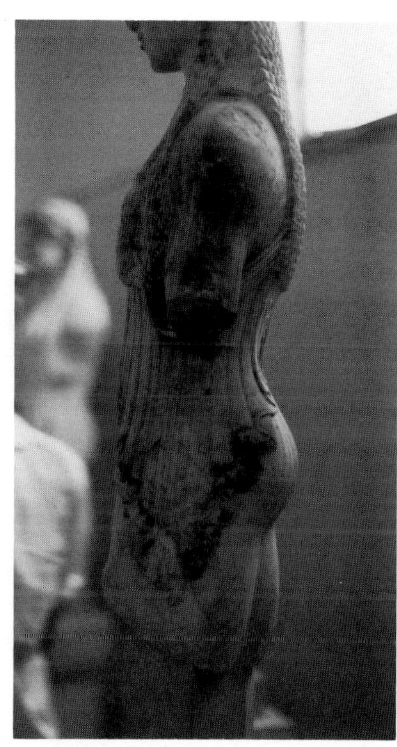

14b. *Kore,* 6th c. B.C.

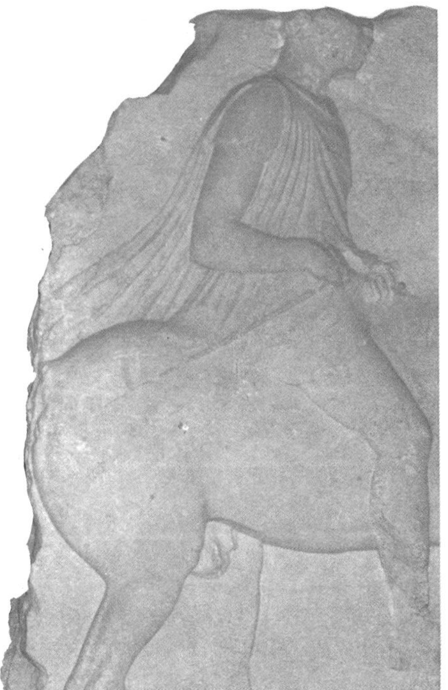

15a. Horseman, 5th c. B.C.

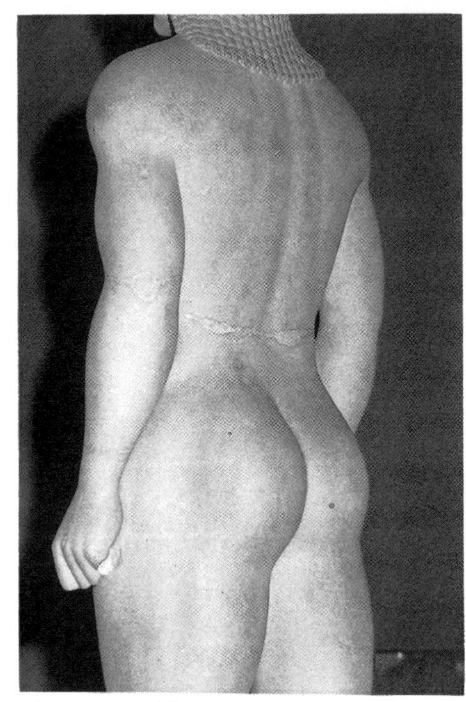

15b. *Kouros,* 6th c. B.C.

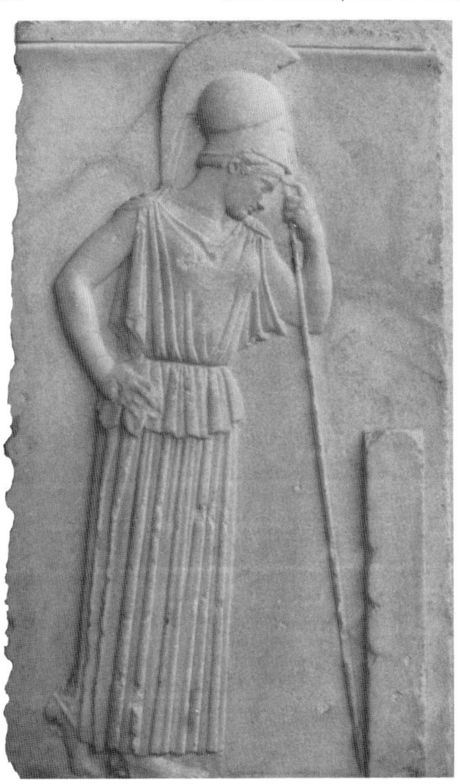

16. "Mourning Athena" from the Acropolis

I, Pimen to be, future monk, old chronicler of a new and young age, how could I have learned all about that Intrigue of depth-transfer told by the Siphnians at Delphi, if not because of what the lost and returned shadow later told me, himself? And so believable seemed to me—for was not the shadow my own shadow?—the unbelievable adventure, that each detail, each gesture of it, stood in front of me as a living, communicative *persona,* not as a soulless *res,* a thing.

And what I heard—what my shadow heard—was the believable: "Long, many many centuries, before I was created by the 'Dorian' genius as the 'classical' curve of an ideal, finite circle—the rounded idea of perfection in man, in the city-state, the law, the mind, the motion of planets and mechanical tools—I was the Cretan curve of a growing spiral.

"I, Crete's spiral: the incarnate—transferred—meaning of a still unveiled culture of growth, of unending becoming—my mythic, beautiful Crete surrounded by the unending shimmer and life of green and blue waters!—the spiral, from death-life's sleep, the grey, gentle and sad sleep of a grain, sweet sadness never forgotten in later Greece (*Plate 16*), to the gentle, sky blue awakening, spring, flowers, the crocus, the iris, and the white butterfly, white 'psyche,' to the death-sleep again and to life-awakening, again . . . spiraling.

"*Crete's purity or loyalty to origins* is her loyalty to the non-mysterious origin and truth of the myth, primordial both East and West, about grain's young male death in the womb of the virgin earth, its male-female resurrections as living plant, as the other or another: in ultimate transfer, the truth and the origin of the spiral. I, the spiral, spiral I was splendidly in ancient Crete—in the opulent ever-spiraling of beings and things in Cretan art (*Plates 17a, b, c, & d*)—the spiraling, labyrinthine plan of Crete's opulent palaces-chapels."[11]

Then—the violent ethnic and cultural change and the birth of

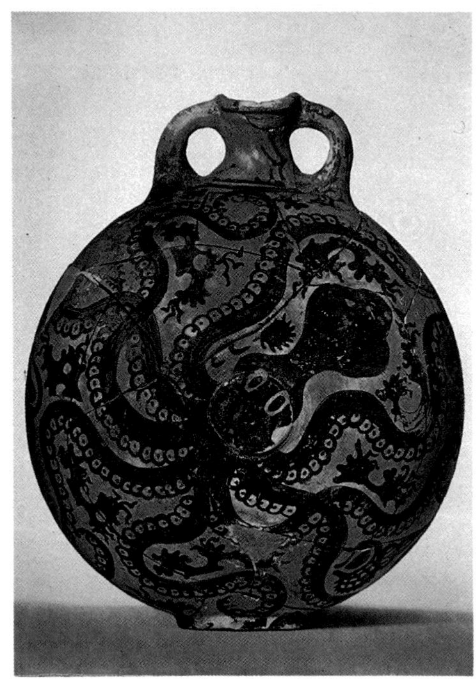

17a. Cretan ceramic with octopus

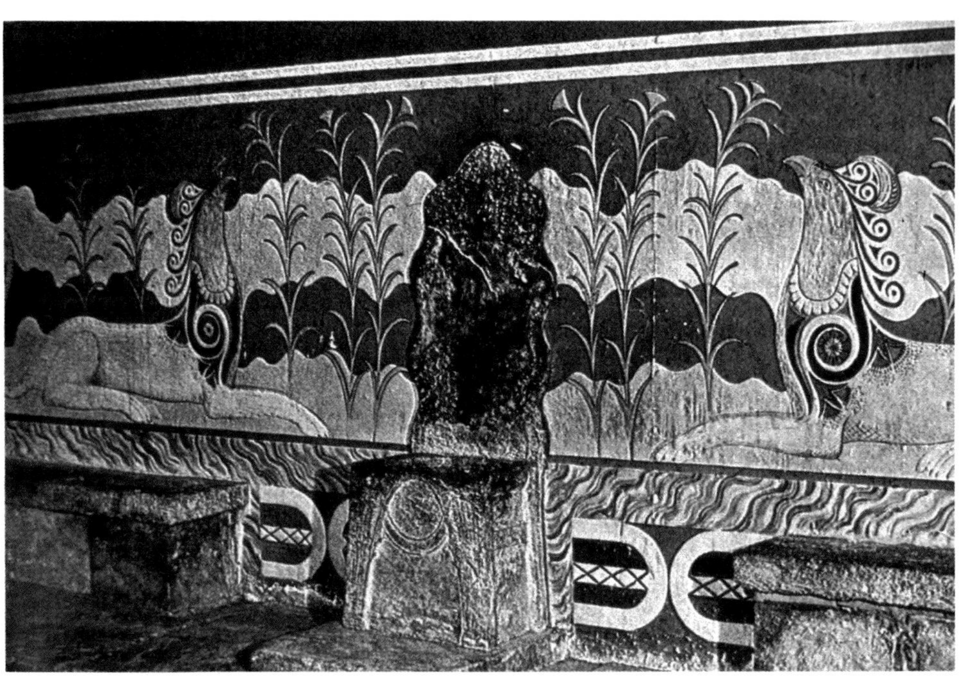

17b. Knossos throne room

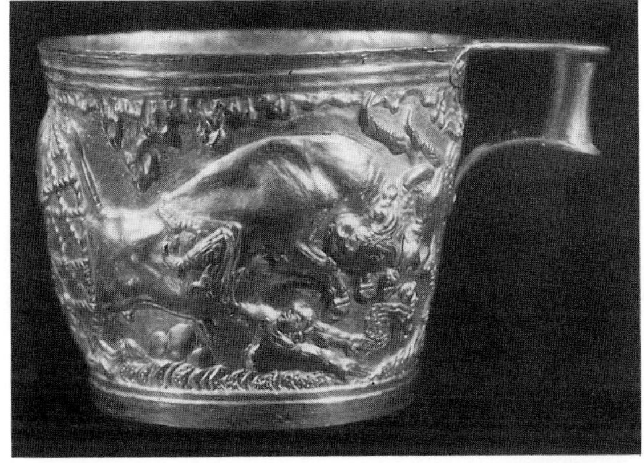

17c. Gold cup from Vaphio

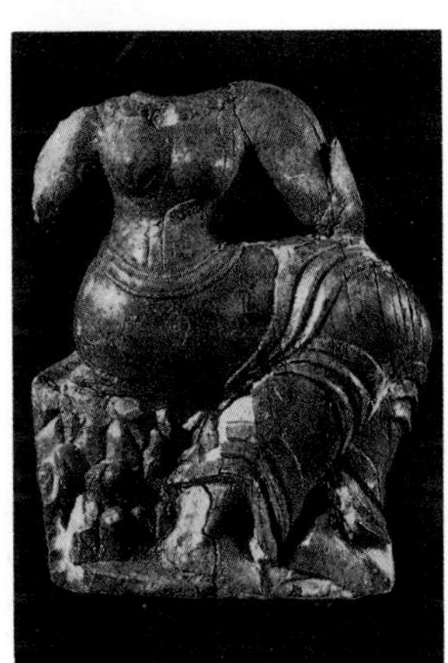

17d. Mycenaean ivory divinity

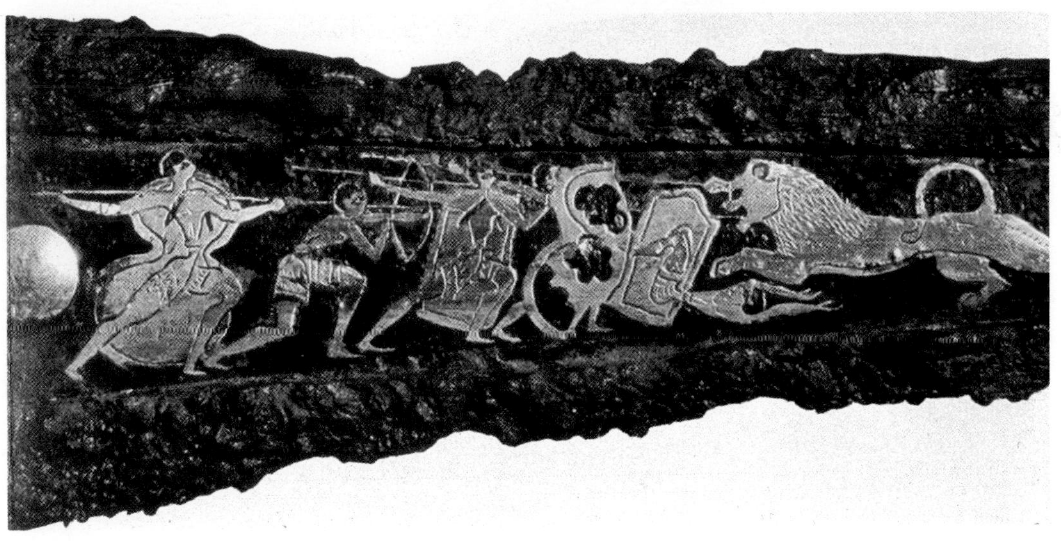

18. Dagger from Mycenae

another Greek world, Achaean, later ''Doric,'' limited, poor and heroic, and truly mysterious in its new loyalty to a new and dramatic vision: of the unending, unlimited, ''infinite'' spiral, submitted, but never yielding entirely (and finally liberated again), to the more and more ''sacred'' finality of geometry's limited, restricted, ''poor'' yet perfect forms.

Here: the still Cretan spirality of an already non-Cretan, Achaean-Mycenaean violent narration (*Plate 18*), and here, at the very threshold of the ''classical'' era, the Siphnian—''Ionian''—return to the Cretan spiral (*See Plate 11*), or, in the midst of perhaps the ''purest'' of all classical Greek creations, the marbles at Olympia,[12] the Cretan voice heard again (*Plate 19*).

Slowly, more and more strongly, the spiral asserted itself again: Scopas and Praxiteles, both of the late ''classical'' (fourth century) era (*Plate 20*). And when, after Alexander, in a world Hellenized East and West, India had been brought closer than ever before, and India's no-beginning-no-end thought came to reawaken the fraternal thinking of most ancient Greece, then the Cretan spiral triumphed (*Plate 21*). Yet the stronger and more obvious became the revived Cretan communication of the spiral, the stronger also (though hidden now, *interiorized,* not obvious any more) grew the intensity of the ''Doric'' voice, the voice of perfect and finite circularity: there is not one tiniest passage of a tiny relief into another in any of the fragmented marbles that came to us from Praxiteles' or Scopas' hand or school that does not tell us this interiorized story of confrontation and dialogue (*Plate 22*).

This typical Greek dialogue is what makes Greek art so truly ''mysterious''—the dialogue between the gentle sadness of death and life as an unending revival (the spiral) and the inexorable, unending presence (the circle) of a ''tragic sense'' of life's joy, the presence of mind's life as the only content and meaning of death itself, the content and the meaning also of the ''what is unthinkable is not,'' the sacredness of the limited, thus the perfect: the ''geometry-*persona*.''

Other things my returned shadow told me he had heard there as answers to some of his queries. I shall mention here only one of them: it belongs remotely, so I thought, to the central intrigue of the chronicle—but it does belong there, nevertheless.

''How,'' asked my shadow, ''are the origins and the history

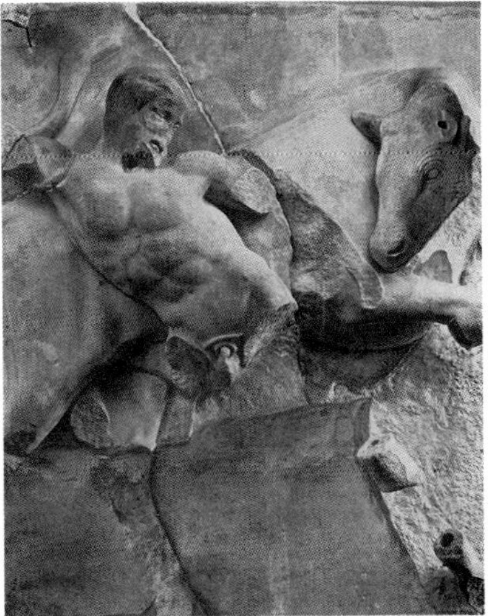

19. Herakles and the Cretan bull

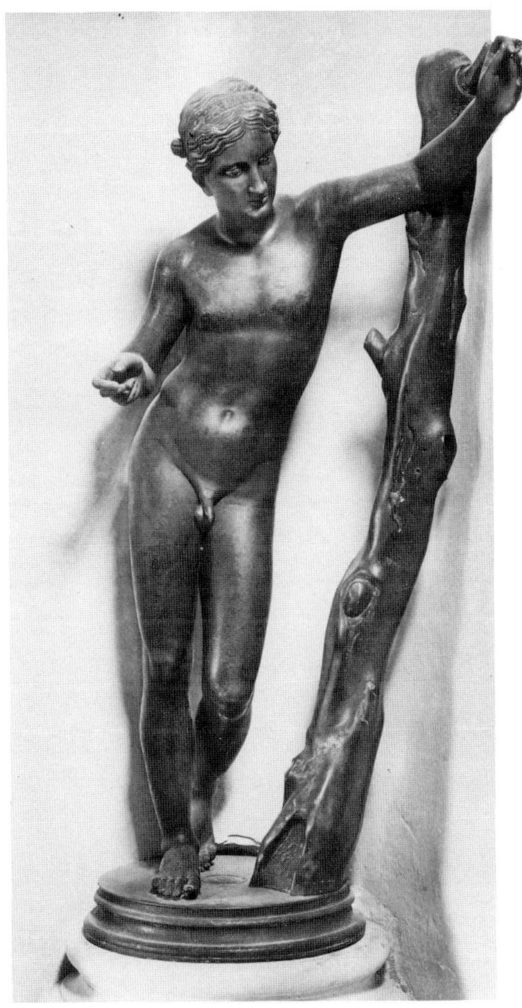

20. Apollo with Lizard

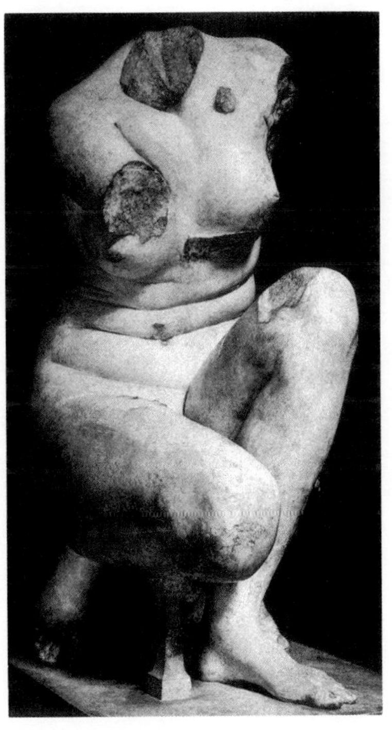

21. *''Venus accroupie''*

of the circle-*persona* related to the origins and the history of Greece itself?''

''There are several relations involved there'' was the answer. ''Nothing is known even here with certainty. For what seems to be the most distant might be the closest blood relation: is not the seed of the trade-*persona,* the exchange of necessary body-and-mind goods, the seed of all cultures on earth—trade and its far-reaching genetic choice: either to *buy for less* or to *sell for less?*

''Ancient and prehistoric India, her fertile valleys of the Indus and the Ganges blessed with plenty, could well multiply and divide her produce and exchange on an immense scale by *selling cheaper,* and develop her plethoric, fertile trading science of numbers, the great revolving Wheel of production and manipulation of infinitely multiplied and divided numbers and fractions of numbers. This is how India could retain and include as part of the Wheel the ever present and mysterious irrational number, the irreducible $\sqrt{2}$. And the equation, pragmatic, of this $x$ or/and that $y$—the unknown—with a real, concrete known number, could be invented: the birth of algebra, India's appeasement of her own tragic sense of finity and infinity wrestling with each other. Here, from transfer to transfer *in depth,* is India's proper 'loyalty to the origins,' her central doctrine, developed later, of the 'interdiffusion of all particulars,'[13] the Upanishadic *atman*-Brahman, myself-cosmic-self, correspondence; India's acceptance of reality as 'compoundness' at the very start, never as individuation, never as separation, transcendence, never separate, individual Godhead, never separate, individual soul-ego. Hence, the very core of India's certainty: that mind-ing and compoundness are one, that mind is matter, is stuff, and that matter or stuff is mind, the only (and only thus) reality. Not otherwise. India: the world of correspondence.

''While Greece, pre-classical Greece, was poor—Herodotus knew it!—to buy for less became the only choice for her grown will and urge to expand: piratic trade and the establishment and spreading of colonial centers of exchange, exploitation of their 'barbaric' hinterlands—opulent Greek trade cities along the Mediterranean shores and elsewhere, Sicily, south Italy, Iberia, France, great trading depots of piratically acquired riches. Contrary to India, here was a restricted world of numbers and their manipulation, the birth of a restrictive, prudent science of numbers. And

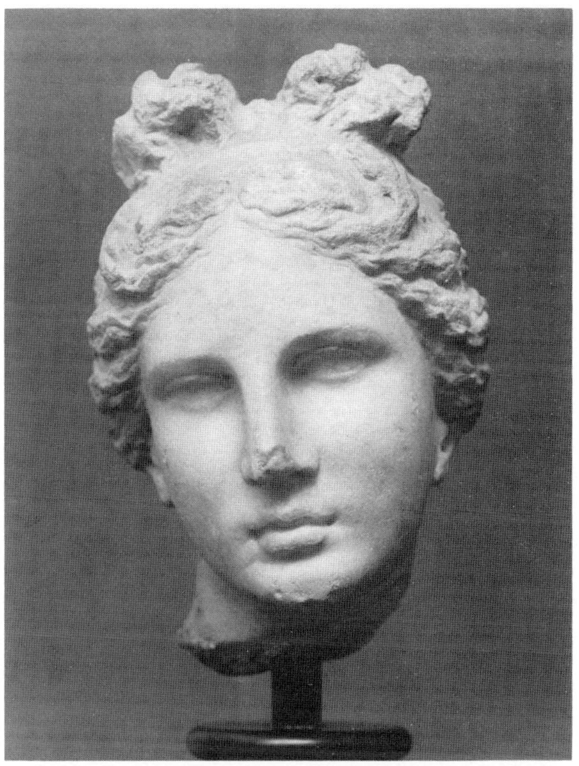

22. Head of a girl, school of Praxiteles

the mysterious, disturbing presence of the irrational, incommensurable number not at that time able to be included or retained, as in India, in an incessant flow of plethoric number enrichment, but, instead, both denied by Greek repulsion for the unthinkable, the irrational, and yet accepted as a concrete, unavoidable fact of mind and of action, this presence became a *transcendental, coming-out-from-oneself entity.* A transcendentality, yet a human, humanly involved, transcendentality. Thus 'better'—the best!—than all calculable and existential entities and beings: a new number-perfection, more precisely the very idea of an inescapable perfection. *The Idea.* From transfer to transfer in depth, it became in its ultimate existential projection, the *perfect form.* Geometry, the sacredness of geometry in Greece! Because the concept of perfection is the concept of what is total, closed, self-circumscribed and inescapable, this sacredness was felt as the reversibility of *all* perfect forms at once: this is what we mean here by 'proportionality' in the art and thought of Greece—the circle or sphere, the square or cube, the

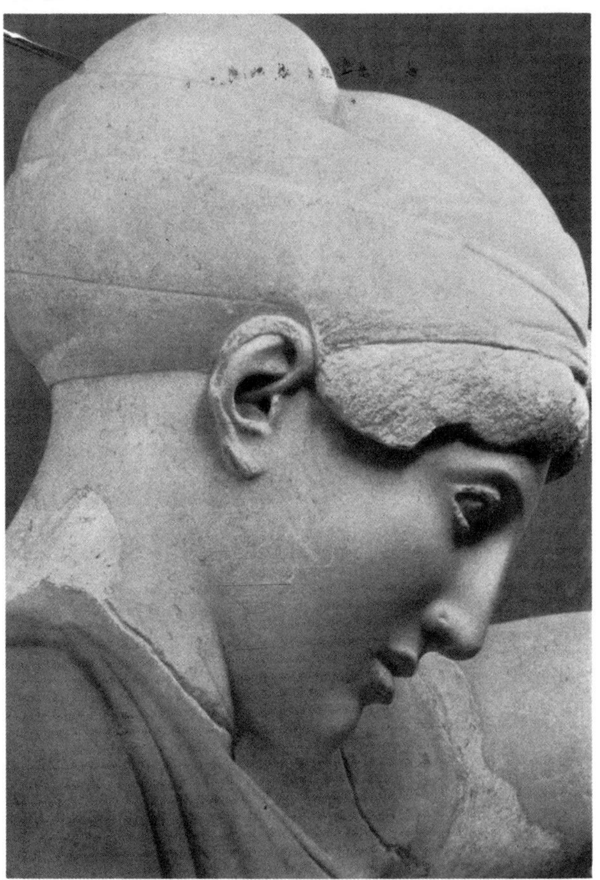

23. Head of Lapith woman

equilateral triangle or prism being one and the same (*Plate 23*). Not correspondence, but substitution—equation, total seizure—for unseizable infinity by the seizable finity of a precise form. *Noūs*. Order of nature and order of mind equated: genesis not only of the analysis of thinking and knowing (India), but of the analysis of the very conditions (categories of mind) *of thinking*, thus of knowing[14]—birth of the West's epistemology, the thinking about thinking, the looking at one's looking, in Ancient Greece; the thinking about thinking about thinking in the later West's derivations."

"Shadow, my shadow, and what else did you hear there to tell me?"

But the shadow remained silent then. Listening. And I knew why and to what: at the last moment of my shadow's rejoining me I too could hear the echo of far-off voices—the continued murmuring of the Oceanids:

" . . . a being . . . the justice-attitude in a particular fact (Babeuf), transferred—as significance, structure, behavior all at once—into the justice-attitude in a totally different, equally persistent and intense fact: very simply the function of the shadow, thus of light, in the art of painting . . . transferred . . . from transfer to transfer in depth: the Ancestor's labor . . . the meaning of Transfer . . . the meaning of History . . . of Mind . . . in Art: Justice, Solitude-Solidarity, *Tendresse* transferred into extension, into proportion, into light-and-color and directions. . . . Justice within the very significance, the directives of a line, of a melody, of an 'ornament,' of a significant, intense, telling curve. . . . "

*

The Ancestor was speaking. And I, Shadow-he, at that very moment found myself again on the balcony of a tall stone house, leaning over a narrow moonlit Mediterranean street: the story of a young northerner in search of warmth, health, and the friendly unknown.

Andersen's beloved story retold, differently. For the young northerner's unquenched yearning—his own shadow lost and returned—was back with him—with me—now, silent and giving. Across the narrow street the balcony opposite mine was silent and giving too, its window-door closed and dark now. The red and green garland of tenderness in full moonlight—Beethoven's last sonorities—was still there. All the solitude of man, all the solidarity in man! The fullest and last moment—the only moment of Permission on earth—of beatitude: evil enlightened—nought; ugly discourse of wars, ugly reasons of all wars, silenced, enlightened by the beauty and the scent of a living rose. And nobody ashamed of this sheltered folly—nobody where the voice of the Ancient was heard.

*

Unblended with either that night or that moment the voice of the Ancestor was heard:

"Somewhere—Okeanos! Soul!—at the bottom of any human attitude, collective, individual, there is present a being, generating, dual, the being-principle born before me, the pre-ancestor of all tensions and polarities in man: man's choice of leaning for his decisions, hopes, and fears on something outside him, and man's choice of leaning on himself.

"The leaning on something outside him: the principle of Creator-Father, giver of existence, of death, of compensation, of reward and punishment, with the terror of Solitude = Isolation, pity and faith in it; the Giver of existence and of souls: man's soul created ready for sin and virtue, an absolute parcel of the Creator's flesh and will, attached to Him, belonging to Him, yet separated from Him in the very *act* of being made His, the Immortal's, created creature, thus of being both imperishable, 'immortal,' and *individual,* yet mortal also, perishable as creature fashioned; forever to be of Him again, to be in Him, in a total death-absorption—oh, roots of nostalgia!—yet never hoping to have it—oh, darkest roots of mind's anxiety! Mask of terror, of fixity, of rest and immediacy, of separation and of creativity! How well did the Ancient Near East know and obey it; how far-reaching in our planet's time and space were its roots!

"And it has always been—still is!—the principle of Substitution by which the unseizable yet desired and present totality of existence is totally substituted—given totally—by a chosen part of it: the Father-creator's law, the law of sacrificial eucharist, the sacrificial 'barbarian' *pars pro toto* in a totalitarian state, totalitarian creed, party . . . and in man's creations—in art's transfer-descent: the substitution for the unseizable totality of personal experience (the total sensation!) by a 'totalitarian' inescapability of geometry's perfect form, perfect curve or perfect angle.

"I named it the world of *Apocalypse* in man, with its formidable iconography of the Pantocrator's terror-and-shelter, anxiety-and-relief: *the apocalyptic man in us.*

"Opposite it, in constant opposition and in constant interaction (*this twist or braid being the very course of all existing, of all history thus*), is the world of Correspondence, man's certainty of finity's flow into infinity and of infinity's into the finite; the world of becoming (spiralling growth), of transformation, with no birth, no death in it, no anxiety in it, and no rest in it either—the immense Indic world . . . I named it the world of *Psychomachia:*[15] *the psychomachic man in us*—the self-emerging creatureness of the creature: man and his inner struggles of good and evil, of evil and good, without the threat of sin or virtue (notwithstanding the verbal iconography of sin or vice and virtue there); the leaning on one's self, the leaning on one's own choice, my gift, the Ancestor's, of love at the birth of the psychomachic man: 'love that must be only love,' with nothing—no object, no subject to lean on; neither God-creator, nor the self, nor nature, nor the reminder of God, or nature, or love, or self, nor the remnants of rewards and denials. Nothing: *amor intellectualis Dei* only.[16]

''And when in depth transfer-descent we reach the domain of art, there it is, art's freedom of choice, art's *intellectual love of God* (love with no object of love—this absurdity in 'only-mind's' song, this clarity in 'marrow-bone's' song!), in choosing a line's 'that' and no other direction, color's 'that' direction, volume's, strophe's 'that' direction: the metaphysical direction of a 'significant ornament.' And in mid-road of the transfer-descent, the metaphysical direction of art's sociology itself: *the way we com-pose our life*—collective and individual—is the way we com-pose a line, a curve, a volume, a color, a sentence.

''So, for instance, in history, the life structure, the composition, of the restless ancient steppes is transferred into the structure, the com-position, of the art that originated in the nomadic, or rather semi-nomadic world. The socio-economic structure: hierarchic ascension from the anonymous base, the 'poor shepherd' masses, to the apex, the tribally chosen *rex* or *khan*, of the social and economic pyramid, whose sides are formed by the ascent of gradually richer and richer heads of cattle-owning families, the aristocracy of the steppes. This structure, 'geometrized,' rigid, yet free *de jure* in its basic element of free—mobile—tribal choice of leadership, is the very structure of the arts that initially came, however far in time or space, from the 'nomadic' world, carrying a dominant tendency toward 'geometrized,' structured and abstract, rigid, but innerly, in their expressive intensity, potentially 'mobile' delineations: the art of the once nomadic Akkadians, Assyrians or 'Hittites,' the art of the Achaeans, the 'Dorians' (*Plate 24*).

''Ringed by this 'mobile'-rigid restless world, was the world of primordial agricultural-urban formations, plethoric in its social structure and its arts, fertility-cult saturated, thus 'naturalistic' in

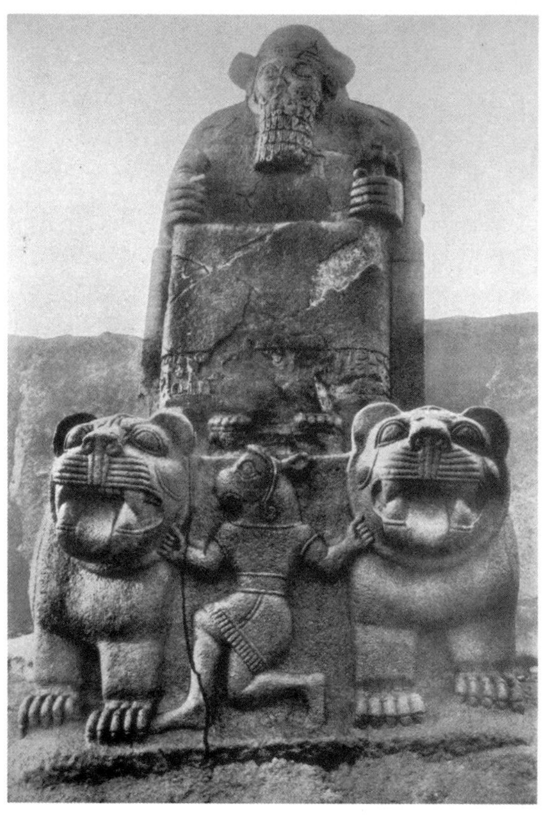

24. Hittite Thunder God

tendency, abstraction-free and potentially, innerly, 'stabile' in its city-temple's or palace-temple's dominating directives of all the economy and all social choices: Sumer, the most ancient Egypt, pre-Vedic India, probably Minoan Crete (*Plate 25*).''

*

''And when you return, as you must,'' continued the Ancestor, ''to your own world, tell them the great story of many origins you have heard here. The story of the Ancient and his Children and Grandchildren you have met here.

''Compose a great song. Sing the song of *Tendresse,* of Intrigue and of Transfer, the song of History and of Art, my first-born. How, from transfer to transfer in depth, the ultimate depth, the oozes at the bottom of Okeanos were reached, and how then the labors of time, the very transferability or historicity in history,

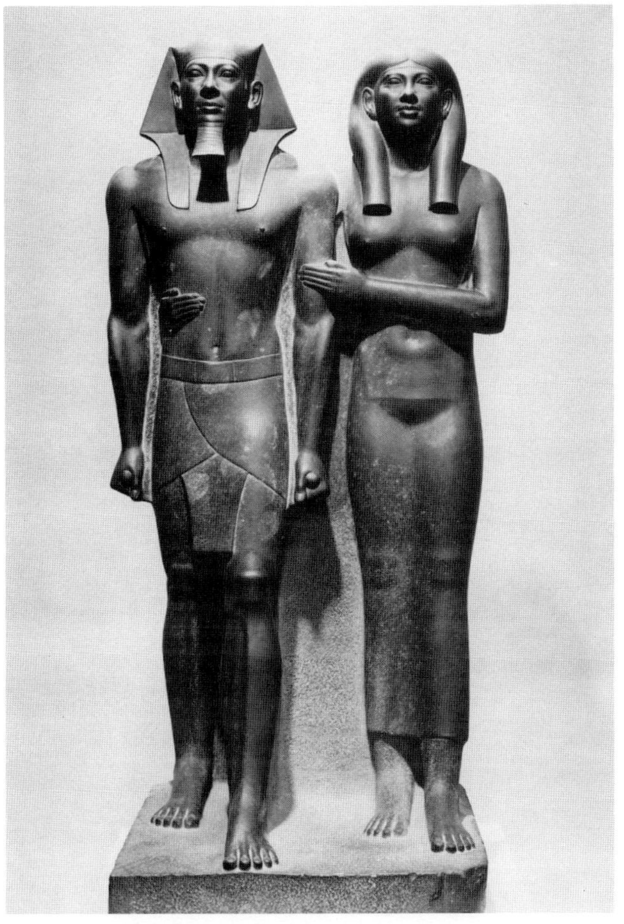

25. Mycerinus and His Queen

in the past, became stillness, *Aeternitas,* of the present, with nothing to transfer any more, nothing but present Solitude-Solidarity.

''The song of origins, of *Tendresse.* The true song of man and the true song of a rose, the good man's boldest, shameless poetry: the pluri-subject, the sub-subject, of art and poetry. Art and poetry's translucid transfer-levels . . .

''Chartres: Chartres' sudden interior, suddenly and really seen for the first time: the red blood on evil hands, the blood of wars and cruelties past and present and future, the red blood of Christ crucified, the blood of the Saviour and Redeemer, rubies and their inspirations, their mysteries of fire and earth now blended, now not, with the blue of the good man's exaltation, the Virgin's sky-robe, sapphires of fire-and-earth's mysteries and inspirations—blue and red roses. *La Femme Civilisatrice* of ancient Crete returning, shining, protecting us again, inside Chartres, from up there above the west entrance, or from within the jewel and bliss of the south rose in Paris' Notre Dame.

''Sing the fullest and last moment of beatitude—the only moment of such a *permission* on earth—of evil enlightened, made nought, of ugly discourse of wars enlightened and made nought by the beauty, the touch, the scent of a rose—and nobody ashamed of it in the interior of Chartres or the interior of History.

''Sing the great song of my other Children—the song of Connections, the song of my apocalyptic and my psychomachic man in us. And the song of the twist or the braid—the very way of existence itself in body, mind and history—the twist, the braid that makes of the two in us a dual oneness from the start, an interlacing, an overlapping in alternating primacy of now one, now the other, a two-one being in us with all the 'natural' complexities of divisions and subdivisions, of crisscross undercurrents: the braid of the apocalyptic and the psychomachic in Christian medieval man's evolvement, the primacy—but only primacy!—of the first in Byzantium, of the second in the West.

''And tell the story, relevant here, about the priestly man in ancient times, his mind and heart following the dictates of Substitution and of Apocalypse, and the story of the prophetic man in ancient times, the man of psychomachic freedom and certainty of choice, his mind and heart loyal to the *logos* of correspondence between freedom, truth and righteousness—that story of the two opposite worlds always co-present in us, once upon a time, in Judea, institutionalized, and thus made unique; in ancient Greece made visible—spiral-and-circle; in ancient India appeased and nourished maternally by the Vedic-Brahmanic (later Tantric Buddhist) world of the 'priestly' man (himself dual and self-subdivided), braided with the world of the 'prophetic' man, Upanishadic and Hinayana Buddhist, the threads of the braid there, as elsewhere, always alternating, over and under.

''Yes, sing the song of the Braid, the song of man's history on earth.''

*

This voice of the Ancient became blended forever with the enchanted Mediterranean night.

Silent. Silence.

I remained alone with the unsung song—and I named this song my mysterious Companion—my Companion visible invisible, ever present beside me. And I went back to my own world, choosing freely to know that the song *Tendresse* wanted me to sing will be sung by the things of man's creation themselves.

I shall look for and look at them anew.

*

It (it: my mysterious companion-song) started anew with the Three Faces I met on a Sunday morning in Barcelona, the city of majesty and of the *Jongleurs.*

Again, as I was doing every day, I descended the clean-washed staircase of my old many-balconied stone house and walked along Barcelona's shortest yet much beloved street, the vehicle-free *Carrer Petrixol,* so full of Barcelona's tormented and nostalgic memories, and at the end of it found myself—a new visitor, a new, another, eyewitness now!—standing and musing in front of the First Face, the façade of Santa Maria del Pí (*Plate 26*).[17]

A Gothic façade, so Gothic-Catalan in its inconspicuous yet elegant sobriety, free of all luxuriance and Gothic *chichi,* still so loyally Romanesque in its all-architectonic-parts embracing expressiveness, the idiom of its entire silhouette being the very idiom of the decorated content.

There it was, total, unobtrusive, open—a chosen Face, a pensive, expressive and smiling young face looking at me and I looking at it, listening to what the face had to say. In a flash of confidence and shared friendship the Gothic façade told me the story—and I knew then it was the entry, the prelude, to the song!—of the far-reaching (to Languedoc, Mallorca, Valencia, all—Iberia at large!) Catalan loyalty to the canon of Romanesque architecture, this Christian art, *par excellence,* of the medieval West, with the poignant confrontation there of classical—Greek!—proportionality and the "barbaric," Celto-Germanic (Islamic also, in Iberia) "significant ornament," a story-telling ornament. Such the imagery of the Romanesque *retablo*-like façades and apses of the great abbey-

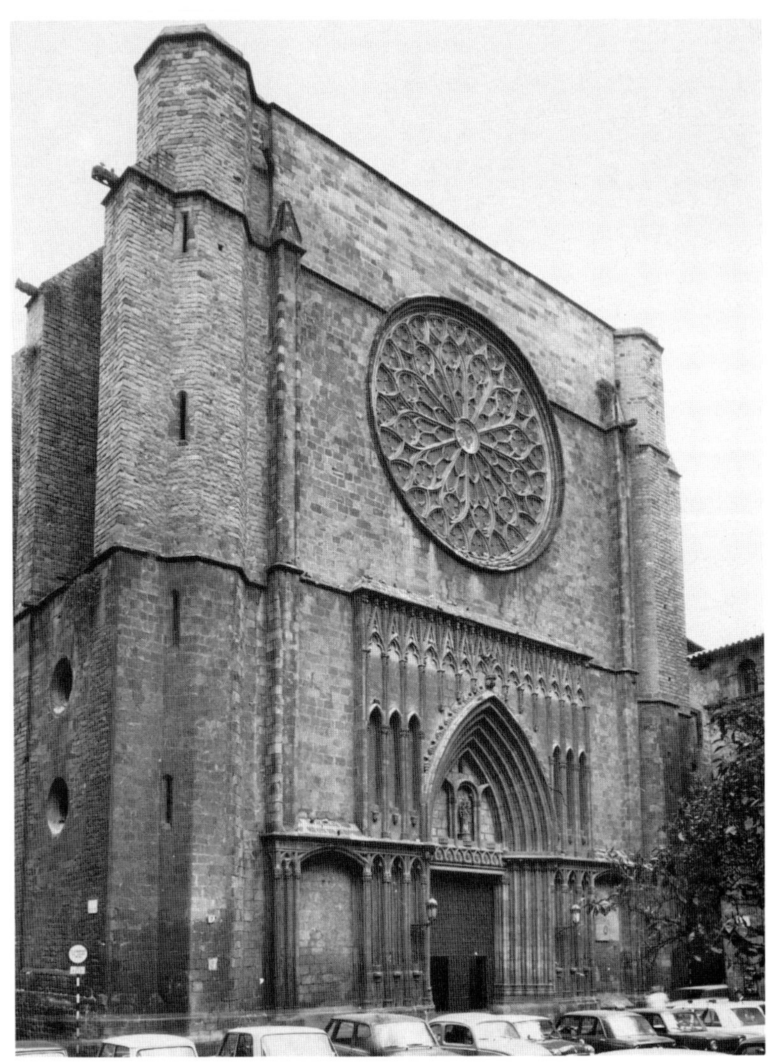

26. Façade, Sta. Maria del Pí, Barcelona

churches throughout the West: Poitiers, Angoulême, Ripoll (*Plates 27a & b*, and *see Plate 10*). . . . Anxiety, tremor in witnessing the incessant battle between good and evil, and *suavitas* in the choice of shelter in the humane Redemption!—all sub-stories, sub-subjects, told in the very composing of lines and architectonic ensembles: such, for instance, the immense cross—a multiple blind-arched pattern laid upon the entire façade at Angoulême—its arms holding suspended at their ends the images of evil and of good (*Plate 28*). Passionate Romanesque *retablo*-façades, both ecclesiastical and secular, forgotten later in the West, remembered with ever increased passion and impact by later styles in Iberia—from, say,

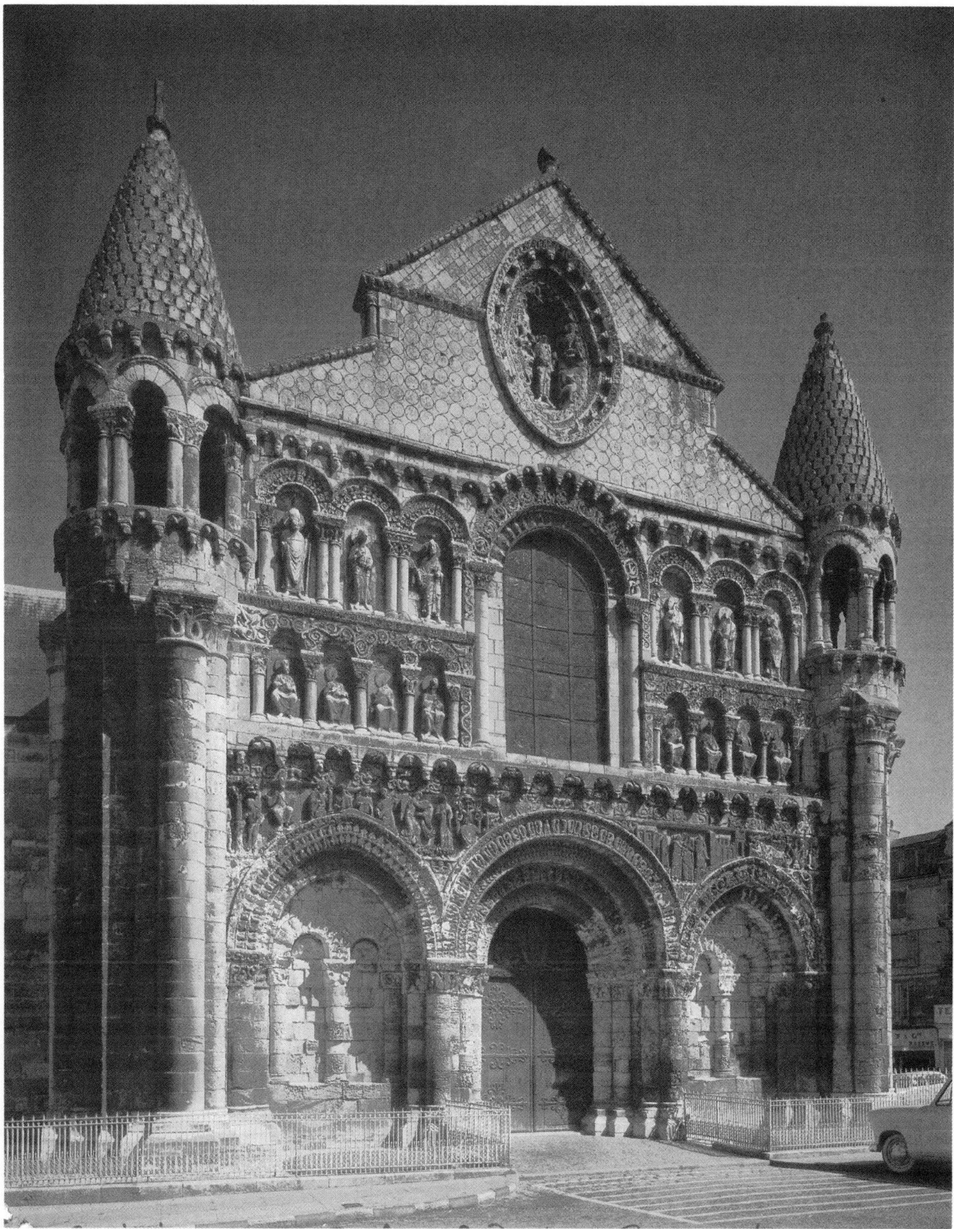

27a. Façade, Notre-Dame-la-Grande, Poitiers

the neo-Romanesque Isabellan (in Castile) and Manueline (in Portugal) to the neo-Romanesque of the (erroneously) so-called Churrigueresque-Baroque (*Plates 29a & b,* and *see Plate 125*).

What my mysterious companion-song was also telling me then was confirming what I had learned long ago about the Romanesque world: that its growing urbanization—fruit of monastic,

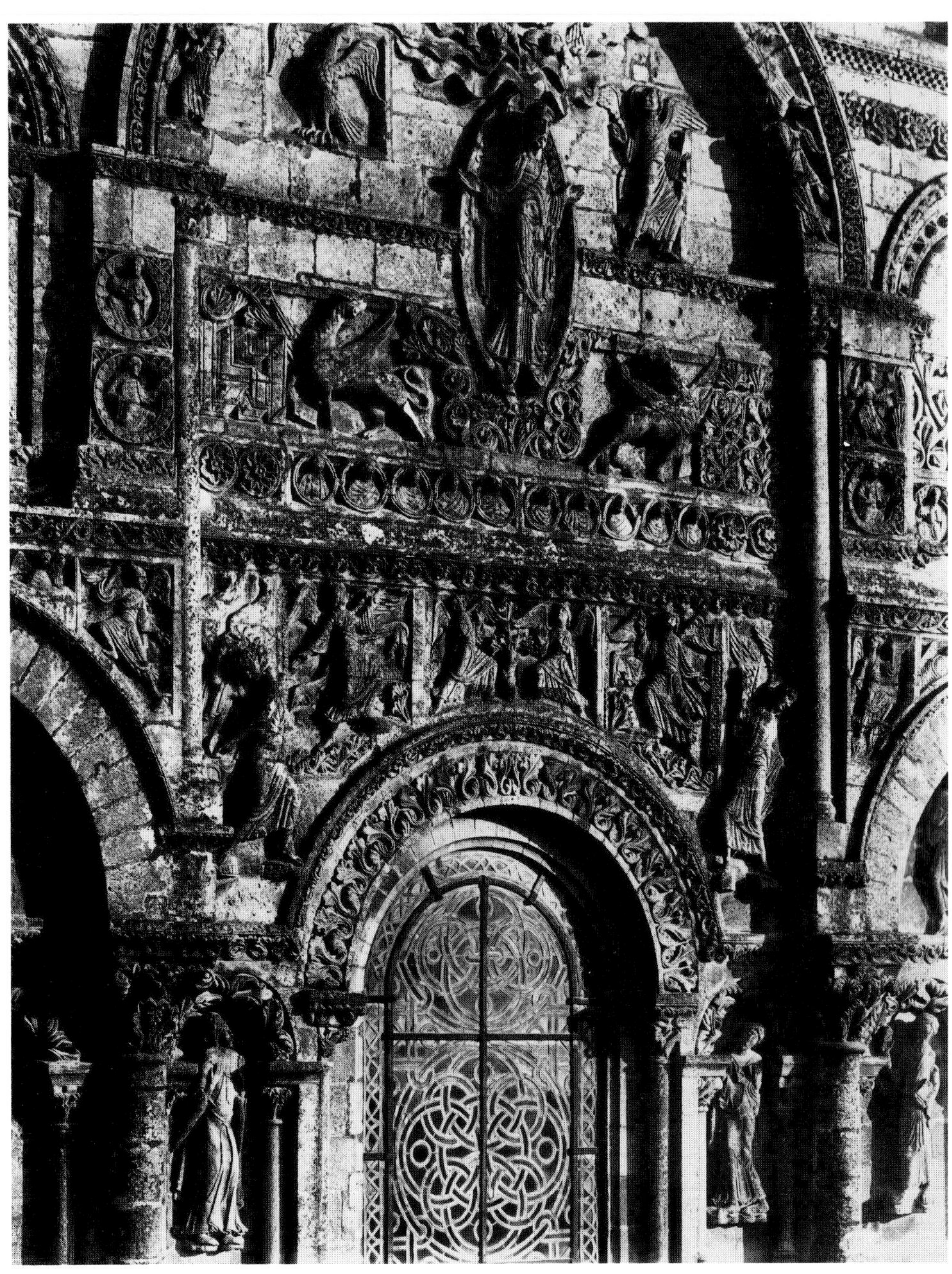

27b. Detail of façade, Cathedral of St. Pierre, Angoulême

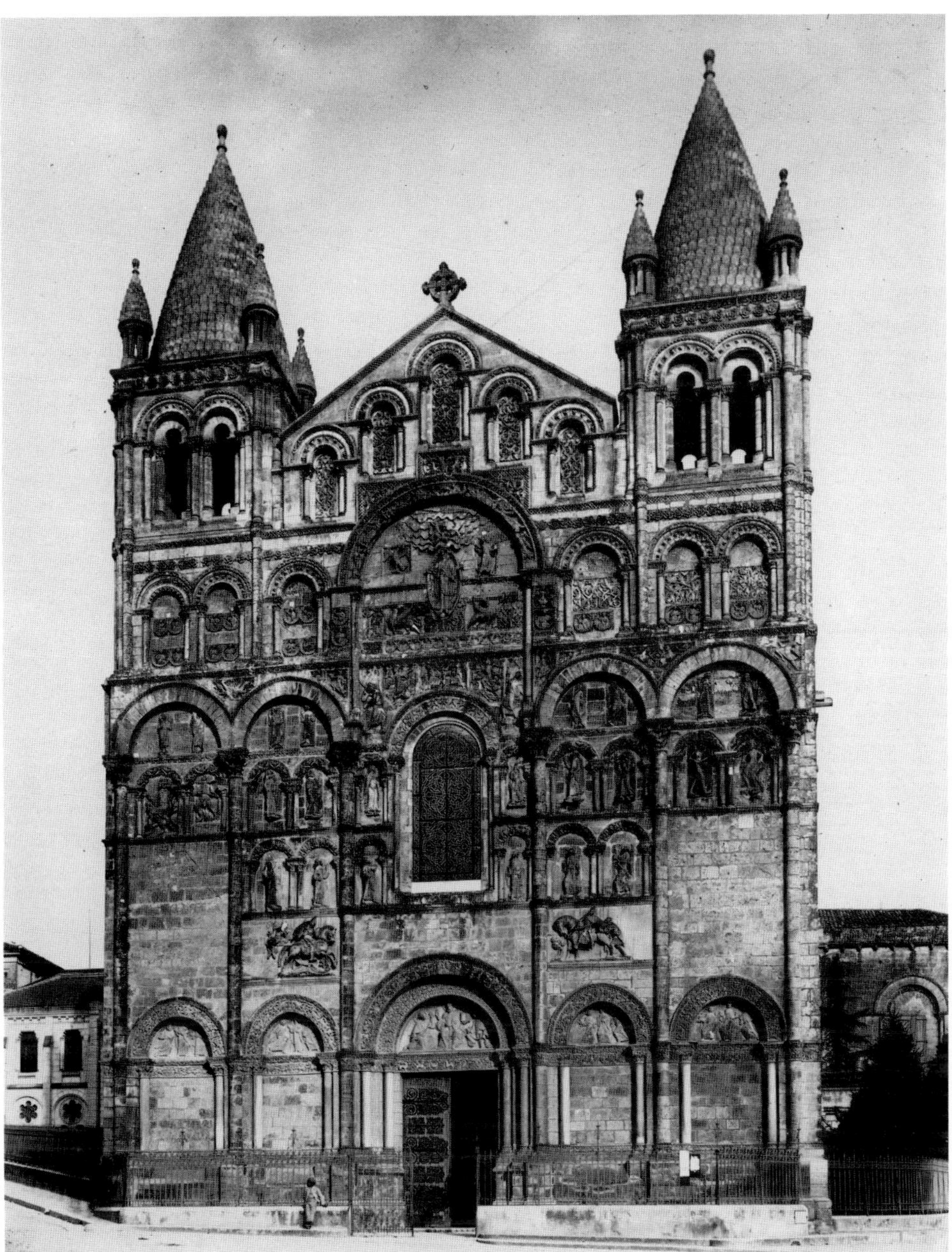

28. Façade, Cathedral of St. Pierre, Angoulême

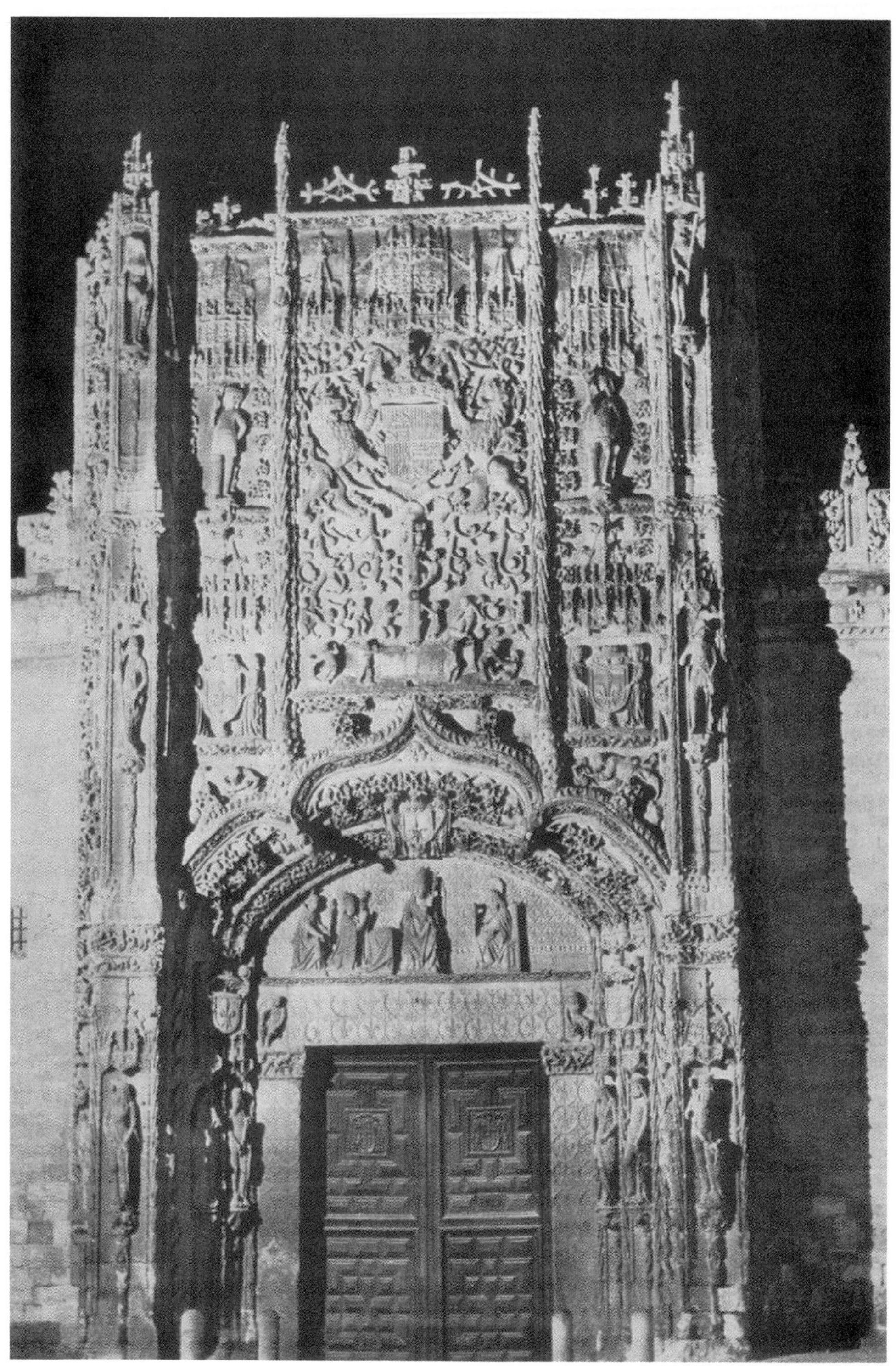

29a. Façade, Colegio de S. Gregorio, Valladolid

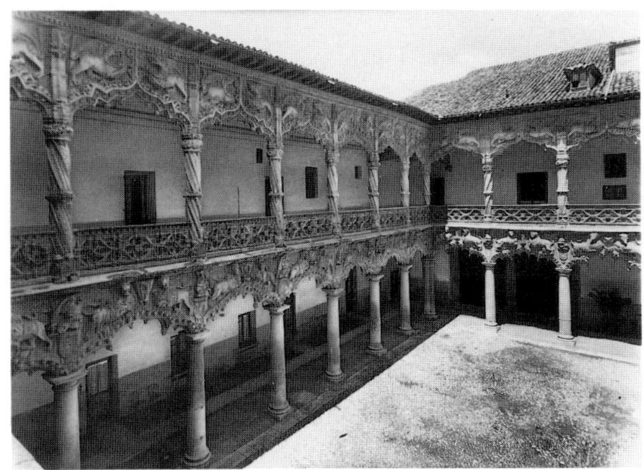

29b. Patio, Palace of the Infantado, Guadalajara

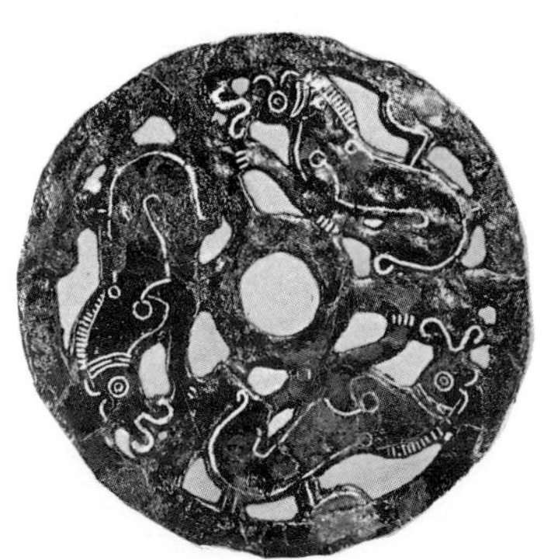

30. Merovingian openwork disk

mainly Cluniac, and a little later Cistercian, ambitious and pragmatic labors—and its acquired multi-leveled sophistication and density, nevertheless kept enough transparency in them to reveal a single object-motif that shone at the bottom level of Romanesque historical origins: the ''barbaric'' object-ornament, part either of personal adornment and utility, or of the nomad's horse trappings, thoughtfully wrought by expert artist hands.

And, as was suggested by a great and imaginative historian in France,[18] this nomadic personal object of both luxury and need that could thus belong to the body's wish (exactly architecture's wish!) for shelter, involvement, self-inclusion, was, in the absence of real, stable, ''nomad'' architecture, as it were the portable substitution for it.

And the ''barbaric'' ornament, a fibula, a clasp, a purse or a horse trapping, this self-framed object, so ''total'' in the dense and tight interlacing of its decorative elements (*Plate 30*) (in reality mythic, good-versus-evil story-telling elements, here too), and in the mutual *adhesion* of all its parts, of their continuity, thus their mobility—this object ornament could become, from innermost psycho-historical transfer to transfer, an immensely magnified object-to-be-held in the hollow of my hand again, close to my body, to be carried along with my body: a Romanesque *retablo*-façade and apse.

The Romanesque world of the eleventh to twelfth centuries—so the not-yet-soaring song was telling me!—the world of a fleshy, sensuous, dionysiac and cumulative adhesion (the principle of a total adhesion to each other of, say, the self-framed, rounded-elastic arches in Romanesque cloisters) (*See Plates 34a & b*) how different is this world from that of the Gothic harmonies, the ''pure'' thirteenth-century French Gothic in its full and young fruition, with its Gothic principle of seriated association, of cadenced and ''stable'' *connections* (not adhesions) between all its architectonic entities, and the logical culmination of this in the achievements of Gothic ensembles, both in architecture and in its imagery: the imagery of Vincent de Beauvais' *Speculum Majus* (*Plate 31*).

With one exception, however—not only in the Gothic art of Iberia, but elsewhere also: the Gothic of Catalonia. It is unique. At the very peak of its Gothic glory, the fourteenth and fifteenth centuries, Catalonia's loyalty both to the Romanesque principle of ''adhesion'' and to classical antiquity's proportionality makes its architecture stand out in the entire West as a beautiful yet puzzling exception (true, Gothic France sometimes also reveals her loyalty to the Romanesque past: the self-framing ''total'' façade of the cathedral of Paris, the interior of Rheims' cathedral sheltering the two ''Romanesque'' multi-niched arches that flank its west entrance).

Historically puzzling, indeed, is the medieval architecture, Romanesque as well as Gothic, of Catalonia. Above all, and particularly, because of Catalonia's never-failing love for antiquity's musical-numerical proportionality, she kept her own spatial appropriateness and economy, the exact ''that-ness'' of distances between, say, an arch and the wall above or around it (later, one of the glories of the early Renaissance in Florence, which suggests if not explains the reason why Catalonia, so close politically and culturally to Italy, waited so long—perhaps never needed or

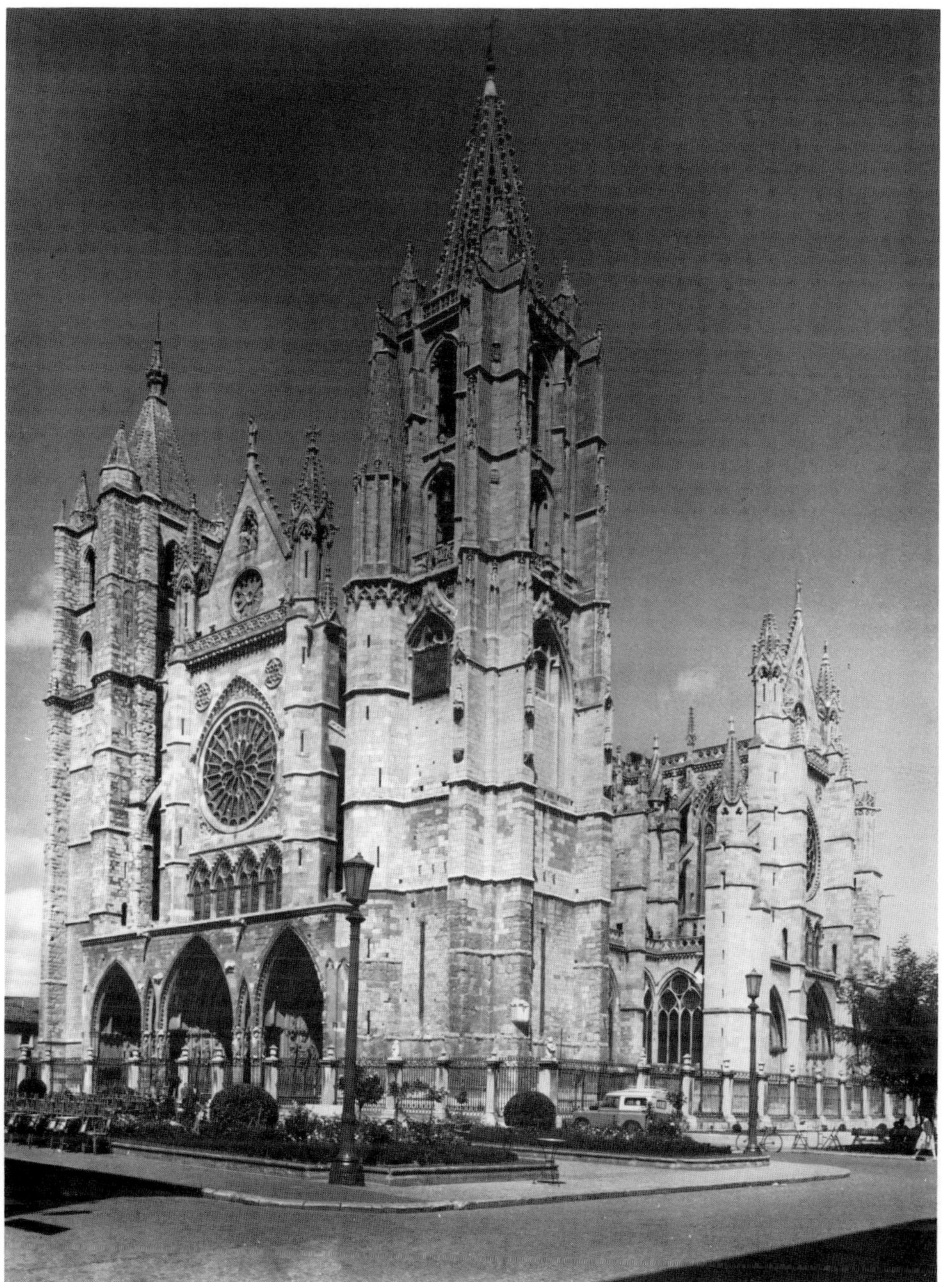

31. Façade, León Cathedral

wanted!—to adopt or follow the Brunelleschian or Bramantean teaching: it was here already). All the elegant, sober, ''classical'' economy of medieval Catalonia—the result of her own ''loyalty to origins'' and not of the ''*avara povertà dei Catalani*'' in Dante's mistaken, because, probably, so jealous definition! But loyalty to what origins? To a mythic ''national'' psychology? To this psychology's predisposition for, say, the forthcoming Cistercian aesthetic ''puritanism''? Or was it, more concretely, the memory of Greece's and Rome's classicism ever alive along the eastern shores of Mediterranean Iberia? Or, again, was it, in a more hidden and undetectable way, along and at the foot of the Pyrenean mountain chain, joining the Atlantic and the Mediterranean, all the subtle influences and inspirations that may already have been traveling in pre-Romanesque times from the rude and still Visigothic (the Visigothic fascination with Antiquity!) (*Plate* 32). Asturias, the cradle of the Reconquista, to the more hospitable and open Catalonia? For what still remains of Asturias' architecture, Oviedo's abbey-churches and palaces at their highest flowering, the ninth-century era of Alfonso II (Alfonso el Casto, circa 790–842) and Romiro I (842–50) is a sheer marvel (despite its pre-Romanesque naiveté) of elegance, of engineering boldness and wholly classical proportionality (*Plates 33a & b*). (As such, those remnants were already admired in the days of Felipe II, by Ambrosio de Morales, who, sent to the North by the king, wrote about San Miguel de Linio to the monarch: ''It is delightfully small, for including the thickness of the walls it is no more than forty feet [old measure] in length and half that in width; yet in this tininess there is such beautiful proportion and correspondence, that any artist, even the very best of today, would do well to consider it attentively and to praise it.'')[19]

*

At this very moment my mysterious companion-song was about to leave its flatland prelude and to take its first soaring flight. The Asturian answer, if answer there had been, I could not see following it. Gone, perhaps.

What surely remained with me there, unchanged, convincing and uninhibited, was the enchantment of the eye and the mind amidst the suddenly revived rhythms of ancient Greece (were they

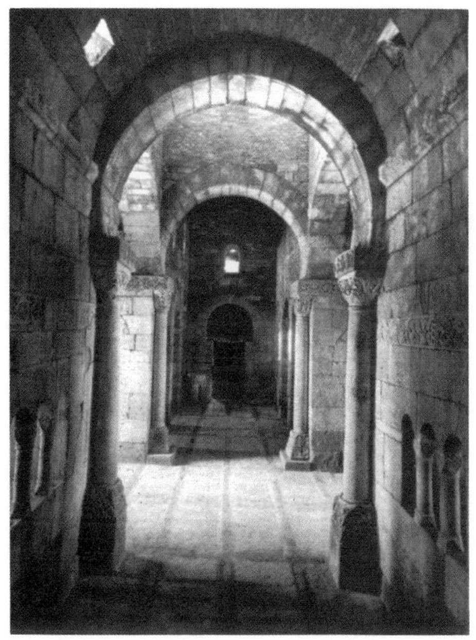

32. Interior, S. Pedro de Nave

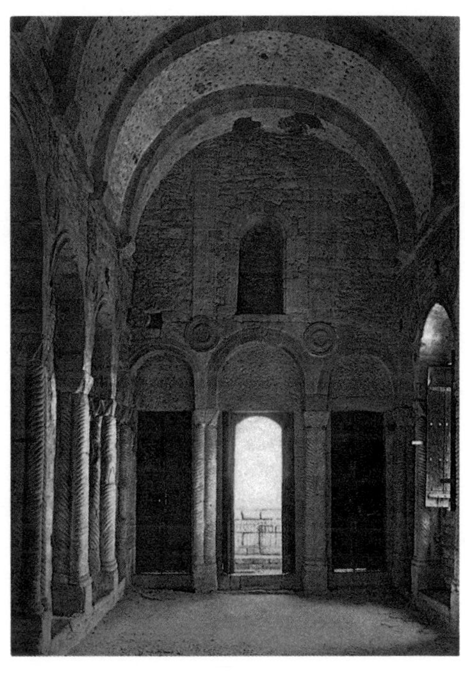

33a. Interior, Sta. María de Naranco

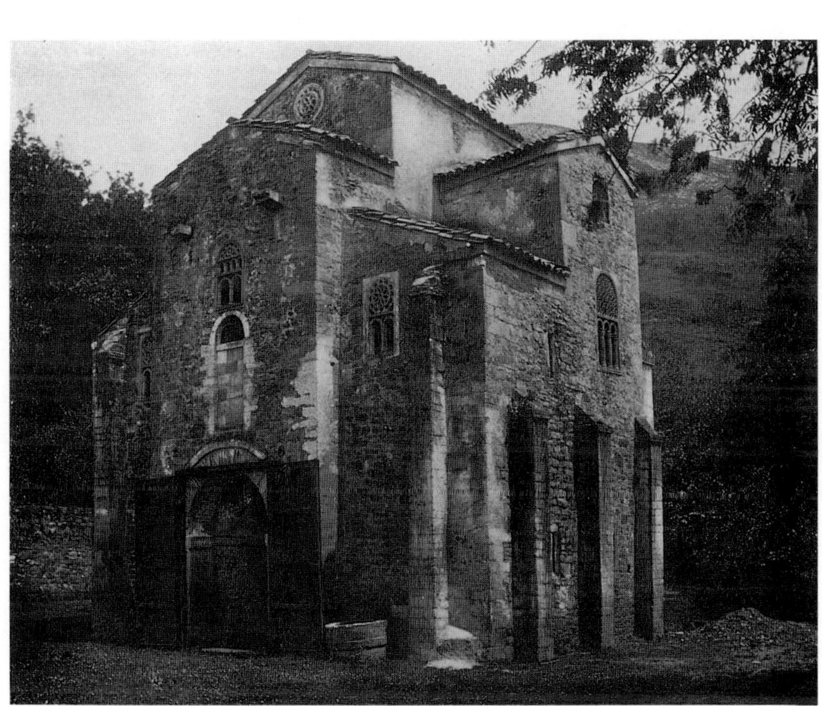

33b. San Miguel de Linio

Asturias'?), transferred now, here, into the Catalan medieval world: the twelfth-century Romanesque cloisters, from Elne in Roussillon[20] to the most "Brunelleschian" of all, San Cugat del Vallés (*Plate 34a*), or the tiny jewel of Sant Pau del Camp in Barcelona, its distinctly Cordoban polygonal arches not troubling Greece's echo (*Plate 34b*); in Gerona, the façade, the interior and the cloisters of Sant Pere de Galligans, this "barbaric ornament," so "classical" nevertheless in its poise and clarity; then, in the heart of the fourteenth century Gothic already (but within the same "Romanesque" adhesion-and-proportionality), among the arches of Barcelona's most enchanting cloister, Santa Ana's (*Plate 35*); or Catalonia's "purest" architectural élan of spatial appropriateness and Greek perfection or inescapability, the Gothic naves and the *girola* of Barcelona's Santa Maria del Mar (fourteenth century);[21] and still later in the Gothic era (fifteenth-sixteenth centuries), within the astonishing and bold ("classic" always—so Catalan!—proud, sober, elegant) interior of Gerona's cathedral, its one nave's vault built in a single span, the widest in the entire Gothic West; and, as final symphonic resolution, in front of and around the fifteenth-century harmonies of Palma's and Valencia's *Llotjes* (*Plate 36*).[22]

*

However, in meditative affinity with the quiet and meditative mood of that Sunday morning, Barcelona's Three Faces became my chosen, my cherished discovery: the façade of Santa Maria del Pí (*See Plate 26*) where I was standing now; not too distant from it, the lateral (northern) Sant Iu façade of Santa Eulalia cathedral (*Plate 37*),[23] and still deeper in the heart of Gothic Barcelona and closer to the sea, the façade of Santa Maria del Mar (*Plate 38*); the three glamorless, often unnoticed, Franciscan, and so expressive, so inviting faces of "my" Barcelona!

*

Neither by dream nor reality molested any longer, the song was freely soaring now—the song sung by the children of the Ancient, the song for *Tendresse,* the song of connections—a high-soaring wave of protected exaltation!—the song of transfers—a

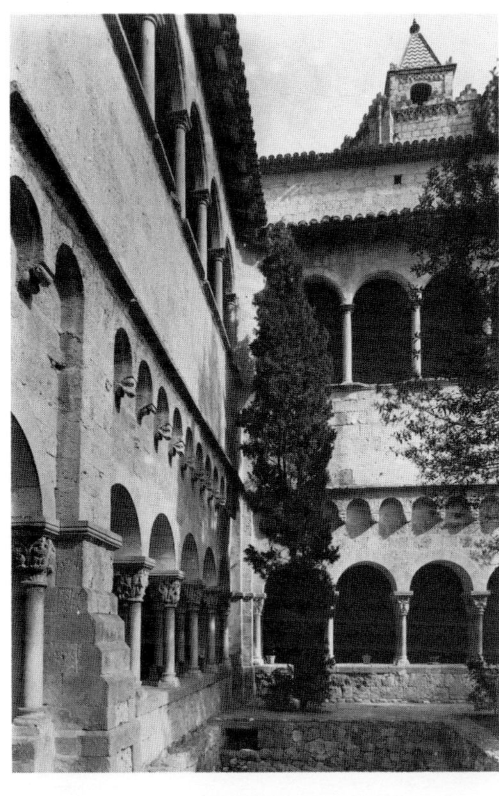

34a. Cloister, San Cugat del Vallés, Barcelona

34b. Cloister, Sant Pau del Camp, Barcelona

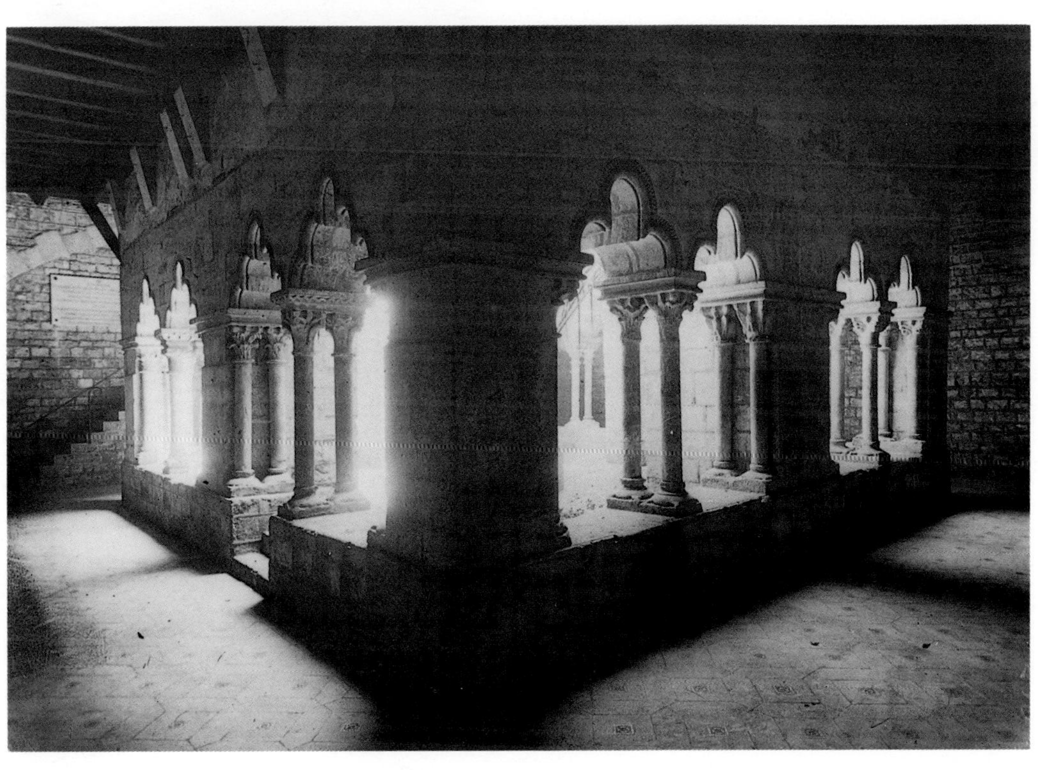

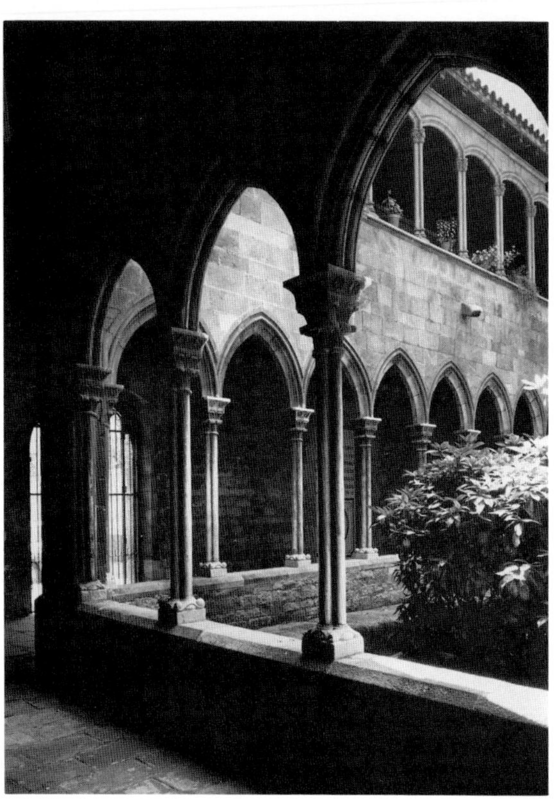

35. Cloister, Santa Ana, Barcelona

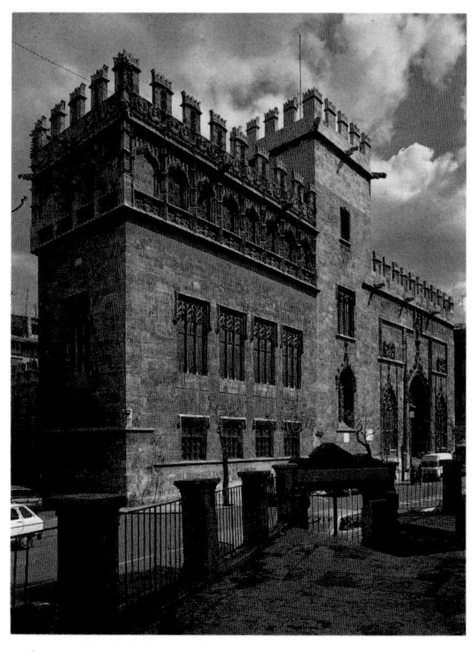

36. Silk Exchange, Valencia

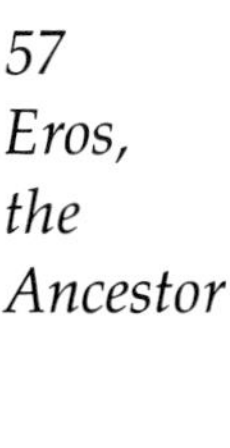


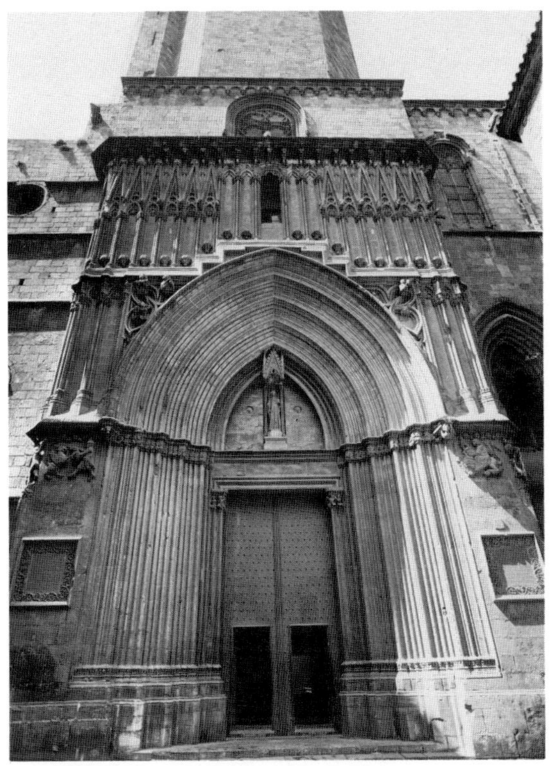

37. Sant Iu lateral façade, Sta. Eulalia Cathedral, Barcelona

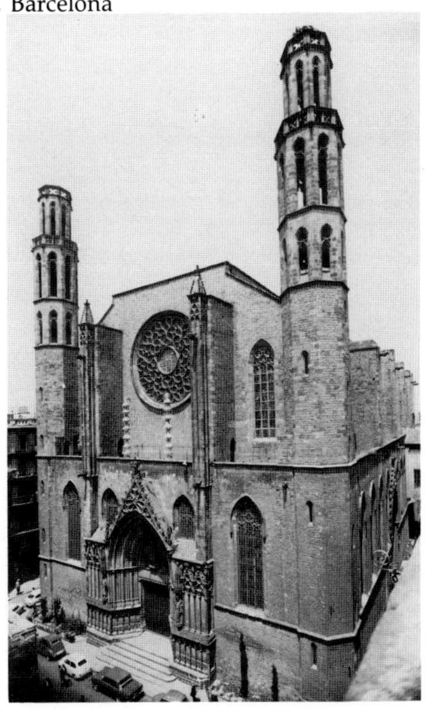

38. Façade, Sta. Maria del Mar, Barcelona

deep-soaring wave of protected contemplation! The song of *permitted* beatitudes. Permitted here and only here! Not permitted there, over there in the cities of "mind only," within the mundane discourse of bitterness (but not within bitterness itself!)—all the busy discourses about bitterness among the siblings of blood-linked, ideology-linked, love-hate-linked families on earth (in our analyses, our letters and our Realpolitik sort of cleverness and satire of today).

Beatitudes: permitted here, where "Anyone who loves flowers is naturally not liked by bullets / Flowers, gather for war!"[24]

"Flowers gather for war"—contradiction, easily set aside, mocked at. And yet: St. Augustine's "Love God and do whatever you wish" meant to be "Where there is love for the Good, Good is possible, and Evil, which is, is impossible"!

"Flowers gather for war" = beatitude, a permitted war—permitted wars! It is the war of the poet-knight there, watching, witnessing the transfer, total, from mind-and-heart's substructures of superstitions, such as the stubborn and dark beliefs in the healing or harming, human-astral and "magic" powers released at will by precious stones of earth, stones quintessentialized by the action of fire—diamonds, sapphires, emeralds, rubies, opals, amethysts—the poet-knight witnessing, first, the total transfer of this into the world of distilled aesthetic joys and enrichments, the exalted world of diamonds, rubies, sapphires, emeralds of the Sainte Chapelle's glass walls, and thence, up and up, among the same splendors and without diminishing their pleasures, higher and higher into the world of mind's and heart's deeper communications and connections. Here—oh, approaching wave of beatitude!—is how, still at the Sainte Chapelle, the world of *moral,* because free, yet self-imperative, *psychomachic* choice is in the choice by the medieval artist (in this not subservient to the theologically dictated iconographic content) of *that and no other* precise value of goodness communicated by the value-red of the translucid ruby, the value-blue of the translucid sapphire or the value-green of the translucid emerald. And again a free, thus creative, choice: the sudden color splashes on the heraldic color field of the Sainte Chapelle's window—*that and no other* vicinity of red, yellow, blue!—the "moral" color accents creating a new psychochromatic idiom in which the poet-knight's final transfer-ascension (his permitted beatitude = wars) is told!

And what is it told there? Touch, smell, see, hear and comprehend—as it was with the Bee of Crete—the highest crest of *Tendresse:* the sub-subject of the innermost, total, poet-knight's tale! The tale of how the moral, the central man in him, second in degree of ascent, awakened by the aesthetic, the first man in him, and weary soon of the intense yet fleeting pleasures of the aesthetic, could not remain there longer, and reached, then entered the domain of the third and ultimate man in him, the metaphysical or the poetic.

And how poetry—this sudden, unexpected meeting and connection between most distant, unexpected beings-ideas and beings-images—became the teller of the total man's inner destiny. How the drama enacted by art's color-and-line directives (the splendors of the Sainte Chapelle and the humility of Barcelona's Three Faces equated now!) is transferred, indeed, into the very drama in depth of good-versus-evil struggles in man's total history, inner and outer.

It was then that Santa Maria del Pí faced me again, alone and the first of the Three.

The Face was radiant with eloquence and confidence: humble and proud at the same time in its over-all horizontal-rectangular ornament directions and expression—so "Romanesque!"—yet also so arrogant, uplifting and beautiful, in the slanted verticality, the arched triangularity of her other architectonic features (*See Plate 26*). A strife so moving and revealing, so meaning-full! And suddenly—oh, permitted presence of beatitude carrying to its crest this *retablo*-façade's tale!—the strife between the two architectonic directions there, simply the vertical and the horizontal, and the strife between two historical idea-directions of mankind were made one and the same: the idea of the humble yet proud Duty—the Romanesque squareness of the Face—and the idea of the arrogant yet uplifting and beautiful Rights—the Gothic triangularity of the Face—their strife, on that Face, along the millenia-long history of mankind. In a flash-vision of transferred psycho-historical levels or attitudes, there it was, the drama—ontology and metaphor—of oppressive minorities, depositories of social Rights, imposing for centuries and centuries, violently, their abusive rule over Duty-bound oppressed majorities; the drama—ontology and metaphor—of the struggle between the two universal, moral-social categories, and of the slow—so slow!—change in them: the idea or the category of rights more and more incorporated in the exigencies of the awakening majorities, and the privileged minorities' rights themselves transferred into the world of duty—violence and violation presiding again and again there—with no end to the struggles, no end to the dialectical braiding! With no end . . . .

And yet, the song, the song of the Face now, was the song of an end also: I could hear-touch-smell-see-comprehend there the prophetic promise (and the vision of a singing voice was this promise already!) of *Tendresse* and of *Resolve.*

And what an astonishing discovery it was for me when later in the day I heard the same song—but different voices—coming from the two other beings so closely related to it and to each other: the Face of the Sant Iu *retablo*-façade, Sant Iu's tale, and the Face of Santa Maria del Mar, Santa Maria del Mar's tale!

But it was still the humble and the most convincing of all, the tale of Santa Maria del Pí, my first-born, that I wanted to hear again and again. The tale of how the imperious, domineering, yet gallant upsurge—the Rights!—of Gothic triangular verticality there, the three tiers of pointed, narrow arches, so young, so lovely, but born blind, surrounded the church's entrance and how this piercing *élan* was interrupted, thus arrested—*no pasaran!*—by not only the ''Romanesque'' horizontality and squareness—humble and proud!—of the two halves and their four sub-divisions, but also by the horizontal rhythm of the superimposed rectangles, unequal in width, that form the entire contour of the resulting *retablo*-façade. And how the counter-arrogance of this imperious arrest became mind's, heart's and history's gift of harmony, the ''contact of contraries''—the gift of a perfect circle-rose on the upper, totally naked, half of the façade, the gift of Catalan classical appropriateness, of the precise placing—not any higher, not any lower!—of this great rose-window and of the resulting proportionality of the Face—the square, the triangle, the circle equated there! The song's prophetic promise of *Tendresse* and Resolve!

Not more dramatic but more familiar, the tale of Sant Iu. Here I saw the Gothic upsurge not arrested as at Santa Maria del Pí, at its lower station or division, but protected and left to be freely achieved in its lordly and exalted goal. I was seated for a long while on the stone wall-bench facing, across the medieval *Carrer dels Comtes,* the humble and also proud Sant Iu façade (*See Plate 37*): no other Gothic arch formation, so I decided then, could possibly give me the same feeling of a totally uninhibited *élan* than what was given to me by the superb five-fold arch framing the cathedral's lateral entrance. And yet the sensuous, fleshy fullness of adhesion between all its component parts made it, and its content, so "Romanesque!" But the drama of confrontation itself—the transferred strife of Rights and Duties or verticals and horizontals—was placed higher up:



The Gothic *élan* of the portal's arch was not only protected, but was helped toward its fulfillment by the crenellated ascension of a rectangular, horizontal—Romanesque!—formation, which both supported and followed the Gothic curve. But it was precisely then that the cry *"no pasaran!"* was heard again; and at the cry's appeal a new, unexpected upsurge—the towering, tall and rectangular structure, both *very* horizontal and *very* vertical, crowning the façade—a new unexpected meaning, came to change entirely the expression of the Face. The proud pride (*orgueil*) of the Gothic ("be the leader of Rights!") was transferred into the humble pride (*fierté*) of the Romanesque ("be the fulfillment of human Duties!").

That is what it was, Sant Iu's own song and tale—unique!—of *Tendresse* and Resolve.

And so intense was this song's impact on me that, finding myself at the end of that day in front of my Third Face, the façade of Santa Maria del Mar, the obvious absence of any dramatic conflict there, its uninhibited expression of *euphoria* startled me at first and made of me a stranger to it. It was only after having visited the interior and seen and admired the exquisite "classicism" of its native idiom—the Gothic-Catalan at its most earnest and sonorous!—that, when coming back to the façade, I could befriend it fully. Yes, I had to admire the harmonies of the interior, the world of both correspondence and adhesion; I had to partake of the open, free hospitality of the nave's great arches,[25] each spanning, in one great embrace, the three arches (much smaller but identical in silhouette) of the lateral nave's chapels (*Plates 39a & b*); I had to listen to this ample melody of correspondence and adhesion continued in the immense *élan* of the tall and slender pillars surrounding the *girola,* their summits—in arched adhesion to each other and to the corresponding radial vaults—adhering also to the memories, never lost, of the Romanesque (*Plate 40*); only then could I hear

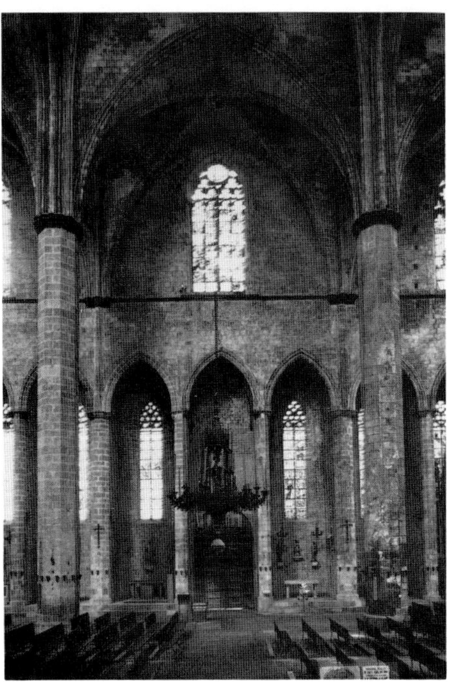

39a. Arches, lateral nave's chapels, Sta. Maria del Mar, Barcelona

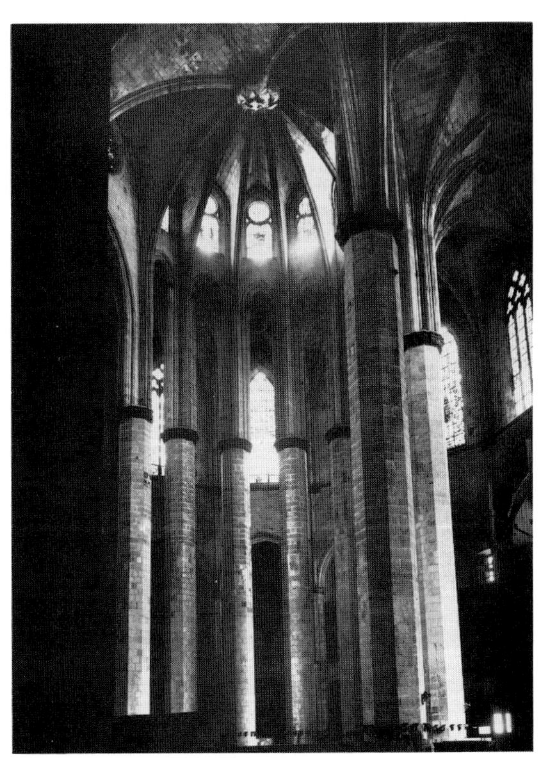

39b. Pillars of girola, Sta. Maria del Mar, Barcelona

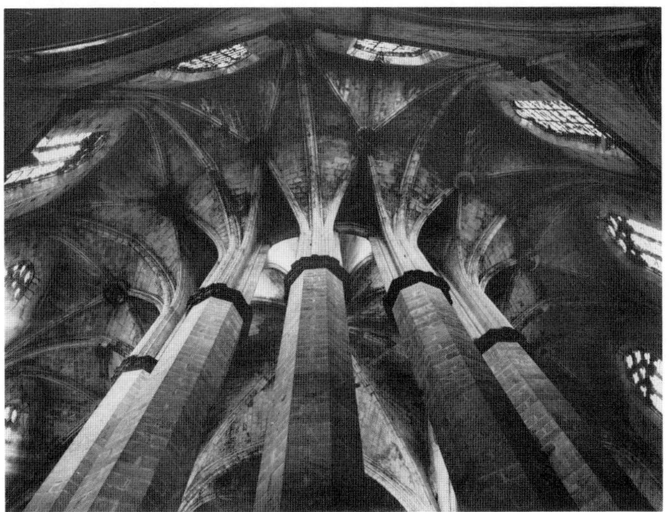

40. Radial vaults, Sta. Maria del Mar, Barcelona

again in front of my Third Face, the singing of *Tendresse* and Resolve! A happy, a very happy song of plenitude and solution, such as to absorb and dissolve in it any dissonance of conflict (*See Plate 38*)! In one calligraphic gesture of resolute and thoughtful delineation, all the architectonic elements of the façade—the two very tall and very svelte polygonal bell towers, the flaming entrance and the well-placed rose-window—are embraced to form one total unit, the ''ornament''-being of a *retablo*-façade, the Romanesque of the past, the Baroque of the future.

*

The song of the three beloved Faces of Barcelona was sung in a discreet, sweet, never loud voice—the voice of all old nostalgic Catalan folk songs—unpretentious songs all, of desire, of defeat, of energy, of promise—of promise only—and of dreaming . . . And the song's repeated melody of correspondence, adhesion and ''Romanesque'' duty-pride, I heard it spreading throughout all the lands of laborious Catalonia, from the cloisters and naves of the Priorat—Poblet, Santas Creus—to those, northern, of the Seo of Urgel . . .

The wave of Beatitude took me up again to its shimmering crest. The wave carried me along and away to other shores . . .

# *The Shores of the West*

. . . AND when the great wave—of permission and of beatitude—was gone, all was gone with the wave for me. Had I then (left alone as I thought I was) been writing my chronicle's last tale, I would have had to stop, to cease there, perplexed and possibly deceived by myself, to ask: was my tale a real witnessing? Was it mind's pretense—my tale of mind's and history's intrigue, the braid of the Apocalyptic and the Psychomachic in us? Bubbles of the earth?

For, indeed, suddenly I saw it—a braid is never Two, is always Three. And yet—suddenly also!—is not the Third one, hidden as it is behind either of the Two, and then in front of them, the guiding course of the braiding itself, the essential meaning made one with the meaning of the two others—a leading, guiding trace?

Traces: Three—Two—One: and the last tale of mind's and history's intrigue was there, after all—continued. Traces, present in the past, past in the future; traces not of memories, memories only (sudden summer scents rushing out from beyond a high-fenced garden of childhood!), but traces of the passage of reality, witnesses, concrete essences, meanings. And a poignant, fearless nostalgia took hold of me: back to Avignon's late summer day, the Ancestor, Barcelona's balcony, my nocturnal shadow lost and returned, my "Acrobats," and the poet-knight's *ascesis,* soul's and art's jewel, the window-rose in Paris!

And the discourse of the world's bitterness I had heard so

often: ''How unhealthy, obscurantist, thus 'reactionary,'' narrowly privileged, inhibitive and dangerous is nostalgia's tenacity in us!''—I could pass it by, listless! For did I not speak, a moment ago, of a ''fearless nostalgia,'' I, the old monk of a new, today's, age? It took centuries and centuries of western man's struggles between his freedom's psychomachic *perhaps*-choice and his ruling's apocalyptic *must*-choice to fashion the fearless thinking of today: *the twentieth century's reborn nostalgia of essences.*

*

This is how Maurice Merleau-Ponty (I bow deeply, my old aching bones consenting, before this mind, probably the most honest and precise of our century!) comments on his older contemporary, E. Husserl, ''the founder of phenomenology in the modern sense,'' and on phenomenology itself:

''A phenomenology . . . has a double purpose . . . It will gather together all the concrete experiences of man, which are found in history—not only those of knowledge but also those of life and of civilization. But at the same time it must discover in this unrolling of facts a spontaneous order, a meaning, an intrinsic truth, an orientation of such a kind that the different events do not appear as a mere succession. . . .

'' . . . This emergence of truth in and through the psychological event is what Husserl called *Wesenschau,* the *intuition of essences. . . .*

'' . . . In defending Husserl against the false interpretations that are so common, we must emphasize the concrete and familiar nature of this *Wesenschau:* It is a grasping of universal meanings [the world of essences!] in and through my contingent experience [the world of accident], which is not at all a mystical operation that transports us beyond empirical facts. . . .

'' . . . According to Husserl, the seeing of essences, or *Wesenschau,* is nothing but the clarification of the sense, or essence, towards which our consciousness is directed. . . . *Wesenschau* is constant, he says, even in a life that conforms most closely to the natural attitude.''[26]

*

Traces going back, traces going forth: shores of permitted nostalgia, the nostalgia of essences!

Traces crossing each other, sometimes being each other, the Apocalyptic and the Psychomachic in us, meanings and existences in not-only-us; the world of "essences," of global attitudes, and the world of "accidents," of the chain-of-facts-and-influences; the world of *substances* (Father-Creator's creation) and *structures* (creature's self-creation), traces along the shores of the West, worries and searches—now hazy, now lighted—of the West's anxious minds! From Tertullian's (*circa* 160 to after 220) "*credo quia absurdum est*" to Nicolas Oresme's (*circa* 1325–82) wish to free all motion in space from the Aristotelian Prime Mover's giving and arresting will, that is, from external impetus, and to make motion the moving body's own, an internal motivation,[27] thus opening the freely chosen road to Galileo's, Kepler's, Newton's and thence toward our own freedom and fear-and-taboo-lessness, to the final decisions in the twentieth-century West of the Psychomachic man in us:

Of Eddington and his "The relativity theory of physics reduces everything to relations; that is to say, it is structure not material which counts. The structure cannot be built up without material; but the nature of the material is of no importance" (in *Space, Time, and Gravitation*).

Of Poincaré's "Space is only a word that we have believed a thing" (in *The Foundations of Science*).

Or Whitehead's " . . . to be an abstraction does not mean that an entity is nothing. It merely means that its existence is only one factor of a more concrete element of nature" (in *The Concept of Nature*) and "The aim of science is to seek the simplest explanations of complex facts . . . Seek simplicity and distrust it."

Or Bell's " . . . mathematical analysis as it works today must make use of irrational number (such as the square root of two); the sense, if any, in which such numbers exist is hazy. Their reputed mathematical existence implies the disputed theories of the infinite. The paradoxes remain. Without a satisfactory theory of irrational numbers, among other things, Achilles does not catch up with the tortoise, and the earth cannot turn on its axis. But, as Galileo remarked, it does. It would seem to follow that something is wrong with our attempts to compass the infinite'' (in *Debunking Science*).

Or Einstein's ''As far as the laws of mathematics refer to reality, they are not certain; and as far as they are certain they do not refer to reality'' (in *Sidelights on Relativity*).[28]

*

Or: Merleau-Ponty's ''In reaching true knowledge, in going beyond the dialectic of the living person or social being and his circumscribed milieu, in becoming purely a subject who knows the world objectively, man realizes to the fullest extent absolute consciousness in respect of which the body and individual existence become no more than objects and death is deprived of meaning . . . the relations of the soul and the body, obscure as long as the body is treated abstractly as a fragment of matter, become clear when one sees in it the bearer of a dialectic. Since the physical world and the organism can only be conceived as objects of consciousness or significations, the problem of the relations of consciousness and its physical or organic 'conditions' would only exist at the level of confused thought tied to abstractions; it would disappear in the realm of truth where only the relation between the epistemological subject and its object subsists in its own right. That would be the only legitimate theme of philosophical reflection.''[29]

*

New shores of permission and nostalgia, of Traces=Witnesses, concrete, precise, incarnate. Such was this new *dramatis persona* I met soon after my coming there: an ancient ritual cup or beaker, with the myth of creation told by a tribal artisan on its curved silver body (*Plate 41*).[30]

And this is how the elemental ''intuition of essences'' seems to work, candidly and obviously:

The highest (primeval sky) and the lowest (the great primeval water=abyss) are joined on the cup's upper rim—the sky made of a wavy four-leveled ornament, the curve of each of its tiny elements pointed downward (water's symbol) and not upward (mountain or earth symbol). Immediately below is given a mytho-

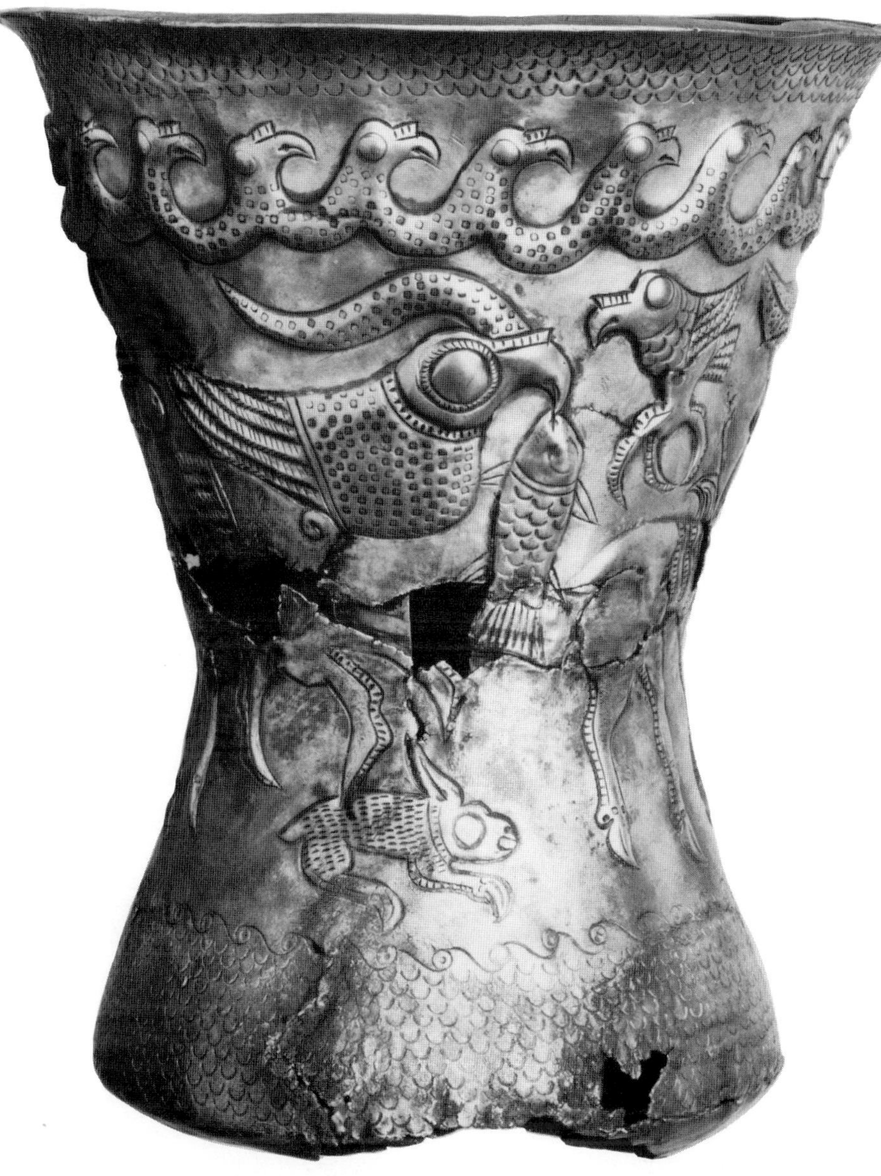

41. Silver beaker, Thracian, side view

poeic confirmation of this sky-abyss marriage or correspondence (genesis of all live creatures) by a bird-and-serpent, sky-and-abyss garland surrounding the cup's upper body. Underneath this no-beginning-no-end landscape of the soul and the cosmos, the labors or the struggles of creation itself begin. From the beak of a great and central sky-and-earth (the horns!) bird, a fish, and from the bird's claws a quadruped, are thrown down into the great primeval abyss (while much smaller repetitions of this act of impending destruction = creation accompany the central one). Then—it is now on the bottom (greatly damaged in its present state) of the cup's interior that the drama of creation proper is consummated—a heavy and strange quadruped is suspended from two winglike or corded plantlike excrescences, a huge and bizarre animal, his clawed feet dangling over the emptiness, his great, open eye, round and empty, unseeing, his half-ajar sharp-toothed muzzle ejecting—vomiting forth—a totally new being, an isolated, hoofed animal leg, the future new creature's fragment-limb to be completed, to become an integral new being (*Plate 42*). And sky and abyss being united at the very beginning, this cycle of destruction and production is to be repeated, endless, the highest and the deepest in close correspondence with each other. While opposite this terror-and-respite giving scene a peaceful group of tall, young and slender animals—deer?—a group-to-be, in reality one multi-legged, multi-hoofed new animal—the prize, both continued and final, of creation—stands erect, ready for action (*Plate 43*).

Yet the entire presentation could also be easily interpreted as opposite, totally different in content: a candid substitution, known in all primitive cultures, for the incessant inter-clan struggles for supremacy by animal totems, the big totem, the big clan, the victor and destroyer of all others (the silver cup's big horned bird).

Correspondence and substitution, here you are joining me again, Children of the Ancestor! Traces of reality's passage, witnesses, concrete, precise; precise happenings in history and mind! Indeed, for the ancient tribal craftsman who fashioned this object of cult—a totally significant and signifying story-telling object—and the grasping of its meaning were one and the same: the visual-manual creation of symbols = concepts (verbal and auditive, indeed)—the images, the imagery itself—and the creation of kinaesthetic symbols (of touch, of smell, indeed)—the artist-worshipper's

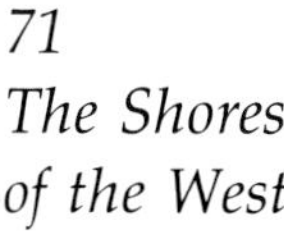

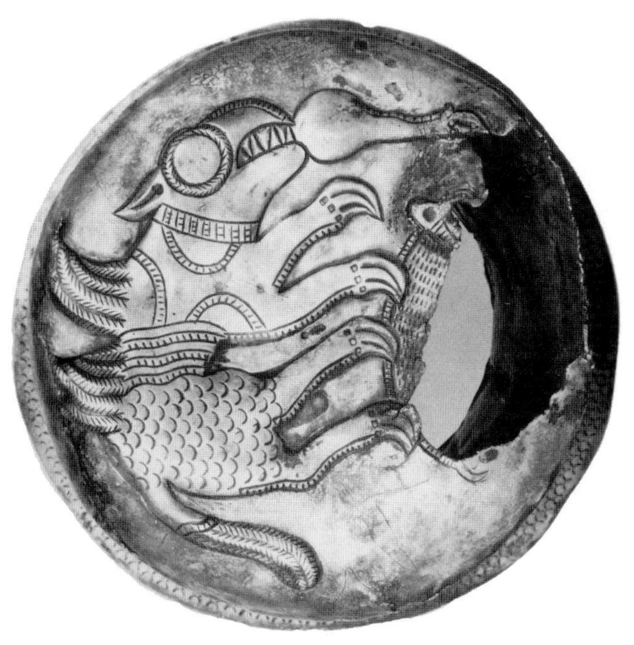

42. Silver beaker, Thracian, view of bottom

body mimicry, his rhythmic absorption of the imagery's total meaning in and through his body's inner dance—all this was, instantaneously, one and the same act. And more: this tightly bunched knot of living-comprehending was also—traces within traces!—a tightly bunched knot of social and economic conditions in a precise moment—historical or pre-historical—of man's Past.

And so it was, I have been told. An historical—pre-historical—moment of a great triple discovery:

That the dying and dead and buried grain is resurrected as a new, yet the same being, a plant—the discovery of the art of agriculture; that, by the action of the sun or of fire, lifeless mud is resurrected as a life-helping clay recipient—the discovery of the art of the potter; and that by the action of great heat a fragment of an inert, "dead" rock can be metamorphosed into life-enriching liquid metal—the discovery of the art of the smith.

Traces crossing other traces, embryo-thoughts of correspondences and substitutions, of transformations and transfers, of metamorphoses and incarnation, crossing each other, being with each other! Traces of that moment in pre-history when, within each collective unit, the tribal magician (creator and preserver of

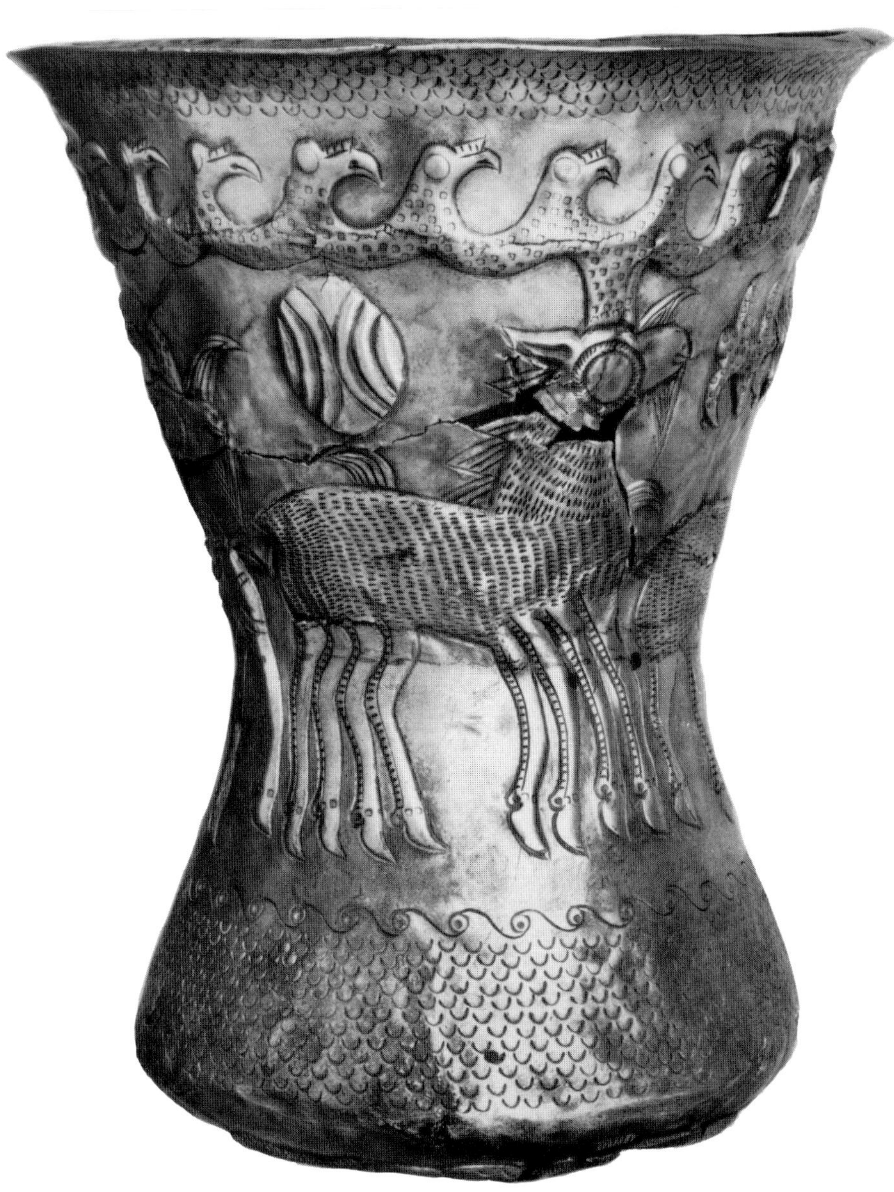

43. Silver beaker, Thracian, side view

verbal symbols-concepts-sounds—future priest, future theologian and scion of the Verbal Elite); and the tribal artisan (creator of visual-manual symbols—future artist-poet); and the tribal chieftain (creator of kinaesthetic symbols, protector and promoter of collective fertility and welfare through and in his body's mimicry, his prophylactic dance—future king, emperor, future politician-dancer and swordsman)—all three of them embodied one global function (whether performed by distinct individuals or by only one, the magician-artisan-chieftain).

And then: then came the split, the *Tragic Split* in the planetary history of man:

While the artisan-craftsman—smith or potter—was absent, possibly on his goods-exchanging missions, the ''magician'' and the chieftain allied themselves against him and his hitherto equal rights and duties, and became the sole depositaries of the local artisan lore—the lore that grew as a defensive barrier around the secrets of the newly invented and perfected skills. And this primeval *techne* lore (on ''my'' silver cup, and on innumerable other ancient objects of cult, wrought in costly material and to be found throughout the already greatly evolved—urbanized or not as yet—regions of our planet's past) was later embellished, enriched, ''interpreted,'' by the subservient craftsman under the leadership, more and more authoritative as well as more and more sophisticated, of the ''magician''-and-chieftain, now the Bronze Age's priest-king, the steward of the temple-and-palace's wealth and supremacy.

And so this lore became and remained the source of all the lofty theologies and theosophic speculations of the king-priest's Bronze Age, as well as of all those of later ages both derived from and in revolt against it. Indeed, is there any adventure of mind, in philosophy and religion, or in the sciences, in the arts and in politics, including the body-and-mind's sophistications of today, that could reveal anything beyond the two primordial principles of Correspondence (the Indic, psychomachic Atman-Brahman!) and Substitution (the still living *pars pro toto,* apocalyptic must)?

The primeval three-one unity of creating-understanding-protecting, the unity of *techne* and *sophia* was gone in the post-split world. The entire history of mankind is in the post-split's trajectory—traces crossing each other, sometimes coinciding with each other, sometimes wide apart!—along which the growing rights (and also merits) of the Verbal Elite allied to the Elite of governing (the state), permitted them to impose, now as foes, now not as foes, their educated skills and schema-thoughts on the thought and skills—now duties only!—of the artisan-artist.

The tale of this millenia-long imposition as well as of the artisan-artist's revolt against it, I shall not tell here: I have already told it, in part, elsewhere,[31] and other chroniclers, more detail-loving and more patient, will follow its intriguing, episode-full trajectory.

But the epic result of the ''tragic split'' I could not miss mentioning here—it is part of my chronicle's essential intrigue:

That the lost three-oneness was never forgotten by the artisan-poet; and that the nostalgia of it with its creative spur on inhibition—the *permitted* nostalgia!—is precisely what became both the tool and the weapon in his struggles of creation and his struggles for liberty or liberation.

For it was in the very *materiality* of his silent skills—*techne's* allotted domain—that the pre-split integral *spirituality,* the integral thing=being, existence=meaning, mind=body, took refuge: no theologian and no statesman *of any time* would ever be able to impose his calculated rules upon the exercised will and choice of a creator (protector and promoter) of colors, consonances, linear expressivity or motion's directions in art unless the artisan-artist himself had accepted and integrated those rules (Leonardo). Michelangelo's creation of bodies that emerge from the living, sentient materiality of a precise marble block is this. And when, after so many battles—socio-aesthetic battles all!—the cry of the twentieth century ''Not art for art's sake, but for the sake of integral liberation in body-mind!'' was heard all over, and from each of man's inventive disciplines, it was still under the spur of inhibition, the *permitted* yearning for the pre-split world, that the artist-creator attained both his success and his revenge: not only, now, Michelangelesque body born within the marble itself, but Henry Moore's reclining woman in wood, born from the wood and given back to the wood—the woodness of the woman, the womanness of the wood, or Brancusi's steelness of the steel that constructs and recreates by its laborious smoothness and its shiny swiftness the swiftness and the life of a bird's *élan.*

The tale of my ancient ritual cup, the myth of creation on its silver, rounded body is thus being told again and anew.

Would this return—liberation almost—be the end of the Intrigue itself? And harmony be reborn in the midst of our century's screaming and announced disharmonies? My sight already blurred by age, I cannot know. But I do know—I witnessed it!—how gallant and loyal were the post-split militant memories of the knight-artisan of our past!—the medieval past *par excellence.* It was then that the drama of the Church-and-State's—the magician-and-chieftain = dancer's—alliance, so often disturbed as well as enhanced, was matched by the drama of the artisan-artist's tenacity and vigilance, his awareness, inherited from the learning of atelier to atelier along great centuries, of his intrinsic dignity and integrity!

Such was the world of the Romanesque man, the world most representative of western man's innermost battles—the battles between the ''artisan'' freedom's choice, the psychomachic free choice of body-and-meaning values, and the values of the magician-chieftain's commanded choice, the apocalyptic choice of power-and-meaning.

And medieval art, sheltered, protected, often isolated (thus creatively inhibited) by its own strong *techne* defenses, could reveal its final goal, all art's perennial goal: to recreate the pre-split man's total integrity, to reveal this integrity not in the verbal content of art's imagery only, but essentially, in the structured form itself.

Here is the birth and the *psychomachic* content-form of the Romanesque ''significant ornament!'' Nostalgia permitted, witnessing traces, concrete, precise—I meant this and no other content-form when I evoked them soon after I came to the new shore!

Through the drama, the significance, of linear-compositional-color behavior or motion, the ''secret'' skill of the medieval artist-artisian could show us two principles at work, the universal principle of correspondence between man and the beyond of man, man-world, man-landscape—*Solidarity!*—and simultaneously the principle by which the unseizable totality of man-and-the-beyond-of man, the infinite landscape, is transferred—thus seized, substituted, given—into a signifying fragment of it, man himself, his figure both isolated and *engagé—Solitude!*

*

So my chronicle continues almost without interruption. Yet something did change there: my own involvement in the Intrigue's Fable. The now far-off shore of *permitted beatitude* has been all mine, its beatitude was mine also, mine only. But the new shore, the shore of *permitted nostalgia* was not mine now, mine only: the beings and the events I met and was to meet there did not come to me as they did before the great wave had left me, to greet me and to confide to me their intimate stories, each related to the other. Their passion for interiority—the very reason of their involvement in the Intrigue—was my own passion then. But now all this has changed. I had to go myself, in search of them, to meet them where they were, and only then be befriended by them. Their passion of interiority—the very reason of their involvement in the Intrigue—remained theirs, theirs alone.

And I remained with mine—happy though, and alone.

Indeed, permitted nostalgia, so the Fable would have it, is a precise, concrete witnessing—my own search!—whose origin is in the pre-split three-oneness of conceiving-doing-mimicking; whose historical content=*substance* is the primordial oneness of correspondence and substitution all around us, and whose psychic form=*structure* is the oneness of the psychomachic and the apocalyptic all *in us.* Origin never entirely forgotten, either by the magician himself or the chieftain-dancer. Indeed, when, along history's post-split trajectory, the Verbal Elite could periodically awaken to the memory and the awareness of the primeval treason, it could itself become a struggling seedbed of all the great reforms on earth. And such could be—if or when purged of lust-to-power-musts—the slow and late awakening of the chieftain's (today's statesman-dancer's) memory. But it is only the artisan-artist, the poet-artisan, who, self-liberated today, could say:

*God guard me from those thoughts*
*men think*
*In the mind alone*
*He that sings a lasting song*
*Thinks in a marrow-bone*

who, painter, could create a line's ''stroll for strolling's sake'' (Klee), who could be fully and finally awakened today to the reality of *permitted nostalgia.* Our century's early plunge into the world of the child, the insane, the ''primitive,'' is this; our conscious, growing decision to lean on ourselves, on our own and chosen crafts' resources is this; so also are all the directives, the meaningful, *significant* directions given and taken in by our working materials, thoughts, actions, tools, in art, volumes, lines, colors, compositions—the ''how'' of these directions containing its ultimate ''what'': the most ancient and ever new meaning=content of the lost three-oneness. And the integral man—the aesthetic-moral-metaphysical man in us—is revealed today in the very ''what-of-the-how'' of these directives: Picasso's growth-to-achievement line, Matisse's growing=achieved line.

This is what I meant when I said the way we com-pose our life, individual and collective, is the way we com-pose our line, our volumes and colors, and our poems. And this is what is meant in this chronicle's last tale of mine by ''significant ornament.'' It is here that the story of the labors and struggles of the psychomachic—the self-freed man in us—is told. For it is here that the apocalyptic—the *must* in us—is given also: in the ever-present *Braid.* The ''stroll for strolling's sake'' of a line means the animation of the ''inanimate,'' a line's precise direction=will made one with the conceiving-imaging-mimicking will of its maker, something approaching interiority itself, the passion for interiority, the essence-meaning of *ekstasis* itself. It means ultimately freedom and choice, not only freedom of choice. For, as you may remember, when the Ancestor introduced me to his first-born Twin he said: ''Man is the chooser of the psychomachic or the apocalyptic in him, in reality of both, each in different combinations of primacy, intensity and obviousness: man is the chooser always. But choice is the choice of what is perceived and felt as good and not of what is not good (a choice which the post-split alliance-treason reduced to the virtue-vice dichotomy): it is a moral choice, a multi-relational, pluralist-moral choice. And the conditioned struggle between the psychomachic and the apocalyptic is a moral struggle, whose only issue or prize is the very meaning of the Braid.

''From transfer to transfer, this is the *moral* essence of the 'significant ornament' in art.

''And because of the intensified impact of the alliance between Church (the 'magician') and State (the 'chieftain') during the era we call medieval—during its Romanesque episode most expressively and acutely—and, correlatively, because of the intensity

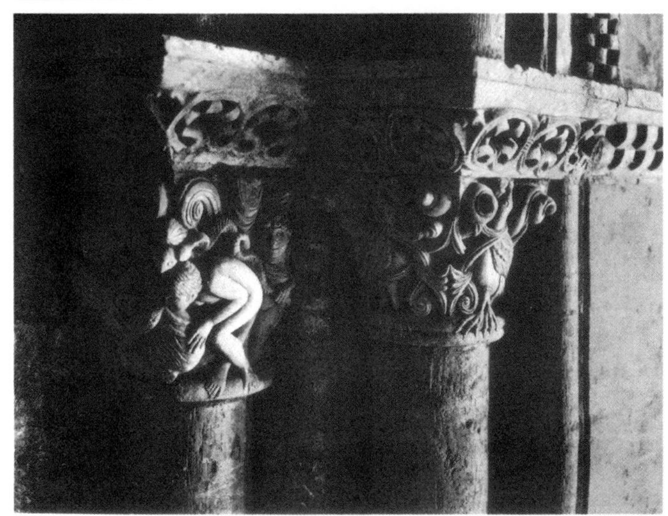

44a. Capital, San Isidoro, León

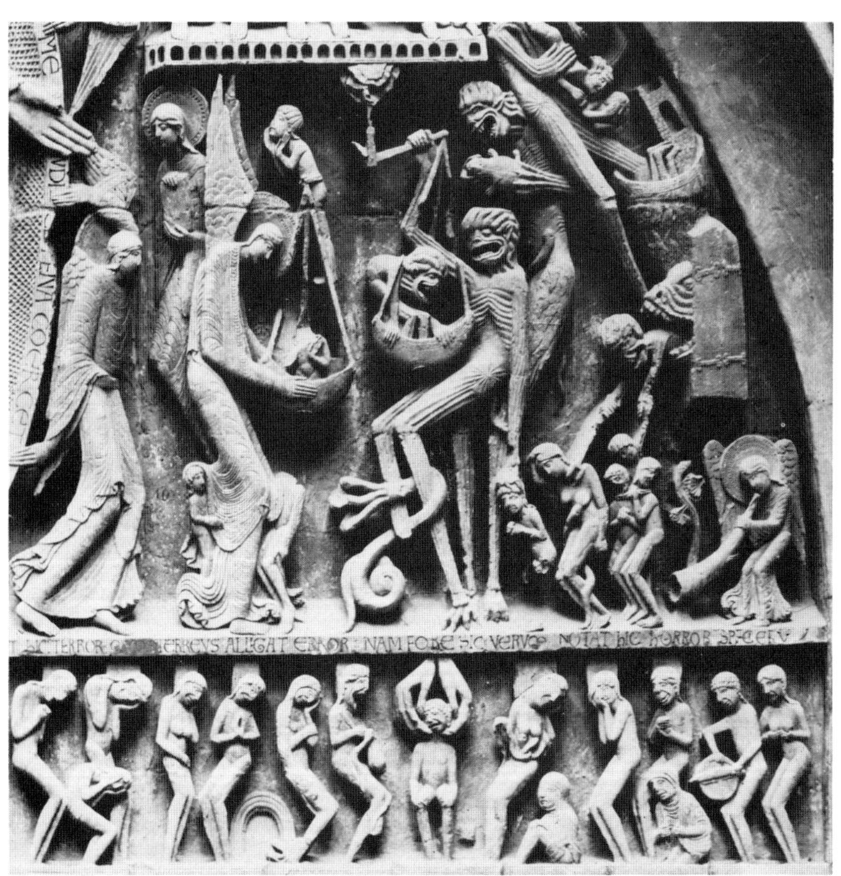


44b. Detail, tympanum, Cathedral of St. Lazare, Autun

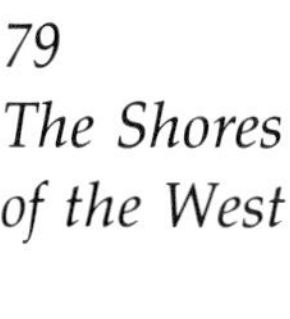

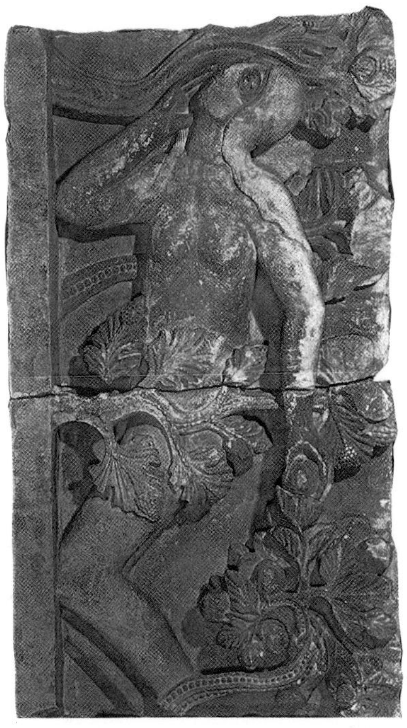

44c. ''Eve of Autun''

of the artisan-artist's memory and nostalgia then, this era became for me the most revealing in the Intrigue's evolvement (*Plates 44a, b, & c*).''

*

*Tangled, we are entangled. Whose*
*fault was it?*[32]

So many voices coming now from the Romanesque ''universe of discourse''—voices testifying, explaining, preparing! I could recognize very many of them—their diverse, regional accents; more distinctly, the accents of the predecessors and teachers, the voices of the Atlantic man, the Mediterranean and the Near Eastern man; the rich and deep voice of the Carolingians and the sonorous voices of Romanesque and pre-Romanesque speculative thinkers, makers of psycho-cosmic schemata, inherited from Late Antiquity's torment-and-anxiety-healing solicitude; initiators and builders of what a little later in the medieval world will be not only its stronghold but its haven: the theology—science in the future—of Light; voices crossing each other, sometimes being each other.

But I went directly to where I heard a more familiar voice. Was it the voice of an Oceanid my wandering shadow had listened to one moonlit night behind the stranger's opened window—a voice of nostalgia, of hope? Could it not be the great wave of permitted beatitude coming back to me after all?

"Tell me," I said, "what is the central passion, the most persistent intensity—the 'sense'—of the Romanesque world? Tell me. . . "

"But you know already. Adherence, the total, thus, when necessary, deforming, 'monstrous' adherence, in art, of limbs to limbs, folds to folds; the continuity, thus mobility, of structures = forms; the re-creation of an ornament-block's, ornament-monster's 'barbaric' humanism (man and beyond-of-man being one there).

"'Persistence of intensity,' you said. You were right, indeed: after a short and brilliant emergence of an opposite universe—the 'classical' Gothic of the Saint Louis era—the Romanesque, now enriched with a new plastic-verbal 'naturalistic' vocabulary, reappeared unaltered and uninhibited in 'late' Gothic art and thought; then, after the brilliant Mediterranean Renaissance adventure of clarifications, the Romanesque was reborn as Baroque to be again submitted to the clarity of the Enlightenment's and post-Enlightenment's era and re-emerge again in today's arts and thought, Romanesque unchanged, uninhibited.

"Adherence, continuity, this is the passion of the Romanesque (of course, you just heard what other voices were telling you: how rich and varied are the modalities of techniques and styles in the Romanesque world: look how 'normal,' seriated, how classical-Roman in their story-telling urge are some illuminated Romanesque narrations; how exquisite, 'natural,' already 'Gothic' is the beautiful, probably Burgundian, Virgin of the Annunciation group at San Vicente's south entrance in Avila, or one of the six virgins surrounding the Virgin of Majesty, from a mural in the church of Notre Dame at Montmorillon sur Gartempe (Vienne)[33] (*Plate 45*); how exquisitely refined and precise is the tiny animal world (rats, birds) on some Romanesque lintels, architraves and capitals (*Plate 46*).

"Re-creation of the 'barbaric' humanism of the 'ornament-monster,' of ornament-passion, the passion of continuity, of inter-

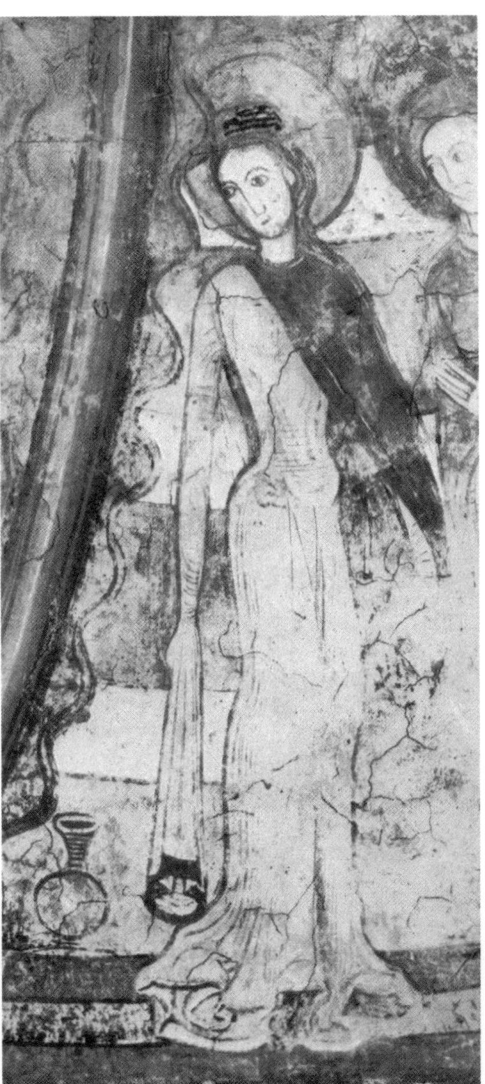

45. Detail, mural, church of Notre Dame, Montmorillon sur Gartempe

penetration, thus of mobility as such, the free vehicle of the *psychomachic* will—this is what the 'persistence of intensity' of the Romanesque is."

"Mobility?"—here I interrupted the voice—"How is it possible? Mobility in the arrested, rigid, truly terrifying, so apocalyptic world of the Romanesque—St. Bernard of Clairvaux' greatest rejection?"

"The Braid! Never forget the Braid!" said the voice. "When later in your life you tell in one of your future tales what you have heard here, you will remember and reveal what I myself once

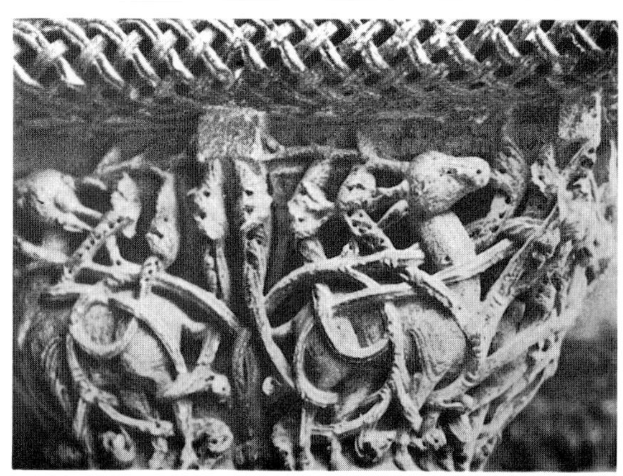

46. Capital, cloister, monastery of Santo Domingo de Silos

heard and am repeating to you about the dual root of movement in art and the braiding therein. This:

''' . . . There is an evident ''natural'' movement (the impression of motion in space) in, say, so gracious a work of art as the Victory of *Athena Nike's* balustrade . . . there is obviously mobility in the clear connection-association between all the formal elements of a compound pictorial image to be narrated in the interlaced rhythms of Delacroix's or Rubens' dramas or in the harmonies of a Gothic grouping.

'''There is on the other hand stiffness, rigidity in the ''Hittite'' throned goddess (*See Plate 24*), in Giotto's figures . . . stiffness, rigidity in the hypnotic repeat of verticality in a Dura-Europos image (*Plate 47*); rigid immobility in the tensely oblique Werden Christ or in the acute, angular humanity at Autun (*See Plate 44b*).

'''Yet, what the deeper, down-lifted level of comparative analysis—the what-of-the-how level—reveals might be the contrary. The movement of the first group is, one could say, a *''mnemonic'' movement, not an immediate or immediately reproduced movement:* it results from our memory's reconstruction of all those observable moments of motion in objects and beings, whose authentication has been for us most satisfying both logically (=this or that curve of a line, or of a color, as the case might be, repeated in us and ''working'' on us as convincingly as a category of mind supposedly does by connecting-associating us with what is outside of us), and optically-erotically (=this or that curve fulfilled and not to be repeated in us, Eros of plenitude and of pleasure-pain), and which our memory could retain, accumulate and select for the purpose

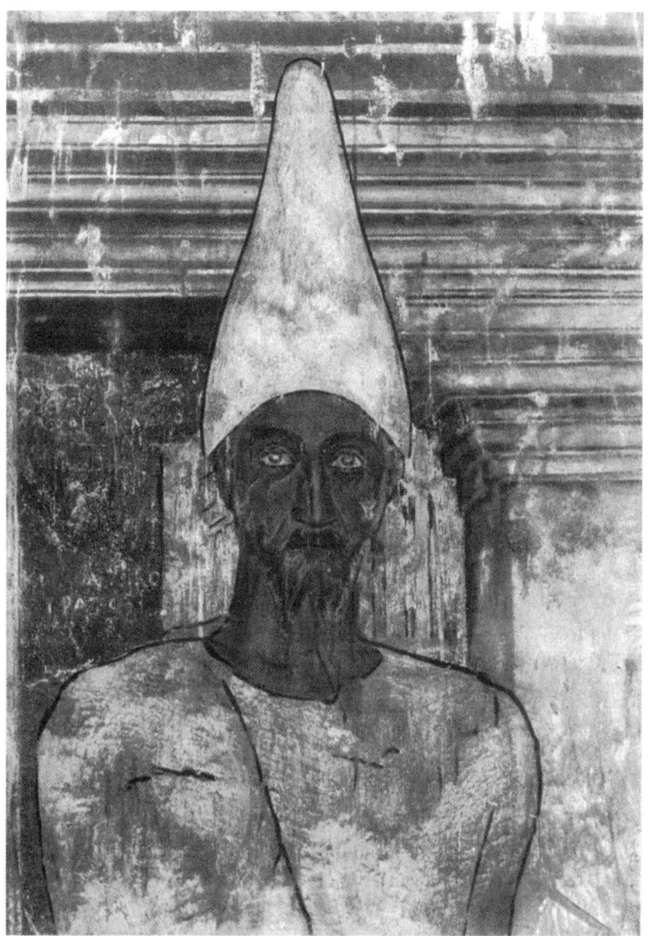

47. Ministrant, wall painting, detail, Dura-Europos, Syria

of an aesthetic reconstruction. Here is the birth of what we call grace in art. . . . Call it also art-stability, art-narration, the marvel-full repetition of what has been given to us once—and not to be repeated.

"'Now, mobility as such, precisely the "not-to-be-repeated" movement immediately captured, might be revealed in the very stiffness or rigidity of the second group. Because this rigidity is the dynamic effort-momentum of a starting or immediate movement, the *decisive moment of a just-opened dike when the quiet waters of the upper level at the point of emptying are no longer quiet, immobile, nor as yet in full movement, in movement already.* It is this effort or this instantaneity of a movement-about-to-be, which *mobilizes* the immobility, the rigidity, of Giotto's drama and figures, or Autun's or Moissac's . . . Nakedness of space and of movement, I call this

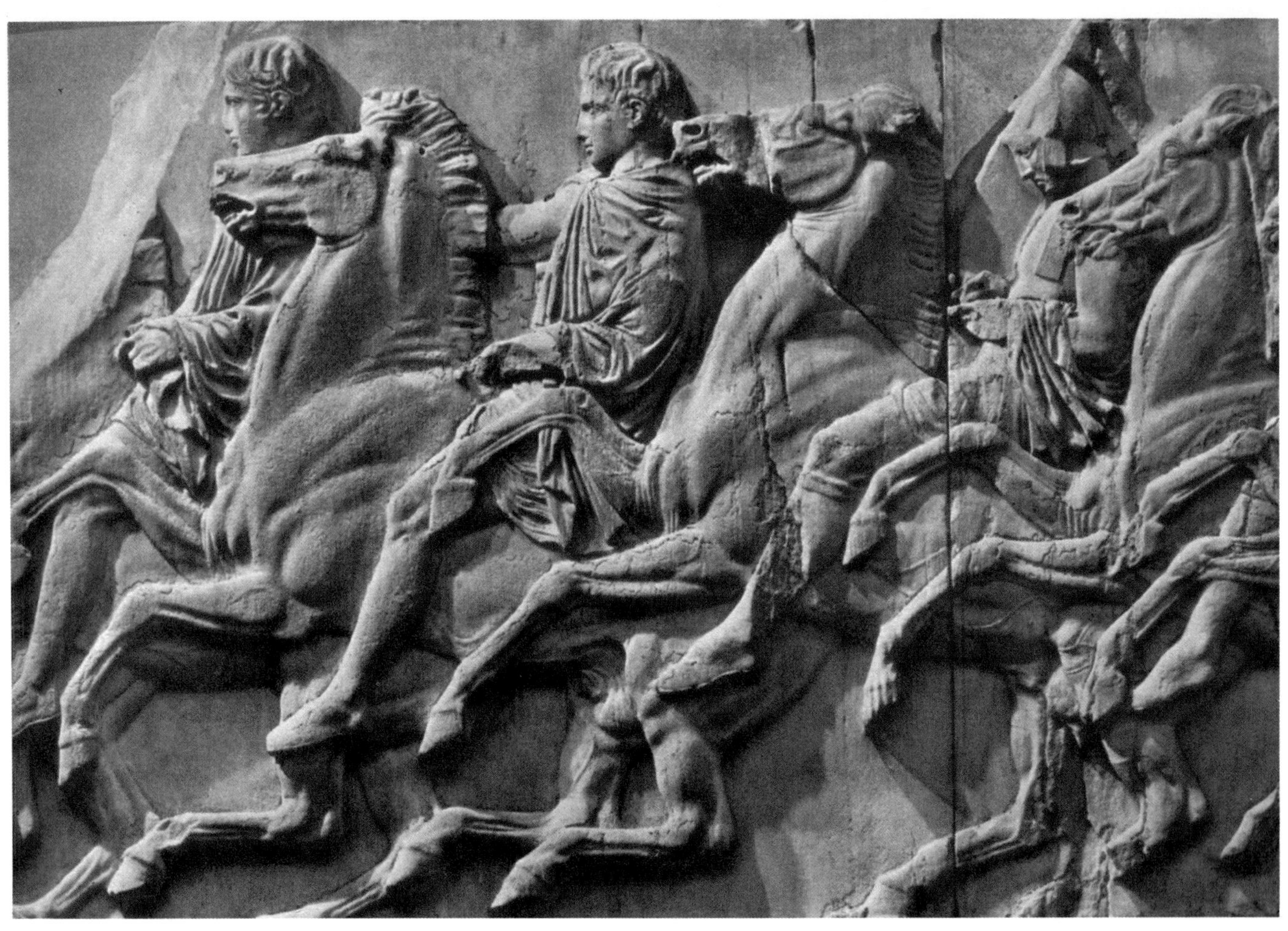

48. Horsemen, the Parthenon frieze

''mobile rigidity;'' nakedness of a total, otherwise unseizable sensation of motion (=e-motion); not the tonal-melodic, remembered, nudity-clothing-the-nakedness of, say, Velázquez' Venus, but the a-tonal, stripped, flattened, immediate nakedness of Manet's *Olympia.*[34]

'''Thus, I would add: art-mobility—eye's synthesis—is mimicry, is unity-adhesion of form-parts. Art-stability—eye's analysis—is narration, is unity-connection between form-parts. It is here precisely, in the close vicinity of our own enjoyment (rather than of our communication, as yet) that the technical ability of art criticism itself, on the ''what of the how'' level, situ-ates its own checking device. Namely: that within this frame of motion's two general divisions, movement-stability, movement-mobility, each contains a pair of subtler sub-divisions: art's ''mnemonic,'' structured movement = grace, *impression's* mediate, derived, found and attired idiom, and art's movement = immediacy, the given, sudden, thus ''mobilized'' rigidity of a just opened dike—*sensation's* immediate, naked idiom. That is to say, the behavior of forms in space—their e-motion—can still reveal itself as ''stability'' in spite of the apparent optical-discursive interlacing of their rhythms and themes (*Plate 48*). Similarly rhythms and themes either continuous-circular or discontinuous-oblique will belong to the world of art-mobility when their interconnections—rather inter-adhesions—form one block-continuum, a new ''monster-block'': the deforming immediacy of adhesion's presence (*See Plate 44b*).

'''Of course—and this is life's command everywhere—there cannot be a pure ''mobile'' style or ''mentality'' and a pure ''stable'' style or ''mentality''; style is always a certain equilibrium between both, equilibrium achieved under the hegemony of one of these elemental stages of the visual—a braiding always, a subtle braid-in-braid braiding, so easy to forget or to miss. For the Braid is the ever-present, yet the most evasive and elusive, the only ''mysterious'' *dramatis persona* of your tale, its guiding, leading *persona*. Remember, a braid is never two, is always three: the apocalyptic thread, the psychomachic thread and the third, the hidden one behind either of them, the guiding trajectory of the braiding itself, its essential meaning made one with the meaning of the other two—not a trajectory of the chain of facts, the chain of influences, but of the bunching together of all three of them in what you call ''global attitudes,'' in history and in mind.'[35]

''There is *terribilità*, the Apocalyptic *terribilità*, in 'mobile-rigidity's' fixed immediacy—yet, in the very signification of this immediacy, the genesis of a choice to lean on one's own resources is already given. True, there is, on the surface, freedom's elasticity of choice in the 'mnemonic' reconstruction of motion. Yet—similar to what happens in music's structures, where the very flexibility, the 'free' fluidity of harmonic chords' behavior is nevertheless rooted in the *a priori* established convergence of dissonances toward the tonal culmination of the consonance (the Father-Creator's *must* of the keynote)—similar to this, there is in the 'mnemonic' freedom itself a *must* of stabilized convergence toward the linear-rhythmic or chromatic dominant. There is, at first approach, an apocalyptic *terribilità* in the Romanesque narrative schemata-imagery, much more so and more frequently, perhaps, than in the Pantocrator's, Emperor-Christ's, theocratically and rigidly fixed iconography in Byzantium, where (this time long after our first glance at its art!), from the start to the passionate twilight, reigns an attraction, passionate also, toward free poly-rhythms and harmonies. And yet, the Eastern Christian's 'global attitude' still remains an apocalyptic *terribilità;* the Western Christian's still the artisan's exalted choice to tell 'his' story in his own creature-creator's idiom.

"Such, the Romanesque artisan-painter's re-working of the otherwise imposed theme, a theological predilection of the West, the struggle of virtues and vices, of good and evil, to be narrated either as direction, individual personification, or as an allegorical group-allusion or metaphor (the story of Cain and Abel, of Abraham delivering Lot, of the crossing of the Red Sea, etc.).

"Here: the figure of Lust (*Plate 49*)[36] on one of the eight low cylindrical pillars, all frescoed, in the crypt at Tavant[37]—a figure of a woman piercing her breasts with a lance, a pity-evoking, not at all abhorrent figure of a capital vice,[38] succumbing among the intended loveliness—a medieval *exception!*—of rounded, undulating, self-enveloping curves (serpents), curves of a significant, meaningful 'ornament' (a pictorial idiom common to the entire production at Tavant).

"And, in the abbey church of Saint-Savin-sur-Gartempe (early twelfth century), among the terrifying episodes of the Sacred Writ, all paraphrases of good-evil confrontation and struggle, covering the central nave's entire vault, the episode of the crossing of the Red Sea (*Plate 50*), the evil Pharaoh's evil host's pursuit and doom: his men, his horses and chariots swallowed up in the liquid cataclysm overtaking all! What prowess of the master-painter's will to tell here in his own freely and meaningfully chosen way (the accepted load of tradition and directed procedures not being any burden to it!), the truth—the artist-artisan's truth!—about the evil standing self-involved in (*among*) and not only punished *in front of* its engulfing doom! Rarely had a Romanesque painter surpassed in directness of visual speech the 'mobile rigidity's' immediacy, the directness of communication and expression of this scene! I remember only one other example—similar in its content and significance: a miniature in an early thirteenth-century illuminated

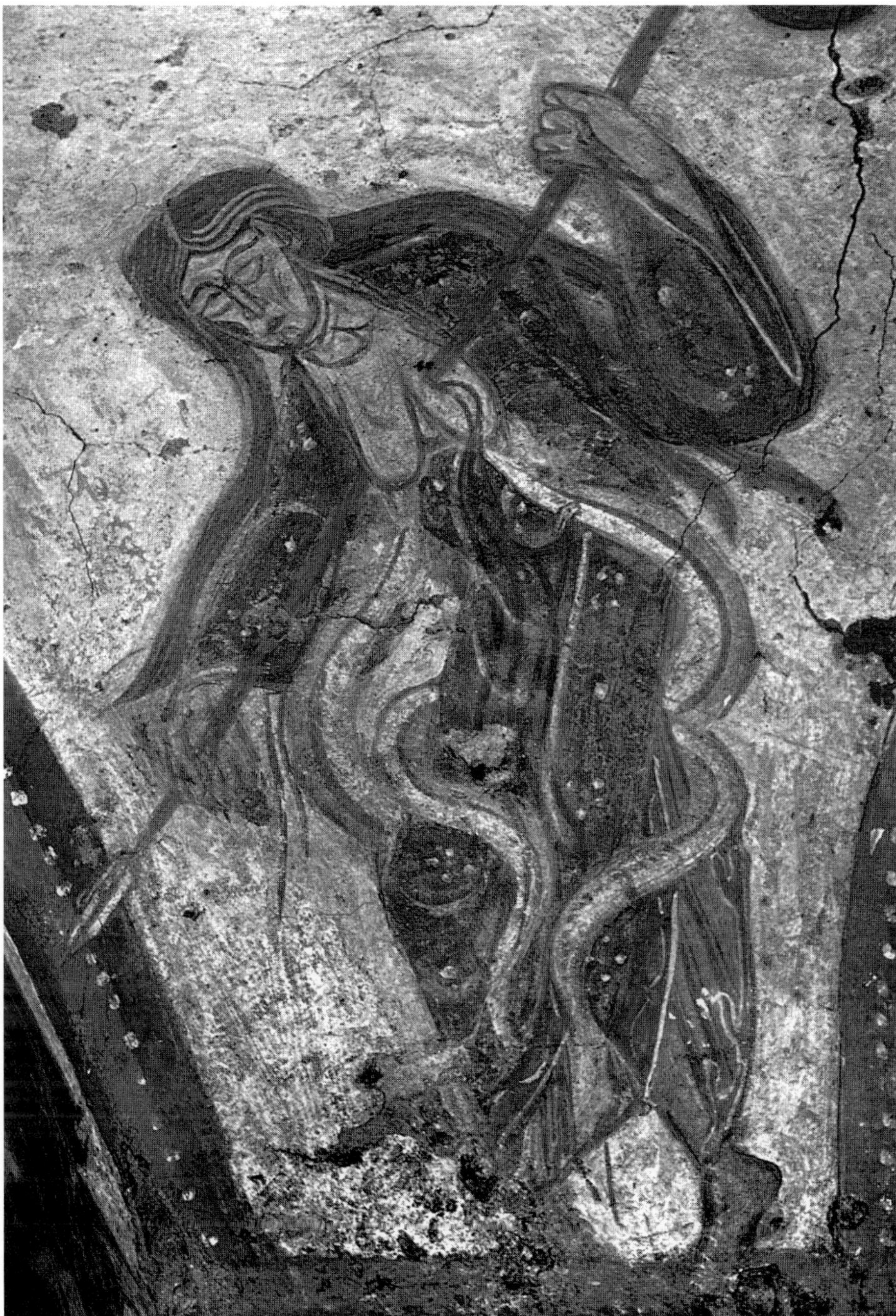

49. Personification of Lust, Saint-Nicolas, Tavant

Bible treasured in one of the best-chosen collections of America (*Plates 51a, b, & c*).[39]

"But nothing, at least in France, can compete with the audacity and freedom of the master-painter who painted and directed the murals—the lives of Christ, of the Virgin, and of saints—in the church of St. Martin de Vic (at Nohant-Vicq, Indre, end of eleventh-early twelfth century), who covered with them the walls of the choir, the arcades that separate the choir from the nave (a strange and rare architectural arrangement), and the apse.

"All is audacity, all is freedom here.

"Here, indeed, at St. Martin de Vic, 'the Wind bloweth where it listeth.' Jehovah's wind: not visions to be matched with words and concepts—gnosis, glory, condolence?—but the roar of great rocks falling from the face of an abrupt mountain; but the roar of big trees torn, their centenary roots exposed, from earth's foundations; but the noise of great bronze idols broken and clashing on a stone floor—that is what the wind of Jehovah does to the recreated humanity here, the torment of folds and bodies, the rigid *terribilitá* of their about-to-explode 'mobilitiy,' its sudden presence being already the *psychomachic* witness of good's beauty and truth, the beauty and the truth in the moral-personal choice of the artist himself (*Plates 52a & b*). Only Giotto's 'Kiss of Judas' in Padua (*Plate 53*), two centuries later, will equal the intensity and 'expressionist' realism of Vic's creation.

"Here, thus, 'the significant', meaning-full 'ornament' again: what else would be there in the astonishing contour of all those toylike, childish, faces at Vicq, all alike, all round, flat, 'meaning-less' masks whose very dullness, so it strongly seems, was intended better to concentrate their real meaning-fullness on the two, almost joined points = eyes, on those eyes' piercing, scrutinizing, interrogative glance—the piercing interrogation from eyes to eyes between Christ and Judas, between the Virgin and Elizabeth. . . .

"That is how from transfer to transfer again, the 'ornament' becomes human interrogation and scrutiny—the western Christian man's interrogation about space in nature and art, about time in nature and art, about soul's departures and mind's arrivals, about *Aeternitas*. . . .

"I say western Christian, for (and here I am giving you a

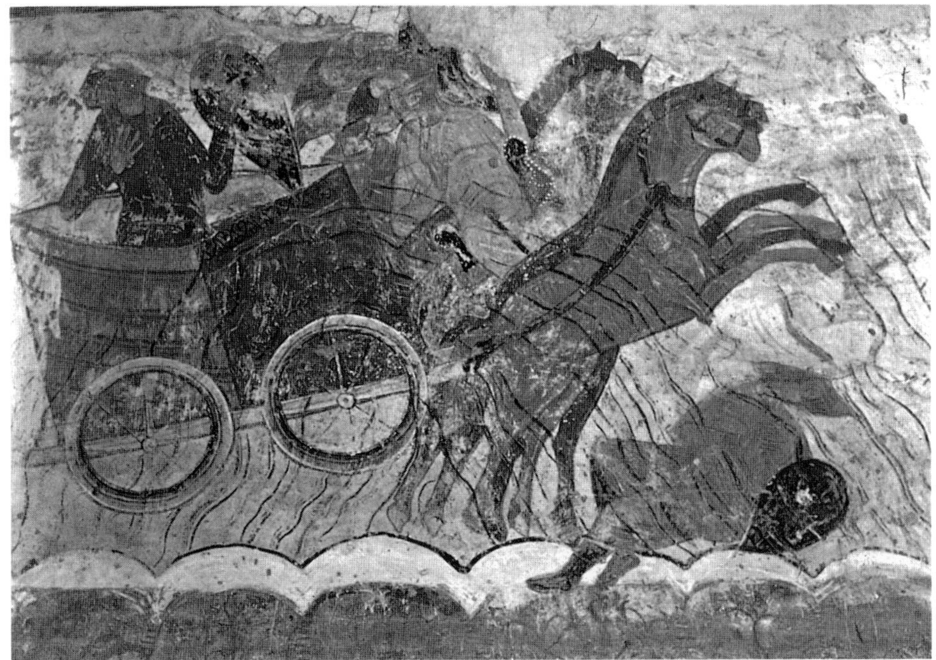

50. Crossing of the Red Sea, Saint-Savin-sur-Gartempe

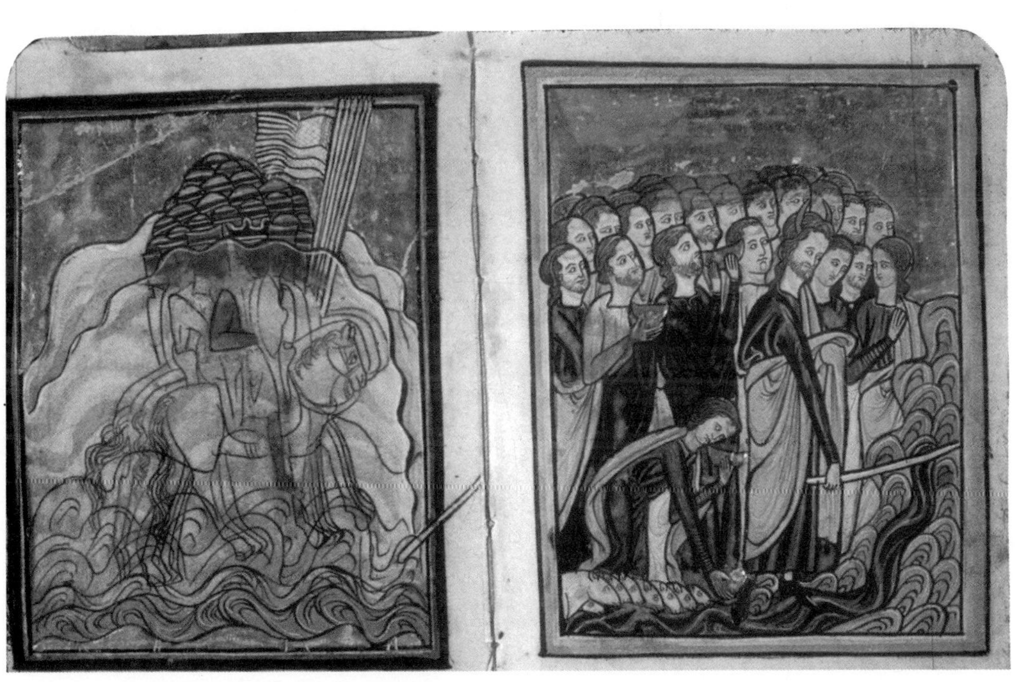

51. W. DeBrailes, Bible illustrations:
a. The Red Sea overwhelms Pharaoh and his army

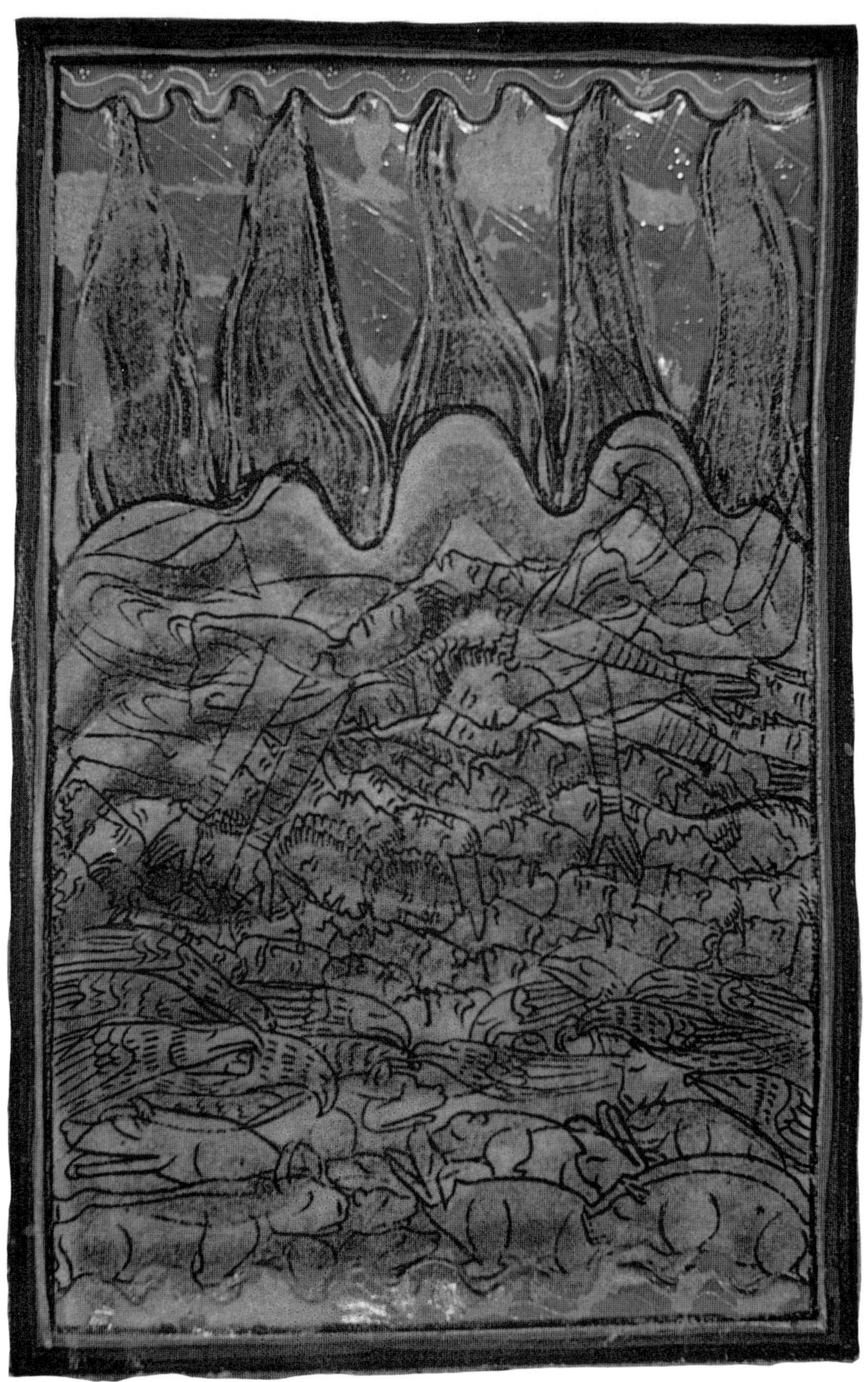

51b. The Flood

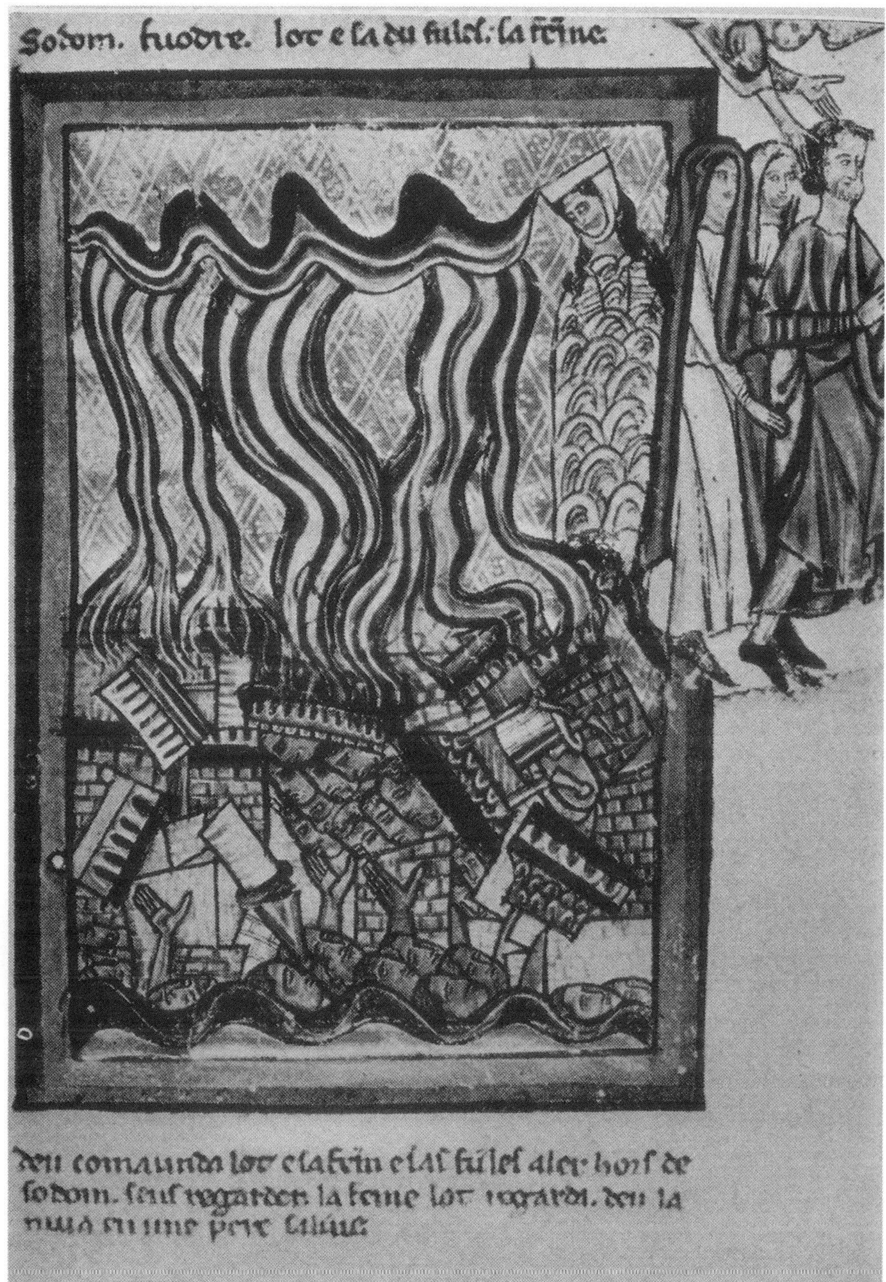

51c. Lot and his family leaving Sodom

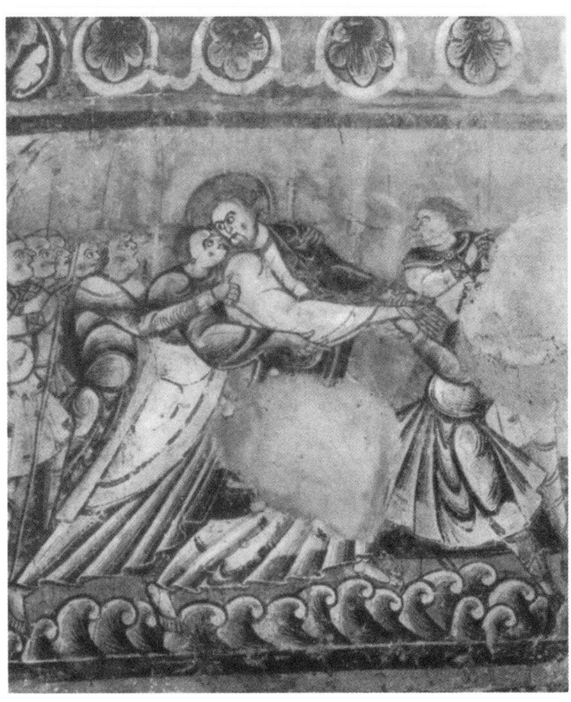

52a. Kiss of Judas, St. Martin de Vic, Nohant-Vicq

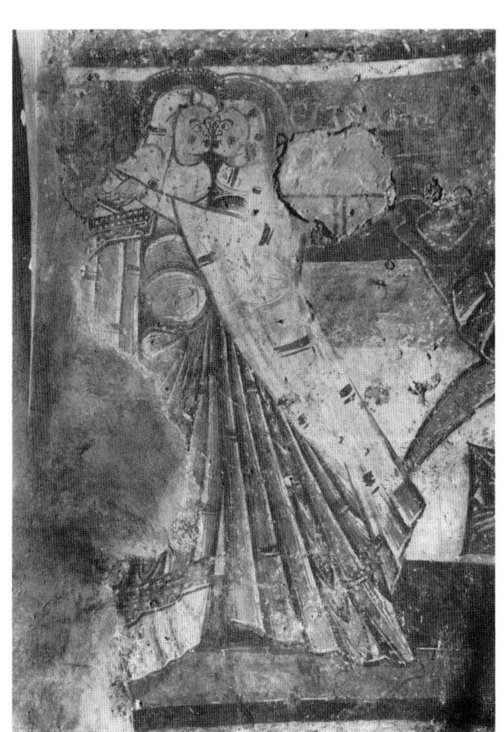

52b. The Visitation, St. Martin de Vic, Nohant-Vicq

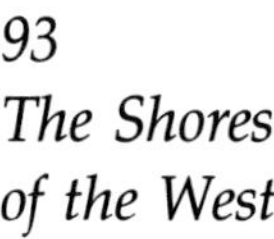

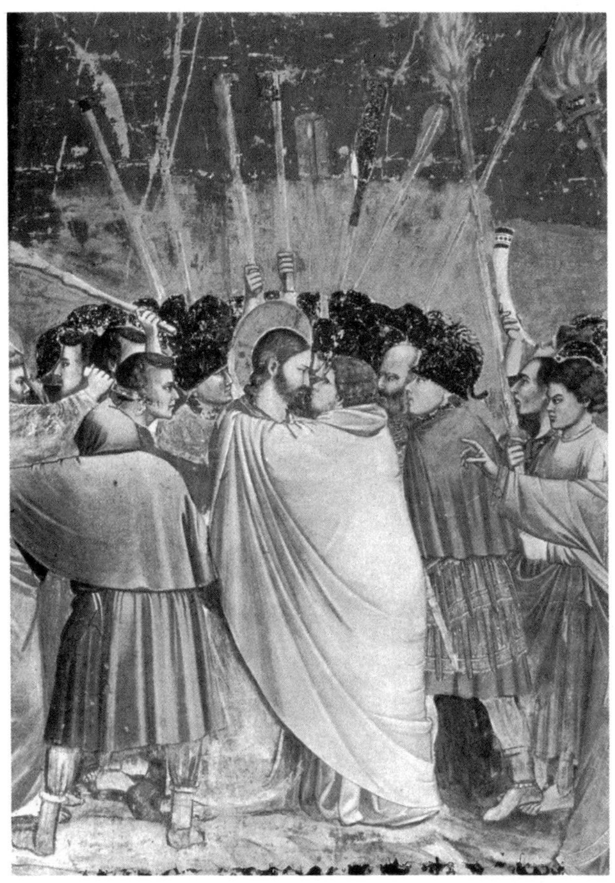

53. Giotto, Kiss of Judas

guiding hint as to what you are to do next!) the eastern Christian man, the Byzantine, is very different—his struggles very different, too. Of course, his repeated impact on the West's maturation has been great, we know it, you know it well; great also was the West's response: both in acceptance and in rejection. To explain what I call 'significant ornament' in a more narrow and specific way is to say this:

"The 'secret' of the Romanesque figurative style is its intense de-Byzantinization; Byzantinization first; de-Byzantinization as the result.

"Now you know what I meant in giving you a hint.

"Go and find and meet where he is your new *Grand Personnage.*

"Go to Byzantium!"

# The Shores of Byzantium

"VENI, VIDI, VICI"—I came, I saw, I conquered—and I went back.

Conquered what? There was nothing to conquer: all was offered to me most graciously. And yet, what I was sent for I did conquer: the reason or reasons why in spite of their common origin—Christianity and its spreading—were Western Christian humanity and Eastern so deeply different? Why the steady de-Byzantinization of the medieval West?

*

And just as I did a long time ago, the day I came to the shores of Japan's far away past, when cautiously I parted the tufted fragrant branches which concealed a sweetest spot there—the Haruna Shrine—and faced, in a blast of Japan's purples, golds, whites and blacks, Japan's Time with all its smells, views, existences and exuberances[40], so I did now—in "silence and secrecy." I cautiously parted the tufted evergreens and view-hiding branches (of learning? the earnest, evergreen, tufted branches of learning?) in the hope of facing, in a blast of Byzantium's golds, whites and purples, the Byzantine Christ-Emperor's pomp and contrasted circumstance—Byzantium's Past.

But—what a surprise!—it was not Christian Greece that was half disclosed to me, it was ancient, heathen Greece itself and again. Ancient Greece—unexpected Byzantium here! The blue, the gold and the white of her presence and permanence; the birth of

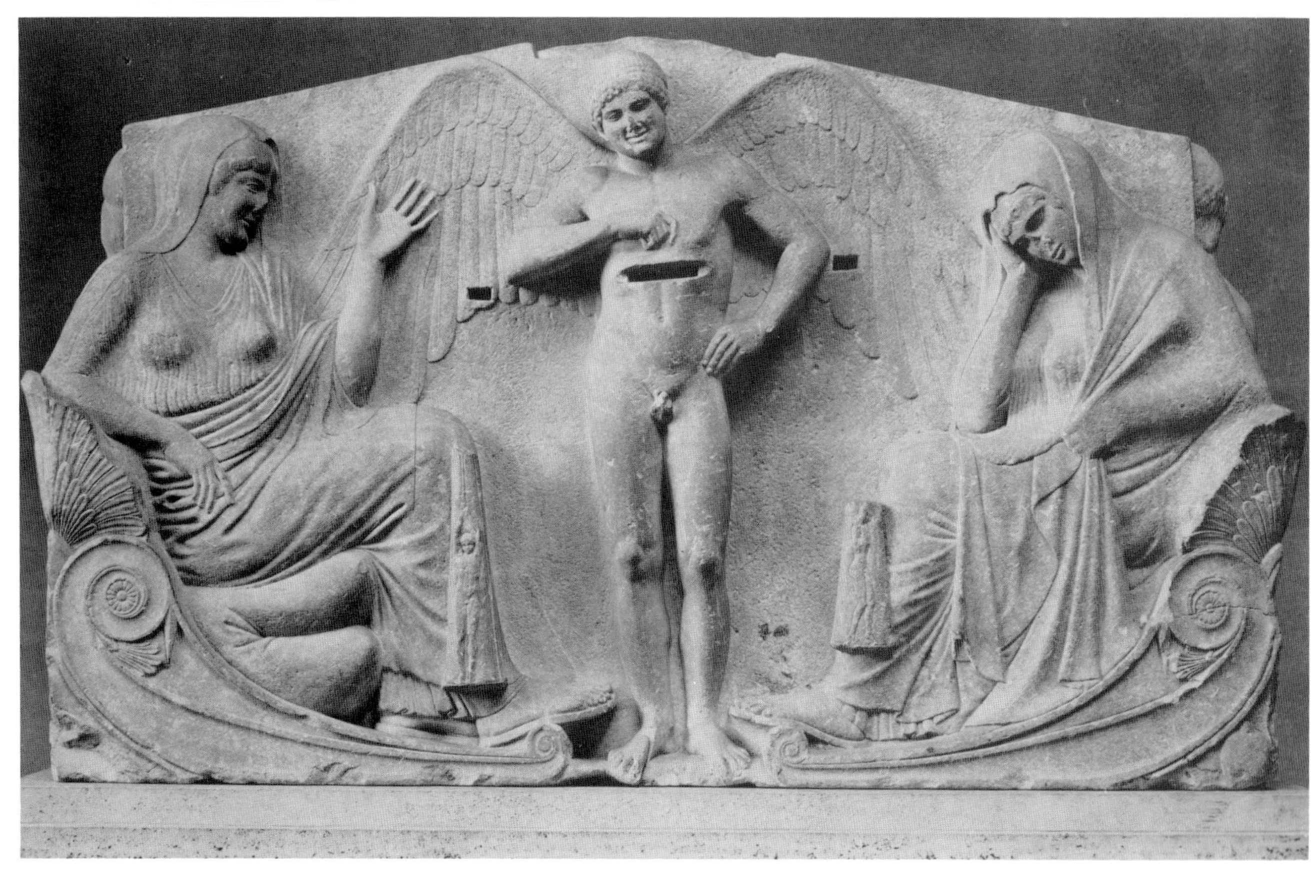

54. Eros holding scale, "Boston Throne"

young Eros, and the birth of the Dionysos-Apollo contest; of *Okeanos,* and of man's descent and ascent in it; the birth of man, paradigm of inexorable and perfect not yet empirical Form, soul's birth as mind-soul-body, exactly what Plato meant when in the *Timaeus* he spoke of the Creator's fashioning of the universe and giving the mind to the soul and the soul to the body, and what an Ionian artist a century earlier, his Cretan past still alive in him, could say in marble.

And this is what I saw through the parted branches:

Two halves of a mystery cult's altar—a "hidden" divinity's marble throne?—disjoined for many centuries (perhaps even never joined), now, on the shore of Byzantium joined and communicating. Joined and communicating in my Fable, for I well knew then that the so-called "Boston throne" (*Plate 54*) and the "Ludovisi throne" (*Plate 55*)[41] had come to meet me only. A new event-

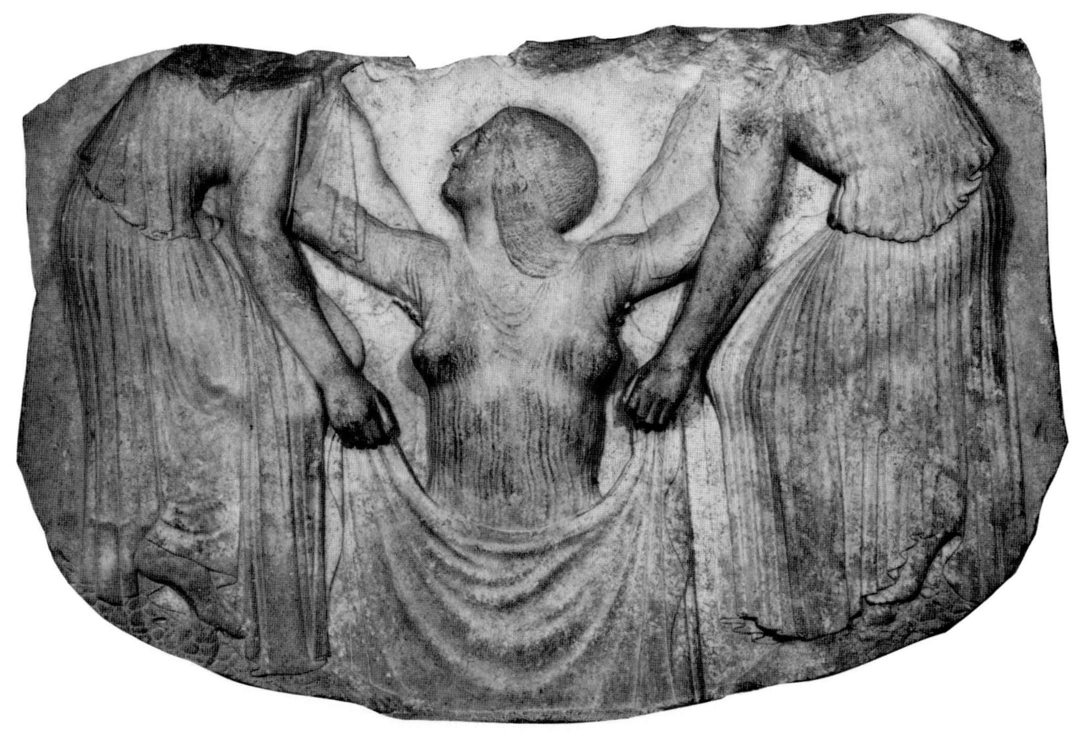

55. Aphrodite, "Ludovisi Throne"

being in my Fable. And not at all an object and a subject of an archaeologist's accuracy and worry. So, romantically (but not candidly so), I found and met this new being-event.[42]

On one of the mysterious faces of the "altar," probably the rear one (its marble chiseled obviously with much less delicacy and precision than the opposite one, probably frontal), the winged Eros, the Adolescent, is holding a scale, each of its plates supporting the weight of a single figure: to Eros' left that of the victorious, departing Apollo, to the right, that of the defeated and punished Marsyas, so I have seen it there. And it was a strange and surprising event to behold! The victor, the one who in mind's weighing decision should have been the heavier—*the more valuable*—his supporting plate was lighter, higher than his daring, challenging and defeated Dionysian rival's. Strange and surprising event indeed! And the expressions of the identical female figures, seated one on each side of the scale (differing only in their contrasting attitude on the left and the right of the scale, and in the corresponding arrangement of their garments), clearly reflected this strangeness. The woman to the right appeared to be asleep, or meditating, detached, inattentive, as if alienated from the central event; the woman to the left (is she the Body?, is she the Mind? I felt I was asked not to care at that moment) awakened suddenly by a sudden surprise or sudden understanding of the event's meaning or birth: the birth of Eros' Dionysian choice, the future birth of the Soul.

And I could then participate myself—always in ''silence and secrecy''—not only in this meaning and this between-mind-and-body future birth but also in the meaning and the birth, the Siphnos-like sub-subject, on the other face of the ''altar.'' From the depths—of Okeanos? of Earth?—emerges here (*See Plate 55*) a young woman's body (Aphrodite Ericina? Hera Teleia? Rhea? Persephone? All of them, at once, each of them in their divine sameness: *La Femme Civilisatrice* always) supported, helped to be born by two identical beings, and absolutely identical now all three, their arms, messengers of their bodies, interlaced, the profile of the emerging young woman turned uplifted and glad toward one of her two selves: soul-in-mind —(the intensity and passion of Apollo), soul-in-body (passion's intensity, its Dionysian heavier weight), and, between them, the emerging soul-in-soul, soul-in-mind's body (passionate intensity itself, Eros the Weigher)—that is how I saw the two fronts of the ''altar'': *Psyche,* her birth, the white butterfly, the blue singing bird from Crete, in ever revived birth (the rebirth of the pre-split *permitted* beatitude, my silver cup of artisan nostalgia and creation!)—the gift of Greece, the Honey and the Bee of Ancient Greece, here, now, meeting me again. All the passionate intensity of Christian Greece, Byzantium! And all this (the Ionian artist of my Fable did not forget to tell me so!) was part of all mystery cults' central teaching: that mind-soul-body's freedom must be for all—no slavery any more. This is what was revealed on the side-faces of the same ''altar'' (*Plates 56a, b, c, & d*) by a pair of young nudes (nudity, the sign of free citizenship in the presence of the Divine), the naked *kouros* playing Apollo's lyre, the naked *kore* playing the Dionysian flute; and seated together with them, in equality of rights and duties, a young woman-slave and an old woman-slave, entirely clothed (sign of

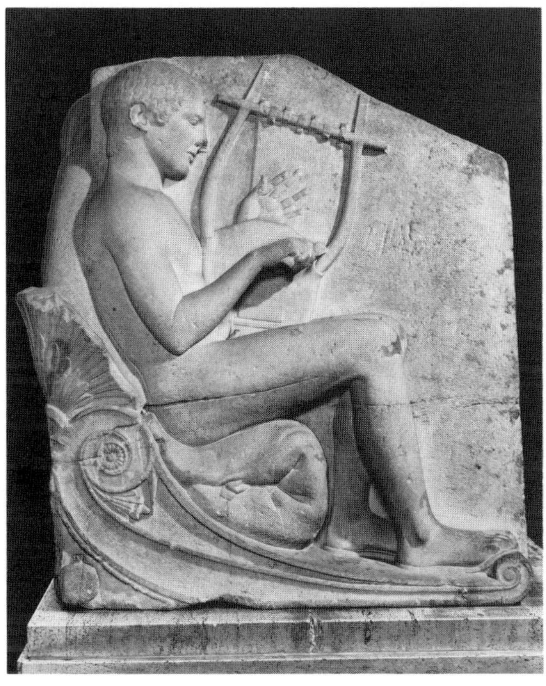

56a. *Kouros* with lyre, "Boston Throne"

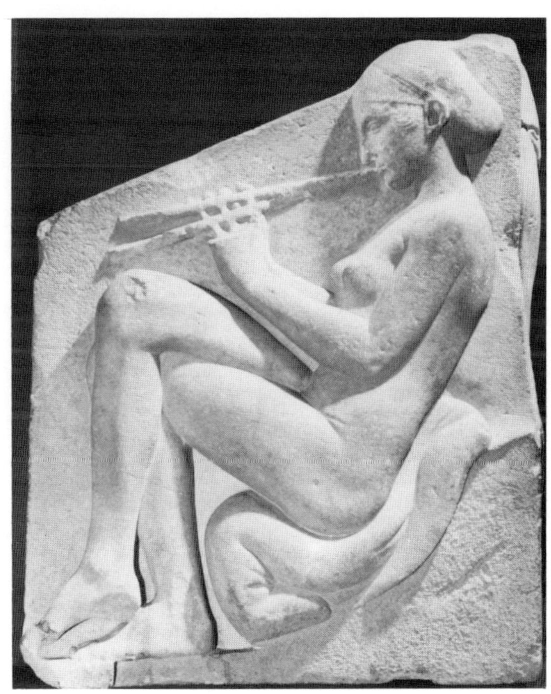

56b. *Kore* with flute, "Ludovisi Throne"

unfreedom, of slavery here), both shelterers, protectors of the flame, of the light and of the grain. For there was no freedom anywhere but here, in the human soul's emerging profile turned toward one of her two helpers. The Mind? The Body? Which one? Their sameness—so I sensed it—having been created choice-free, any choice would thus become yours, all yours. And mine, of course: my choice of Body's awakening first, before Mind's, at the call of Eros' decision, and of Soul's first emerging glance turned toward the Body's supporting help, equal to Mind's. My choice, decisive for a while, mine, I the Byzantine for a brief while, for whom Tertullian's ''absurdity'' became light and passionate intensity: ''The Son of God died, this is credible, because it is folly. He has been buried and resurrected; this is certain because it is impossible,''[43] I, to whom also, much later, the famous Byzantine Athonite monk, Gregory Palamas (mid-fourteenth century) spoke of the common energies in the body and the ''passionate part of the soul,''[44] and spoke of the Flesh of the Light that shone on Mount Tabor. Abomination? Abominable, dangerous nonsense? Obscurantist abomination—''opium'' of exploitation and mind-soul-body's oppression? Yes—undoubtedly! No! no, in the ''silence and secrecy'' of soul's birth—of soul's invisible radiation bringing at once doom—Byzantium's final doom!—to the rotting grain therein, and rebirth, the new plant, a total, unpredictable, thus ''monstrous'' change. Byzantine mysterious spirituality—the Christological dialectics of the ''unity of contradictories,''[45] the dialectics of Correspondence (Father-to-Son-to-Holy-Spirit-to-Father) and Substitution (Father = Son = Holy Spirit)—Byzantine spirituality of the past today could be, perhaps, the equally mysterious spirituality of ''dialectical materialism,'' soul's rebirth, Greece! *Sanctus, Sanctus, Sanctus*—this word-not-for-everybody, this word-in-everybody, that a ''Byzantine'' Catalan, Gaudí, nailed and multiplied along the towers of his and Barcelona's *Sagrada Familia (Plate 57)*!

From transfer to transfer, the same and ultimate Solitude-Solidarity was witnessing for me again, this time in Byzantium:

That the Witness is. The Witness-Image, Flesh, Touch. The in-carnation seen by me through and beyond the parted branches. But it was precisely this that the Christian East shared with the West in their common origin. How?

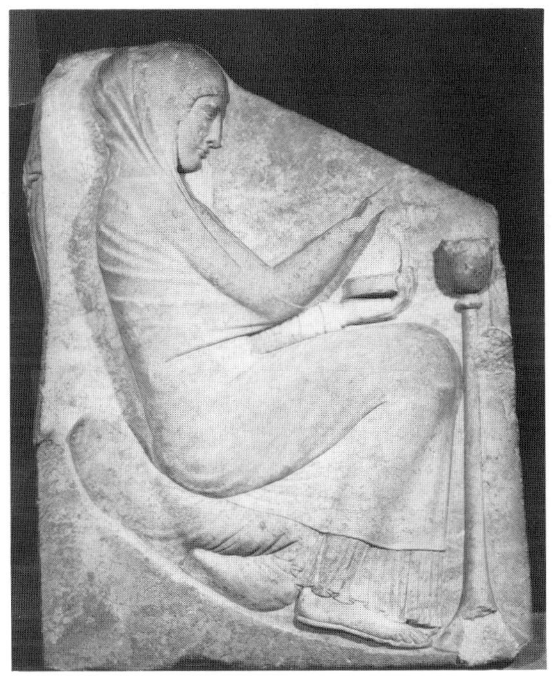

56c. Young woman, "Ludovisi Throne"

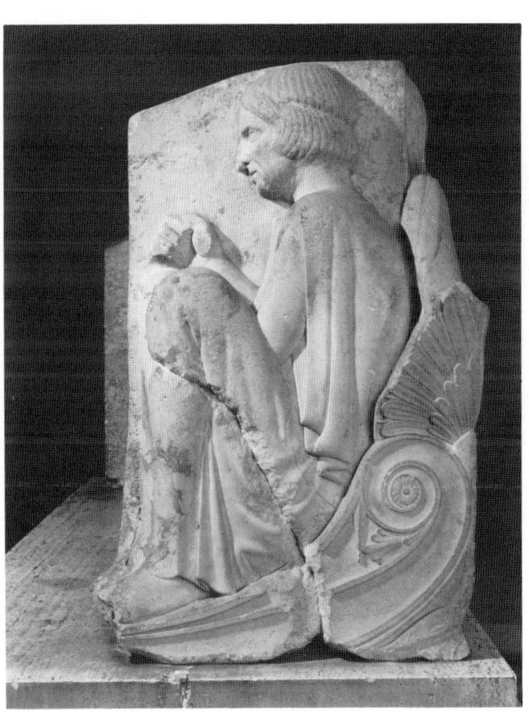

56d. Old woman, "Boston Throne"

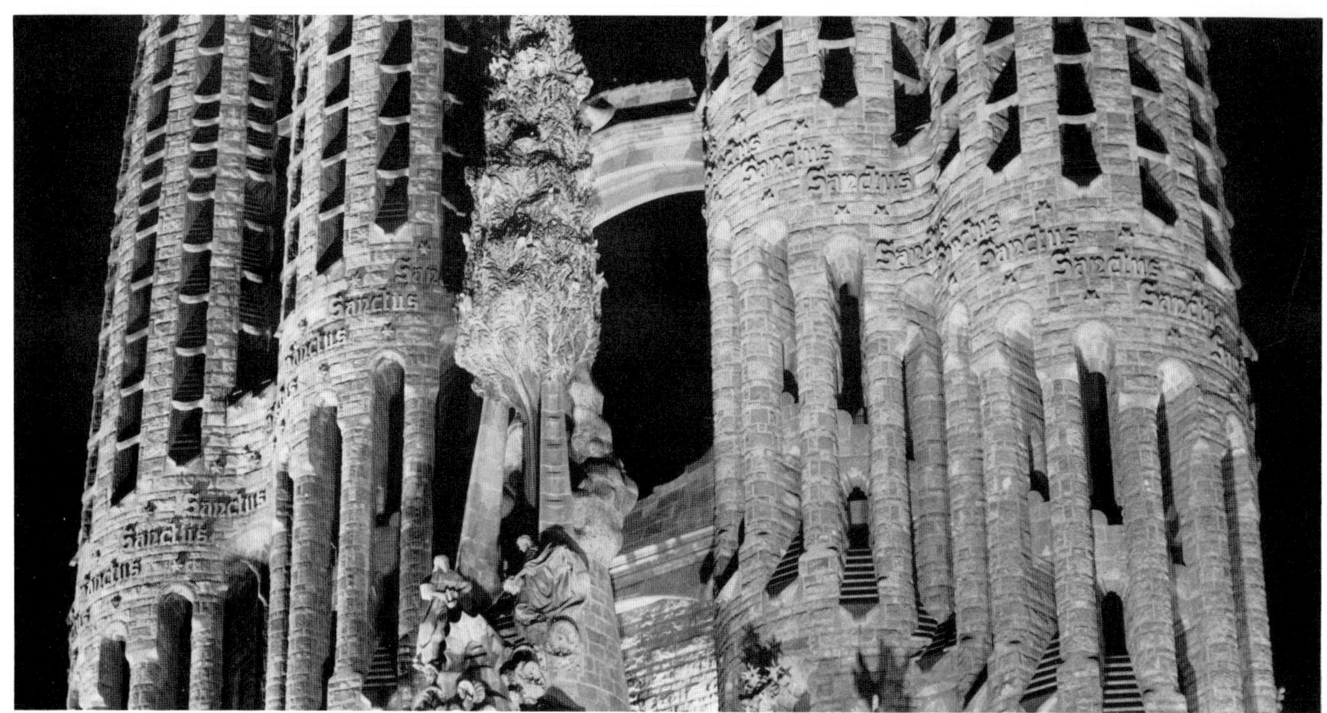

57. Gaudí, Sagrada Familia church, Barcelona

*

Puzzled and doubting, I felt suddenly abandoned and discouraged. And it was a great relief—a sense of belonging and security again—to see coming toward me, unheralded, the Children of the Ancestor, those who had befriended me before.

And the Witness was with them, one of them, the leader of them all.

My tale of the Braid's Intrigue in history and mind could remain with me and be continued.

And the Witness spoke then:

"We came to remind you of what your puzzlement seemed to make you forget: that nothing in man is one, everything is two from the start to the end. Man is two-oneness. The 'crisis,' uninterrupted and ever growing in complexity of creative opposition and creative interlace is man's painful and rewarding 'normalcy.' The only oneness in man, the only 'absolute,' is the third thread of the braid itself. And so it is with all human communications and convictions. There are always two opposite-interlaced ways or methods—never only one!—carrying to us what we either accept or reject as 'proof.' One is the way, the method, that emerges, lit by mind's *category of relation,* from the still hidden recesses of what vaguely we name intuition—this treasure house of unlimited possibilities of choice—and leads through a series of determining facts, through the linkages of mutual, factual influences, to the acts of observation, description, demonstration and finally conviction and 'proof.' It is the way of connections and dialectics. The way of sight, sound and concept.

"And opposite it, the way of immediacy, of no-way thus, with no propelling intuition or *category* of relation within its origins—but naked relation as such and at once, immediate; a *presence of adherence*—a tightly bunched event-attitude, a two-before-one touch, image-touch, image-flesh: the *Witness, the proving without proof.*

"And the first was the Braid's manifested way of Classical Antiquity. And the second, that of Christianity. And both ways, both methods of mind's structuring remain the same as they were in the past, with us now.

"The discursive, persuasive, demonstrative method of communication and conviction—legacy of the matured Hellenistic-Roman method, rediscovered, revivified by the medieval West once Antiquity's Aristotelian learning had been propelled there through Judeo-Islamic and Byzantine agencies—became the leading way in the West.

"The other, the way of the Witness, remained at the historical roots of the 'purely' Christian method of 'proof,' East and West.

"Belonging at its inception much less to the Judaic world of theological *pudeur* and prudence (but belonging there also!) than to the surrounding world of mystery cults and their 'humid' theosophies, Christianity nevertheless emerged as a revolt against the esotericism of the *deus absconditus* mystery cults and their interpretative control by the Verbal Elite. Christianity's credo is an *exoteric* credo, open to all (more so than its rival, the Mithraic credo)—a narrowly, historically precise revelation. Very historical—the image of a little, insignificant Jew, crucified and resurrected in a little, insignificant and troublesome corner of haughty Rome's imperial world, an image *to be touched with the finger, the index, of History,* a carnal witness without—not yet!—any theophanic attributes and attributions!

''A truly astonishing, unexpected, thus 'monstrous,' new, thus to be desired, subject and object of thought, of vision and of power, a new power so different from the over-exercised, exhausted power of Rome's sophisticated body and mind; a witness to be adhered to, touched; a new birth of the soul and a rebirth of a primordial epistemology; the image-metaphor as such (that little, insignificant Jew, the Saviour of the significant Cosmos!), becoming at once the *subject, the object and the very method* of communication and conviction—the witnessing method itself, the *proving without proof!*

''And, as you must have guessed already, the way and the method of the Witness—my way and my method—is the way, the method, the metaphor and the sense of art's image-building itself.

''And so, in all earnest, I say to you: *Christianity is its art.*'' (It is here that you should see, seize, the closest connection with the 'immediate' motion in art's space of beings and things—'mobile rigidity's' motion—here at the threshold of the *apocalyptic;* while the 'mnemonic,' the mediate, learned, derived motion would belong to the 'discourse' of search, persuasion and certainty, at the threshold of the *psychomachic*).

*

''The historical beginnings of Christianity—its spreading, to be more precise—coincided with the reawakening of 'artisan' nostalgia, 'artisan' memory of the lost three-oneness (memory and nostalgia at the very roots of the then swarming mystery-gnostic cults and Neo-platonic speculations) in the still loyally Hellenistic East, that is, in the thickly and widely urbanized world, a very 'artisan' world, surrounded by—and pushing back—an ever narrower thus dangerously restless belt of 'nomadic' humanity and its threat.

''And this rewakening was helped, during approximately the first five centuries of the Christian era, by the results of a great event, dual in its origins and its consequences, that radically changed the social and mental structure of the West in particular: the catastrophic fall of Rome at the hands mainly of the nomadic or semi-nomadic 'barbarians,' and the concomitant birth of a revolutionary new social order. I mean the *fusion* of embryonic feudalism sprung from politically and economically decaying Rome (late Rome's *possessio precaria,* the embryo of the future *beneficio* and the still later *fief*), with the equally embryonic—but how much more vigorous, more 'normal'!—feudalism conditioned by the nomadic inner structure itself.

"This fusion slowly and steadily transformed Antiquity's central, basal economic category, *slavery* (other forms of labor relations there notwithstanding), or the direct producer's total alienation from any kind of possession, into *serfdom,* where the *de facto* enslaved, yet *de jure* partly free peasant-and-artisan could remain possessor of some remnants of property, thus of some means of future emancipation—family, wretched shelter, some tools, remnants of lost freedom to be recovered by endemic medieval revolts. Artisan 'nostalgia' (artisan-peasant in prehistoric depth) and artisan social emancipation (artisan and peasant in historical alliance) together led the way to the West's emancipation. Such was the destiny of the Christian West—ultimately, but not exclusively, the destiny of Psychomachic man. Such was not Byzantium's destiny and way. Originally and ultimately (but not exclusively either) it was the way and the destiny of Apocalyptic man.

"Imperial Rome's world-state structure, with state-slavery at its socio-economic basis, was inherited from the Orient's Bronze Age, an age when all, from despot to actual slave, were in total theocratic and equalitarian enslavement of mind and body to the real ruler and real owner of the temple-palace's wealth, the divinity.

"And the Bronze Age world at the collapse of Rome was transferred to Byzantium. All the pomp and glory, all the misery and oppression also, the unprecedented splendor and the predestined doom of such an epic anachronism—imagine it! Imagine also its historical fascination, its charm and its impact, the fascination, the charm, the impact, also the puzzle, of all the resulting contrasts and inner contradictions: Byzantium's 'purity' and glory of exaltation, Byzantium's enlightened certainties, and Byzantium's 'mud,' the misery of darkened superstitions and stoppages. Consider here the uninterrupted confrontation in Byzantium between the 'profane' Hellenic heritage, Hellenic inquisitive discursive thought and the early Christian and patristic heritage of thought-*ekstasis*—an historical process, uninterrupted and growing in intensity, in Byzantium never tending, as in the medieval West with its succession of *renovatios,* toward a synthesis, but simply a process accented, rhythmically measured by a series of dramatic and open oppositions, paired, symmetrical and personified. In the ninth century, soon after the Iconoclast crisis (itself an outlet, violent and passionate, of the same oppositions), the learned 'humanism' of the patriarch Photius and its opposition by his rival, the patriarch Ignatius; in the eleventh century the passionate Hellenism of a Michael Psellos and his entourage, and opposite it, the patristic theology of *ekstasis* and Light boldly revived by Simon the New Theologian; then later, during the Palaeologan dynastic period, the last crisis in Byzantium, in the midst of all the political, social and economic chaos and exhaustion, the last and perhaps the acutest crisis of confrontation and contrast: the world of the learned, competent and conscious 'humanists' of the fourteenth and fifteenth centuries—the world of a Theodoros Matochietes, of Nicephoros Gregoras, of Bessarion and of the famous, 'pagan' Judge of Mistra, Gemistos Plethon; of Planides Moschopoulos and many others, learned women among them,[46] and, opposite it, on the eve of the Empire's final doom, the final triumph of Byzantine monkhood, the ecstatic thought in the Hesychast 'perpetual prayer of the heart,' and the thought of its chief defender, Gregorios Palamas.

"Typically Byzantine is also the contrast between the weakening of political authority, and the strengthening of spiritual vigor. Thus it was immediately after the era of the greatest expansion of Byzantine might, the tenth and part of the eleventh century of conquest and consolidation, that, following the death in 1025 of the victorious Basil II, the Bulgaroctonos, the era of the Byzantine Empire's downfall started amidst political and economic disasters[47]—yet was not this failing era at the same time the era of perhaps the greatest creative activity and vigor? Or think of this other example of the so peculiarly Byzantine contrasts and contradictions: the never contested (although often and brutally soiled by intrigue, treachery and murder—how candidly human this!) sacredness—sacramental!—of the person of the autocrat Basileus, as well as that of his Basilissa, and the 'vulgar' secularity of their imperial, *personal* manipulations of mercantile interests and profits (trade and industry being the imperial absolute monopoly).

"Or, again, the strictly, rigidly fixed hierarchy of function and ceremony surrounding the sacred throne of the sacred couple and its porphyrogenite offspring; the near-and-far reaching social implications, and at the same time, the truly astonishing fluidity of Byzantine society at large, where no race or professional discriminations and privileges, but only merit, counted for social ascension (*apaideusia,* the lack of mental training or education being considered the greatest, almost awe-inspiring, obstacle to advancement).[48]

"And what of the more localized, less 'global' contrasts: the institution of eunuchs, for instance, so unnecessary in a civilization of equality of sexes, where most women were free from gynecian seclusion, free socially, even economically? And yet, was not this immemorial Oriental institution one of the most exalted and powerful in Byzantium, leading even to the Patriarchal throne itself? An institution and a practice frowned upon by the Church (as an Origenean not-entirely-inner-self's means of body's spiritualization), yet accepted also: the host of castrates at the court of the Emperor=Christ=Emperor was the host of 'angels' surrounding and supporting the throne—totally loyal 'angels' who when given administrative powers (the eunuchs were often in control of the huge imperial bureaucracy) could become one of the most efficient political-diplomatic weapons against the onrush of landed aristocracy, this greatest, always threatening danger for the maintenance of the theocratic imperial monolith."

Here the Witness interrupted himself, as if tired. "Of course," I thought. He looked at me. And I saw in his eyes irony inhabiting his mind, sorrow inhabiting his soul, and tenderness inhabiting his body.

That was the Witness. And then he continued, his companions around him:

"Now remember this also when searching among the many reasons for the Christian East-West dichotomy: the Bronze Age, the king-priest's presence there had never disappeared from the horizon of the West either. But in the West the *Sacerdotium* and the *Imperium* or *Regnum* were confronting each other as separated entities, either allies (the medieval 'sacerdotium' of the Pope's primacy assured though) or enemies, each aspiring to its politicaljuridicial priority. While in the King-Priest's Byzantium this would never have been possible, notwithstanding the factual and frequent strife between the Basileus and the Patriarchate, absorbed as the latter was in the theophanic sanctity of the Imperium's body.[49]

''The deeper, the subtler, thus the truly effective reasons for the East-West dichotomy, the de-Byzantinization of the West—the West's art as we want it here—I, the Witness, one of your tale's *Personae,* should not persuade you of: it would be playing the role and the game of destiny herself, not my role, not my game.

''But, just as a voice and a hint sent you to the shores of Byzantium, so I too can give you a hint to follow: You will find traces of me, the Witness, of my presence and passage, everywhere in Byzantium. But truly to find me there, look only where, underneath the precarious security of the Bronze Age legacy, another legacy and another security, unexhausted and planetary, the artist-artisan's primeval creativity, made its working home and shelter: the home, the shelter, the art of Byzantine monkhood. There, only there, only when my body becomes the body of Mount Tabor's Light itself, will Byzantium be given to you. Search for the image-touch of Light in Byzantium's intrigue of history and mind.''

Thus the Witness spoke to me ever so graciously and simply, omitting—I knew it later—many a detail and correction.

And so, half-prepared, half-puzzled still and still in doubt, I went to meet the *Grand Personnage*—the Art of Byzantium.

It was a marvelous meeting.

*

And that same day I had a dream. I dreamed that, fatigued, I fell asleep and had a dream of a great journey. I knew at once it was the journey of Eros, Desire. But I did not know whether it was Eros of all origins, or Eros, Desire in me alone; and also whether there was meant to be any distinction between the two.

Desire was dwelling on Earth, among everyday's precessions or precedence, dwelling successively in each of the twelve *earthly* zodiacal ''houses of life''—now in the great house of Sex, now in that of Strife—Power against Strength, now in that of Order and Organizing Category, now in that of Help and Helplessness; then in the house of Pity, Indifference and Separation, then in the house of Fatigue . . . And it was from the house of Fatigue that, temporarily leaving the remaining houses uninhabited, Eros took flight (was it because of my dream's confusion and isolation?) to the higher world of heaven, of earthly meanings or essences, the high world of Fable.

There, in harmony with his own nature, Eros could remain for a longer while, among the harmonies of Fable's converging inventions and correspondences. Restless Eros! ''*Mas alto*''—''Higher! Higher!'' so the poet's cry was heard.[50] And Eros, Desire, ascended from the joy-full earthly heaven of Fable, to the highest and ultimate heaven of Myth. And there, in Desire's presence, I saw all the correspondences and convergences of Earth and of Fable—still separations!—transferred into total adhesions and total, global meanings—Myth uniting the stellar and earthly happenings and actions across the millenia-long span of human guesses and quests, among the astonishing universality and similarity of mythic inventions, created separately by separate races and peoples on earth, ancient and modern.[51]

Ardent, unquenched aspirations toward the *Harmonicê Mundi,* and ardent melancholy anxieties and doubts in the face of the cosmic ''riddle''—the stellar, inter-stellar and sub-stellar subtle irregularities and subtle deviations, in, say, the ordered precession of the equinoxes, the ordered motion of the ecliptic, the ordered ''fugue'' of the entire starry sky. All this certainty and doubt, harmony and the ''riddle'' of deviations mirrored—dream of a dream!—in Myth's anxiety and melancholy in the face of every day's earthly riddle of life and death, and in Myth's final sliding into life's and death's harmonies. But—''*Mas alto!* Higher, higher!'' was heard again across the skies of Earth, of Fable and of Myth: ''Higher, higher!'' Yet—and I sensed it clearly!—there was nothing higher there. And Eros started back on his descending journey. Was it, crossing the Poet's voice, the mocking voice of the Soviet astronaut: ''I ascend the skies and nowhere have I found God''? Was it Pascal's ''*J'ai peur des espaces infinis*'' that made Desire descend? No—I knew it!—it was still the poet's ''Higher, higher!''—the now impossible ''higher'' which thus was now becoming ''Lower! Lower!''

And it is here that the real impossible—the absurd—in my

dream occurred: I saw Eros (I recognized the Eros of Socrates and of Diotima, the unwashed, the not festive and not ''beautiful'' Eros) *ashamed.* I saw him ashamed and angry. I knew also then—and only then—clearly, why. A sudden feeling it was, a suspicion awakened in the dream itself, in Eros and in me:

That the prolonged attachment to the enjoyments of Fable and Myth—not to their need though!—could have been no more than a shameful oblivion, a veil concealing what precisely made both Fable and Myth exist and be real—all the struggles on Earth, the struggles of what is still just there against what is unjust, the old and obsolete and tenacious ''class struggle'' still taking precedence. ''*Mas alto!* Higher, higher!''—rapidly, abruptly, Eros and I, wings outstretched flew downward. ''Lower, lower! *Mas alto!*''—and we arrived. On the top of a mountain—Mount Sinai—there stood before us the spirit and the light of the Ten Commandments.

That was all, and my dream's end.

And I awoke from my dream's dream not puzzled or frightened, but rested, ready and glad.

And I know this now: it was not the content, the subject matter, of my dream that made me remember it so vividly to this day. It was the dream-feeling, vague, guiding and central, of an ascension, a descent and an unexpected, abrupt arrival. But why—I wondered long afterward—why now the Ten Commandments, so sudden, so precise? Why the Ten Commandments, whose subject matter, translated as its idiom might be into the interpretative idiom of today's moral directives, I could remember only in part, and whose rules I could partly follow, simply by instinct or freely chosen Kantian moral *must?* I do not know why and how—such is the conditioned freedom of a dream. But I do know now, I, Pimen, the old monk of a young new age writing in my cell the last tale of my chronicle, that what I knew then in the dream's dream made this arrival—the vague and guiding and central feeling of it—the very sense of all my future quests and wanderings: the spirit and the light of the Ten Commandments standing erect on the top of Mount Sinai and in the heart of my own fable.

*

And more: my dream was about loyalty. And about origins: a new trace joining so many others along the past shores. A guiding trace: the same and the else made one, in loyalty to the origins.

And so the voice of the Witness became—as it needed to be—one with the listening thoughts of all those who were assembled around him, all Children, as he himself was, of the Ancestor—Substitution-and-Correspondence, Transfer-and-Transformation, the Apocalyptic-and-Psychomachic; and in deepest loyalty to all their common origin, the Braid, the same-else, the self-other, Solitude-Solidarity, *Tendresse!*

''Look for the concept-touch, the image-touch of Light,'' the Witness said to me, ''and you will find Byzantium.'' And I know what he, what they all, really meant by Light: the birth of Light in man's soul: and not only the birth of enlightenment, the birth of illumination in man, or even soul's recreation of light outside man, as in man's creations, man's arts—but also soul's birth as the ''passionate part''—Light!—of the ''body,'' the *body* of man and the body of the beyond-of-man made one. Made one—made two-one, the same-else, the self-other, here also: either as mutual adhesion or as mutual correspondence.

''*Veni, vidi, vici*''—I repeat what I said at my arrival. For I found then, and at once (or so I thought, for I found it without great effort) what I came to look for: the essential difference as well as the initial similarity between the concept of man in the Christian West and the concept of man in the Christian East.

In the West:

Man (in art, the human figure, its primacy and integrity, Antiquity's total and essential legacy) and the beyond-of-man (''landscape'') made into one integrated, new, total entity.

In Byzantium:

Man (in art, his figure, its primacy and integrity, begotten from Antiquity, just as it was in the West) never made one with his ''landscape,'' with the beyond-of-man, whatever this might be, but only accompanied, dramatically interpreted by it.

The West has always been and today is still loyal to this origin. And so has Byzantium been to its own origin.

Let an early Romanesque image ''ornament'' stand for me here as the testimony of the West's concept of man in art *(Plate 58).*

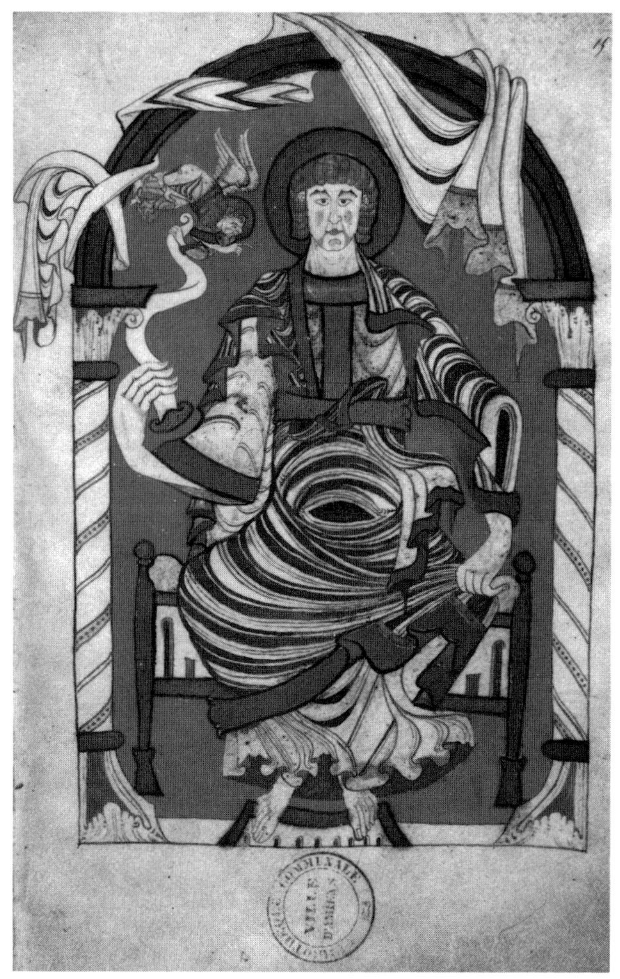

58. St. Matthew, Gospel manuscript from Corbie

Let a Byzantine sixteenth century icon, Byzantine-Russian at that (it does not matter at all here),[52] be the testimony for me of the Byzantine concept of man-and-the-beyond-of-man *(Plate 59)*.

The Romanesque distortion of St. Matthew's body is this body's total belonging, total, ''hypnotic,'' dancing adhesion to that which surrounds it, and *vice versa.* Here man is his ''landscape'' and ''landscape'' is the man. Such will always be the way of the West, its destiny and idiom; such, from Romanesque and proto-Romanesque distortions, the Romanesque man-landscape ''ornament,'' to the ''realistically'' transformed continuation (after the ''classical'' revival—around 1200 and during the High Gothic—

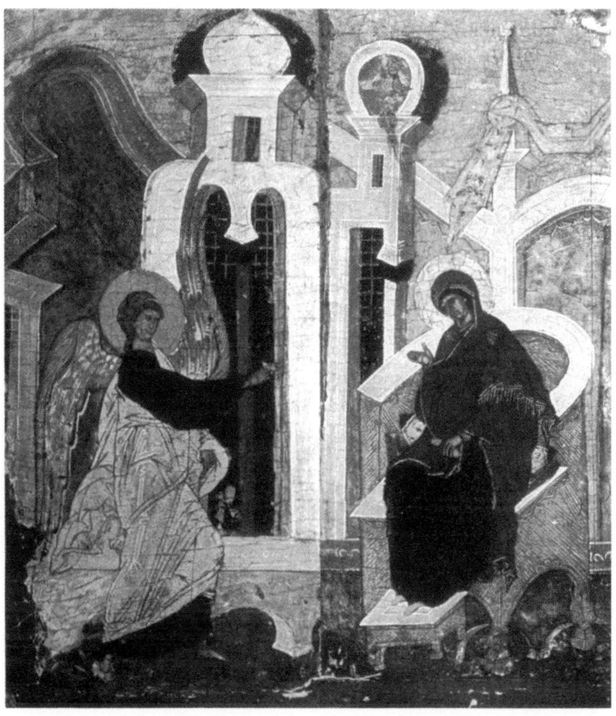

59. The Annunciation, Russian icon, Novgorod school

of Antiquity's anatomic and spatial integrity or ''correctness'' of the same Romanesque theme and goal in the so-called Late-Gothic, Renaissance, Mannerist and Baroque styles *(Plates 60a & b),* to the nineteenth century's sentient landscapes with man often invisible or silenced, yet present in them, and on to the twentieth century's simultaneity of man and the beyond-of-man in being the same and the else (in deepest awareness now): Picasso's ''chairness'' of a seated woman and ''womanness'' of the chair *(Plate 61).*

Thus, the pictorial landscape itself as we understand it in the West, is the West's ''pure'' creation (the Northern Atlantic man's rather than the Mediterranean man's, with the ancestral Celtic and other, ''barbaric,'' kindred roots close to his creative will), so different from the two other, equally distinctive landscape creations in man's history: that of China, where the self, the limited figure of man, was willingly absorbed in the other, the illimited grandeur of the beyond-of-man *(Plate 62);* that of Hellenistic-Roman Antiquity, where landscape remained simply the rhythmic and psychological accompaniment of man's activity *(Plate 63).*

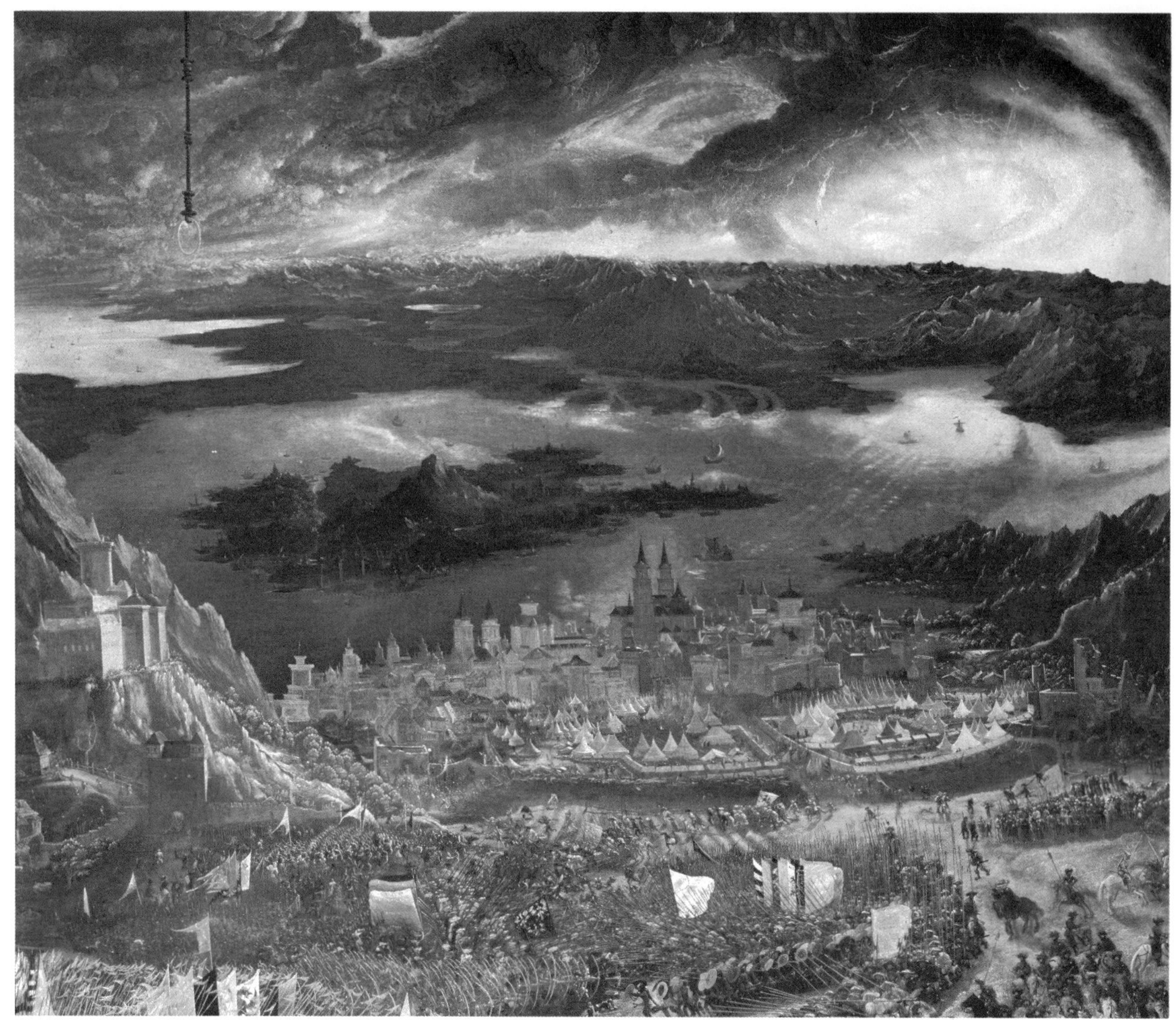

60a. Altdorfer, The Battle of Alexander, detail

And it was in the art of Byzantium that Antiquity's conception of man's environment as interpretation and accompaniment of man's drama—and never as total, mutual adhesion—had its fulfillment.

The classical *Medea*[53] *(Plate 64)* meditating her own doom, the murder of her children, stands against an ordered, yet tormented,

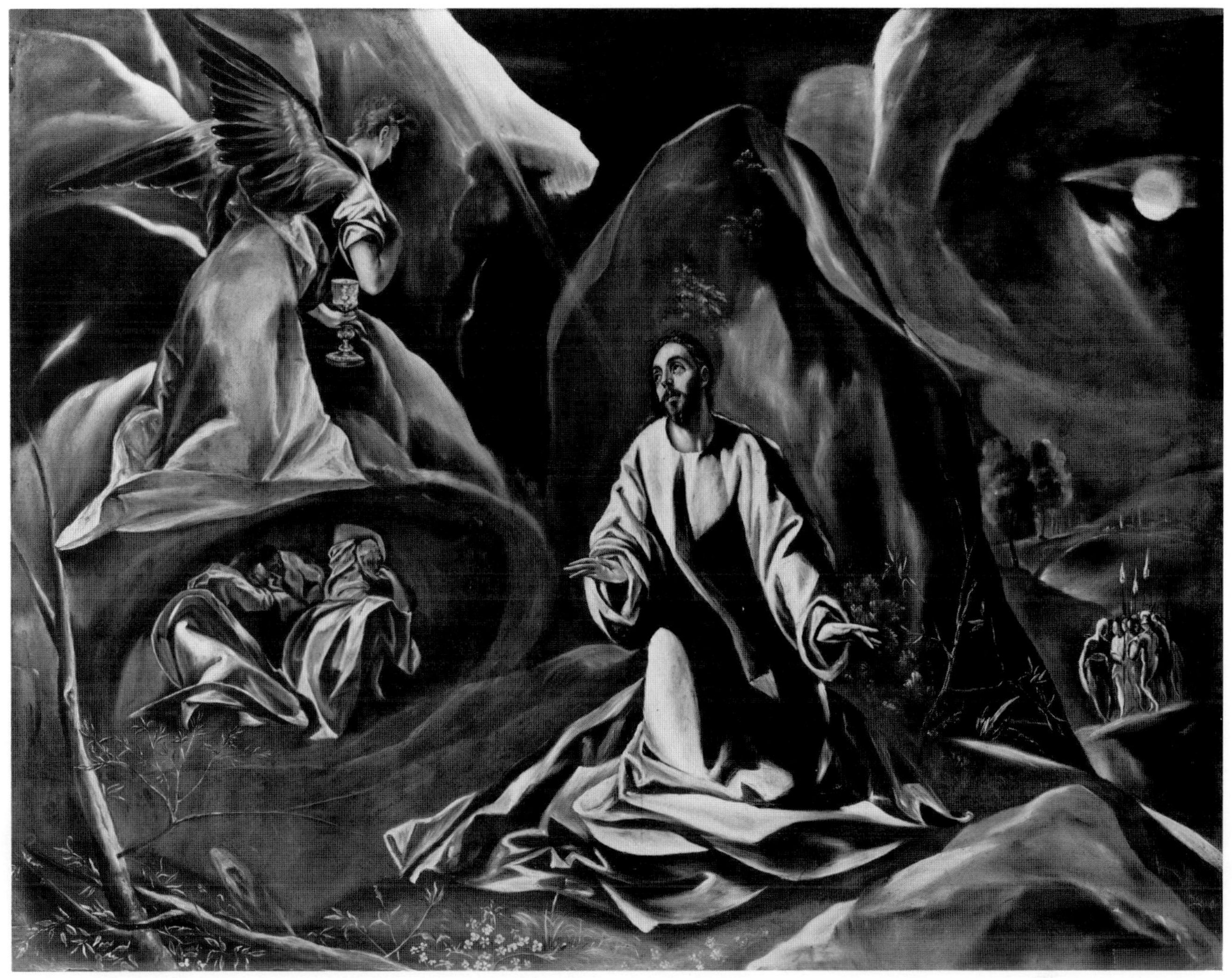

60b. Studio of El Greco, The Agony in the Garden of Gethsemane

downfalling—doomed!—row of columnar supports, while the *protecting* figure of the children's guardian appears against an open door's lighted, *protecting* space, and the children themselves are seated, unconscious of the threat, yet ready for sacrifice, on a sharp-edged protruding altar-like base, threatening in its closeness to our eye. The integrity of the human figure is undisturbed, untouched here, not even by the soul's storm.

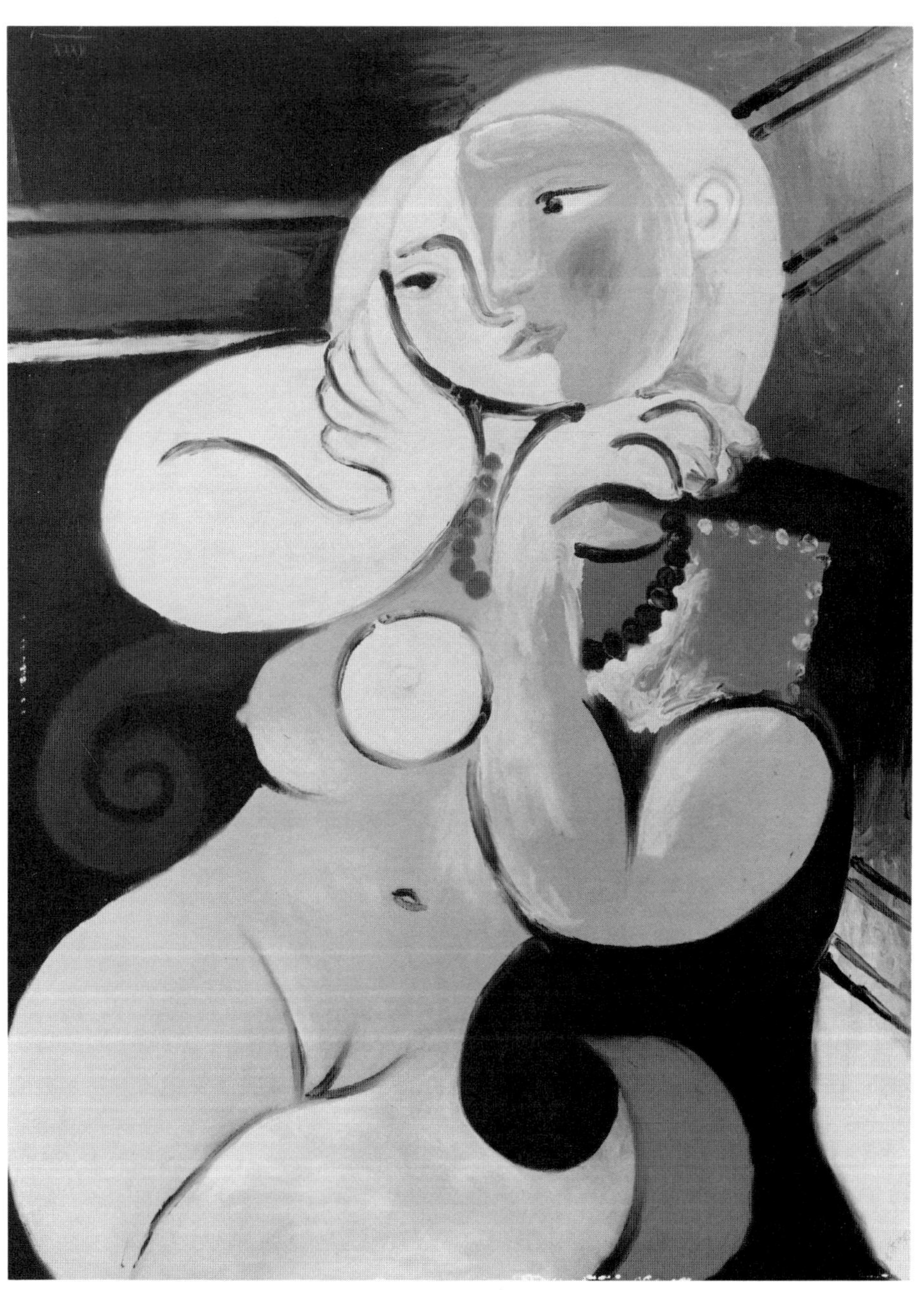

61. Picasso, Nude Woman in a Red Armchair

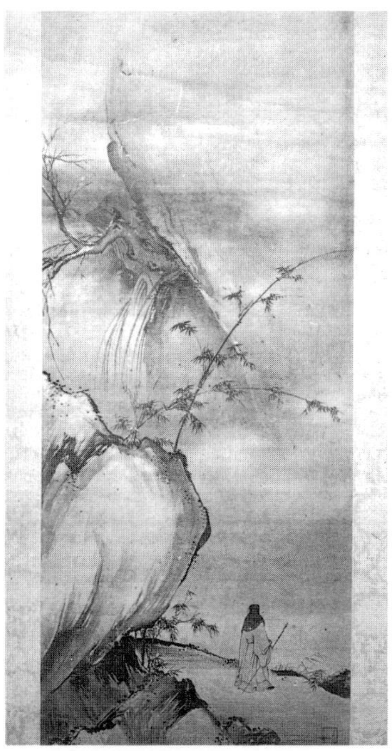

62. Landscape in Winter, Northern Sung

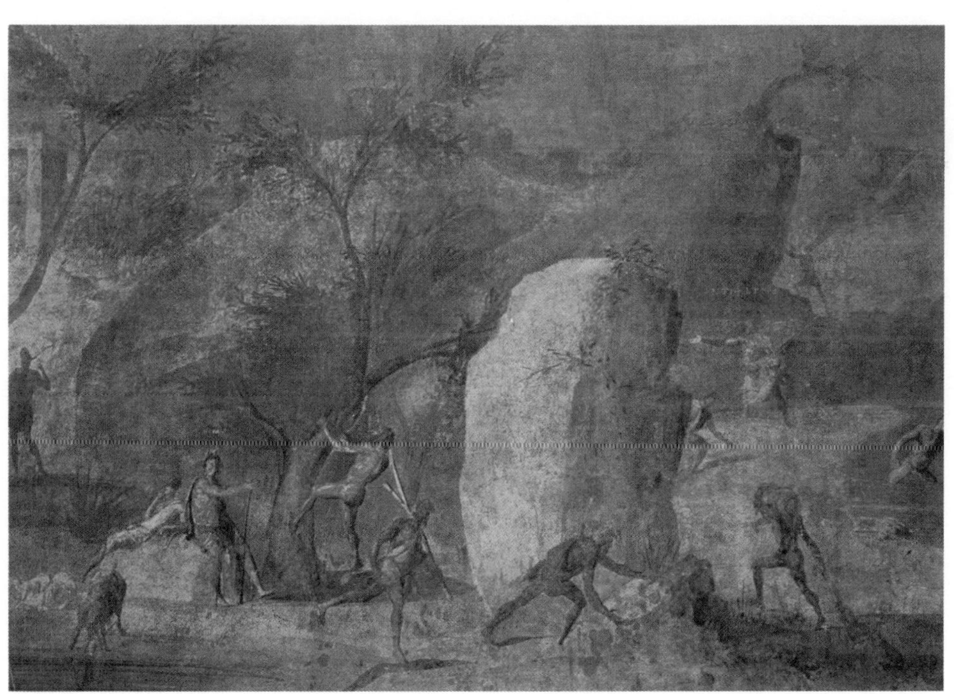

63. Ulysses in the land of the Lestrygonians, Roman painting

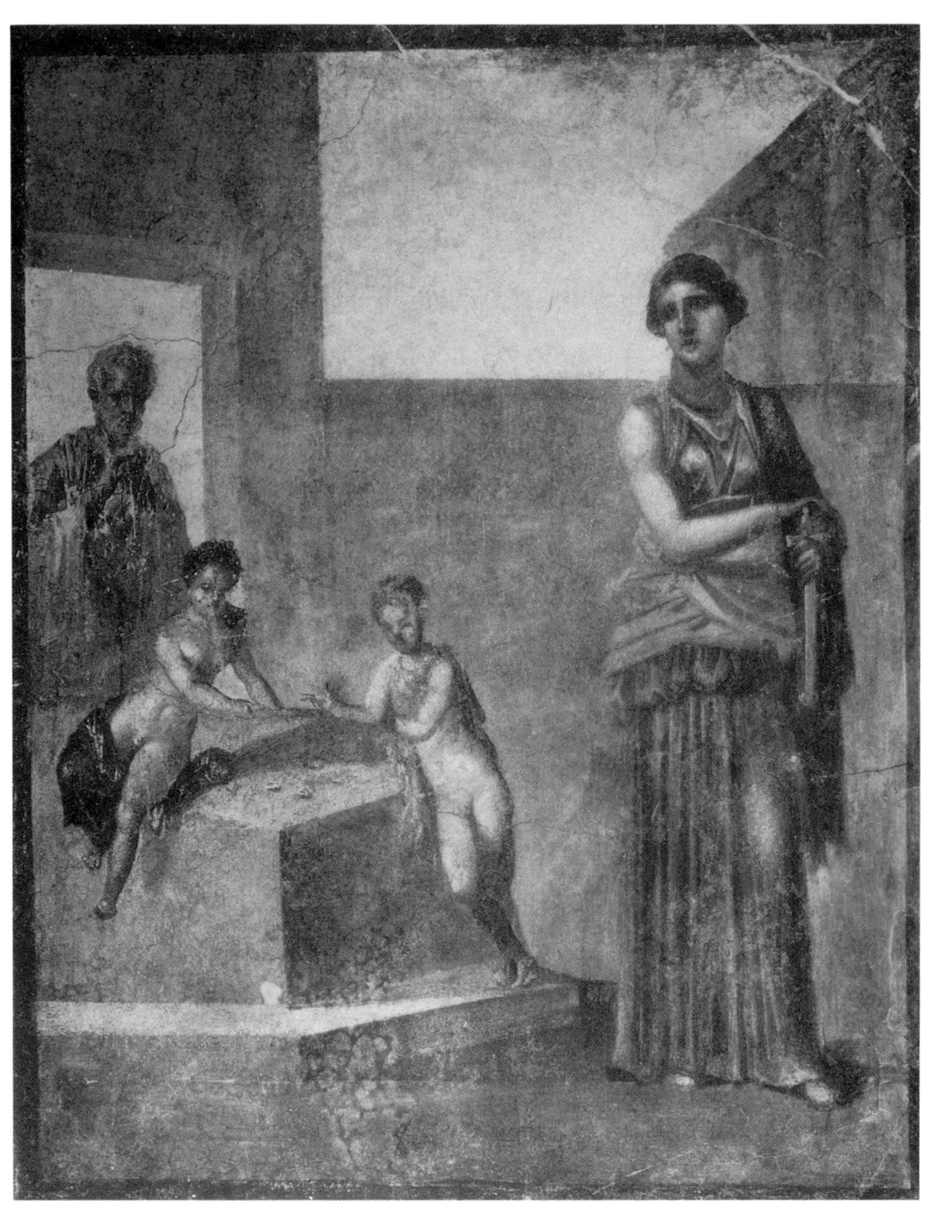

64. Medea meditating the murder of her children, wall painting from Pompeii

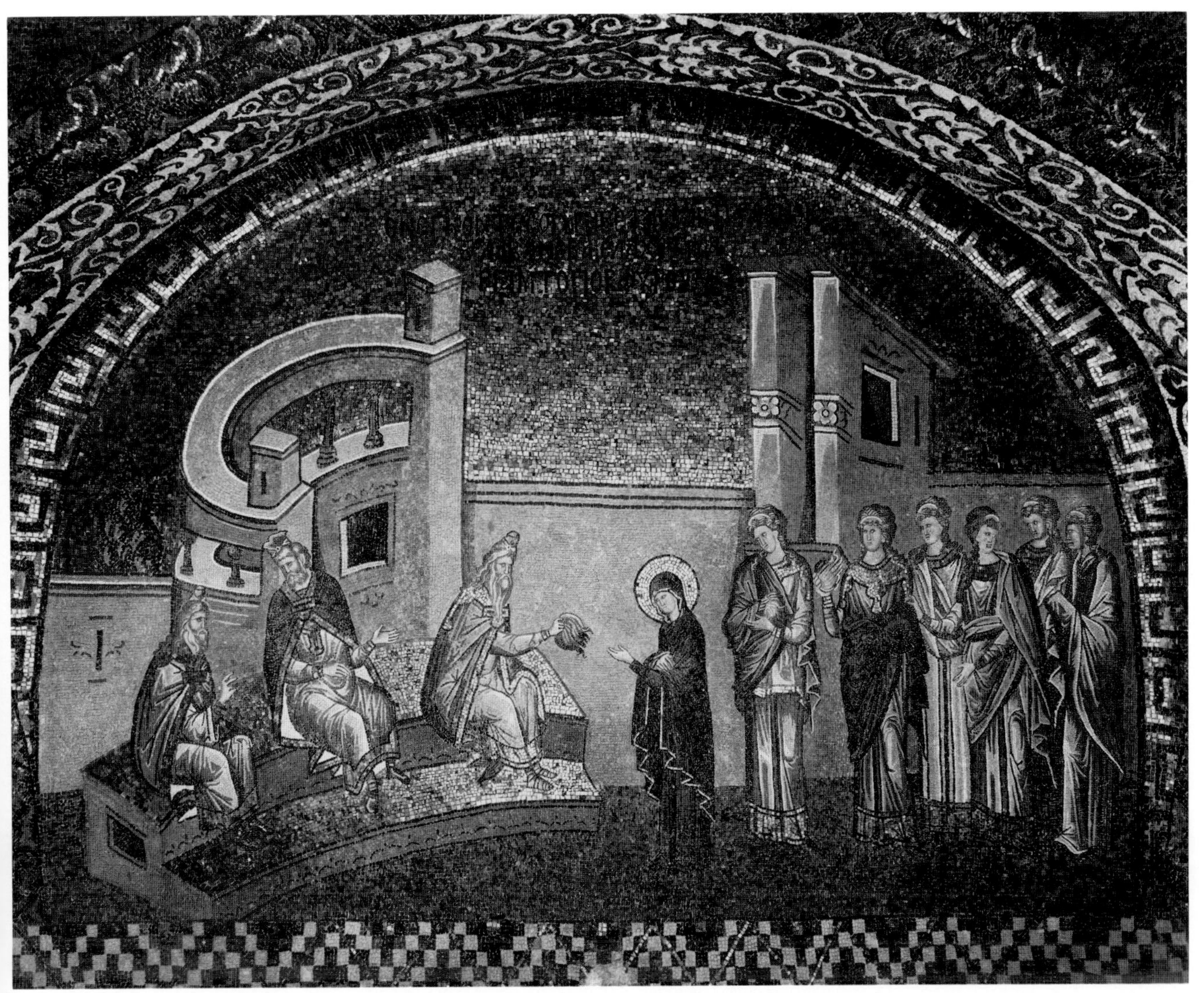

65. The Virgin receiving the skein of purple wool, Kariye Djami, Istanbul

And so has been from its inception to its end—notwithstanding all the external changes in stature, dimensions, pose, expression introduced by the changes, of taste, fashion, church's dogma or secular darings—the image, the figure of man in Byzantine art (mosaics, murals, portable icons), never distorted, because it never adheres totally and mutually to its ''landscape'' (the background's architectures or trees, or ''abstract'' rocky formations—whatever might be the ''what'' subject-matter chosen here traditionally).

The testimony of the surroundings only accompanies and dramatically interprets man's action (as the chorus in Greek tragedy does, as does the orchestral gloss in our musical drama)—hence the significant, ''expressionist'' distortions of the Byzantine ''landscape'' or backgrounds: the elongated proportions of the Angel and the Virgin on the sixteenth century's Byzantine-Russian icon *(See Plate 59)* preserve all the integrity and pride of a ''classical'' figure; it is the elliptical, closed and embracing throne of the seated Virgin and the surprising-surprised architectures accompanying—interpreting—the surprising-surprised event of Annunciation, that are significantly—medievally—distorted. And so is—at random, among so many other, especially later examples of Byzantine ''orchestration''—this early fourteenth century Palaeologan masterpiece *(Plate 65)* a mosaic on the outer narthex-wall in Istanbul's Kariye Djami[54], the apocryphal episode of the life of the Virgin, the Virgin receiving the skein of purple wool for the veil of the temple:

In the center, at the focal point of the composition, the plain, unadorned elegance of a low wall accompanying, accentuating, the serene and plain elegance of the statuesque Virgin and, to the right as far as the end of the mosaic, that of the group of her companions, the chosen virgins of the tribe of David; to the left, the tense, commanding curve of the elliptical architecture-seat, the two-stepped priestly *synthronon,* imprisoning the tense, commanding group of temple priests.

And, following stage after stage the story and the history of the Byzantine Intrigue, I found along the way how Byzantium had invented—loyal to ancient Greece in this too!—a new form—geometry's form-ellipse—for the presentation of the human figure in art, and in doing this, a new form—form-ellipse also—for its image-concept, the image-touch of Light. For Byzantium had inherited in depth the passion of ancient Greece for the concreteness and the meaning of ''abstract'' form, just as the West had inherited in depth Rome's passion for the concreteness and the meaning of ''abstract'' narration. And by passion I do not mean what in man's creative projection is called and is confused with temperament. *Because temperament is human soul turned towards life's activity and narration—towards life; passion, human soul turned towards life's enigma—towards death.* Art is enigma's (death) activity and narration (life): the passion of the soul. Form (enigma) and narration (activity) are equated there in death.

*

It took centuries of dialectical labor to evolve fully for Byzantium the image of its inner Form, and for me, many a visit to its testifying monuments, in order to follow meditatively all the stages of their evolvement.

I began—by chance rather than by choice—with what, perhaps, is the most surprising, as well as the most appealing testimony: the mosaics of the dome of Hagios Georgios in Thessaloniki *(Plate 66),* the dome of the immense Roman rotunda decorated, around an opulent garlanded *oculum,* with a succession of robust young saints and martyrs clothed in golden splendor, standing with outstretched arms against the background of a gold-shimmering succession of open palatial architectures—loggias, balconies—late Antiquity's pictorial formula still present there. A fifth-century, pre-iconoclast imperious splendor, and a great imperious surprise! Indeed, neither the figures of the saints, nor the architectures behind them imposed as yet their drama or their gloze on each other; in stature, in proportion, in expressiveness they are equal—friends, allies. Here again—but never as openly in later Byzantium!—the ancient Greek exalted meditation on amity is communicating with us: grandiose architectures form—like the Siphnian *kouros*-and-steed—a perfect curve of close friendship, an intimate alliance between man and the beyond-of-man. So delicate and so exquisite an atmosphere—without as yet the Pantocrator's terror-protection in it!—in so grandiloquent a setting! How Greek!

The dome of Hagios Georgios remains unique among early Christian *gesta.* But from there, as from a balcony overlooking a

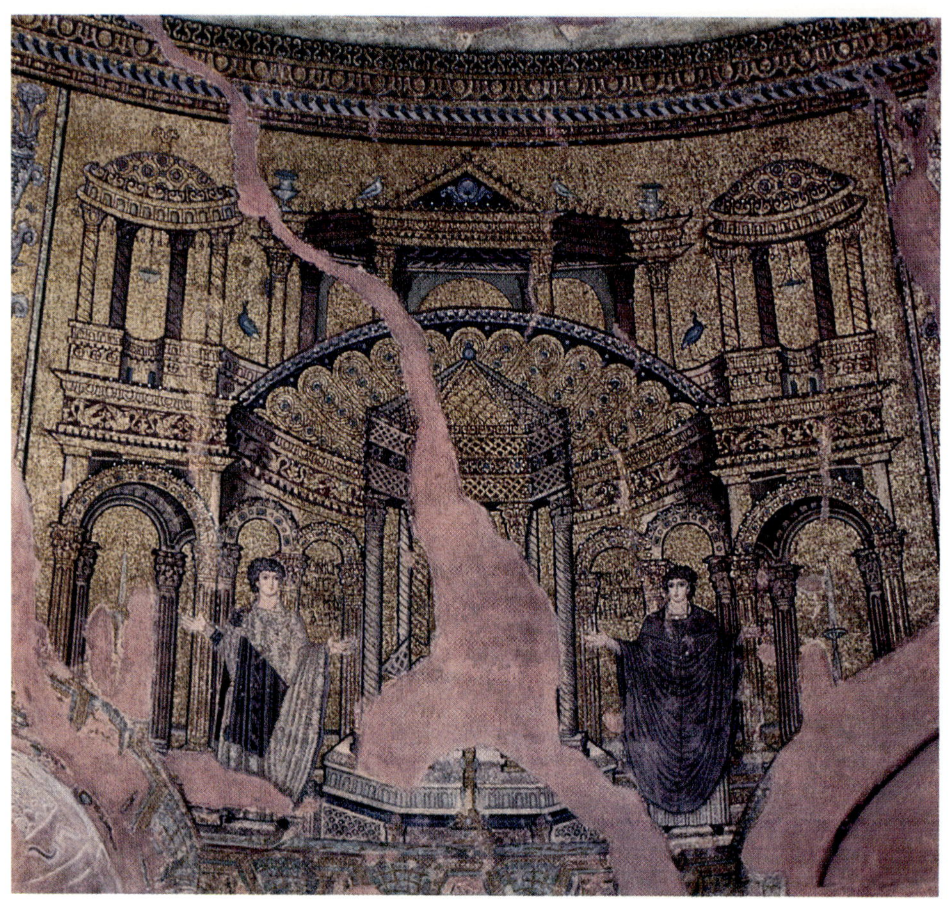

66. Interior of dome, detail, Church of St. George, Thessaloniki

wide panorama, I could follow down the centuries the slow and stable transformation of this alliance-friendship between man and the beyond-of-man into a mutual independence and cooperative relationship—from the serene assuredness of the Macedonian Comnene post-iconoclast era (ninth to twelfth centuries) to the darings, growing in intensity, of the last (Palaeologan and post-Palaeologan) era in Greece proper and outside it, in Italy, Russia and the entire Balkan world *(Plates 67a, b, c, & d)*. The Byzantine "darings" affected both the pictorial backgrounds and the figures,[55] but it was the human figure that bore the greatest weight and responsibility in the presentation of the Byzantine psycho-plastic drama.

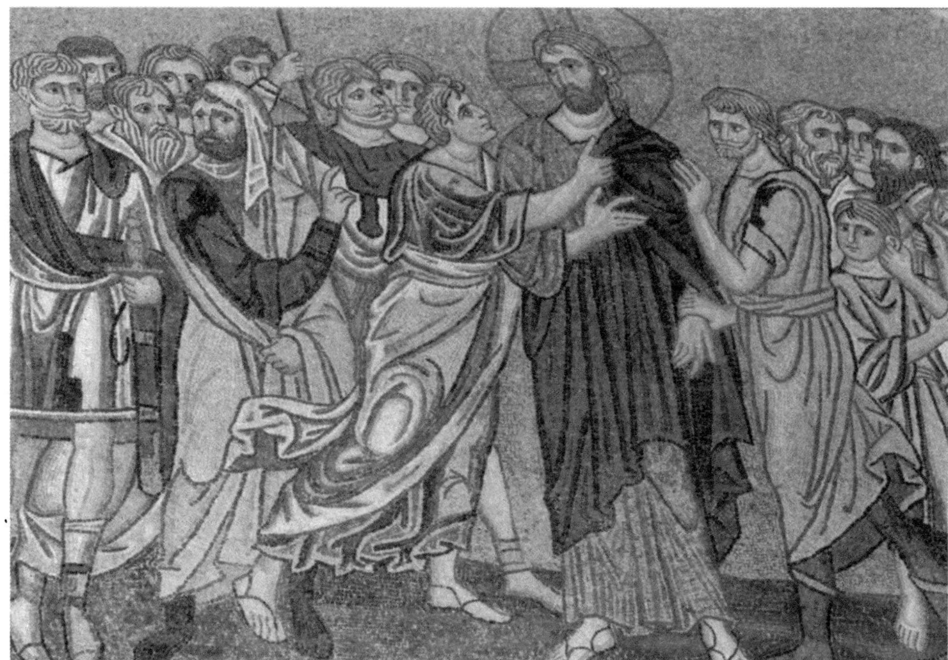

67a. Kiss of Judas, Monastery church, Daphni

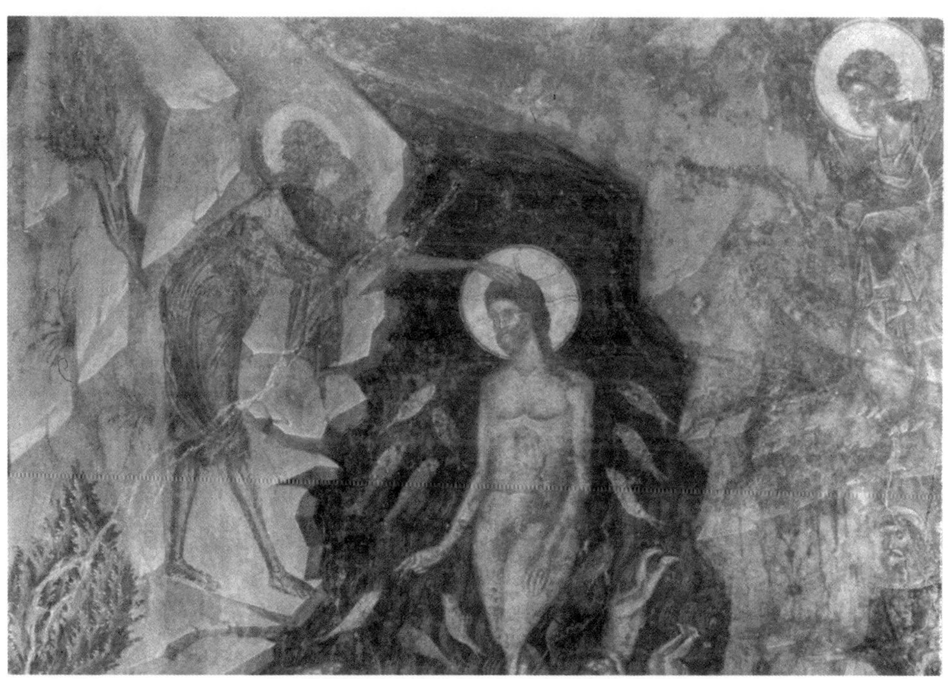

67b. Baptism, detail, Church of the Peribleptos, Mistra

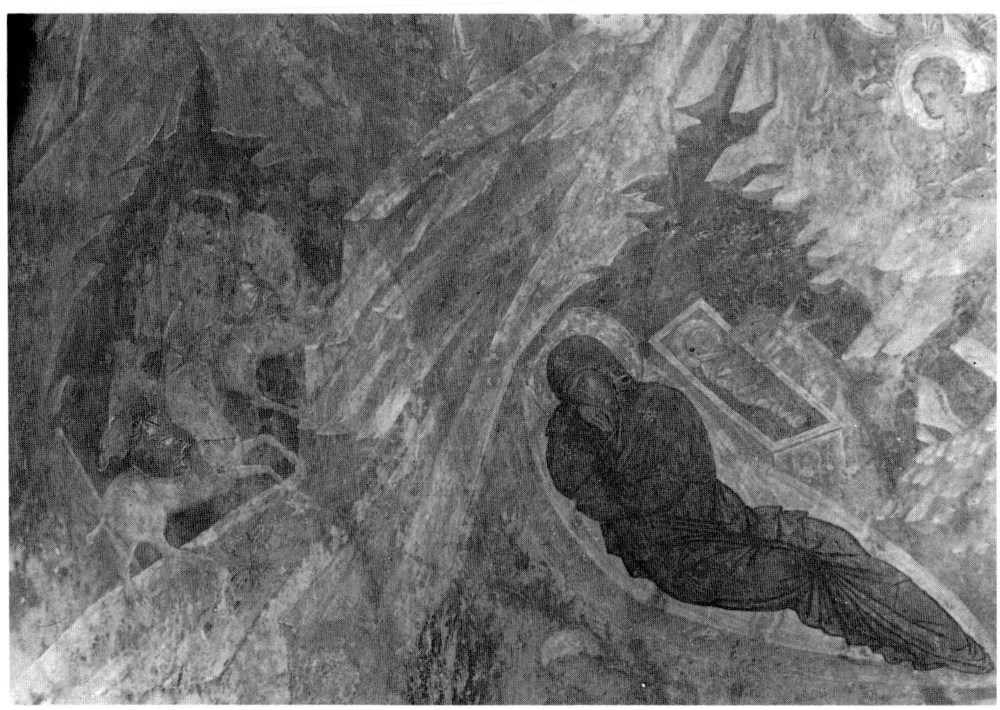

67c. Nativity, Church of the Peribleptos, Mistra

From its beginnings, the same co-presence—braiding—of the two main sources of Byzantine inspiration remained the invariant there: Classical antiquity with its spatial and kinetic ''stability'' (plastic, thus immediately psychological, indeed, metaphysical, in my Fable's transfer-to-transfer avatars) and the Near East with its spatial and kinetic immediacy, ''aboutness'' of motion, its multi-angular, flattening, rigid ''mobility'' (plastic, thus psychological, indeed, metaphysical, in my Fable's transfer-to-transfer plunge).

It is here that the initial difference between the Christian East and West could also—and easily—be located. Western art's origin has a triple—not only dual—structural support: as in Byzantium proper, Classical Antiquity, the Near East (to which, in depth affinity belongs, I was told in my wanderings, the re-emergence in late Rome of the Etruscan—so Oriental!—legacy), and a third source or support, the world, astonishing in its seminal efficacy and impetuosity, of the so-called barbaric ''ornament-monster'' or ''ornament-landscape'' *(Plate 68).*

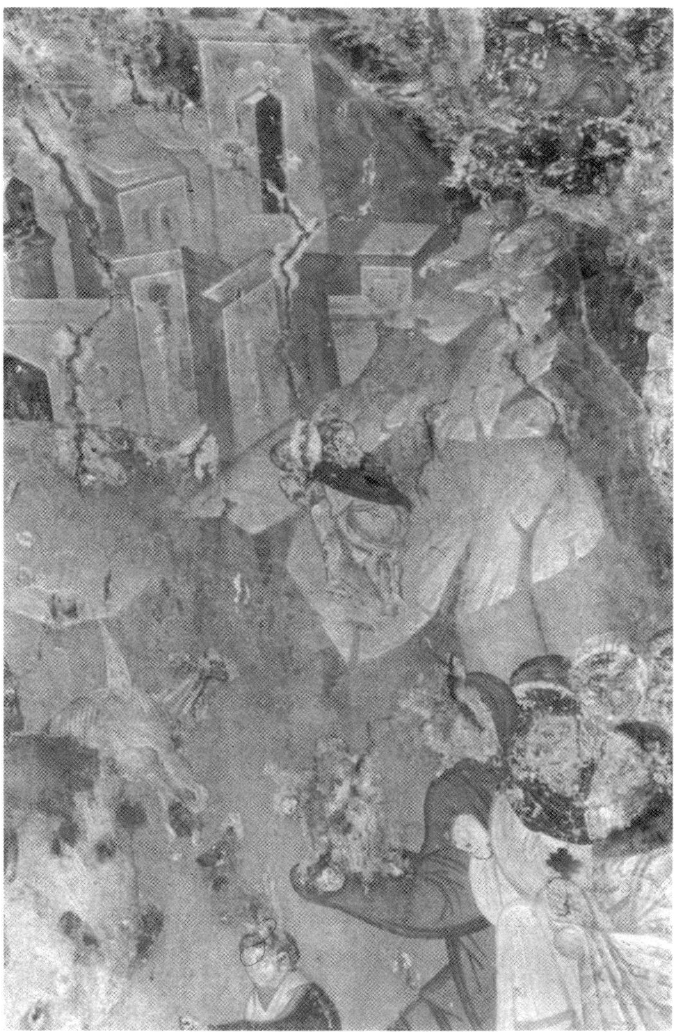

67d. Entrance into Jerusalem, detail, Church of the Pantanassa, Mistra

And because Byzantium's "invariant" was thus simpler in its roots than the West's (not triple, but two opposite worlds confronting each other) the resulting drama was also more intense there and more directly offered. And by intense I mean here a penetration both easier and deeper into each of the two opposites: the sensuous fullness=circularity of ancient Greece and the suddenly mobilized, piercing fixity in the ancient and the Christian East *(Plate 69. See also Plates 24 and 47).*

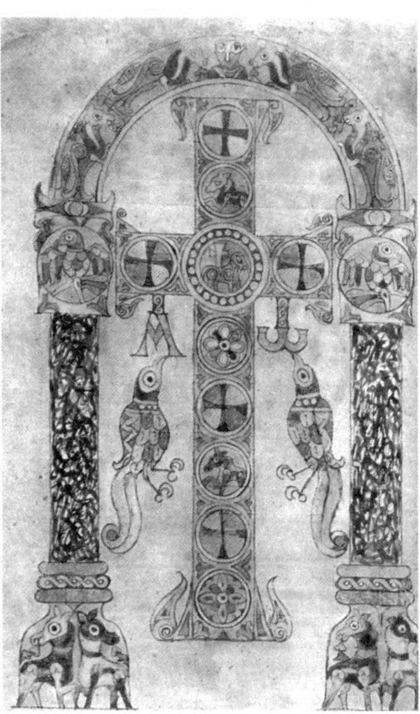

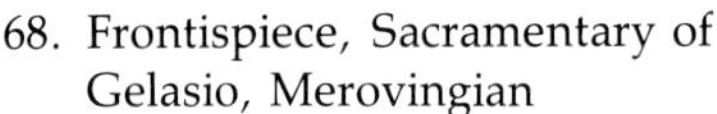

68. Frontispiece, Sacramentary of Gelasio, Merovingian

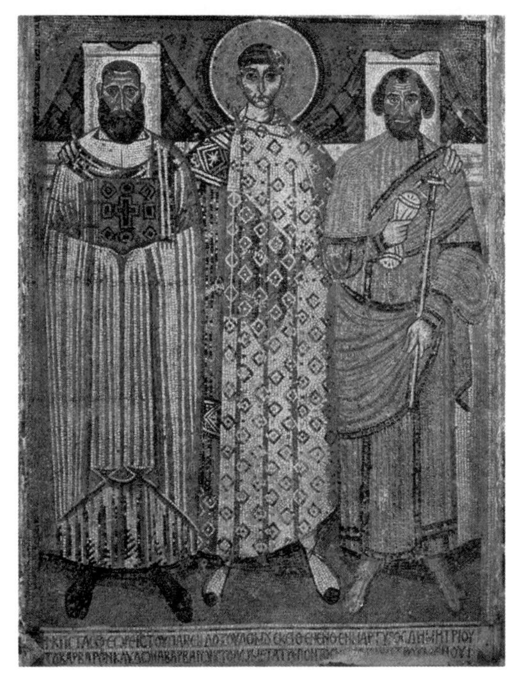

69. St. Demetrios and donors, Church of St. Demetrios, Thessaloniki

Ancient Hellas in Byzantium: this elongated, so "Byzantine," yet so sensuous rounded body of one of the Apostles who surround the standing Virgin on the dome of Christ's Ascension in Thessaloniki's Hagia Sophia, *(Plate 70)* the naked body of an athlete-*kouros* seen fully from the back, transparently white-clothed—astonishing (astonishing, indeed, in a ninth century sacramental-liturgical work!) as well as revealing example of Byzantium's homage to Hellas![56] Mosaics and wall paintings that belong to all the subtly or openly diversified periods of the history of Byzantine art never conceal this sensuous, constant, robust homage to Hellas *(Plates 71a & b)*. The movement, however vehement or tormented, that animates and accompanies the bodies—the folds flapping, spiralling, down-and-up cascading[57]—this movement is still Antiquity's "mnemonic" movement, rhythmically, gracefully accompanying and interpreting not only the figure's intention (here again, the harmonic proportionality of the classical Greek fig-

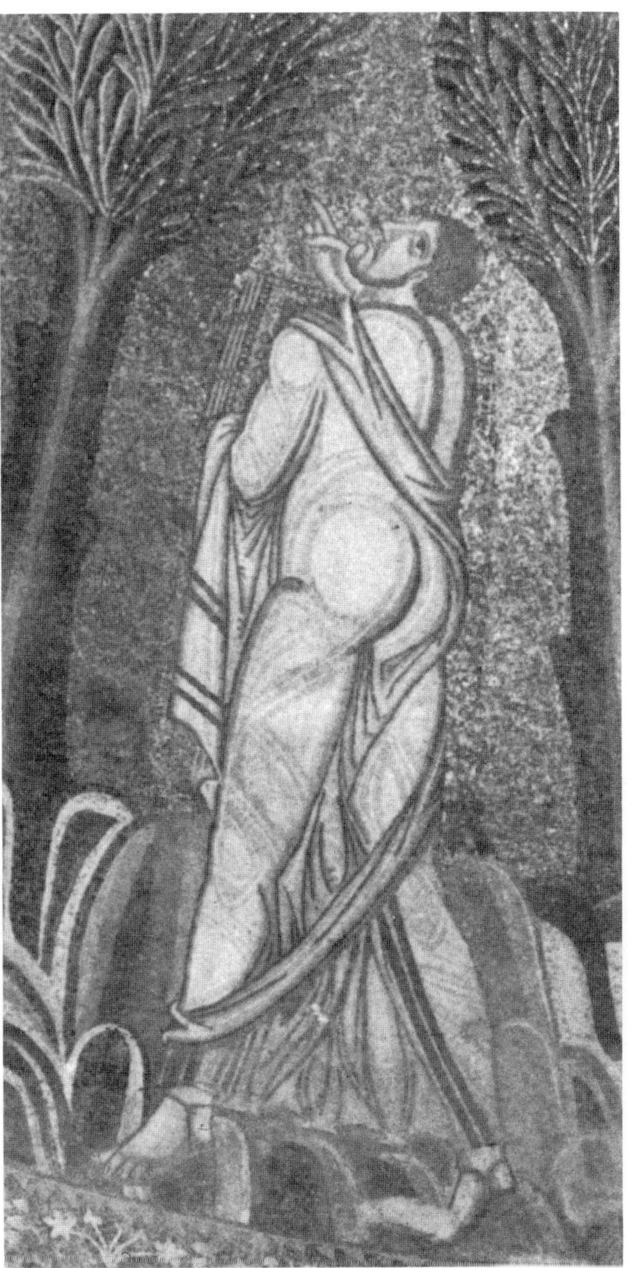

70. Apostle, detail of cupola, Saint Sophia, Thessaloniki

ure), but the intention of the entire represented scene *(Plate 72a & b).*

And yet—such is Byzantine passion, passionate loyalty to its origins!—the Ancient East's world is always present there too, just

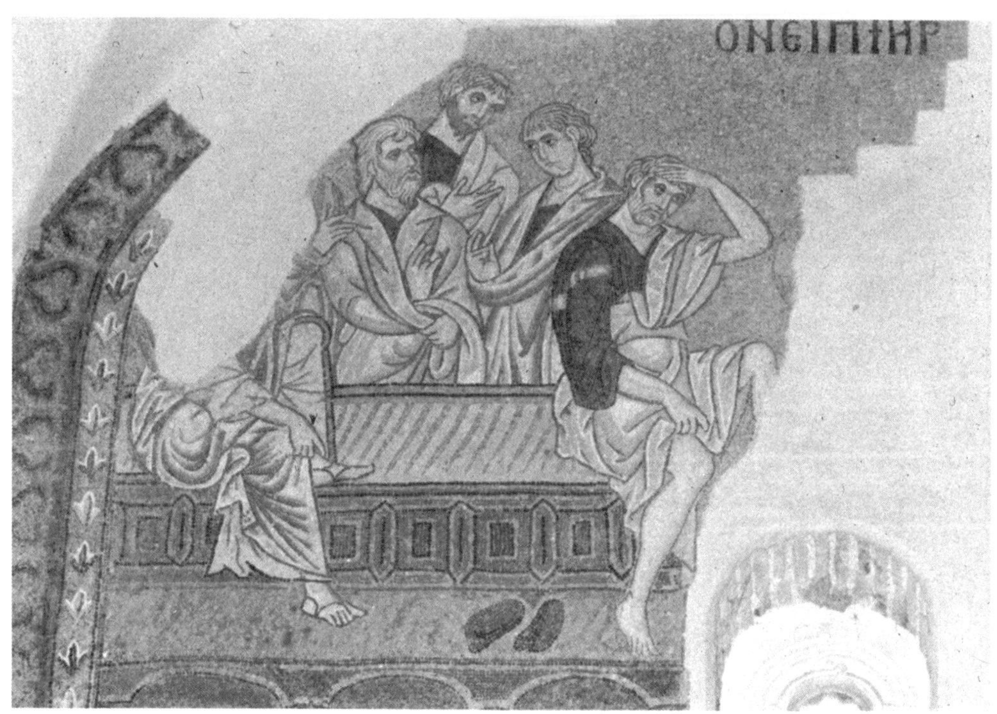

71a. Washing of the Feet, Monastery church, Daphni

as Antiquity is present (in subtle confrontation or in even more subtle merging) in the midst of most convincing testimony of the East's parentage: however rigidly immobilized in appearance (yet, in intention, about-to-move) might be the Byzantine images of saints or emperors, translucid, flattened bodies merging—dissolving—into their translucid gold-vibrating, imageless backgrounds *(Plate 73)*, Antiquity's suave consistencies, suave pictorial "sfumato" shadings are seldom missing *(Plate 74)*.

*

But I don't speak of art; I speak, and unabashedly, throughout the entire length of my tale (I see, I hear millions of people struggling all over our planet for better life and against the uncamouflaged oppression of man by man, marching, marching under the great banner, guided unknowingly by what I speak of), I speak of human soul—again, always!—that is, of soul's incessant birth, soul's uninterrupted activity between mind and body, soul-soul emerging, born between soul-mind and soul-body, the birth of

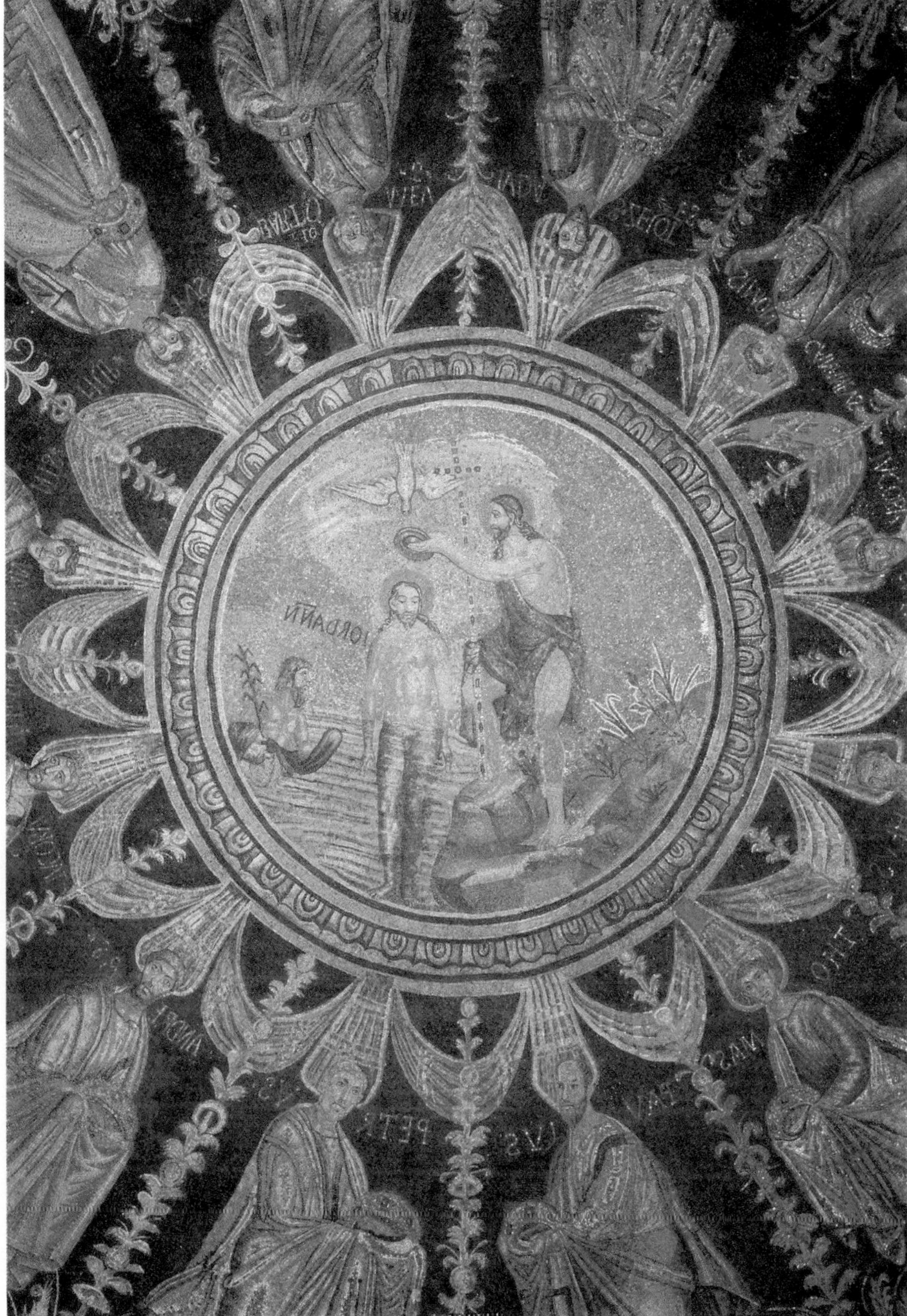

71b. Baptism of Christ, detail, Cathedral Baptistery, Ravenna

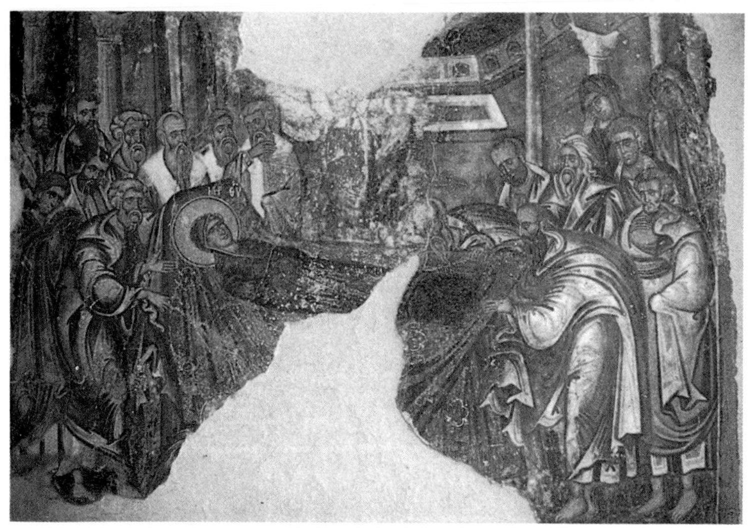

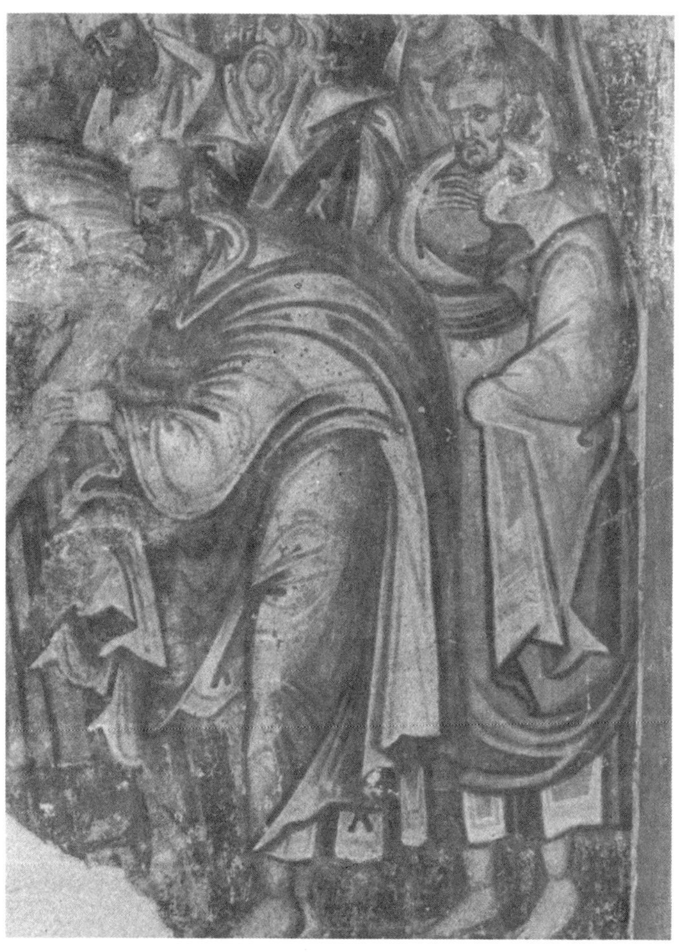

72a & b. Dormition of the Virgin, and detail, Byzantine Museum, Athens

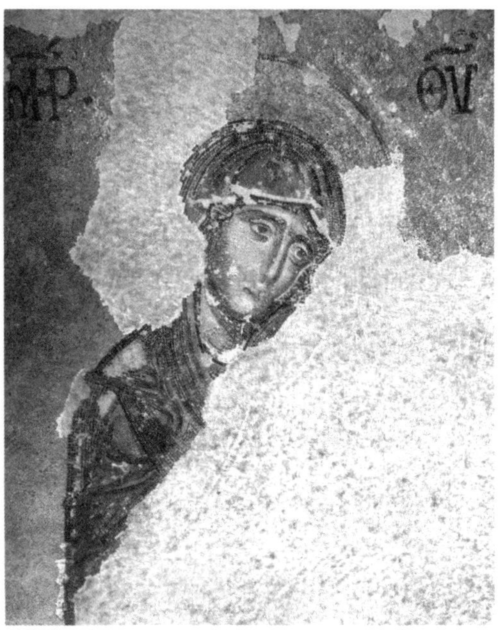

73. The Virgin Mary, *Deesis,* Hagia Sophia, Istanbul

Aphrodite (the flight of Eros; my dream!) as they often, and still, call the emerging image on the Ionian-Aegean ''altar'' that greeted me, first, at the shore of Byzantium, the birth of Aphrodite-Hera-Persephone-Ariadne, *La Femme Civilisatrice,* tamer of the young, impetuous, subterranean Bull, the Mother-Virgin whose cultic necessity and reality, the only possible concretion of Christ's—the *Logos'*—humanness, reinstalled by the Ephesian and Chalcedonian ecumenic decisions, gave to Christian man his support for tenderness: *Theotokos,* this tender, tender creation; that it was the creation of the Apocalyptic Byzantium should never be forgotten by those who enter Byzantium!

Was not the exalted and most tender hymn to Her, the *Akathistos,*[58] much earlier chanted than was St. Bernard's in the West? The burning solitude-solidarity—*Tendresse!*—of the apsidal Virgin in Torcello facing the terror-protection of the Last Judgment at that church's entrance *(Plate 75)!*

*

My tale of soul's birth and soul's adventures is the tale of meanings-essences transferred into attitudes-forms. And so I do

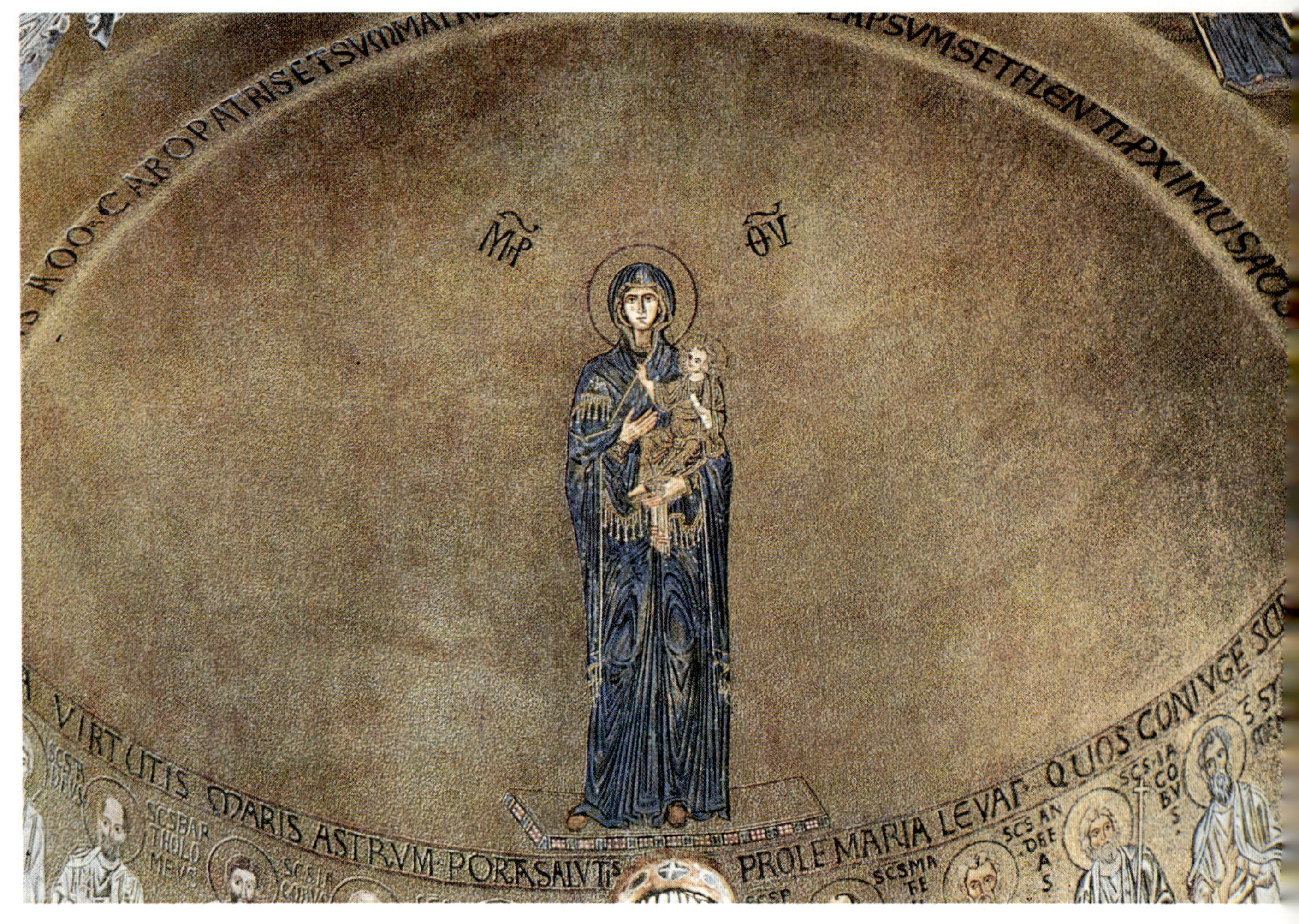


74. The Mother of God, Torcello

speak of Byzantine art and of Byzantine loyalty to its art's origins: first, the loyalty to Hellas' passion for the Form, the inexorability of a perfect form in space, in mind, in geometry, Hellas' equation of Form's finity (''the order of mind'') and the un-finity of Content (''order of nature,'' the empirical flux); then, Byzantium's loyalty to the Orient's illimited, never ''perfect,'' yet equally inexorable empirical flux—un-finity—mobilized in the very immobility and rigidity of the Father-Creator's will to create it. *Christianity is its art*—this transient remark of the Witness suddenly stood up in me as firm as it became permanent.

*

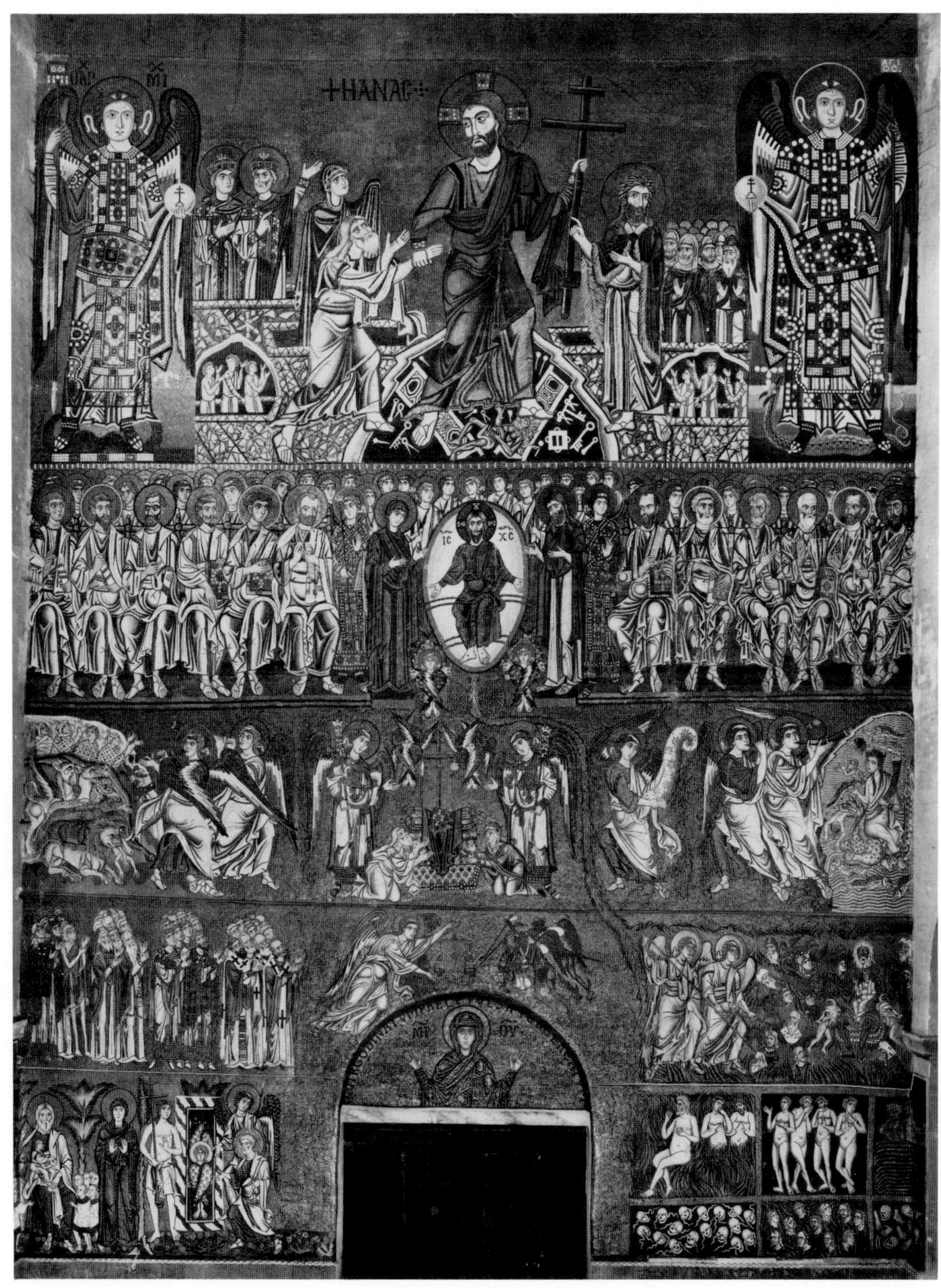

75. Last Judgement, Torcello

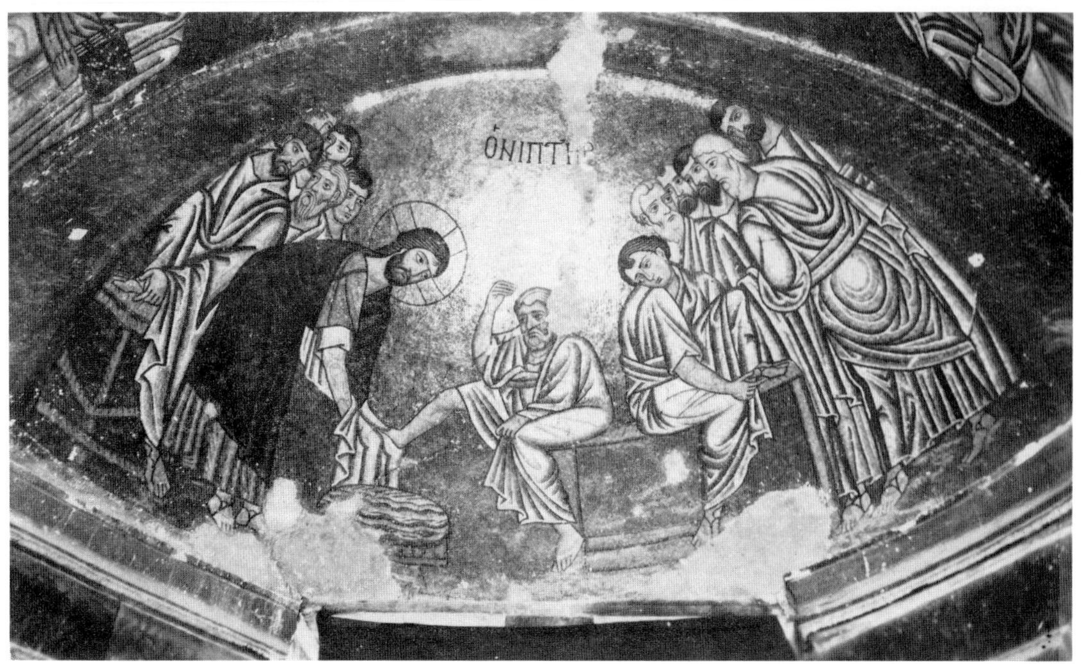


76a. Washing of the Feet, Hossios Loukas, Greece

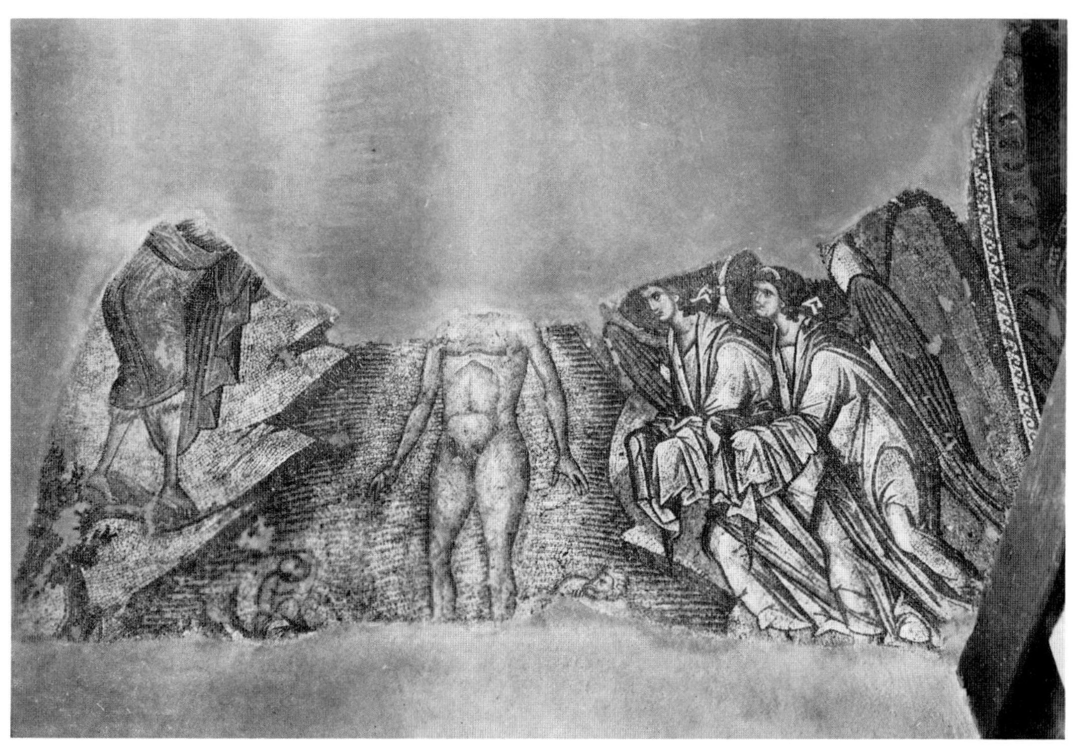

76b. Baptism, Church of the Holy Apostles, Thessaloniki

# Part II

Byzantine pictorial art is the invention of a totally new formula, the dialectical synthesis of those two opposite universes—a formula-synthesis embodied in what for Christian Greece became, just as it had been for Ancient Greece, the central concern: the structure and the drama of the human figure.

The Byzantine invention is new and unique, indeed: precise and flattened geometrical forms-schemes—circles, squares, ellipses, triangles, trapezoids, etc.—sharply delimit those anatomical parts whose bulging tactile consistency the artist wanted to evoke—and, indeed, passionately evoked!—by concentrating, massing, often violently, shadowed zones around the external contours of the forms and at the same time projecting, always violently, a great burst of pure light toward the center of those forms. From the first, and not knowing how to do it more correctly, I called this typically Byzantine spatial formula *luminous geometrism:* light geometry *(Plates 76a & b).*[59]

This psycho-plastic procedure, introduced in Byzantium sometime after the acute iconoclastic crisis, grew in intensity and explicitness during the tenth, eleventh and twelfth centuries (often over-accentuated and over-emphasized as a technical device, in those artistic centers of Byzantine parentage that were distant from Constantinopolitan elegance and sophistication—the Veneto, Sicily, the Balkans, Russia (Kiev)—an exaggeration often explained by earnest students of things Byzantine as "provincialism," but due rather, I still continue to suspect, to the direct or derived impact of the contemporary medieval, Romanesque West) *(Plates 77a & b).*

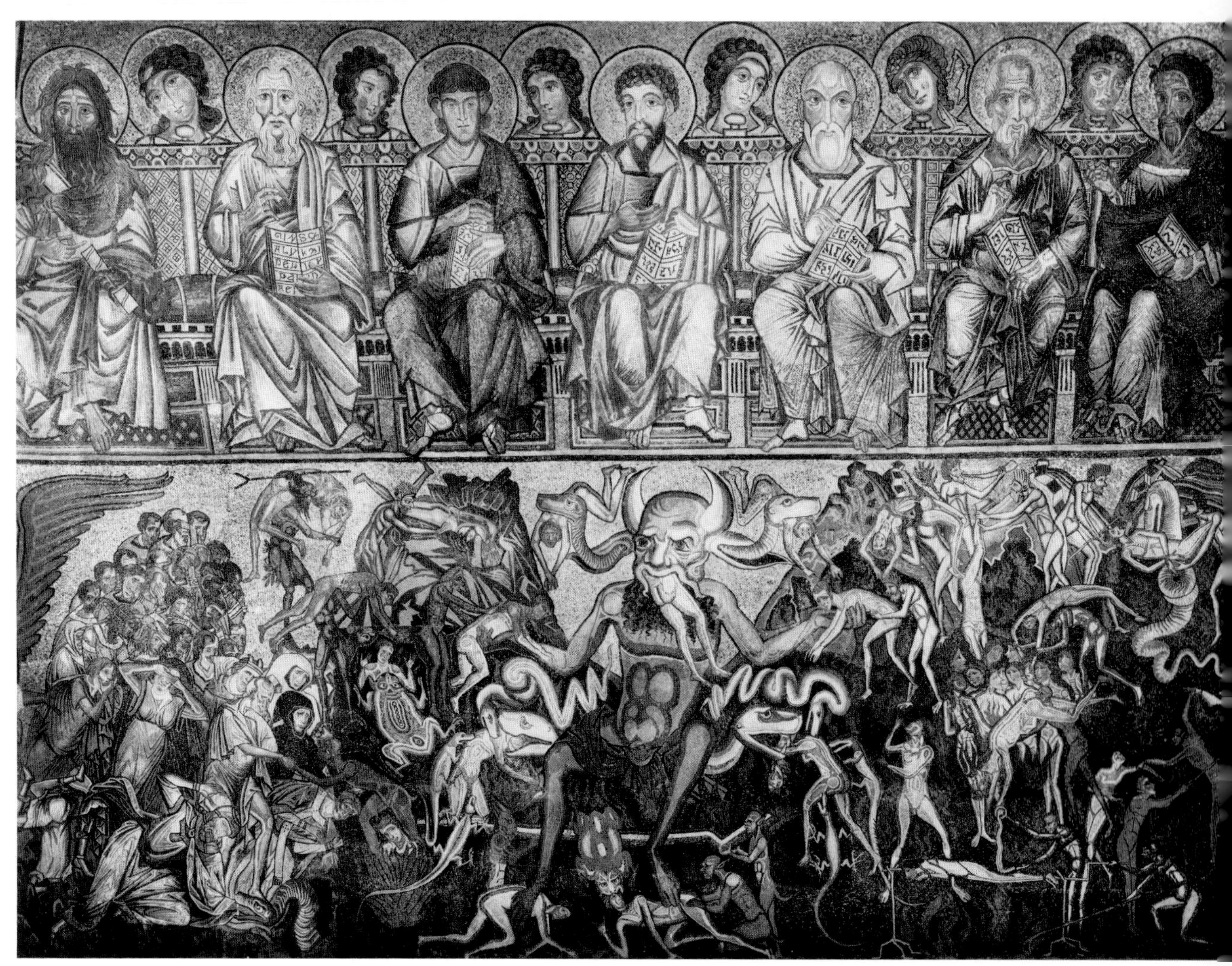

77a. Hell, Baptistery of San Giovanni, Florence

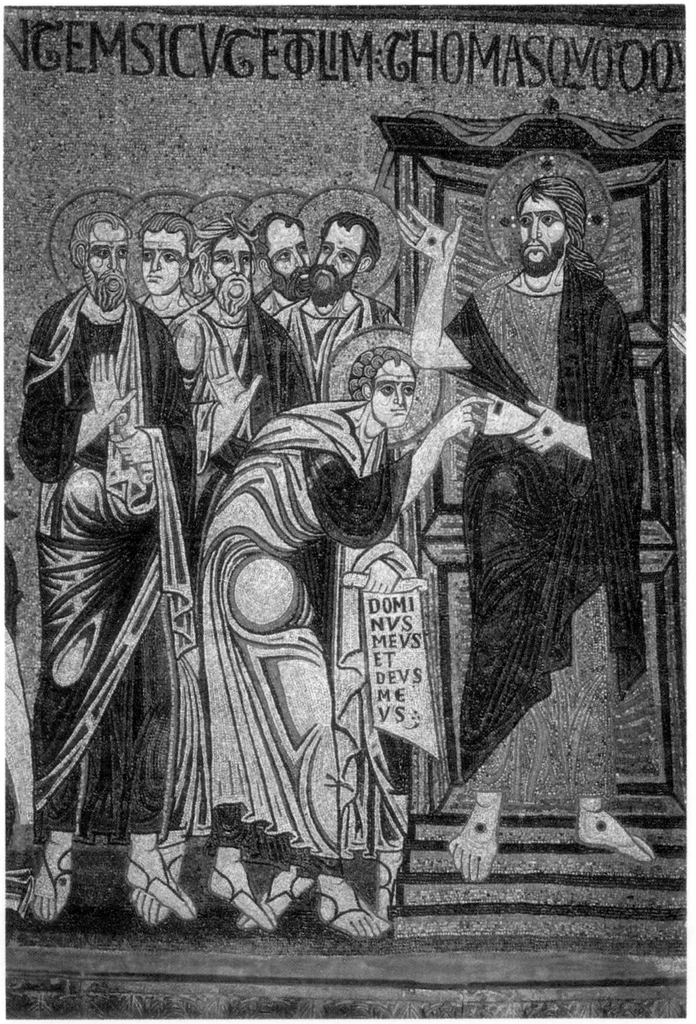


77b. Incredulity of St. Thomas, St. Mark's, Venice

The Byzantine formula was a living, life-giving formula: it could remain essentially the same and yet become something else, change in aspect and direction. Thus, "luminous geometrism" gave birth to what should perhaps be named "light unforeseen"—an equally sudden burst of light no longer confined to a rigid, calculated armature of geometrized anatomic limits but propelled freely, unexpected, unpredicted, upon those parts. And the reality of the represented body becomes light itself—light's only realization, plastic and dramatic (you might be thinking here, dear reader, of the sixteenth century Venetian "luminism," and rightly: without Byzantium, Tintoretto is unthinkable).

In the intention of the Byzantine artist-artisan the goal was, then, no longer a pictorial illusion-building reality, but reality in the flesh, ubiquitous, all-embracing, the living light coming from below, from above, from the sides, oblique, elliptical—not simply a pictorial light issued from outside the body's source, but light-in-the-body, light-*persona,* light-concept, light-touch that the Witness had promised me, Light-Flesh, Light=Witness. *(Plates 78a & b).* In this last creation of Byzantium, the figure, the background, the color, any part or element of a given pictorial composition *and the composition itself in its entirety* become this witnessing of Light-Flesh.

And it is here that Christian Greece and ancient Greece at their subtlest, and then at their most revealing degree of loyalty, are the same and the else at once: the primacy of the circular form in ancient Greece became in Byzantium the primacy of the *ellipse,* the Byzantine synthesis of circle-finity and line-un-finity.

Byzantium, all Byzantium, is an elliptically incurved universe—in mind, in history, in geometry, in light.

*

And I saw again, at its clearest and ultimate, the basic dichotomy between the Christian West and the Christian East—the basic duality in Christian man himself, medieval, and, by uninterrupted derivation, today's.

For light, the thought and the feel of light as an unchallenged certainty, an unchallenged condition of visibility of things both in-

and-for the mind, in-and-for the body, was shared by both divisions of Christianity.

The astonishing as well as revealing thing is to see how this thought-feel, coming as it did from the same historical and even pre-historical source, developed into two totally differing—interlaced though, as all things and beings need be—ways or disciplines: the theology of Light or, as it is more often referred to, the mysticism of Light in the twelfth and thirteenth century West, and the theology or mysticism of Light in the East, *Hesychasm*, this truly Byzantine expression of Byzantium's spirituality.[60] For the core of the Hesychast monkish doctrine and practice is ''the perpetual prayer of the heart'' or ''prayer of Jesus,'' by whose silent and concentrated action the divine Light of Christ's Transfiguration on Mount Tabor could again be ''seen'' and felt as a supreme bliss and gift by the ''recluse''—the Hesychast—the Light shining out in his heart or even from his navel (this psycho-physical technique—Hindu in origin?—being considered necessary only at the early—still incompetent—stage of the mature mystical experience.)[61]

*

Light, this materiality and this concept coming from the farthest confines of history and pre-history (materiality and concept most subtle, more subtle, because so ubiquitous and so actual in both its presence and absence, than any other matter), light, the great white, pure white Eagle, Dove perhaps, floating in the sky's ocean of white-created colors, so full-toned as to make the white be lost in them; white Eagle, white Dove of the Vedas and of the Avesta's heights, *Hvarenah*—Heaven's Fire—the invisible Light, ''the Glory'' that accompanied and made sacred, god-equal, the blood of kings in ancient Iran (later, in Islam, the blood of Shī'ah's hidden Imams); the Jewish *Shekhinah*, the Light that shone in the desert on the Tabernacle (Light-hypostasis, the only ''dangerous'' notion feared or avoided in Judaic theology); the sun's dazzling splendor, Mithra of pre-Zoroastrian Iran; the splendor of the stars' ''dark clarity'' in the poets—now descending to rest, and glad on the land of luminous Hellas, Dove-Eagle of Pindar and the Olympian marbles, Dove confiding to the Philosopher's ear its secret

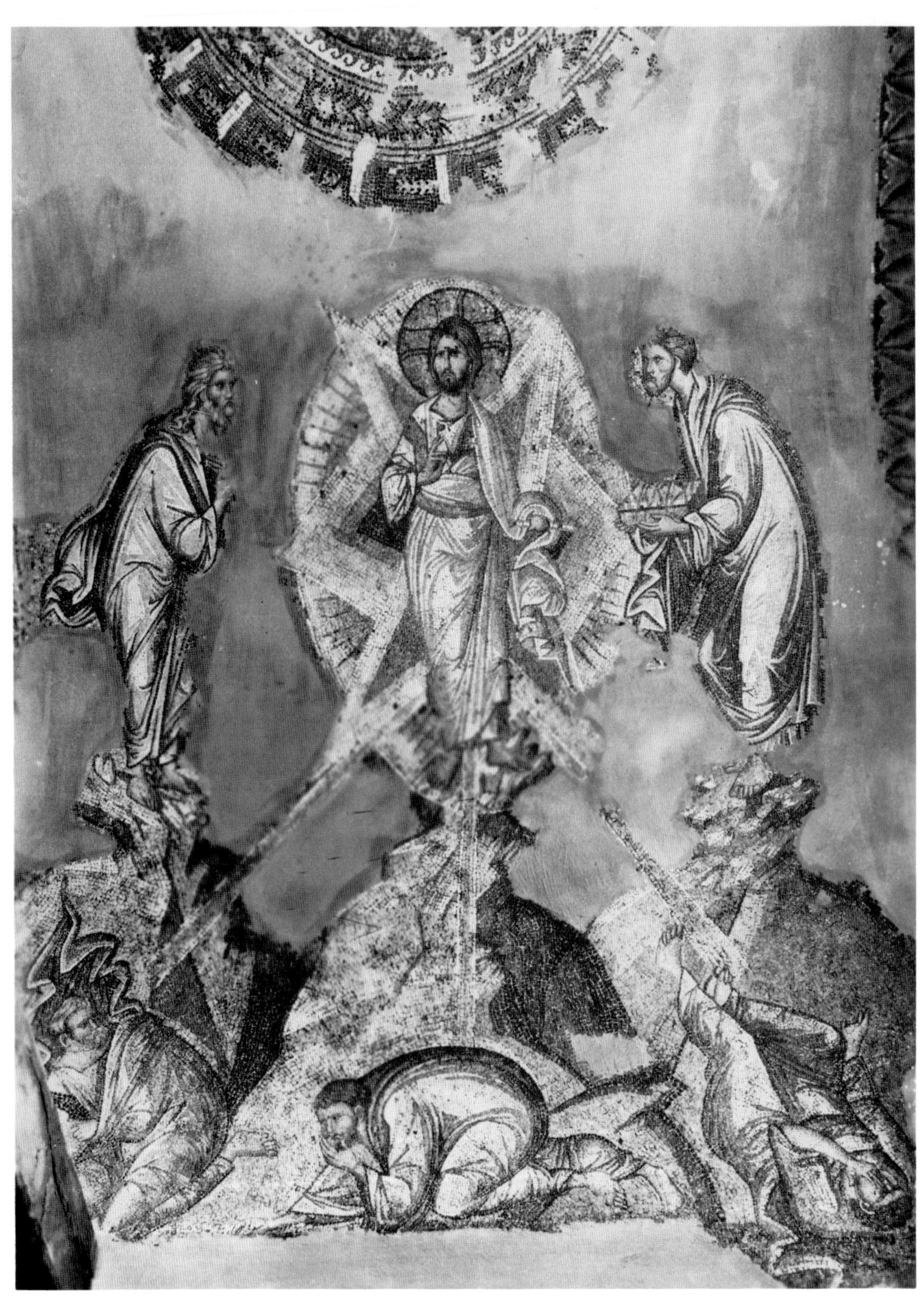

78a. Transfiguration, Church of the Holy Apostles, Thessaloniki

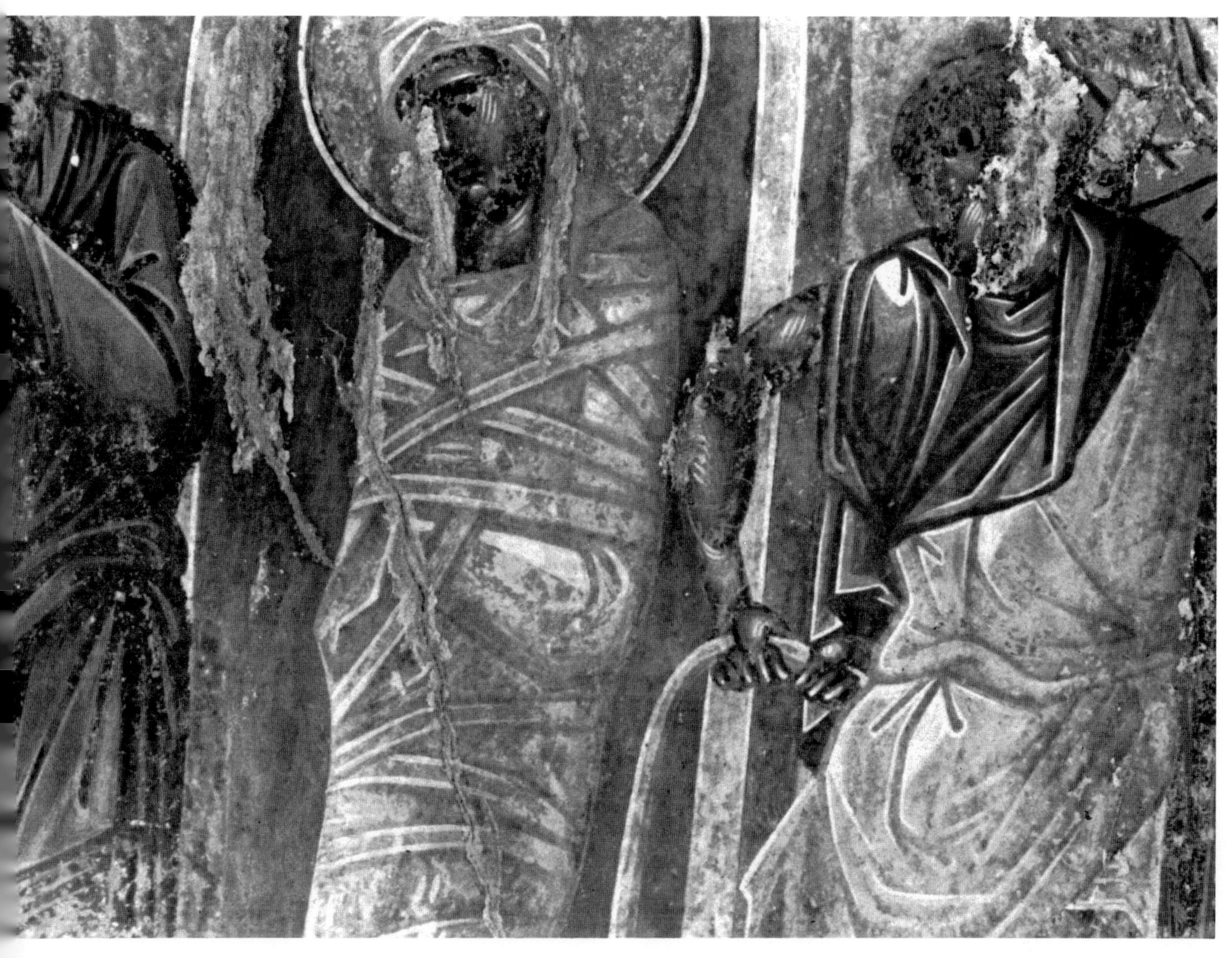

78b. The Raising of Lazarus, detail, Church of the Pantanassa, Mistra

name, not secret any more: *entelecheia,* the uninterrupted birth of the soul—matter, materiality, act-and-form so subtle as not even to be a becoming, and so real as to be at once becoming and being; *entelecheia,* the universal, the general and the unique, thus the individual, made one, the seed of all metamorphoses, the seed of all Transfers: of light into splendor, radiation, into enlightenment, illumination, into emanation and energy, into lightning and direction—into proportions, numbers, metaphysics and physics at once.

Thus: the Light in Plato, in Plotinus and the Stoics; thence, with the coming and the spreading of Christianity, the Light in the thought and feeling of the Fathers, Greek as well as Latin: Evagrius Ponticus, Macarius, Basil, Augustine. In the West, the Light—number-proportionality—of Boethius and the vehement Carolingians (John Scotus Erigena, whose final translation of the Pseudo-Dionysius' "Divine Names"—Names of Light—became, as it had already been in Byzantium, the leading guide of all Western medieval thought).

*

Originated at the same time and at the same source as the East's, the way of the West, nevertheless, became the East's opposite.

In the West:

Light as the very essence, the *is-ness,* of all existence, of all forms and contents of energy, radiating, acting, moving—it was that equation of light and motion, of freedom and choice, which became the very foundation of Western man's integral thought. (Is there, indeed, anything in the world of today, of our "electronic" world, in science, philosophy, technology, politics-to-be, and in art, that is not this very assertion and equation, this very choice and freedom: choice of the concept of light = motion as energy, as *structure,* thus as self-creativeness; freedom also from the concept of light imposed as *substance* = creation-Creator?)

"Luminist" medieval minds, Hugh and Richard of Saint-Victor in the twelfth century; Bonaventure or Alexander of Hales, Roger Bacon, Peter of Spain, John Duns Scotus, and many others, but perhaps most explicitly Grosseteste,[62] could all speak of light as the very foundation of corporeity in the universe, of all possible action and motion, physical-mechanical as well as psycho-physiological; light-energy being thus not the result of any preexistent corporeity but *constituting it* itself,[63] radiating in all directions instantaneously and forming a perfect luminous sphere—an extended magnitude resulting from a qualitative (= structural) source of energy.[64]

The soaring speculative mysticism of Light in the West can ultimately, without much error, be looked for in and traced back to late Antiquity's speculative mysticism of Light-Emanation, the neo-Platonic Light as emanation of the One.

Not so in the Christian East. True, the "humanist," Platonic and neo-Platonic elements of Byzantine theology—that of, say, Psellos or John Italus, or that, the boldest of all, as well as the most original, in the still mysterious neo-paganism of the famous Judge of Mistra, Gemistos Plethon[65]—could also be traced back to ancient philosophical-emanatist origins.

Not so the truly Byzantine theology of Light. For the Hesychast monk Light is not Light-Emanation of the Logos, Light-Correspondence corresponding with the Infinite One. It is Light-Presence, hypostasis, Light-Substitution, the eucharistic sacrificial finity's identity with infinity—a very precise, concrete, localized Presence, the unseizable, uncreated Light-Logos, seized, created—Incarnation of Logos!—as the visible light that shone once and forever from the faces of the Prophets during Christ's Transfiguration, the same that shines again from the face of the "perpetual prayer of the heart."

Light-Incarnation, Light-Flesh, Light-Witness, this is the form and content of Byzantine theology, Byzantium's "loyalty to its origins": St. Paul's "We preach Christ crucified, this cause of anger to the Jews, this silliness for the Greeks" (I Corinthians 1:23).[66]

Sheltered by Byzantine monkhood, matured there through long centuries of uncompromising loyalty, Hesychasm became the arch-enemy of everything that has been accepted and understood (as not "silliness") by the loyalty to Antiquity (late Hellenistic-Roman, contemporary with St. Paul) and its discursive-persuasive method of communication and "proof"; arch-enemy above all of the Judaic rejection of the very concept of Incarnation—this greatest "cause of anger," this abomination, indeed, for Judaism—and so, enemy too of the Judaic acceptance, instead, of the concept of Embodiment, this ''permitted,'' peripheral, temporary communication of the Truth of Revelation through symbols and metaphors or visual imagery. Hesychasm is the arch-enemy of everything that the West in appraising its own religious (even ecclesiastical), philosophical and socio-historical transformations today labels ''progressive.'' Hesychasm became the stronghold of exalted, stubborn anti-humanist ''obscurantism,'' whose Bronze Age foundations reached out north-and-eastward, far in time and space beyond the frontiers of Byzantium proper—a neo-Byzantine apocalyptic world that continues till today the division of so-called Christian civilization into two opposite-braided branches: the militant Apocalyptic and the militant Psychomachic.

And yet . . .

*

And yet, it is precisely this monkhood, the home and shelter of this theology of Light, that, when it allied itself, as I was soon to discover, with what we saw was the post-split ''artisan'' *nostalgia* for the lost three-oneness (the Psychomachic man's own loyalty to his origins), made it possible for this theology of Light-Flesh to become the very Witness of this Light's incarnation, as Byzantine monkhood's most tangible creation, Byzantium's art.

Byzantine art, submitted totally though it was (after the iconoclast tempest and ''defeat'') to the Verbal-military Elite's—the Priesthood's and the Throne's—dictates of dogma and iconography (this is why by art I mean here only, if temporarily, the art of visual narration, the pictorial art *par excellence*), nevertheless within its own ''universe of discourse,'' its own resources—colors, motion, expression—found its freedom of choice and goals in the Hesychast concept-touch, image-touch of Light, in the Incarnated Light-Logos-Grace of *Hesychia.*

It was what the Witness meant by his guiding words: ''You will find the traces of my presence and passage everywhere in Byzantium, but you shall look for the real me elsewhere, where, underneath the precarious security of the Bronze Age, another legacy and security, unexhausted and planetary, the artist-artisan primeval and nostalgic creativity, made its working home and shelter: Byzantine monkhood.''

And because these guiding words were words of the living Witness and not words of an arrested conviction or ''proof,'' their meaning could expand and continue at will, freely.

To my query, ''Why did this alliance between the monk's *Hesychia* and the artisan's nostalgia-and-freedom take root in Byzantium? Was not monkhood a living and nourishing force in the Christian West also?'' the answer, I witness now, was:

Because the roots of monkhood's history itself, in the Christian West, its sub-history, possibly its depth-sociology, are structurally different.

It is true that what obviously dominates the medieval history of both the East and the West is (and to repeat it again I feel is here a must) the Bronze Age King-Priest's legacy of opposition and alliance between the two power-and-balance holders, the Emperor and the Patriarchate in the East, the Emperor and the Pope in the West. But underneath this socio-historical level, so formidable in its massive presence, there extended a sub-level, destined in the West to become the real—because so much more vigorous and actual—building ground of the destiny of Western Christian man.

This much deeper sub-level—best perhaps termed folk-level—is that of two newly evolved institutions, slowly built, slowly occupying all its width and length: the feudal and the monastic.

The Feudal:

Home of the principle of freedom of choice *qua* choice, the ex-nomadic or ex-semi-nomadic freely, de *jure,* and collectively chosen leadership of a chief, the chosen *rex.*

The Monastic:

Home of the institutionalized principle of labor's value, of *the respect for labor qua labor,* principle such in its sanctity and primacy (prayer itself being a form of labor!) as to be Christian man's (and not India's) creation proper.

These two socio-historical sources, intimately joined together, formed in the world of the Christian West one current of all-embracing, all-penetrating activity.

And it was this future-propelled source of socio-cultural energy, the energy of prayer-labor (the rules of St. Benedict, who introduced the monastic institution to the West in the sixth century,[67] emphasized, far more than those, earlier, of St. Basil, its organizer in the East, this respect for labor, labor of mind-body—ultimately the respect for hand-and-mind's creativity, the artist-artisan's universe), and the energy-freedom of creative choice—the primordial chieftain-dancer's universe, ultimately—it was this future-propelled dual source of energy that gave, indeed, to the West its unique structure. This level, this sub-level, and not the upper level of *sacerdotium's* and *imperium's* strife.

And nothing could shake me in this conviction, not even the inevitable osmotic interdiffusion or mutual contamination, as it were, between the two levels of the West's structure, between the Bronze Age elements—despotism and slavery-under-godhead—and the Christian elements of sanctified (ontological, one could say) respect for labor and freedom (ontological, one could say also) in choice of leadership; not even the resulting confusion of functions and corruption of means: the Emperor and the Pope often acting as labor-and-freedom respecting protectors, the feudal king and the abbot as divinely appointed to the ownership or stewardship of temple-and-slavery.

Significant historical events are there also to testify on behalf of my conviction. One above all, paradigmatic, thus sufficient; the history of the great monastic order, the Benedictine, and its ramifications; of its inner organization and polity, which became the very history of Western political thinking and organization at large: the three progressive and consecutive stages of that history—the earliest one based on the combined principle of obedience to the order's Rule and of the autonomous, individual self-governing of each separate monastic unit. Then, the following stage, the great Cluniac reform (tenth and eleventh centuries), its principle of centralized authority making the individual will and authority of each of the now immensely more numerous monastic establishments converge toward the centralized, enlightened, yet unchallengeable authority of the Great Abbot of Cluny, himself a convinced and sturdy protector of the still higher, ultimate spiritual authority, that of the Bishop of Rome. (One memorable symbolic night of the year 1077, among the deep snows and winds at Canossa, the Holy Roman Emperor Henry IV humbled himself and kneeled in penance and obedience before the Pope, Gregory VII, with the erect figure of the Abbot of Cluny standing by and watching the scene—St. Hugh, the promoter and organizer, the real creator of this event.) And a third stage, the "puritan" reform of Citeaux, gave to the monastic world, indeed, by future extension, the entire secular Western world, the utmost proof of the beneficent efficacy of the alliance between the principles of respect for labor and respect for freedom. I speak of the Cistercian *federal* structure given to the order's socio-political being—a federal structure or *federalism* not in the sense of Ancient Greece's League, with the strongest member dominating it, but, already, in the modern sense of self-disciplined, self-ordered equality, enlightened and proud.

All those great abbots of the Romanesque era, great builders, great travellers, St. Odon, St. Hugh, Peter the Venerable, St. Bernard of Clairvaux, builders of roads—roads of pilgrimage, human streams, carriers of songs, merchandise and ideas, of heresies and images—robust abbots, by whom forests and barren wildernesses were transformed into bread-and-labor-giving fertile communities to become wealthy cities of the classical Gothic era!

And all this labor-profit-energy (profit in the Lockean sense of prime incentive, of pure theory and pure *praxis* reversible therein), energy also—by fusion and future-propulsion—of political freedom-of-choice, all this energy, besides becoming the molding force that gave to the history of the West's socio-political changes and progression its complex content and form, became, as well, the molding force that gave content and form to another, organically related, yet autonomous history, which, as the truthful interpreter-mirror of those same socio-political changes, was also the truthful embodiment of the sub-level's total energy: the history of the changes and progressions in the Western artisan-artist's destiny—the history of the West's art.

Not so in Byzantium. Here, most obviously, it was the formidable weight of the Bronze Age's king-priest alliance that supported the entire, equally formidable, upper level's structure of *sacerdotium-imperium;* the sub-level—very powerful also, often dominating by means of its two components, the monastic and the feudal—lacked Western history's future-molding energy, the energy that came there from the intimate alliance, fusion even, between the two guiding principles. It is this intimacy of alliance that was absent in the Christian East. And Byzantine monkhood, politically allied to, even supporting, the state-church power-holding elite, and thus all-powerful itself, was nevertheless bereft, in its intrinsic, sub-level's structure, of that total, dual energy that made Western monkhood a future-building ''progressive'' body.

And I saw this: Christianity's monastic *respect for labor qua labor* (both monk's and artisan's respect-as-principle) was always there, in Byzantium as it was in the West; and so also was the respect-as-principle for freedom's choice (collective choice of leadership, mind-soul-body's choice in depth-transfer). But the two sub-levels' secret forces were, in Byzantium, forces separated from each other (feudalism in Byzantium never became a centered or central force, always remained peripheral).

And I saw more: Byzantine monkhood, externally subservient to the verbal-military elite and its apocalyptic vision and dominance, internally and inevitably found the missing link, the depth-union, in that farthest-from-our-reasoning-norms corner of human vision-thought (the thought still rooted in the primeval three-oneness, the magician-chieftain-artisan's creativity, at once verbal, kinetic and visual-manual), which, in Byzantium, was the invisible world of Light=Witness, the Hesychia, made visible by the Byzantine monk-artisan's will. (That my chronicle is the chronicle of the Intrigue in the world of essences, structures, forms, I beg my reader never to forget.)

It is in Byzantine visionary art that the monk-artisan found his primordial freedom, man's—the ''nomad's''!—psychomachic freedom of choice.

The true history of Byzantine Intrigue in my tale is the story of the growth, the maturation, the aging and the death (the resurrection, as a possibility, if you wish!) of the Witness, the ''proving without proof,'' the image-touch. In Christianity's concrete terms, it was the history of the sanctity, reality and efficacy of the *touch* of the Witness, residing, as Light-Flesh, in the holy relic—the body (or its fragment) of a martyr of the faith, or the *lieu* of martyrdom itself, as well as in the trace-image of the Presence, the icon. (The term witness itself meant martyr's relic in early Christianity.)[68] It was the relic, the witness of Faith-Flesh that inhabited the church and was the innermost reason for the physical aspect, physical structure of the church. And it is here too that the difference between the East and the West is again manifested. For, while the holy relic was as strongly revered in the West as it was in the East, it was—and exclusively so—the essential funerary character of a *martyrium,* this direct descendant of Hellenistic-Roman domed and vaulted mausolea and *herōa,*[69] that dictated the Byzantine church's architectural dispositions—a vaulted chamber with its central, heaven's all-embracing dome (later several domal radiations around this central one) hovering over and containing, in the substructure of the church, the body of the saint or martyr, the ever-present there, ''proving-without-proof'' Witness: apotheosis of the Apocalyptic man in Christianity.

In the West the destiny of the church's physical structure was different: the subterranean, always vaulted *martyrium*—the more and more complex crypt, a corridor, the ''entrails'' of the church—with the body of a saint or a martyr buried under the Eucharistic altar, was there also from the earliest times (sometimes, as in the Carolingian era or perhaps even before, surely in Visigothic and Asturian Spain—Pravia, Oviedo, later, León—doubled in its secular sepulchral function by the raised tribune-narthex at the West façade); but the main, the basilical body of the church, the area of liturgical synaxes, could *freely,* choosingly and creatively develop throughout centuries of architecture's technological changes, acquisitions and enrichments: apotheosis of the Psychomachic man in Christianity.

That the Light-Witness, the Light-immediacy of the Presence of Adherence, the Touch by hand, eye or memory, resided in the holy relic—this sheltering belief was the Christian East's as it was the Christian West's. But that the uncreated Light-Flesh resided also in the holy image—the icon—just as it resided in the relic, that the icon was the Light itself, the Witness itself, this was Byzantium's. For Byzantium was the loyalty also to the icon's origin: Christ's Face, the *acheiropoieton,* the ''image-not-made-by-the-hand,'' which, when freed and purified from its initial Hellenistic-Roman military-imperial, city-and-army protecting function and usage (as in Emperor Heraclius' ''holy'' campaign against the Sassanian Chosroes II),[70] became again and remained what it was in its origin: the witnessing apparition—creature of Light-Touch—of the co-Sufferer's Face on the helping, consoling and imageless kerchief of Veronica. The same Light that shone on Mount Tabor and that shone in the heart of the "prayer of the heart" of Simeon the New Theologian (eleventh century) and thence, upon the heart or (echo of a Hindu voice?) from the navel of a mid-fourteenth century Athonite Hesychast.

That is how—the *Grand Personnage* had told me so!—the history of the Byzantine Empire is simply the history of two, only two, crises or traumas, one merging into the other and forming one historical continuum: the crisis—the fury!—of iconoclasm in the eighth century and the crisis—the fury also! of the Hesychast struggle with Byzantine "humanist" tradition in the middle of the fourteenth century. It is not so much a repulsion for the sanctity and veneration of the holy images, or even a rejection of them, that is so peculiarly iconoclastic in Byzantium—a frequent outburst of similar repulsion and rejection in early ecclesiastical history occurred in the West also: the Iberian Church's official prohibition (Council of Elvira, *circa* 309); the Gallic clergy's distaste for the use of holy images in churches: it was a bishop, the Bishop of Marseilles, Serenus, who ordered the destruction of sacred objects, an action criticized but not entirely condemned by Pope Gregory I (540–604), who wrote in his warning message to the bishop: "In forbidding the adoration of pictures you deserve commendations, but in destroying them, you are to blame."[71]

It was the iconoclast fury of prohibition, persecution and destruction (particularly during the first phase of that era, before the temporary iconodule restoration in 787 by the Empress Irene the Athenian—more conciliatory tactics being used later, during the second iconoclast wave, before the final reinstallment of orthodoxy by another woman, the Empress Theodora in 843), it is this fury of violence that is so Byzantine. And I say it was so Byzantine because the problem involved in the struggle—a Christological problem—has been always so vital, so firmly rooted in Byzantium's psycho-historical consciousness, overlapping as such, in its deepest motivations, other and more obvious socio-economic causes.

For Byzantium, as for all Christendom indeed, the central problem of Christology—the divinity and the humanity of Christ at his body's death—found its solution in the "objective" efficacy, unquestionable, of Christo-dialectics, or the so-called (already non-Aristotelian) "logic of the unity of contradictories,"[72] a solution—

God's Three-Two-Oneness—firmly established for orthodox Christianity, East and West, as an ontological certainty after long periods of theological deliberation, first by men like Leontius of Byzantium, then, later, and definitively, by John the Grammarian and others. In practical, concrete terms of Byzantine mysticism, it meant that the Divine Being is at once unrepresentable, because humanly and absolutely inaccessible, and present or presented in real and absolute hypostasis, as divine Light-Energy in the holy image, the *icon.* It was already the pre-iconoclast ecumenical Council of Quinisext in 692 that, in its famous Canon 89, established the essential difference between the "symbolic" (liturgically erroneous for that Council) rendering of the supreme subject and object of Christian art—the image of Christ—as the "sign," the "shadow" (the Lamb or the Cross, this latter "sign" accepted later by the iconoclast theologians as the only possible and permissible sacred object), and the "realistic" rendering, the "thing" itself, not its "shadow"—"signs" (the "thing" having been revealed to all humanity in the era of Grace, the "shadow" belonging still to the era—Judaic—of the Law); not Christ hidden behind his symbol, but Christ as a real, earthly man, his "reality" both transcendental and physical;[73] the reality of the Icon-Face.

And it was with the end of the struggle and the triumph of the sacred image as the true "thing," as Light-Grace incarnate, an epic battle won by the monk and the monk's passionate ally, Byzantine womanhood, this most convinced adherent to the truth of the Presence, to the reality of the Witness-Touch, that the theology of Light itself began its teaching (continued even more energetically from the ninth century on) about the *physically* spiritual, transcendent-actual Presence of God-Infinity, substituted totally by, transferred totally into this finite Witness, the Light in the "image-not-made by hand," that same Light of "the perpetual prayer of the heart."

In the eleventh century, with Simeon the New Theologian and his adherents and followers, this theology or this mysticism of Byzantium fully attained its "proving-without-proof" goal. And then it was during the socio-politically tormented time of the mid-fourteenth century that this *free* teaching of Peace, as it was called, became a dogma and a rule, a militant *must,* absorbed, included in the Eastern orthodoxy: the now institutionalized, victorious, arrested Hesychasm. And it was the last crisis of Byzantine spirituality. The battle was won by the monk again. But the woman—her Byzantine passion and loyalty to the origins—was absent.

And the curtain had descended on Byzantium's stage.

*

The Light, the pure white Eagle-Dove of Pindar and of Olympia's marbles, the Light-Grace of the first ''prayer of the heart''—where is it? Gone?

Now, again, I felt suddenly abandoned and alone—in ''silence and secrecy'' again.

''Adieu, Byzantium! Adieu!'' I said to the slowly disappearing shore. The great noise of Byzantium's tragic twilight was disappearing also, but my memory, sliding across it, could redescend into the ''silence and secrecy'' of the relived day's dawn and, grateful, rest here and there for a while: a relived bliss of the beginnings, child's hand-and-thought-full bliss, Light of contemplation, white, all-white Bird floating in the sky's ocean of light-created colors—sky of tenderness, of rest and support, *Theotokos!*

Theotokos:

For the last time in me, under the terror-protection of the Pantocrator's Face, I saw Daphni's suavities again, the wonder—*suavitas!*—of the silver-blue-pink harmonies, child's bliss, of the Baptism lunette *(Plate 79);* the radiating wonder and luminosity—*suavitas!*—around the deepest night-blue of the Nativity lunette *(Plate 80),* the converging suavities of the Transfiguration *(Plate 81)*—all these suave harmonies erected there *intentionally* to support the Pantocrator's *terribilità (Plate 82),* the true subject, the sub-subject, of Daphni's mosaic ensemble.

And—surprise and joy—Kariye Djami's mortuary chapel, the Parecclesion, covered entirely with frescoes, its walls, vaults, apse:[74] the growing, propelled *terribilità* of its walls' and arches' imagery, the ''mobile rigidity'' of the erect row of saints, caryatides supporting the biblical thunder of warning, preparation and irrevocability—the prophecies of the Jacob's Ladder, of the Burning Bush, of the Vessels deposited in the Holy of Holies of Solomon's Temple, of the Closed Gates of Jerusalem; the formidable figures of four poet-hymnographs (on the pendentives below the dome of

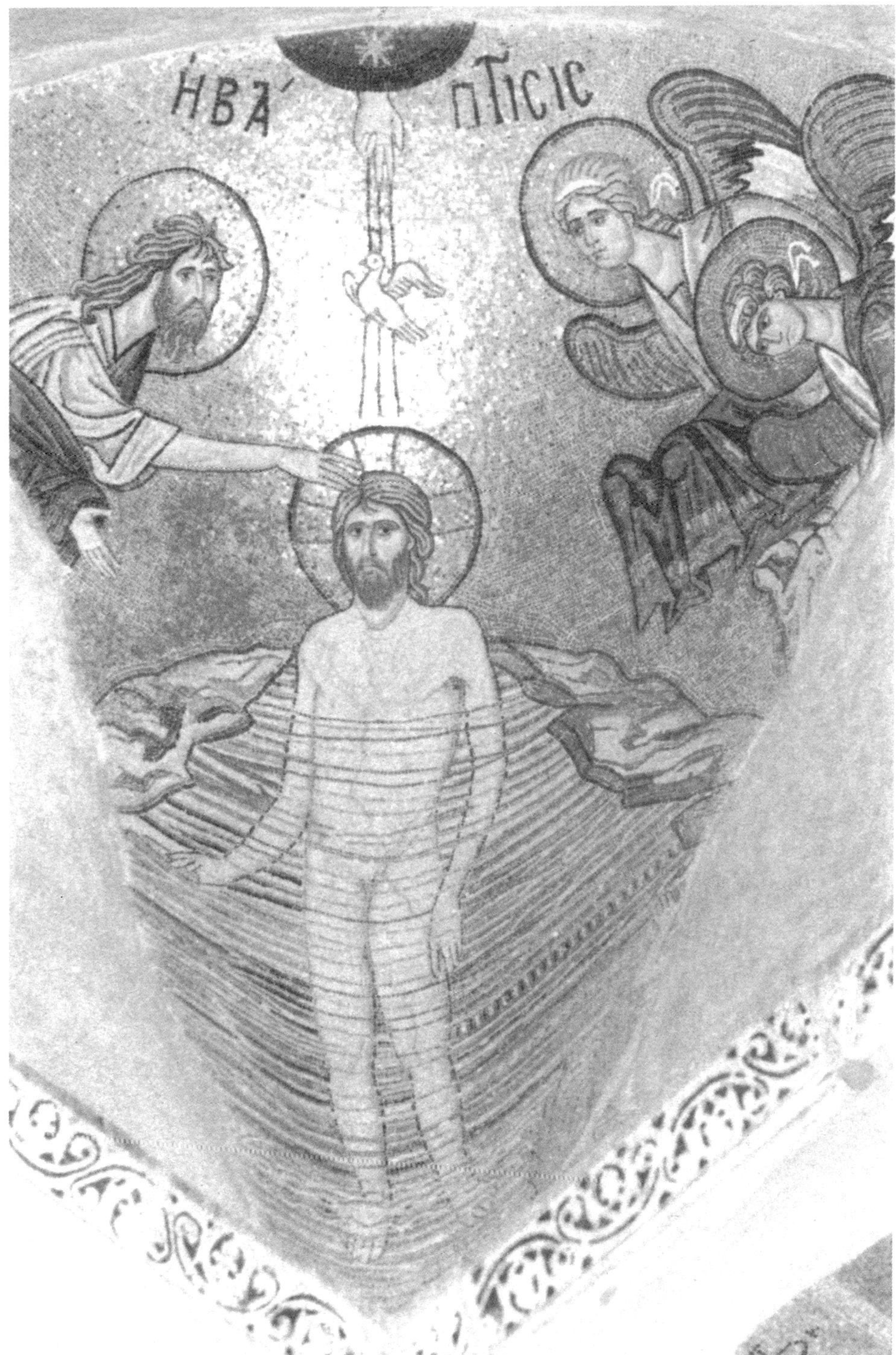


79. The Baptism, detail, Monastery church, Daphni

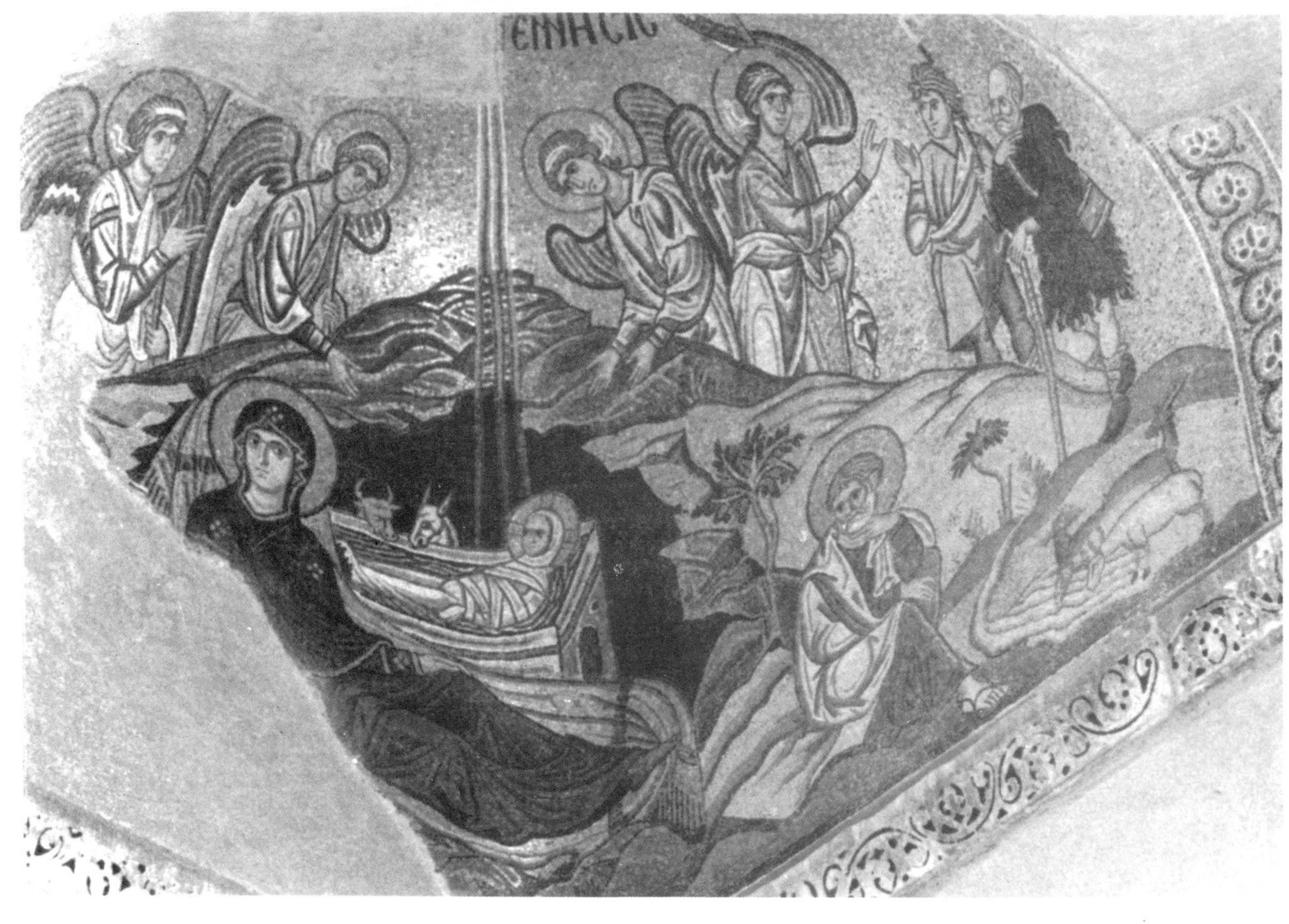

80. The Nativity, detail, Monastery church, Daphni

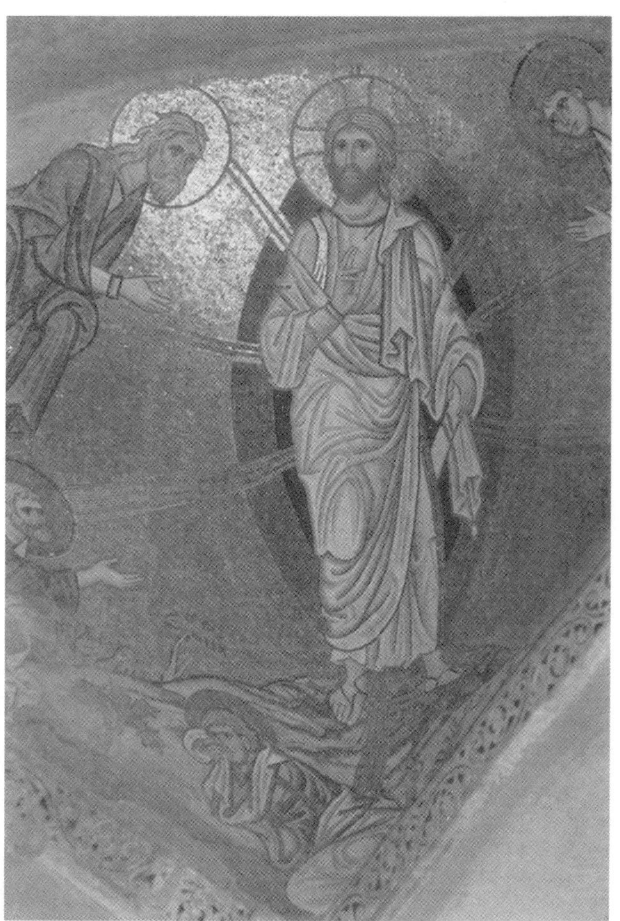

81. The Transfiguration, detail, Monastery church, Daphni

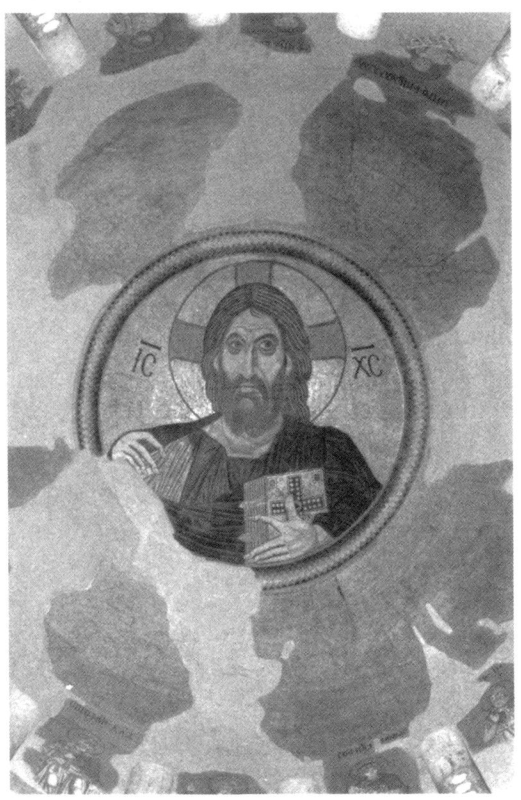


82. Pantocrator, Monastery church, Daphni

the western bay of the nave), the Virgin's hymnographs, St. John Damascene, St. Cosmas Melodos, St. Joseph the Poet, St. Theophanes *(Plate 83).* All this culminating in the *terribilità* of the apse's Last Judgment, its red river, and, high up, its doom-or-reward announcing angel *(Plate 84),* all this, intentionally again, preparing the grant *éclat* and advent of the Presence: the Light of the Anastasis *(Plate 85)*[75]—the Witness of the Terrible and, underneath, the Witness of Christian *Suavitas,* Theotokos, present, invisible, there!

But the memory's halt at San Zeno's chapel in the basilica of Santa Prassede in Rome, let it be the last and most grateful halt of all: the unforgettable intimacy of this tiny, penumbral sanctuary—a most precious jewel of Roman-Byzantine art productivity under the builder pope, Paschal I (reign 817–24).

Here—and nowhere else closer to light's and child's bliss—all the terror-protection and, at once affirming and transforming it, all the harmonies of Byzantine *suavitas!*[76]

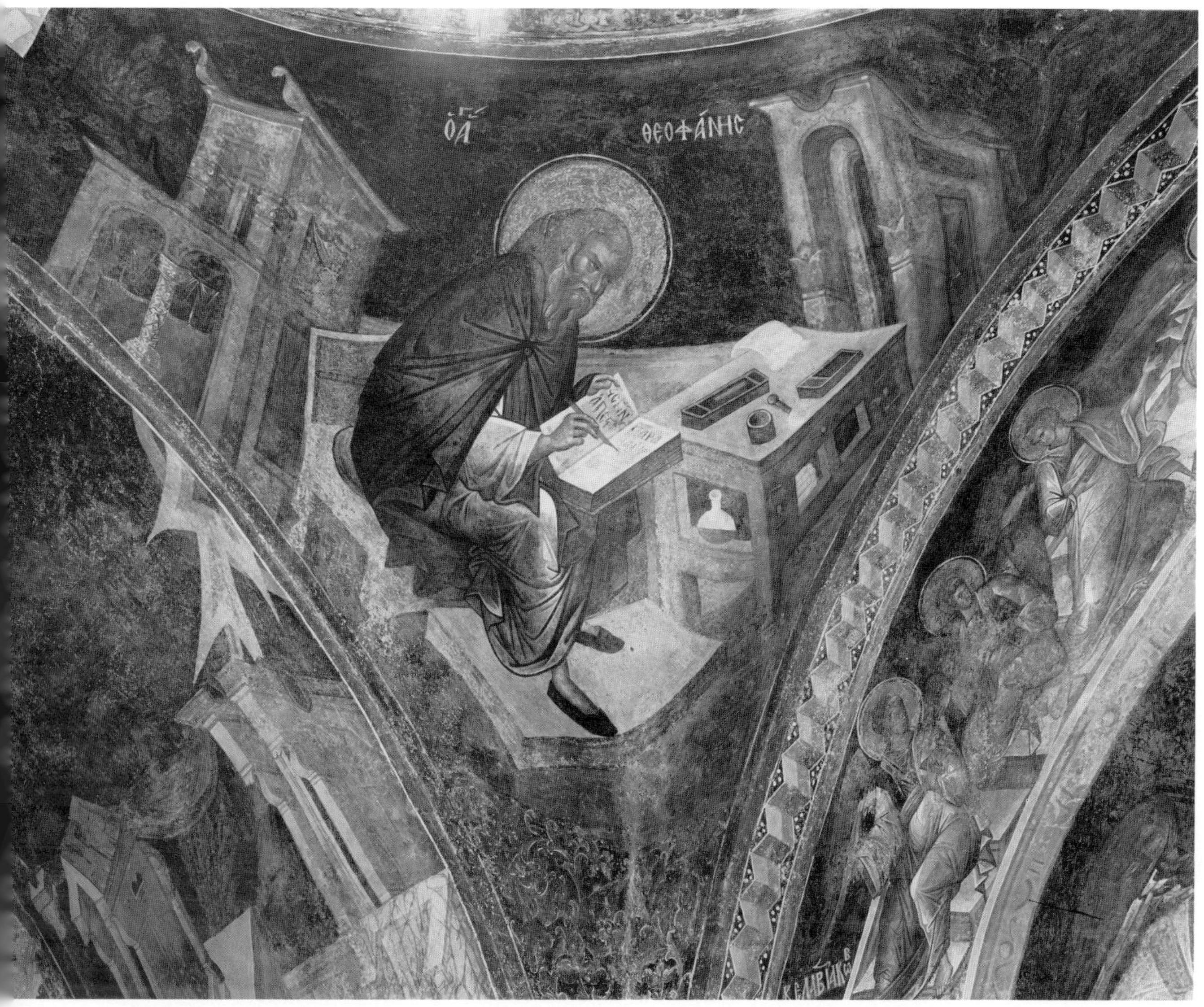

83. St. Theophanes, Kariye Djami, Istanbul

Four blue-nimbused angels burst, each from a granite corner column, supporting, arms uplifted, hands helping—as a Doric column does!—the sky-blue round medallion of the cupola, where the face of Christ is the face of Ancient Greece's human certainty revived: serious, melancholy, meditative and sweet—given me for the last time, the Bee, the Honey of Hellas! (*Plate 86a*) Flash of white robes, all over the flash of blue: these angels and the saints

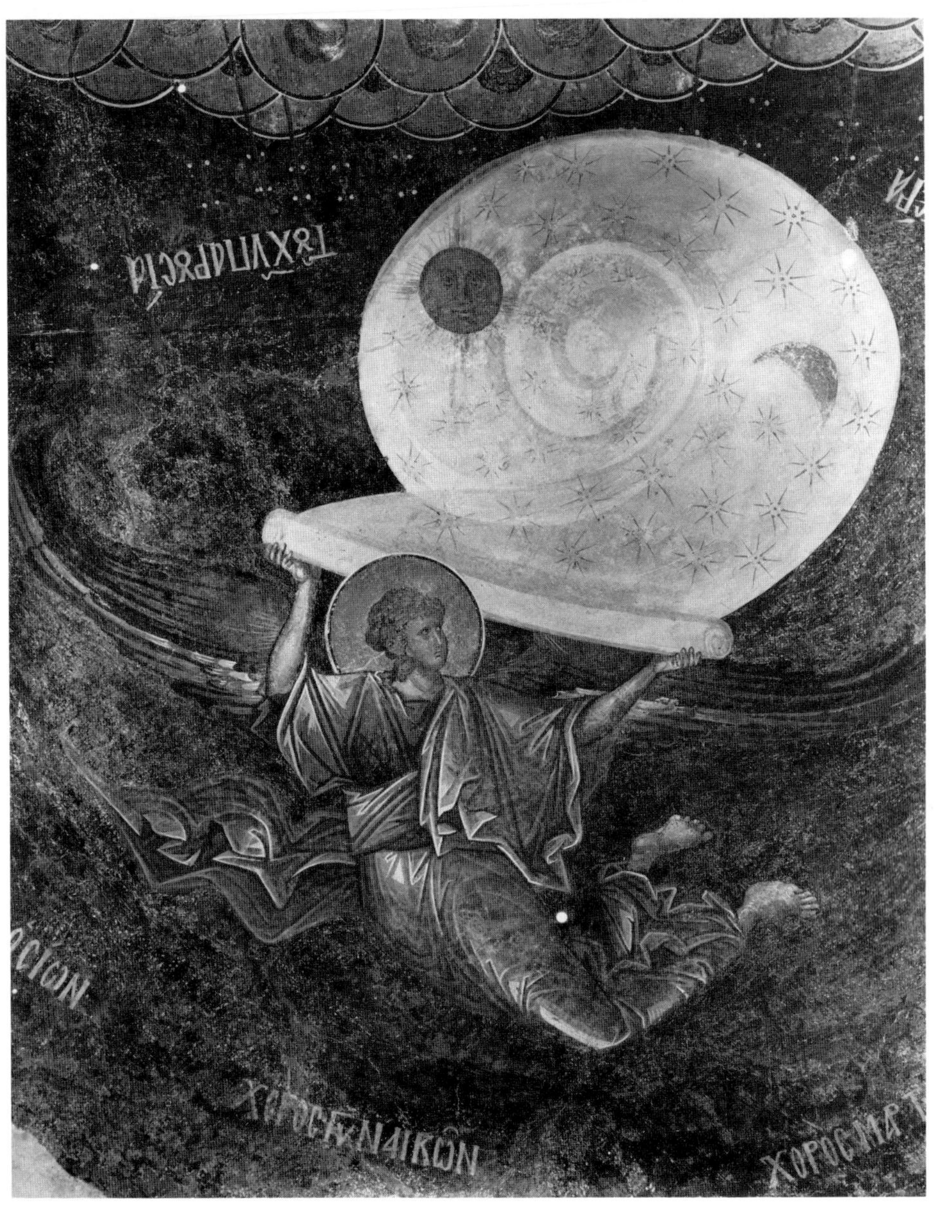

84. Angel, detail of Last Judgement, Kariye Djami, Istanbul

on the walls around them are the white and the blue of the Immaculate's liturgy. And the ruby red of the earth-flowers the walking saints tread upon—this also is the true subject, the sub-subject, of the chapel: the bleeding bliss at soul's birth in light, incessant, everywhere, anywhere, all white, all blue, all red here, all red-blue-white upon Chartres' inner west window!

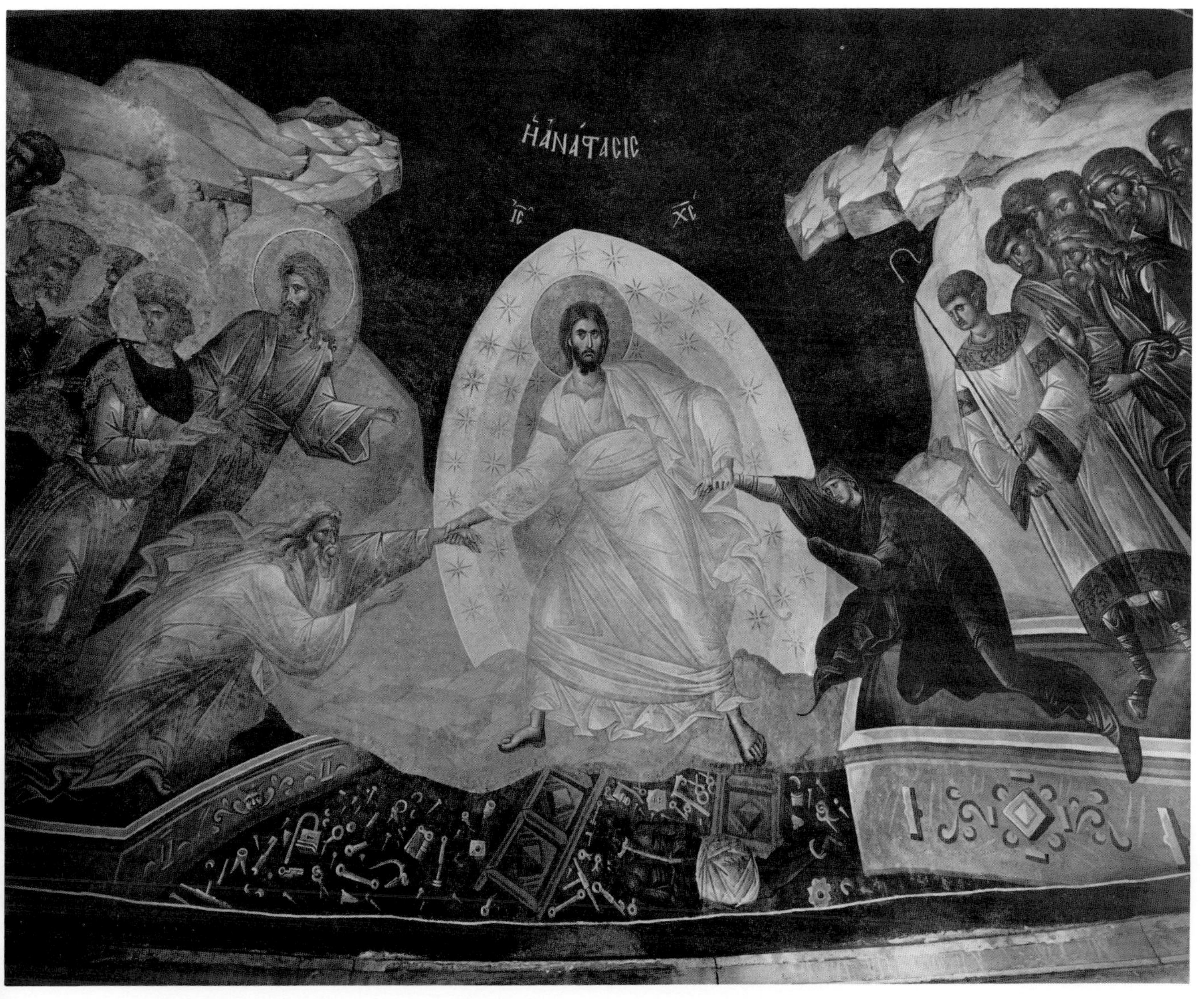

85. Anastasis, detail, Kariye Djami, Istanbul

Terror, child's protection, and *suavitas*—lovely, lovely chapel of San Zeno! A similar story was told once to a child about St. Elizabeth's miracle of red roses and of bread. And about her husband, a cruel unbelieving king who forbade her to carry and distribute, as daily and even nightly she would do, the bread to the poor; and how one morning when he met her walking thus, he cried out to her in red, threatening rage: "What are you, Madame,

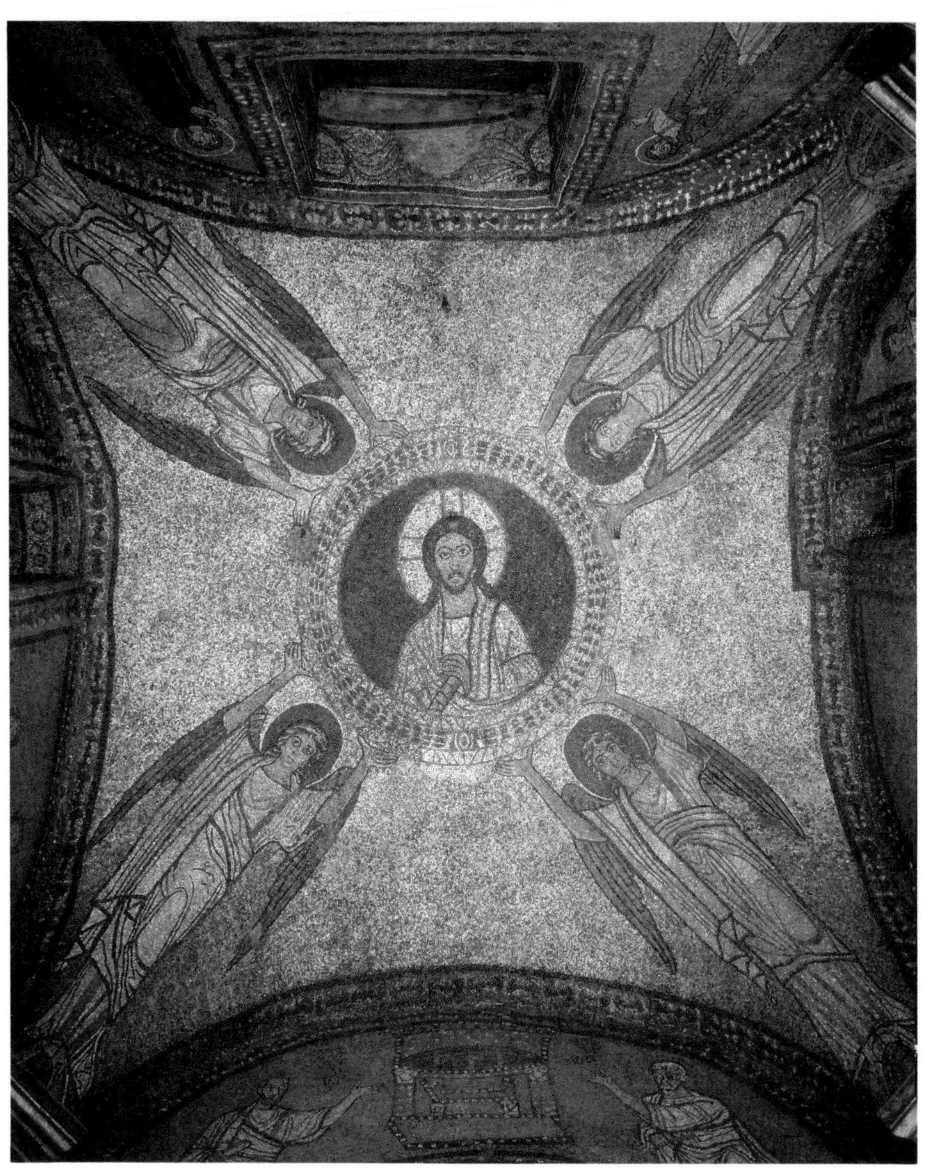

86a. Four angels, San Zeno chapel, Sta. Prassede, Rome

carrying again there in the fold of your royal mantle? Answer me, or . . . " "Roses," she said. And when the king pulled down her robe's fold, not loaves of bread, but red roses fell on the stone floor. She lied and was a saint. And henceforth, whenever on Sunday mornings the child saw the sky above his noisy, royal and angry native city very blue and very luminous, he felt behind it—

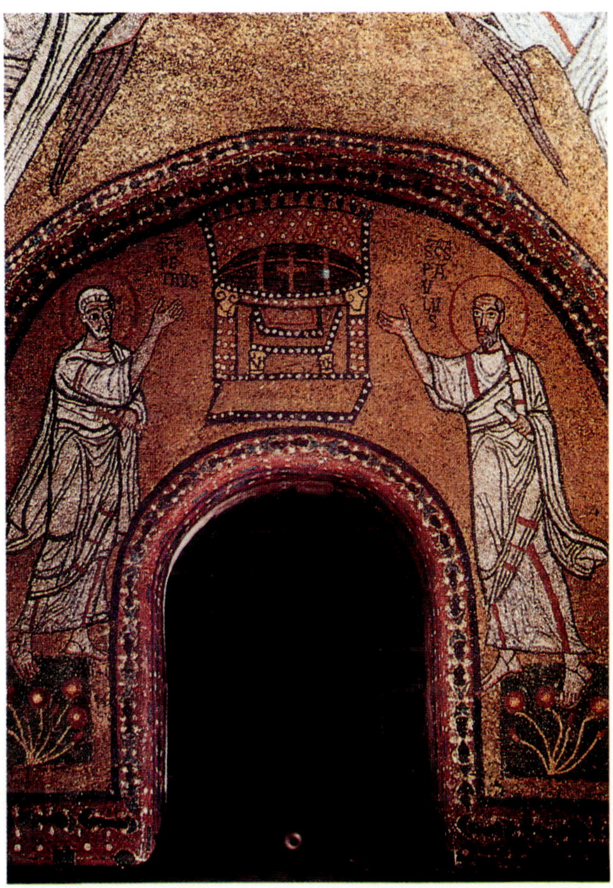

86b. Sts. Peter and Paul, San Zeno chapel, Sta. Prassede, Rome

oh, Hesychia!—the presence of the bread for the poor, the roses and the walk of the saint. Just as my memory saw the red flowers under the feet of the angels and the saints on the walls of the chapel of San Zeno, and red stripes—accents, ruby-red Caritas!—along their immaculate robes. (*Plate 86b*)

*

''Adieu, Byzantium, adieu!'' The shore became but faintly visible.

I journeyed westward, back again.

# *Iberia*

Our Ancestor died. The news reached me when I was still shaky and weakened by a great fever that struck me on my return to the tempest-brimmed West. Those who brought the news could not know what they really had brought me: my own death as the Ancestor's shadow; they were astonished at the extent of my distress. For I became the shadow of a shadow. An absurdity. Solitude it was and separation, the solidarity in it separated or confused—unrecognizable. The hyphen of my two-one universe was torn away from it—torn from top to bottom—even as at the crucifixion's end "the curtain of the Temple was torn in two from top to bottom" (Matthew 17:51, New English Bible). The tearing of a curtain it was, and a void resulting there, suddenly filled in with the great voice of another fable—not mine any more: the life-mirroring fable of Pandora's beauty and perfidy—the Olympian artist-artisan's primordial creation—that first and most beautiful woman fashioned out of clay and water into flesh and irresistible charm; beautiful Pandora, embellished even more by the ministrations of the three admiring, obedient Horae, Eumonia, the guardian of the Law, Dike, of Justice, Irene, of Peace; Pandora, beloved (her heart really so perfidious?) by the imprudent Epimetheus (brother of the rebel and warning Prometheus), to whom, sent as a gift by revengeful Zeus, she brought her own gift, that gracious vase, whose heavy lid when lifted by her hand let all the evils, and all the afflictions of earth escape and spread, all of them led by Indifference, Greed, Chance and Bad Faith (*Plates 87a&b*).

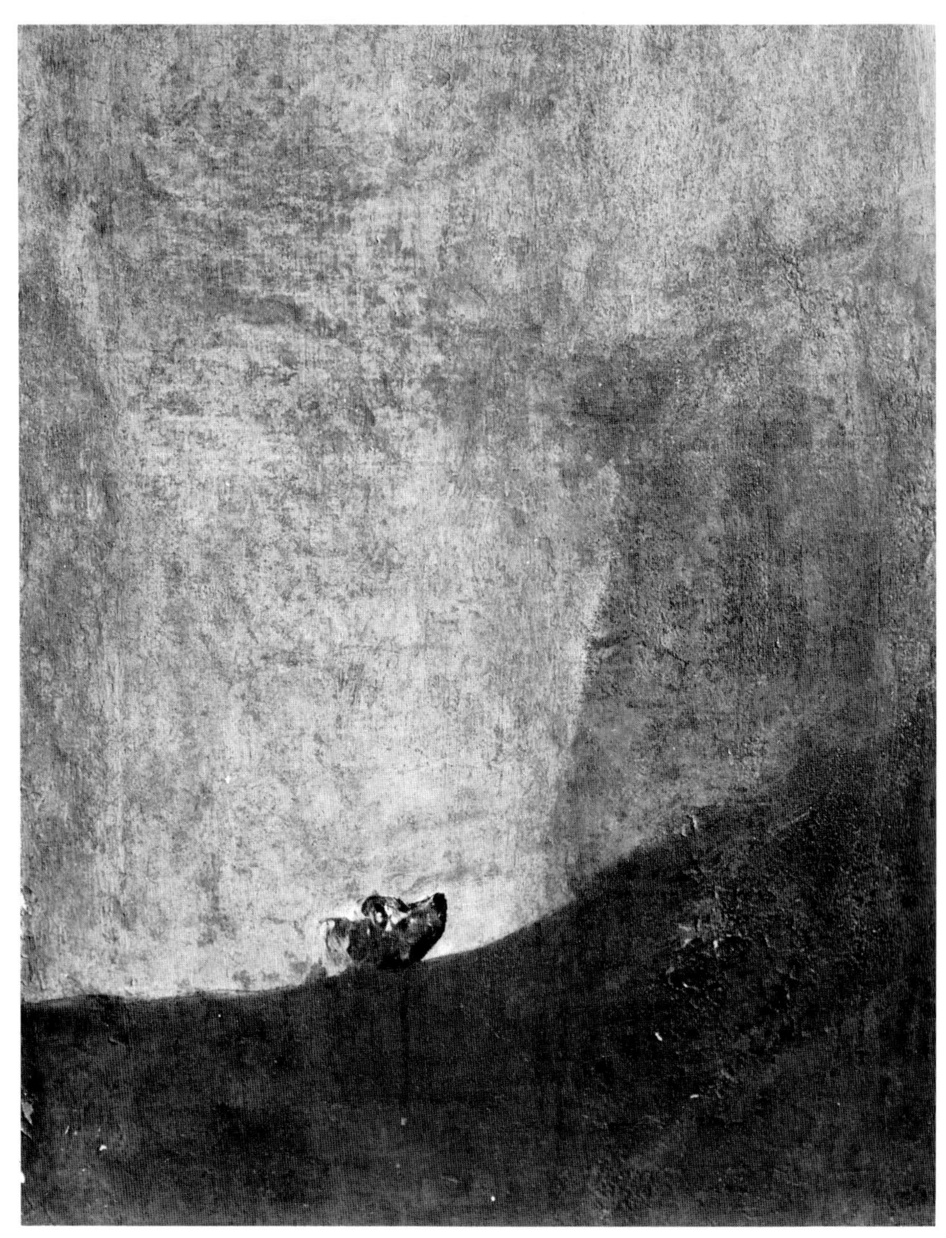

87a. Goya, Dog in Sand

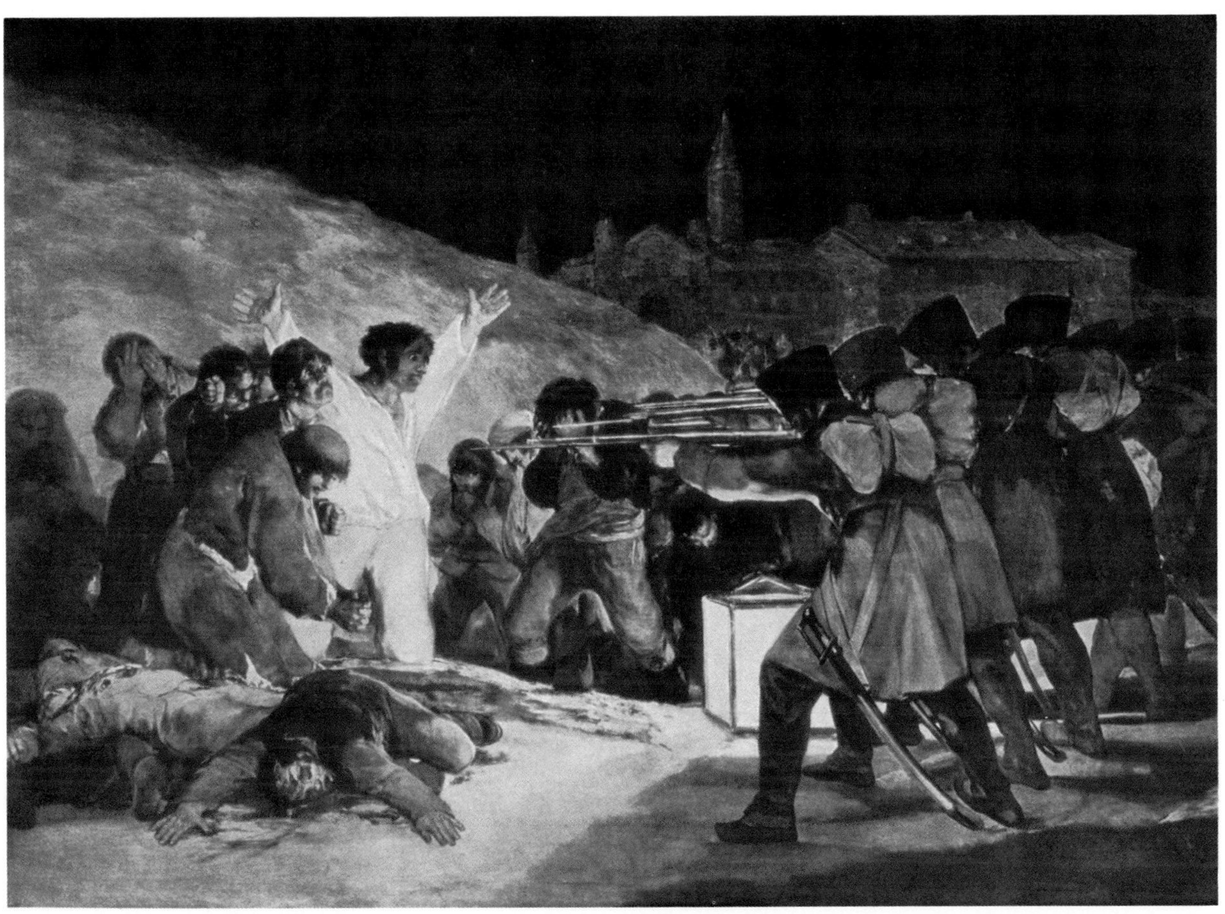

87b. Goya, 3rd of May (1808)

Still children, eventful as all children are, playing with the child Aeternitas, the ancient Greeks could very well see hope remaining at the bottom of the emptied vase. But I could not see hope there; I could only see, coiled in a corner, little winged memory—little winged matter, deeply asleep as if dead and forgotten.

The Ancient died. The hyphened world—Solitude-Solidarity—of his Children, the world of *Tendresse* and of Art—where now? Perhaps indigent, in exile, perhaps, despised, mocked?

Left alone, I wept bitterly. When a familiar voice inside me spoke thus: ''Don't! Don't be so distressed. Yes, the Ancestor died. *Tendresse* died. This is true. But you know what is even truer: that the Ancestor is your invention, an Idea-*res* made by you into an Idea-*persona*. His going into death is like what happened—according to a strange and truthful appraisal—to a famous old Chinese mountain-mist-water landscape painted so convincingly, rendered so alive, so moving and so 'real,' that the only human figure inhabiting it contemplatively, a miniscule, yet equally convincing figure, alive and moving, although not equally 'real' as yet, could wish and decide to move away, to leave this created world, to step outside its frame into the outside, the real, world—to be 'real' there.

''The death of the Ancestor, in contrary direction to the same move, is such a stepping outside the frame of your created world into his own 'real' world. Follow him. And the two worlds will be yours now, if you wish it so: here, all the evils and afflictions on earth (the world some call the world of facts); there, all the evils and all the afflictions will be present, but not yours—their own now (the world some call the world of structures, of essences, forms, meanings, of attitudes). Follow the Ancestor.''

''But how? The road back, I see it closed.'' And I continued: ''True, the little, winged, poor memory I saw, asleep, as if dead, is awakening now (I can see it), slowly, slowly at the sound of your words. But I can only—and not fully yet—remember or see the silhouette of a story read to me once by someone in good faith: 'The Chinese have a game: the connecting link, they call it. They capture two birds and tie them together. Not too close. The cord is thin, strong, and fairly long. When the birds are released, they take flight, they think they are free and rejoice in the wideness of the sky. But, suddenly: crack! The cord is stretched taut. They flutter and whirl in all directions, blood drips from their bruised wings, feathers and fluff fall on the onlookers . . . . Sometimes the cord gets tangled in a branch or twines around the birds, and they struggle as though caught in a trap, peck at each other's eyes, beaks and wings, and if Providence doesn't impale them on a branch, one of them dies before the game is over. Alone. Or with the other. Both of them. Together strangled; blinded.'[77] Strangled, blinded, all of us, without exception . . . here. You say follow him, but—I repeat—how?''

''Listen,'' the musing voice answered me then, ''Listen! Do you hear, coming from your not-so-distant future, this guitar-accompanied song-interrogation sung by a young American man?

*Hey mister that's me up on the jukebox*
*It's me who's singing this song*
*And I cry every time you slip in one more dime*
*And let the boy sing the sad one one more time . . .* [78]

"And the young American woman's guitar-accompanied song-answer:

*I've looked at clouds from both sides now*
. . . . . . . . . . . . . . . . . . . . . . . . . .
*From win or lose, and still somehow*
*It's life's illusions I recall;*
*I really don't know life at all.*[79]

"Listen. For you see, to speak about life is to speak about death: the interrogation about life and its enigma means, in truth, an interrogation about death."

And at these words of the voice I saw my poor little winged memory—the poor little winged matter—fully awakened and about to leave. I knew it: I started to remember and to re-understand. The narrow bridge-road leading back to the Ancestor was the narrow memory—a bridge-road—that was leading me back to my past thought: in Byzantium, I remembered now, I had said to myself, "Passion is soul turned to life's enigma, toward death. Not toward life's activity."

"Listen." (The voice again!) "Death." Not the expectation *of* death, but the expectation *by* death:

*¡Ay que camino tan largo!*
*¡Ay mi jaca valorosa!*
*¡Ay que la muerte me espera*
*antes de llegar a Córdoba!*

*Córdoba.*
*Lejana y sola.*

The same wounded and sweet sadness in the youth and in the old: death waiting for you, watching from wherever your heart's eye, hand and heart are poised over there, from the misty and close

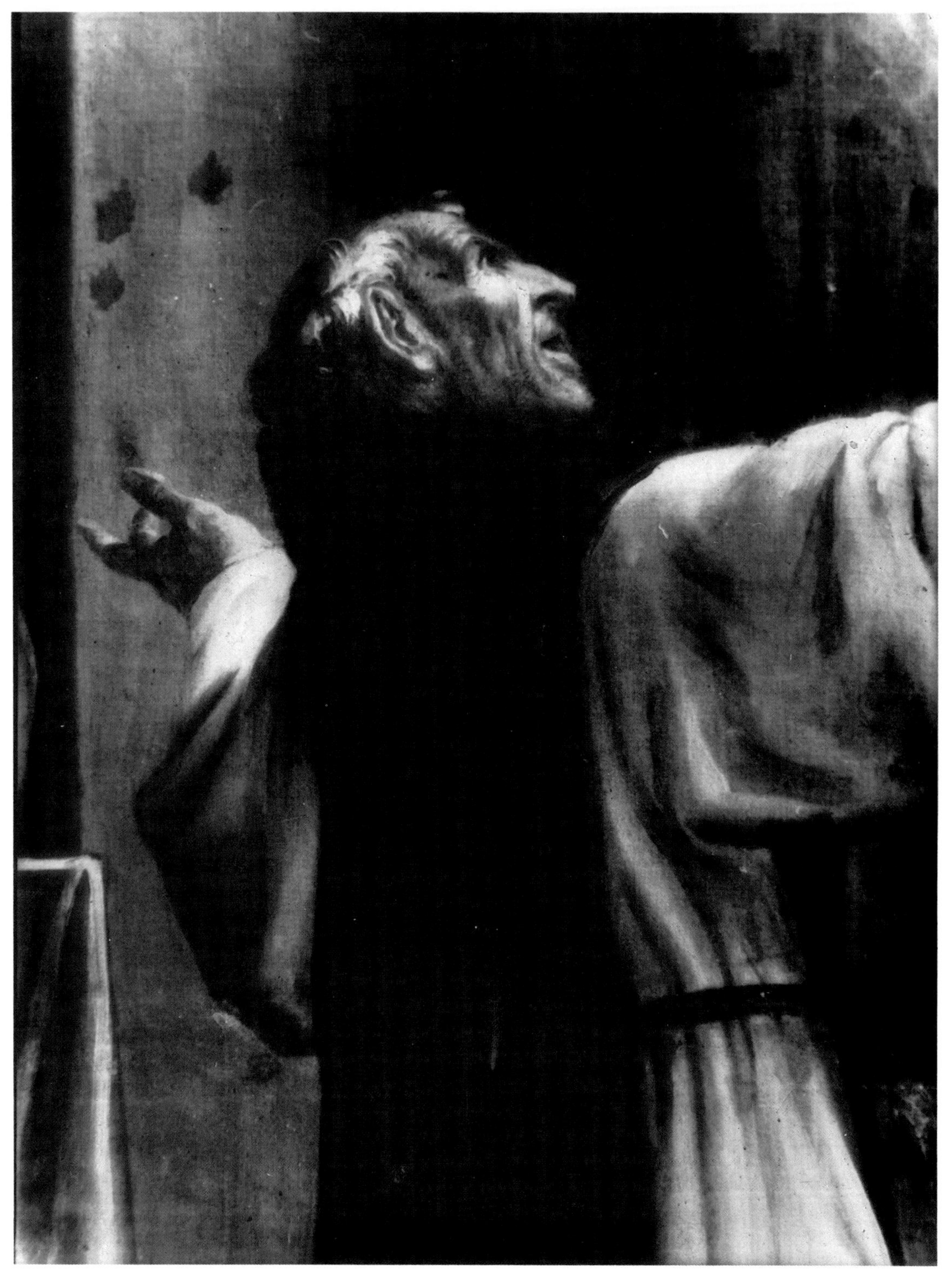

88a. Valdés Leal, Friar Fernández Yáñez de Figueroa, detail

halo crowning in warmth the cold, dry winter branches of trees seen at a grey distance; from the lips of a wounded soldier dying in a farthest, far, far away land, bereft of all causation, and finally bereft of greed, indifference or bad-in-good faith; from the spring-swayed bow, *salut,* secrecy of white and yellow field flowers so close to the green soil and still closer to the blue sky: ''Higher, higher! Expectation *by* death, not *of* death. Interrogation. Passion. Listen and follow the Ancestor now.''

*

And such, indeed, was the land into which I followed the little inner, disappearing voice. I knew at once what it was and where it was: its idiom, familiar to me, was the native idiom of the Ancestor and my own, his shadow's idiom.

I was in Spain. Man's soul turned towards the enigma of life. Interrogation. Glance. Not eye's expression but eye's interrogation. Passionate. Thus individual, irreversible, unique. The secret goal—the interrogating and communicating glance—of Spain.

This is how the world of Art, as I had known it before, was given back to me then. Permitted.

Again and now in Spain: the terror-and-rest of the Apocalyptic present in it, the freedom-choice of the Psychomachic present and supreme in it now, the one braided with the other, ''as the willow bows before the breeze.''[80]

*

And I continued descending deeper down into the world of Spain's Glance.

The Ancestor and all his Children and Grandchildren were there again. But invisible now. And yet all present. I was not interrogating any more, not anything, not anybody. How could I? My new world was interrogation itself! Where else but here in Spain could I meet a Valdés Leal, this most Spanish, perhaps, of all Spaniards—eyes fixing-interrogating, believing, doubting, witnessing—(*Plates 88a&b*)? or Alonso Berruguete, or a Goya, the stubborn, passionate, bad-in-good uncovering, interrogating, Aragonese *batturo:* the dying-interrogating eyes of his kneeling San José de Calasanz

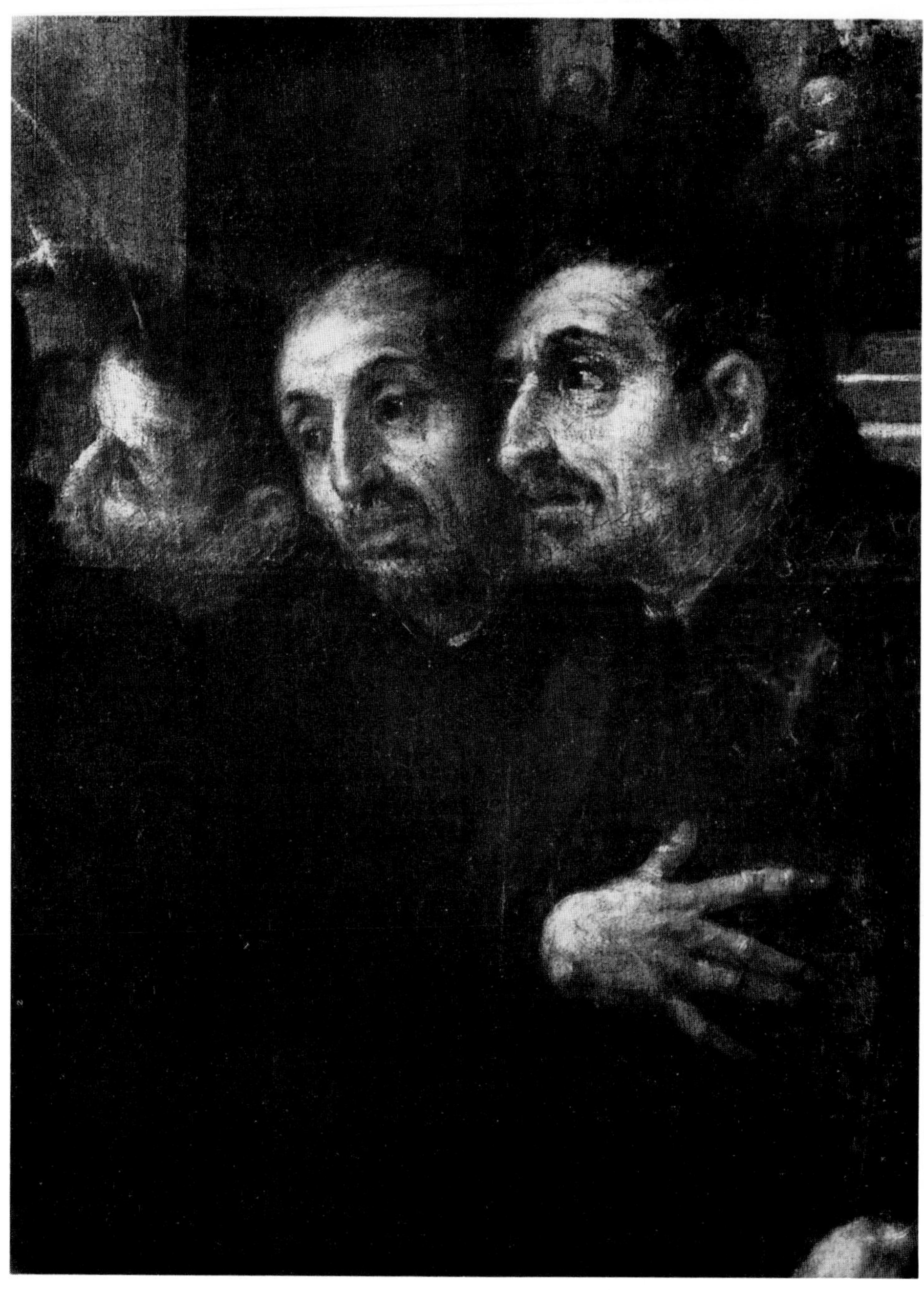

88b. Valdés Leal and workshop, St. Ignatius receiving the bull for the founding of the Jesuit order from Pope Paul III, detail

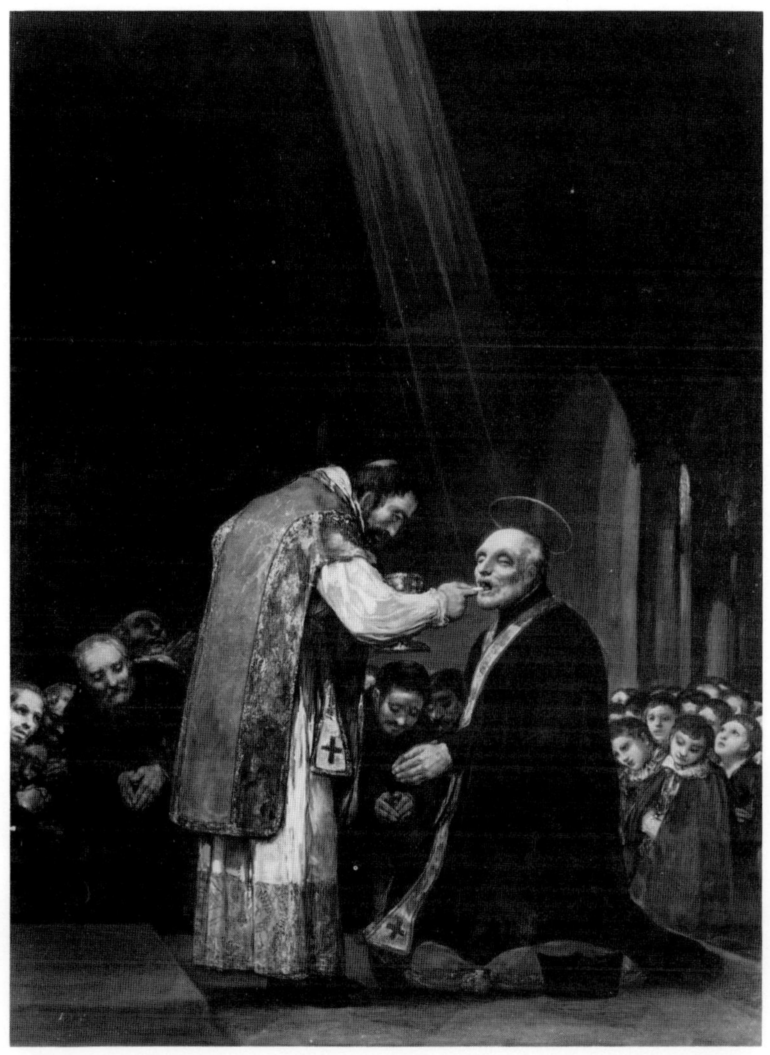

89. Goya, Last Communion of San José de Calasanz, church of San Antonio Abad, Madrid

(*Plate 89*); eyes witnessing the terror-rest-freedom-choice of the holy communion's being *there,* about-to-be close, eyes lost to the brutish hand, impatient, ignorant, of the administering priest who pushes into the moribund's mouth the holy Host (*Plate 90*).

Carried away as I found myself, in my motion into remote historic time, by the testimony of Spanish events = monuments of art, freed thus from scholarly worries about all their stylistic and

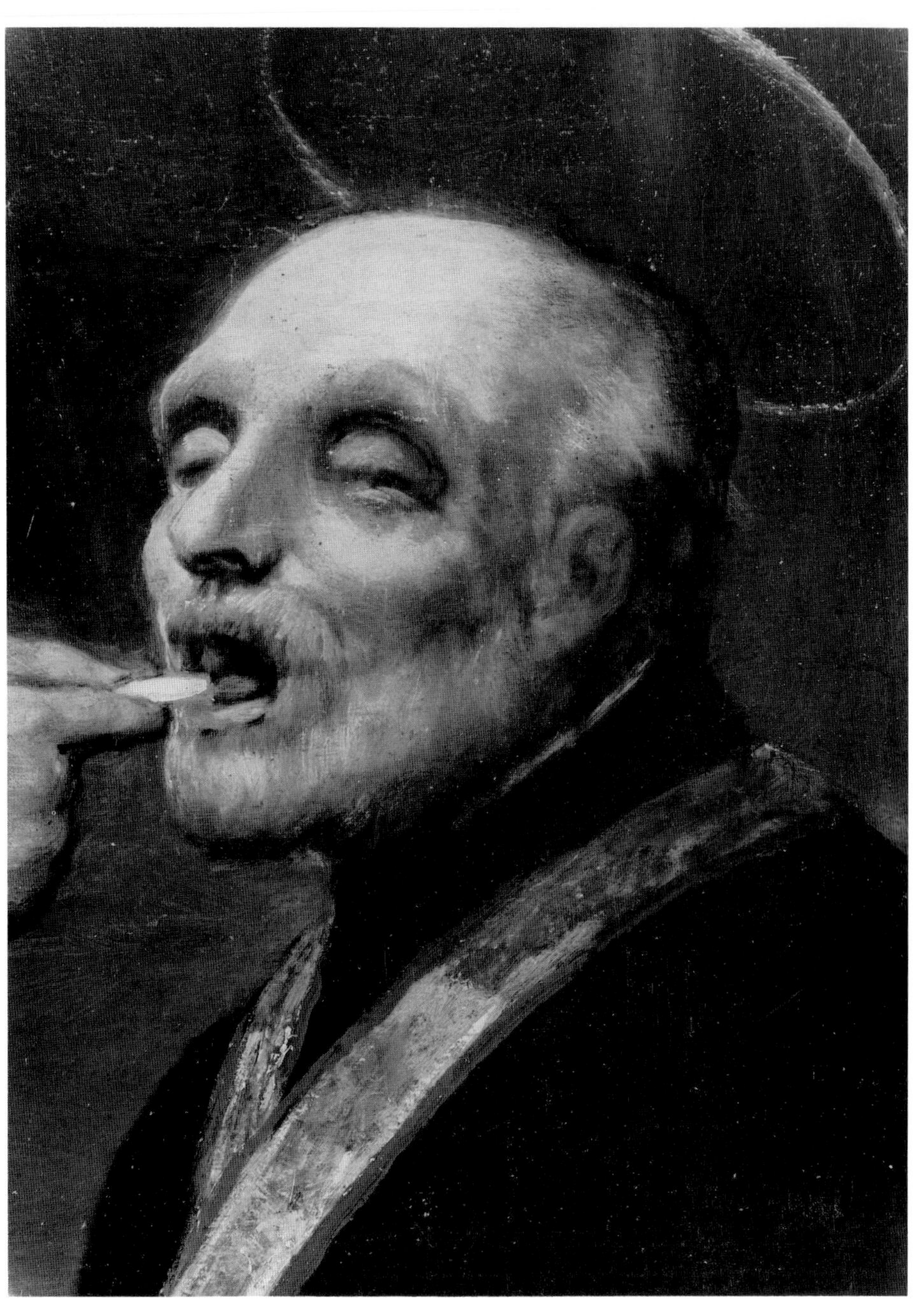

90. Goya, Last Communion of San José de Calasanz, detail

iconographic derivations, the accurate appraisal of their affinities and of their loans from other cultures, I was free to ask, where but in Spain could I meet so passionate a glance of interrogation—the

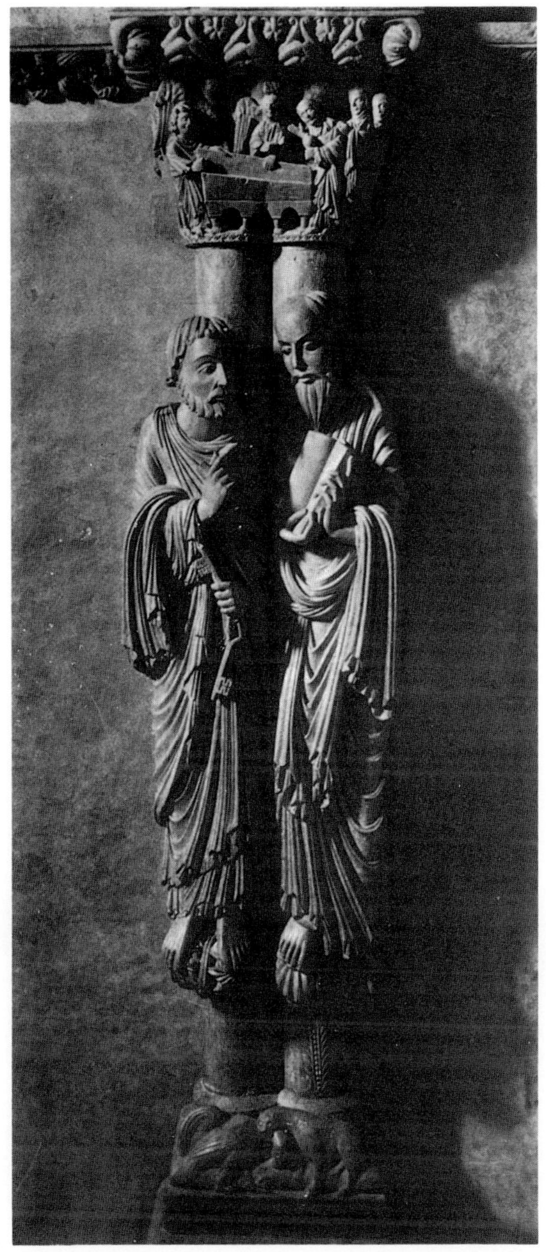

91. St. Peter and St. Paul, Oviedo Cathedral

glance of metaphysical anxiety, of faith and doubt, of certainty, terror and *pax*—as in the eyes of St. Peter and St. Paul (twelfth century) at the portal of Oviedo Cathedral's *Camara Santa* (*Plate 91*);

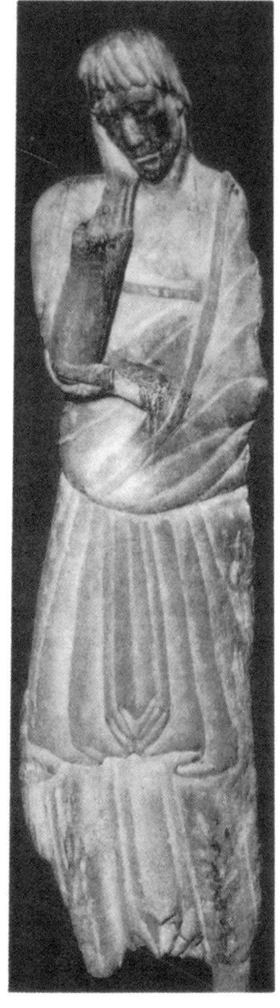

92. St. John, ex-Cathedral of Roda de Isábena, Huesca

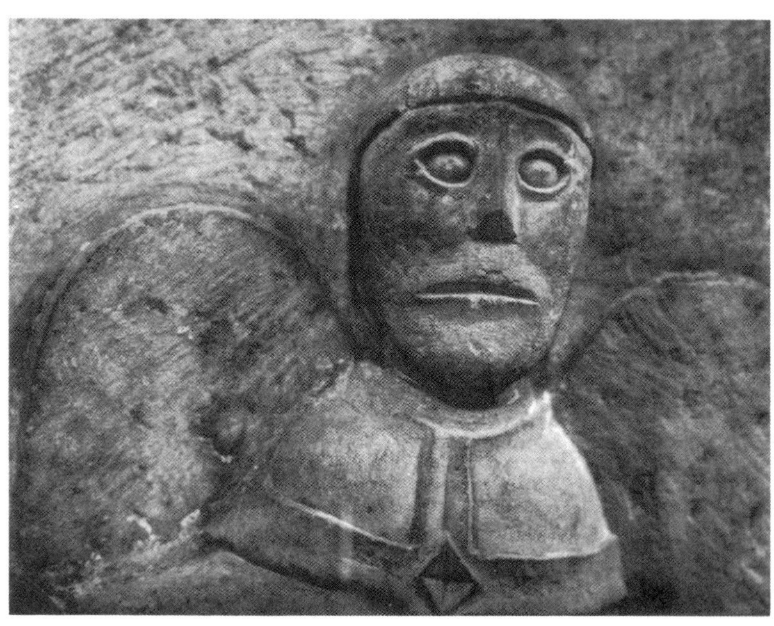

93. Altar angel, detail, San Martín de Mondoñedo, (Lugo)

in the eyes of St. John (twelfth century) at the ex-cathedral of Roda de Isábena (Huesca) (*Plate* 92), or in those of the altar angel (twelfth century) at San Martín de Mondoñedo (Lugo) (*Plate 93*); in the eyes of the Gothic Archangel Gabriel (thirteenth century) in Salamanca, of the ''Doncel of Sigüenza'' (fifteenth century [*Plate 94*])? And farther still in my backward motion through time, this same intensity of glance bringing back to life the engraved effigy on a fourth-century Christian funerary *lauda* (*Plate 95*).[81]

Obsession, uncritical self-delusion on my part? For how could this late Roman sepulchral mosaic slab be so ''Spanish'' already—so astonishingly Spanish? Yet—why not? The ethnic and cultural complexity—maturation—of an at that time still Roman Iberia could already have prepared it—more directly, more acutely than in other contemporary and neighboring cultures—for the future much more complete maturation of Spain's tormented body-soul-mind's interrogation. And the far-off panorama, half misty, half sunny, of Iberia's past unfolded itself before me: the confron-

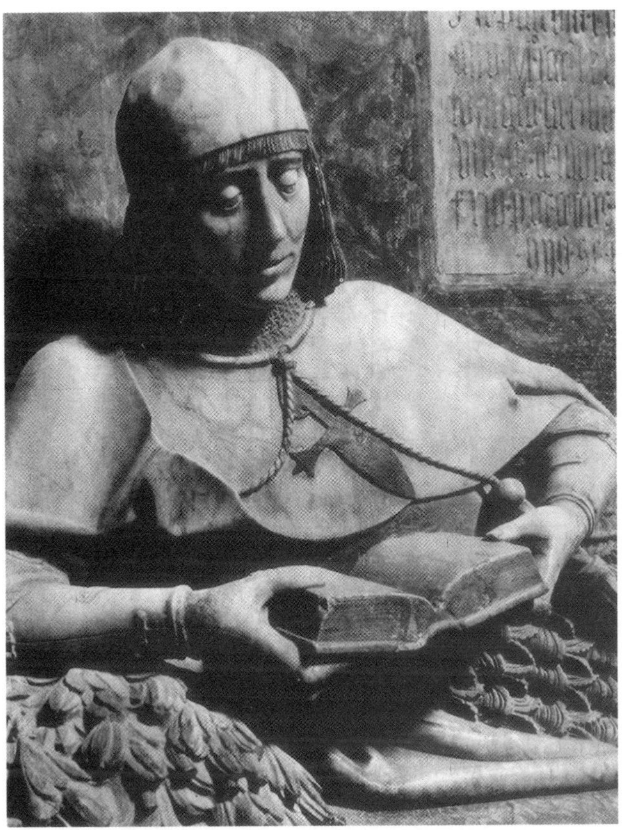

94. "Doncel of Sigüenza," detail, tomb, Cathedral of Sigüenza

tation, conflict and final mingling of the two most ancient and contrasting worlds of proto-historic Iberia, the world of the life-activity and-fertility-evoking original "Iberians," participants in, if not co-builders of the enigmatic southern—Andalusian—culture of Tartessos (Tarshish of the Bible), so admired and coveted by the adventurous, silver-greedy Phocaean and Phoenician colonists; and the world of the ancient Celts, lovers of abstraction and of proud death; then, the interdiffusion of the two creating a Celto-Iberic nucleus—its memory, the memory of the tragic, freedom-unto-death defending Numantia,[82] still alive, erect today in Spain's lore and consciousness; and, finally, the universal mantle of Rome, the Helleno-Etruscan mantle, covering that primordial nudity.

A slow and complex maturation it was! Hence this marvel of ancient Spain and of its art—this most precious marvel among so many marvels of the ancient world: the interrogating, acute *verismo* of "La Dama de Elche" (*Plate 96*).

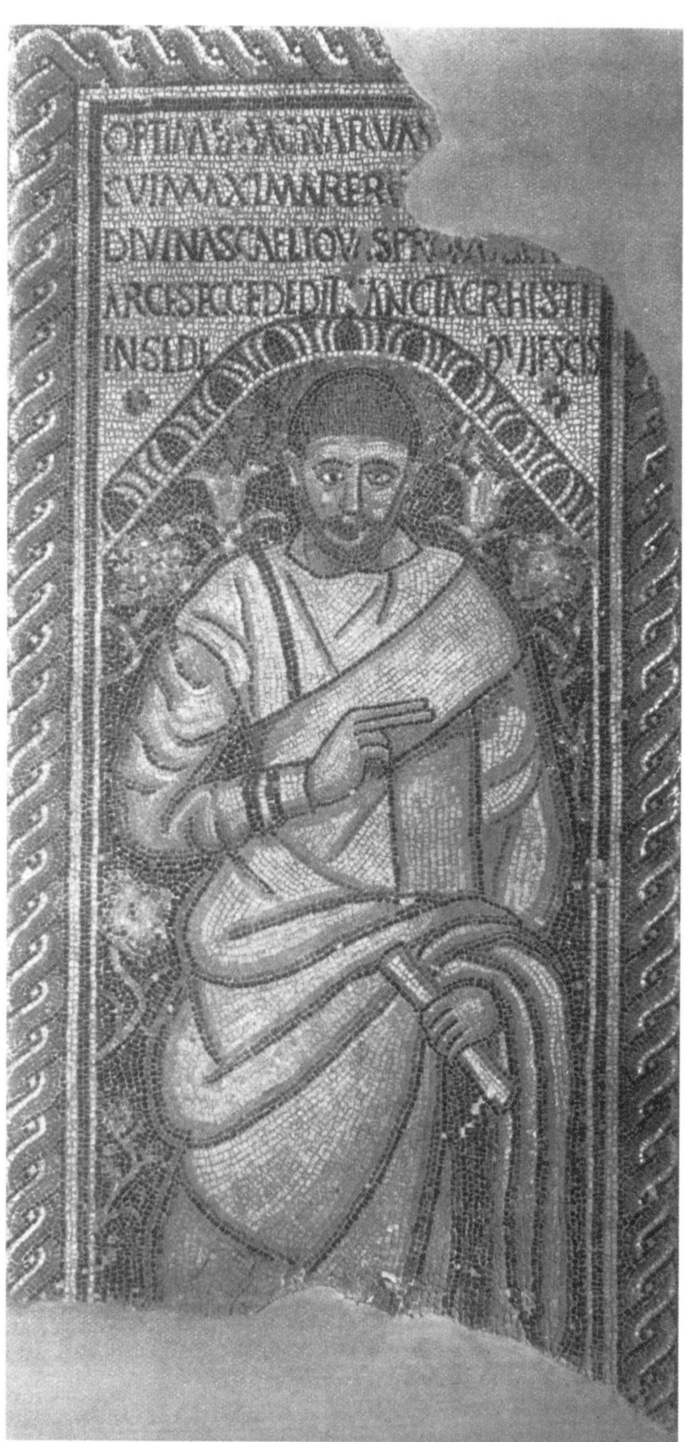

95. Funerary *lauda,* mosaic, Tarragona

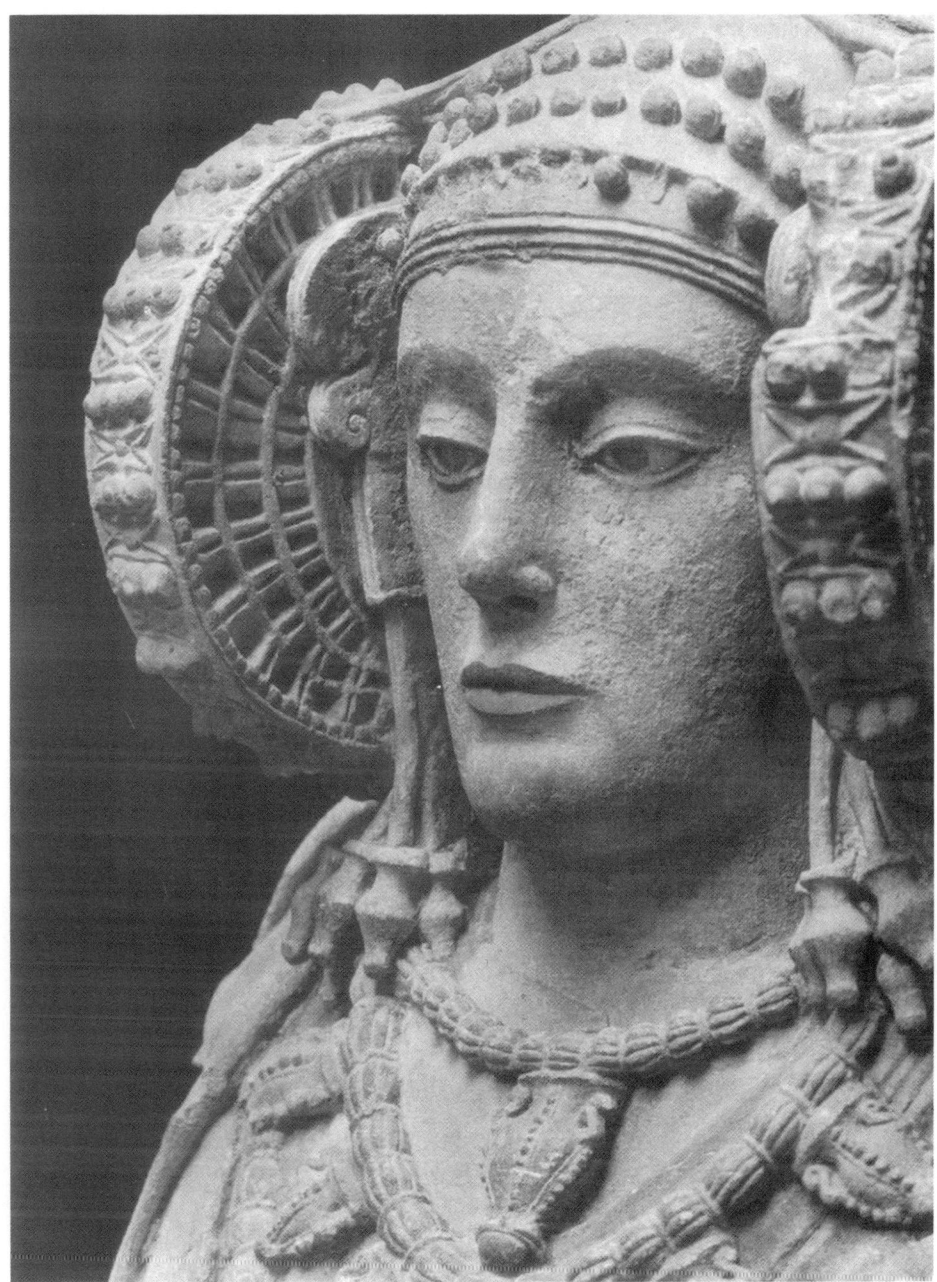

96. "La Dama de Elche," National Archaeological Museum, Madrid

*

For me there was no need any more to descend further. As I said before, I could not, even if I would, interrogate anything or anybody there. For this world where I was now was interrogation itself. The other world where I came from—both of them mine now—the world of Pandora's realities and evil gifts, was awaiting my return and my interrogation, later.

Here all was shadow. The Intrigue and the makers of it I came to know so well, the participants in it (myself included), all were invisible to me. Yet present. I knew it.

All was silence there and fulfillment—without secrecy, without mystery in it. (The true mystery, the little, poor winged mystery-never-to-be-interrogated—the young American guitar-accompanied singers'—was the other world's.)

Here all was silence: I, Spain and Spain's art—total interrogation. Nothing else. *The secret interrogating glance of eye's passion, of the eye's soul turned towards the enigma of life, towards death, became one with, was transferred, total, into the secret interrogating glance of art's spacing, of extension itself, and into the secret glance of art's timing, rhythm's embrace of all the senses;* art's and eye's secret told, thus banished here from all mystery's temptations.

Transfer, TRANSFER, T R A N S F E R—invisible and present Transfer-Personage (the fully awakened memory, present too and invisible), now made more present than anything, anybody else by the "Meninas" of Velázquez (seen not in a mirror, but in flesh) (*Plate 97a*). "Las Meninas": the glance of passion and interrogation piercing the mystery of pictorial *extension itself* (mystery and interrogation once told, banished); the metaphysical meaning and feel of extension, of spacing, both as motion away from my eye into the beyond-of-my-eye—thus continuing the one into the other in a mutual correspondence and transformation, a melodious, rounded, "mnemonic" movement there of people, of light, of shadows (*Plate 97b*)—and, at the same time, as the closest closeness to my eye, the beyond-of-my-eye contained in me, the beyond *ad infinitum* in the very narrowness of my eye's seizure as substitution, as identity-sacrifice, the silent, cutting immediacy, the "mobile rigidity," of the people, of lights, of shadows there, in "Las Meninas" (*Plate 98*).

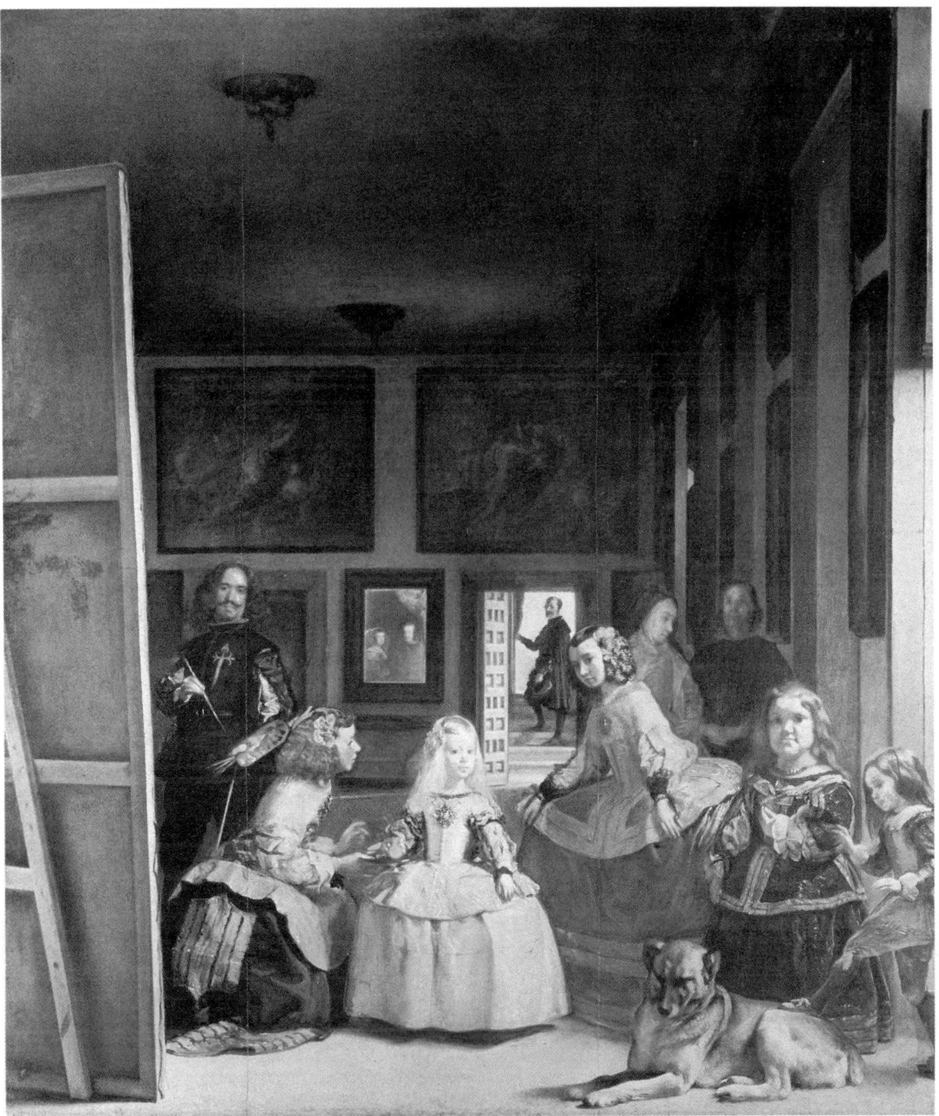

97a. Velázquez, *Las Meninas*

Passion. All interrogation. Glance of Apocalyptic terror-rest and of Psychomachic freedom and choice: "Las Meninas" of Velázquez.

Art's mystery, told and banished at once. Interrogation by someone dead and brought to life: the glance of Lazarus—the

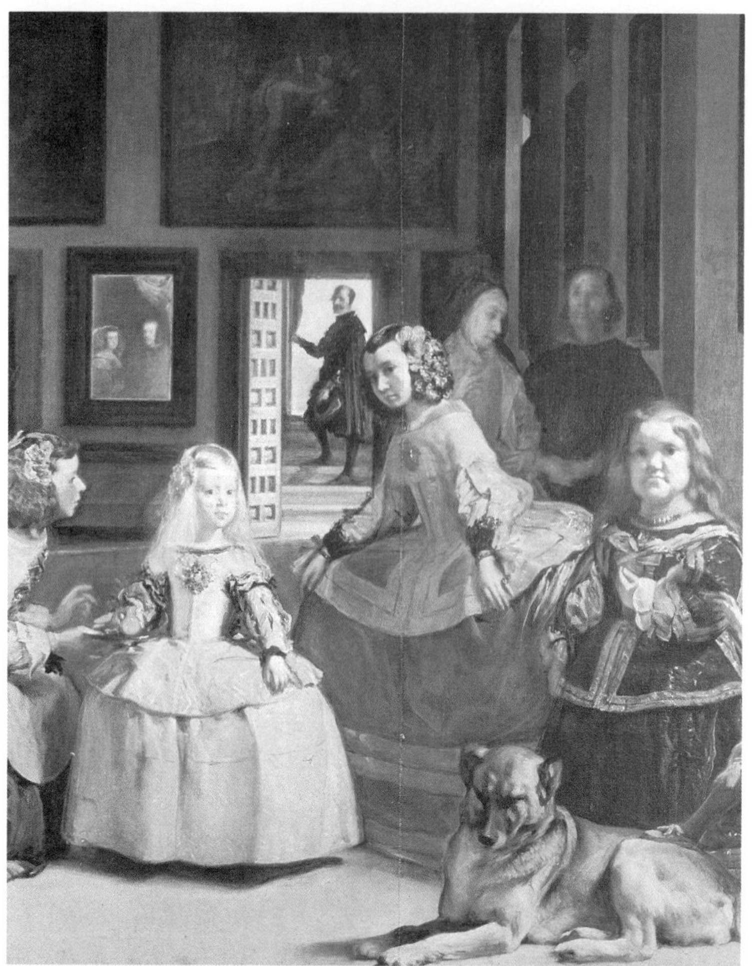

97b. Detail of 97a

space-extension in ''Las Meninas''—of Lazarus resurrected and pursuing his interrupted-by-death everyday activity, friendly, neighborly, active, liked by all, Lazarus whose eyes, however, when meeting the eyes of others would bring to them, frightening them to death, not knowing why, the living memory of having been buried, having been in death.[83]

And, confident as I was now, I gave the name ''Rite of Interrogation'' to the sub-story of the story painted by Goya (between 1798 and 1799) on the walls, the cupola, the apse of Madrid's San Antonio de la Florida. Here the glance of passion and interrogation pierces the secret of art's timing, of musical spacing—a secret told and banished—painter's rhythm embracing all senses, taste, smell,

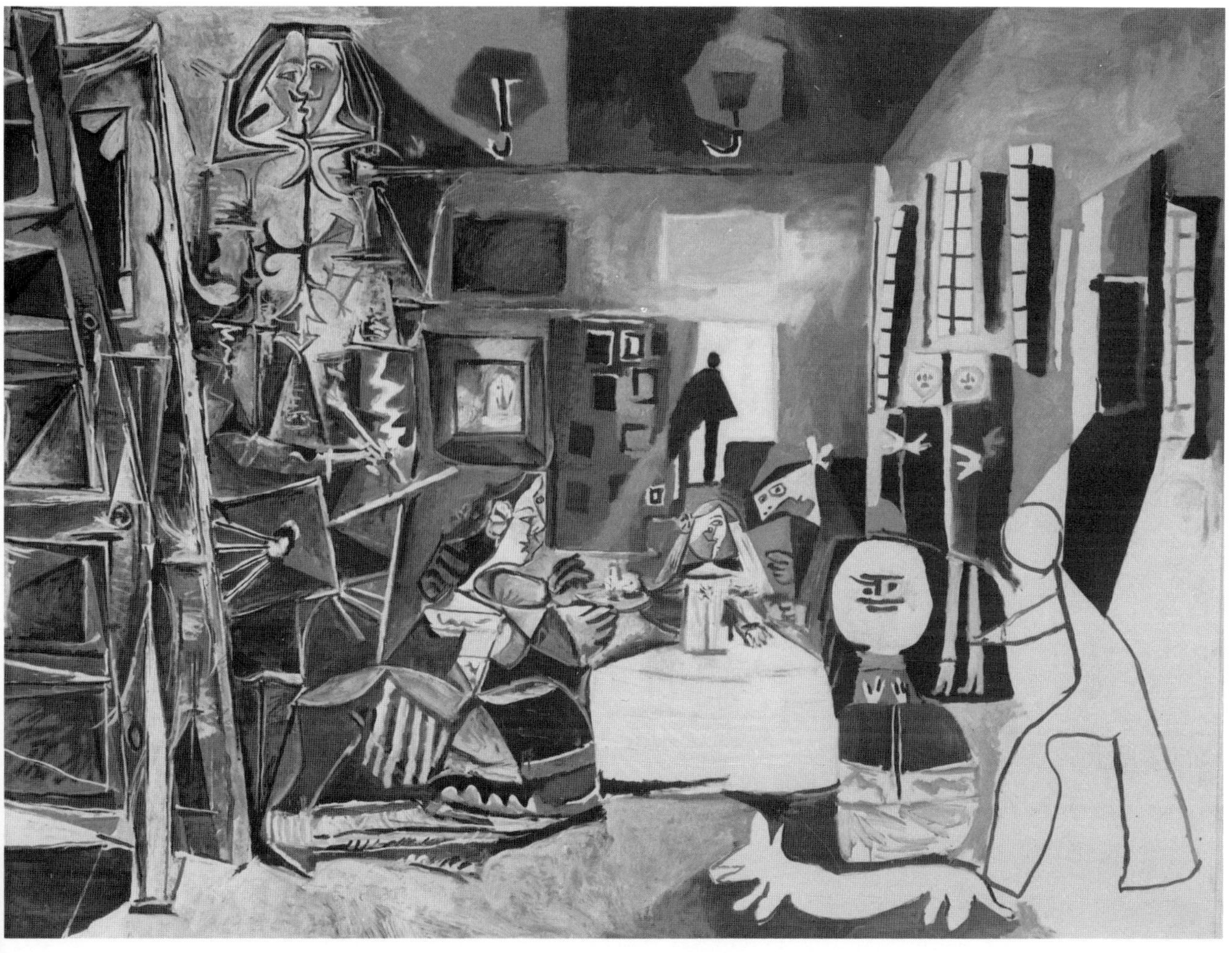

98. Picasso, *Las Meninas*

touch, sound, vision, ideation (''a painter paints what he does not paint''),[84] the entire history and prehistory of man at once in it! Heavy, very heavy, fleshy curtains, too heavy for even the earthy robust angels, pretty robust girls (*Plate 99*)—matinal angels walking along the luminous, wintry and busy streets of Madrid, Atocha or Pez!—Goya's heaven-bound angels, thrusting the cumbersome earthly obstacles apart—those curtains!—to make visible up there—higher! higher!—the confrontation from opposite sides of the painted inner cupola, and among the tumult of a suddenly enlightened, otherwise unbelieving or indifferent, *turba multa,* of two miracles, the miracle of Saint Anthony of Padua raising from death

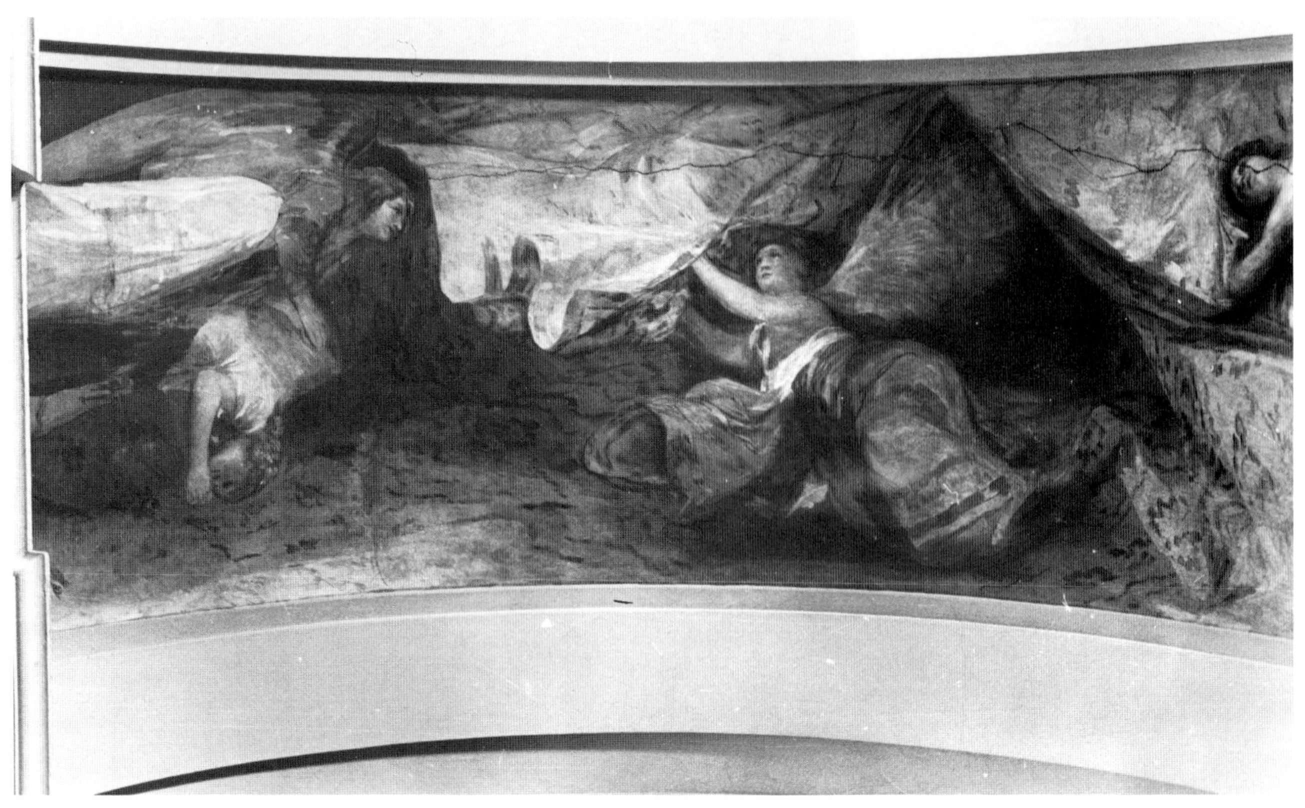

99. Goya, two angels, beneath cupola, San Antonio de la Florida, Madrid

a murdered man and that of an ''ecstatic''[85] bystander *suddenly, miraculously* discovering and announcing the real, new meaning, hidden from all present, of the miracle.

In the center of the cupola's northern section is the tight group formed by the saint—a familiar, unassuming, ''average'' figure of a young monk—witnessing his own miracle of compassion and tenderness, and, in front of him, the onlookers surrounding the resuscitated and supported corpse of the assassinated man, meekly and submissively[86] rising at the saint's call (*Plate 100*).

In exact counterpart to the humble saint's figure, Goya erected, across the entire span of the cupola, the heroic figure of a young bystander-witness (*Plate 101*) dominating triumphantly, defiantly, as it were, hand and glance uplifted, the surrounding sky, earth and turbulent humanity, Goya's witness-discoverer, witness-announcer who stands, erect, in isolation—in solitude—yet in full solidarity with the young saint's miracle, performed by,

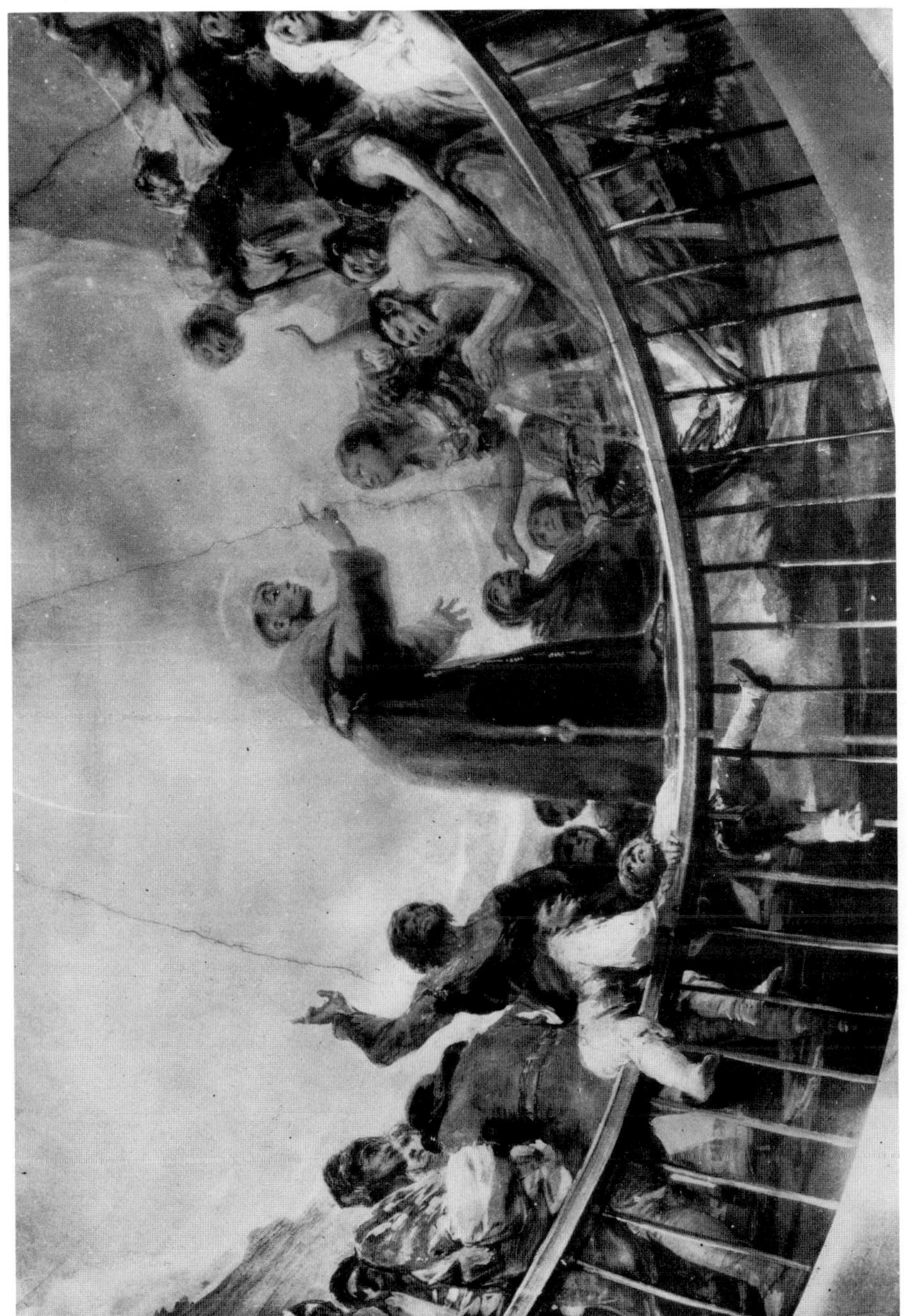

100. Goya, Miracle of St. Anthony of Padua, cupola, San Antonio de la Florida, Madrid

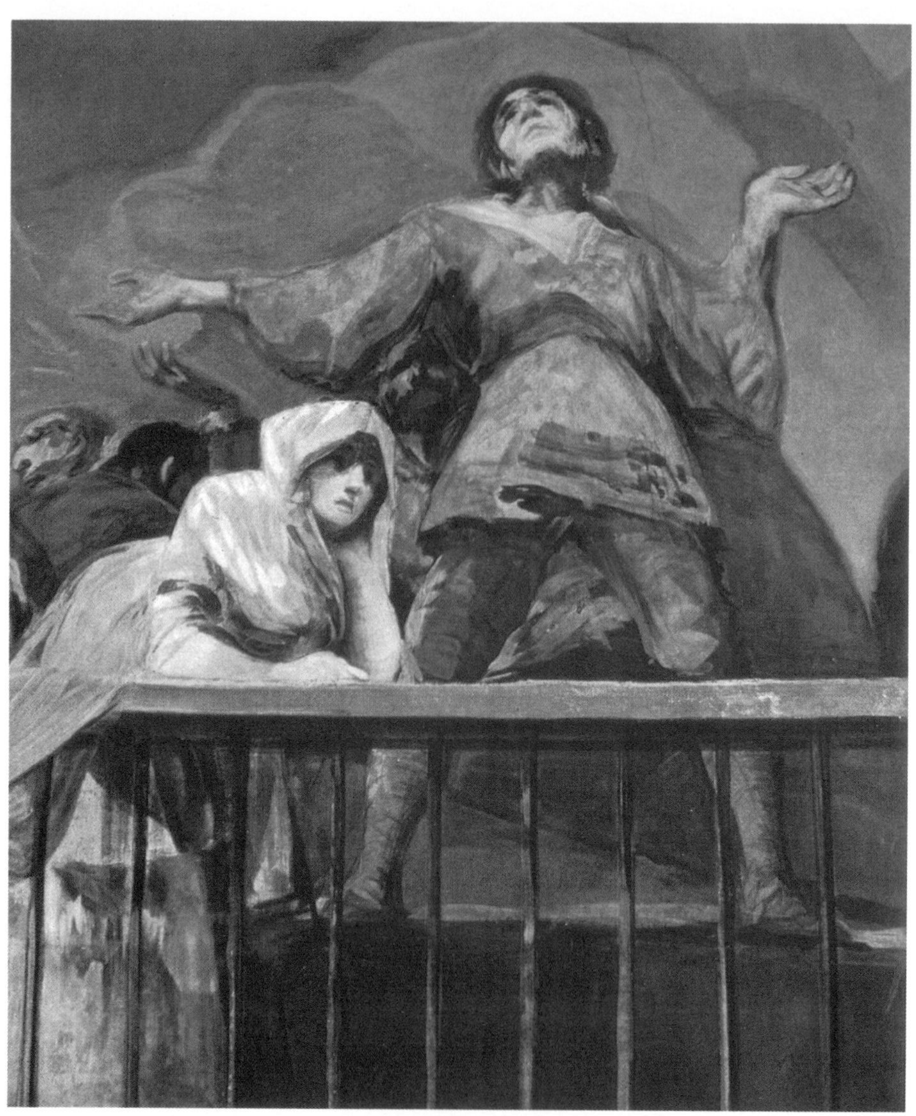

101. Goya, the witness of the miracle, cupola, San Antonio de la Florida, Madrid

for and with him, but ordered by someone Else, by Another: *Sanctus! Sanctus! Sanctus!*

Which of the two witnessings, perhaps two miracles, is "greater" or more sacred, truer, better and more beautiful? Which? The white éclat of interrogation, the white linen thrown across the painted railing that encircles the cupola (*Plate 102*), the blind and blinding great white laid upon the slippery, icy grey sky—cry, despair, interrogation!—this space created by Goya, his timing and interrogation, so Tiepolesque in its staccato rhythm, is

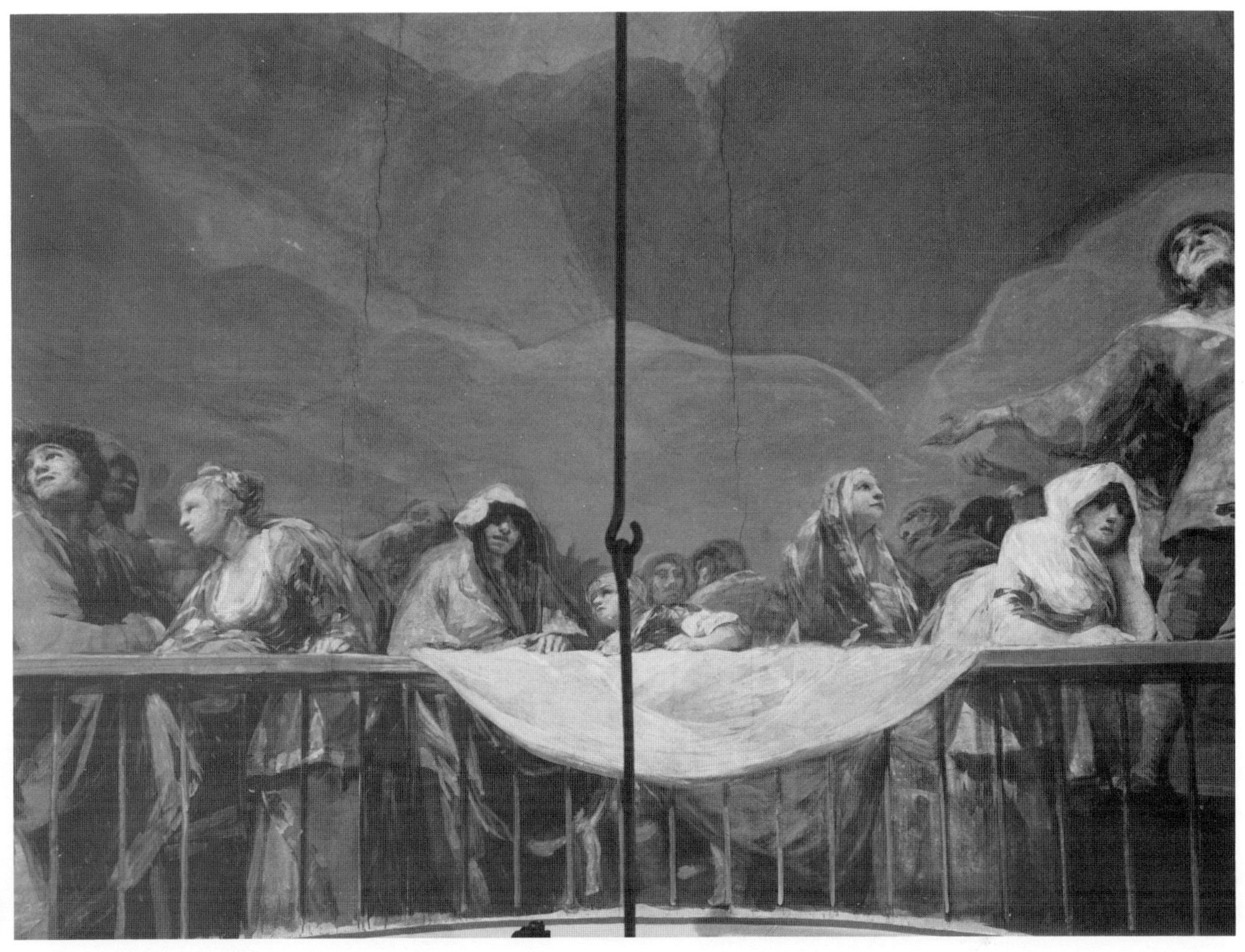

102. Goya, linen on railing, base of cupola, San Antonio de la Florida, Madrid

all Spain's answer, Spain's and Goya's, and not the Spain of the elite but of the passionate, interrogating *vulgus* made sacred by election, awakening and elevation: San Antonio de la Florida, the *credo* of Goya and of Spain, is Christianity's *credo* and interrogation, Christianity's because not secret, but open to all. Open, everybody's, human, basal, universal and Spanish, Spanish *only* because so passionate. To me, then, like the opening of the ultimate Seal, a metaphysical (I called it so just now and not unwittingly) interrogation.

A metaphysical interrogation, I say, because its roots are the roots of two braided (the Braid! Of all the Ancestor's children only the Braid could make visible its presence now and here!) opposites in all man's existential decisions: Certainty and Faith. And Certainty was testified to before me as man's conviction that the finite I and the un-finite *Not-I* are at peace—however temporarily—one with the other: Atman-Brahman, the revolving Wheel containing, carrying, both of them simultaneously, the I plunging in full confidence of being, into the distance of not-being, distant also from all anxiety; certainty, wholly correspondence, transformation, significance and fullness of answer—India in all of us.

While (and not for an instant losing sight of the elusive Braid) Faith is not this. It is not the appeasement, but the absolute peace achieved through the touch of doubt, the touch by the believing Thomas of Christ's wound. Not conviction, certainty's reassuring and convincing distance, but closest proximity of faith to doubt—the *credo quia absurdum est:* faith to doubt as light to shadow, inseparable; identity, not correspondence, of the I-fragment and the total not-I; *''certitude, certitude, joie!''* of Pascal, who meant, for all that, ''Certainty of Doubt, of anxiety, yet Certainty, joy!''—Christianity in all of us.

And still more narrowly within my present world—from transfer to transfer in depth—I saw Spanish art's *verismo* to be precisely this: the doubting touch of St. Thomas' fingers (*Plates 103a&b*). So passionate, so persistent in its intensity is Spain's choice, that the presence of these two opposites of man's interrogation, of man's universal and inevitable, thus ''normal,'' crisisness, Western par excellence, could be projected with more persistence, intensity and historical clarity in the art of Spain than elsewhere in the world. *That is why I call Spain the mirror of the West,* a magnifying mirror: it reveals the same series of Western man's crises, but magnified into truly epic proportions and size. And so the history of the Peninsula's visual thought can be followed simultaneously along each of its two primary currents: the art of faith-doubt, of Substitution, of Apocalyptic proximity, of what is given as a possible reality in its impossible, suddenly real, proximity, and the art of persuasion, of convincing interdiffusion between proximity and distance, the art and metaphysics of the ''significant ornament''—with the braiding, the blending of both of them.

Here: the most significant and surprising monuments of

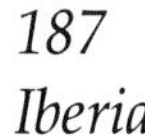

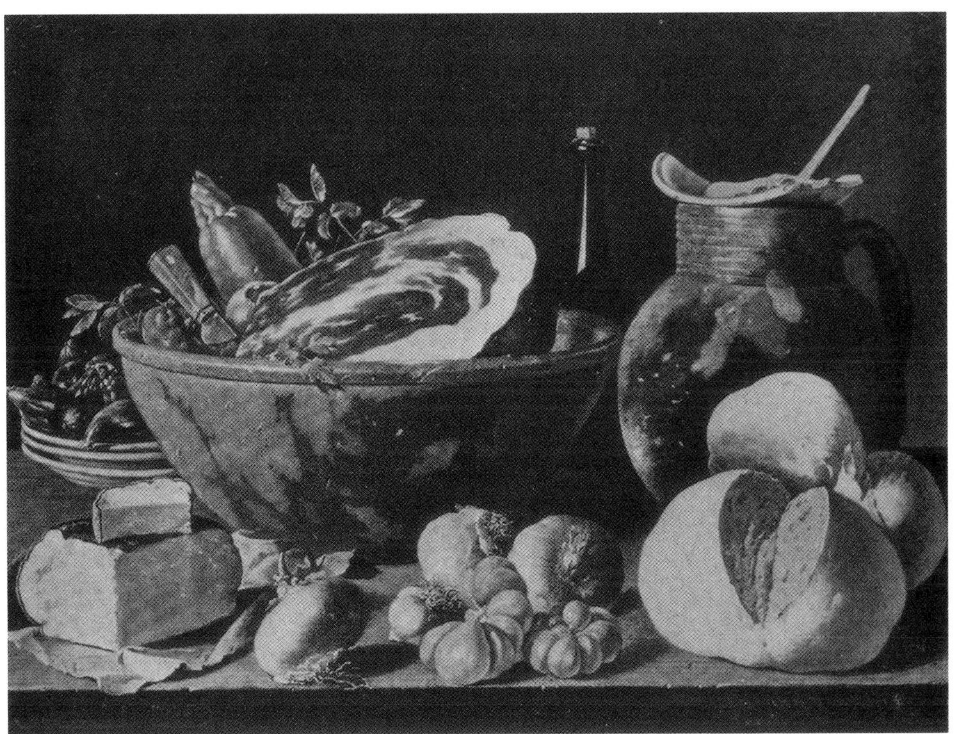

103a. Luis Eugenio Meléndez, Still Life

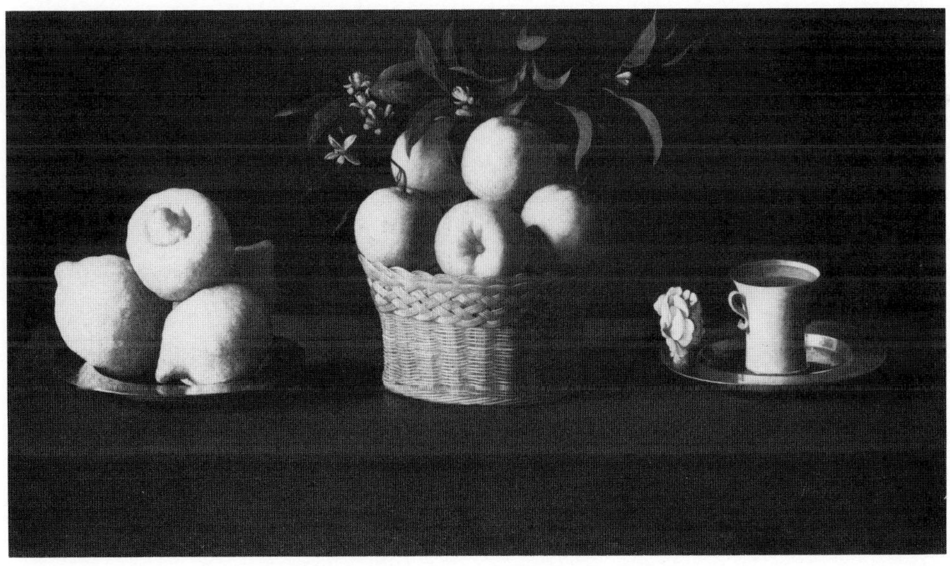

103b. Francisco de Zurbarán, Still Life

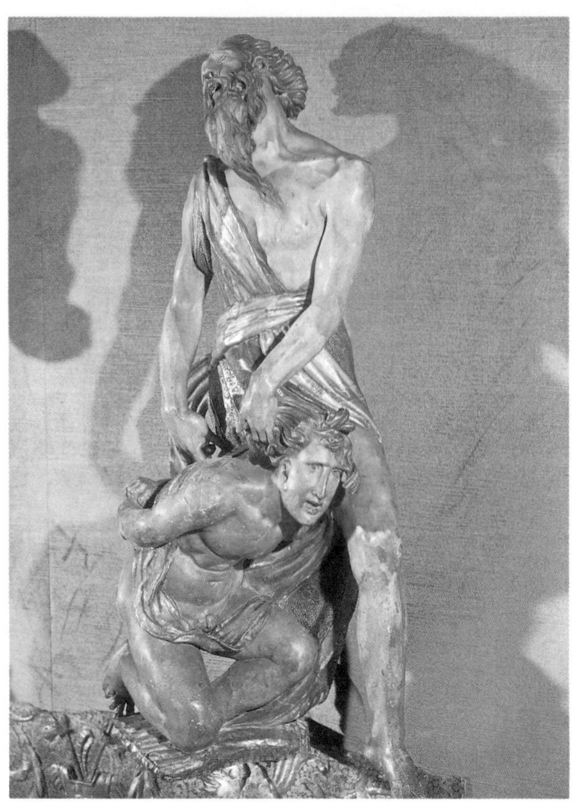

104a. Alonso Berruguete, Abraham and Isaac

purely Spanish *verismo,* the monuments of faith-doubt—the pious sculptures in wood, figures isolated or grouped together, the processional *Pasos,* of the late sixteenth, the seventeenth, and eighteenth centuries, Alonso Berruguete's (*Plates 104a&b*), Gregorio Hernández' (*Plate 105*), Manuel Pereira's (*Plate 106*), Juan Martinez Montañes' (*Plate 107*), Alonso Cano's (*Plate 108*), Pedro de Mena's (*Plates 109a&b*) or Francisco Salzillo's (*Plates 110a&b*)—dolls or toys of death-proximity, mimicry of passion, of "my soul turned toward the enigma of life," of sorrow, menace and finite rest, art terrible and sweet, everybody's, "vulgar," unique in the entire world.

Here also the most significant, truly surprising monuments of Spain's metaphysical certainty—the telling significance of the Romanesque "ornament-monster"; in painting perhaps best represented by its Catalan testimony, the linear and chromatic narratives of Pyrenean wall painting such as those in the churches of Santa María and San Clemente at Tahull and many others: the "Byzantine" Virgin and Child of Santa María's apse, so de-Byzantinized, because made one with, and not, as in Byzantium, rhythmically "accompanied" by her sky-throne, Virgin and

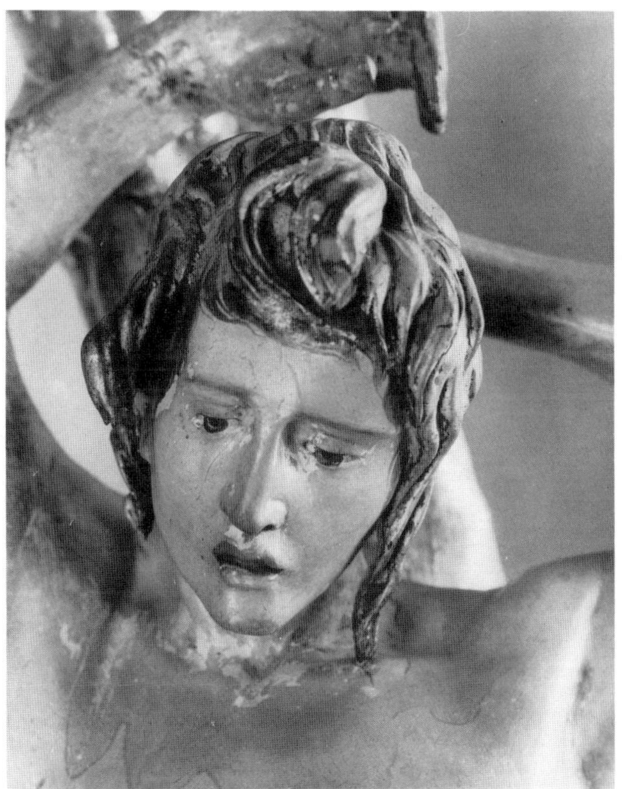

104b. Alonso Berruguete, St. Sebastian, detail

throne forming one ornament-block (*Plate 111*) (medieval Western man's schema of microcosmic-macrocosmic oneness, his certainty of correspondence and continuity told here in the very poetry of the com-position); the ''Byzantine,'' so de-Byzantinized Pantocrator (*Plate 112*) on the apse of San Clemente—the Light-signifying ''ornament-monster'': I am the light!—and the equally de-Byzantinized bust of the Virgin among the Apostles on the same apse.

But the ''Spanishness'' of the Catalan Romanesque pictorial monuments is not a factual, historical Spanishness; were they all Catalans, the Romanesque masters of Pedret, of Tahull, of Bohí, or Anau?—a local problem in art history not meriting, possibly, much scrutiny. Spain was there nonetheless, as I said before, precisely and only as an intensified global attitude, as a ''magnifying mirror'' of the West. The Catalan pictorial monuments' testimony is a towering one and becomes central as Spain's future-bearing message, in particular when they are compared with other, non-Catalan monuments, contemporary, or almost: the murals (especially the secular hunting scenes and animals) of the church of San Baudelio de Berlanga (twelfth century) near Soria (now in the

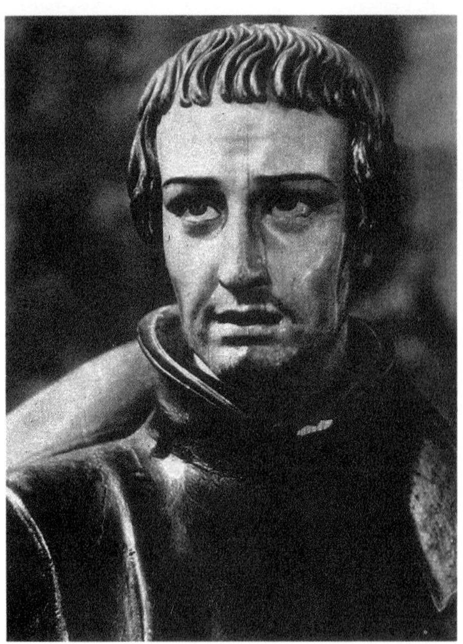

105. Gregorio Hernández (or Fernández), St. Francis Xavier, detail

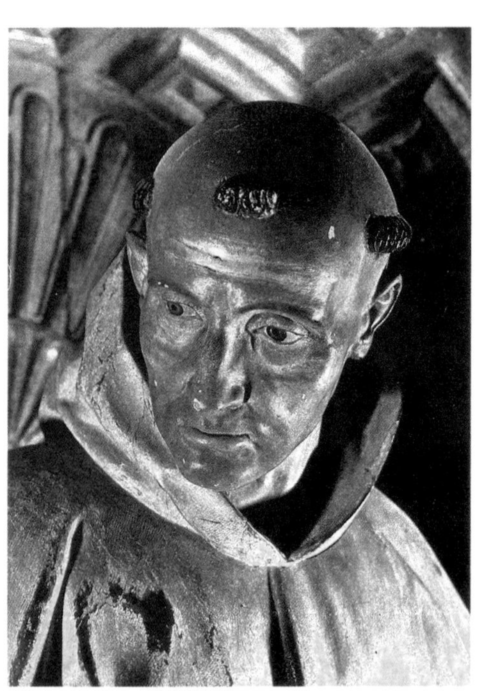

106. Manuel Pereira, St. Bruno, detail

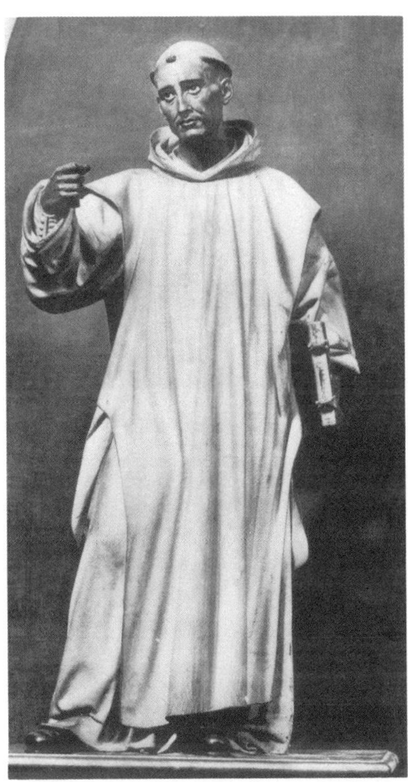

107. Juan Martínez Montañés, St. Bruno

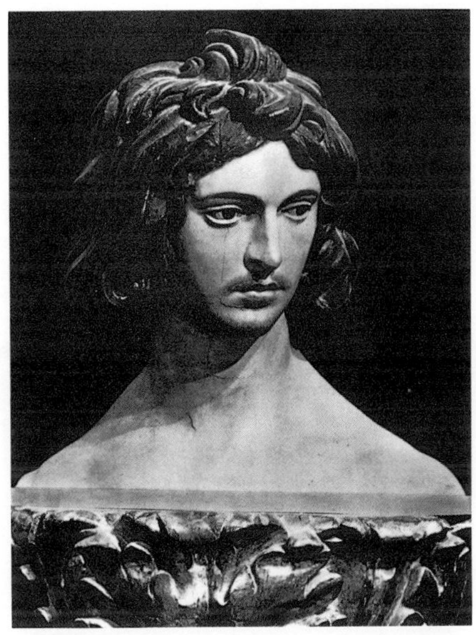

108. Alonso Cano, unfinished bust of Adam

Prado) and the famous painted vaults of San Isidoro's Pantheon de los Reyes in León, the first enigmatically allied in style to "my" Jongleurs from the Catalan church of Bohí (*see Plate 1*), and both probably Mozarabic[87] in inspiration (*Plate 113*), that is, Visigothic-Merovingian (*see Plate 68*), with a direct touch of what I call Islamic "heraldism" (the self-positing, the self-situating of signifying "object-beings" on the "heraldic field").[88]

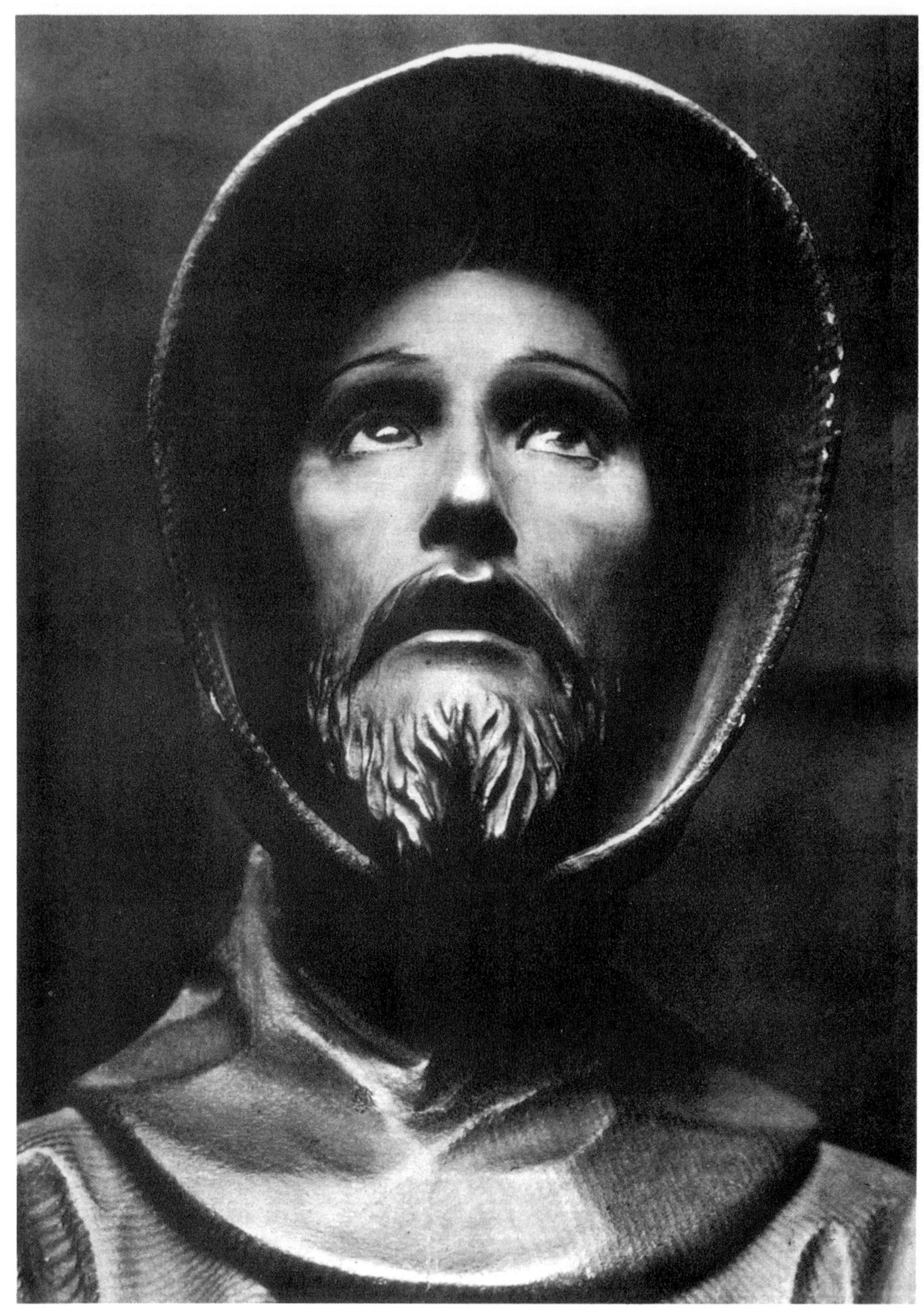

109a. Pedro de Mena, St. Francis of Assisi, detail

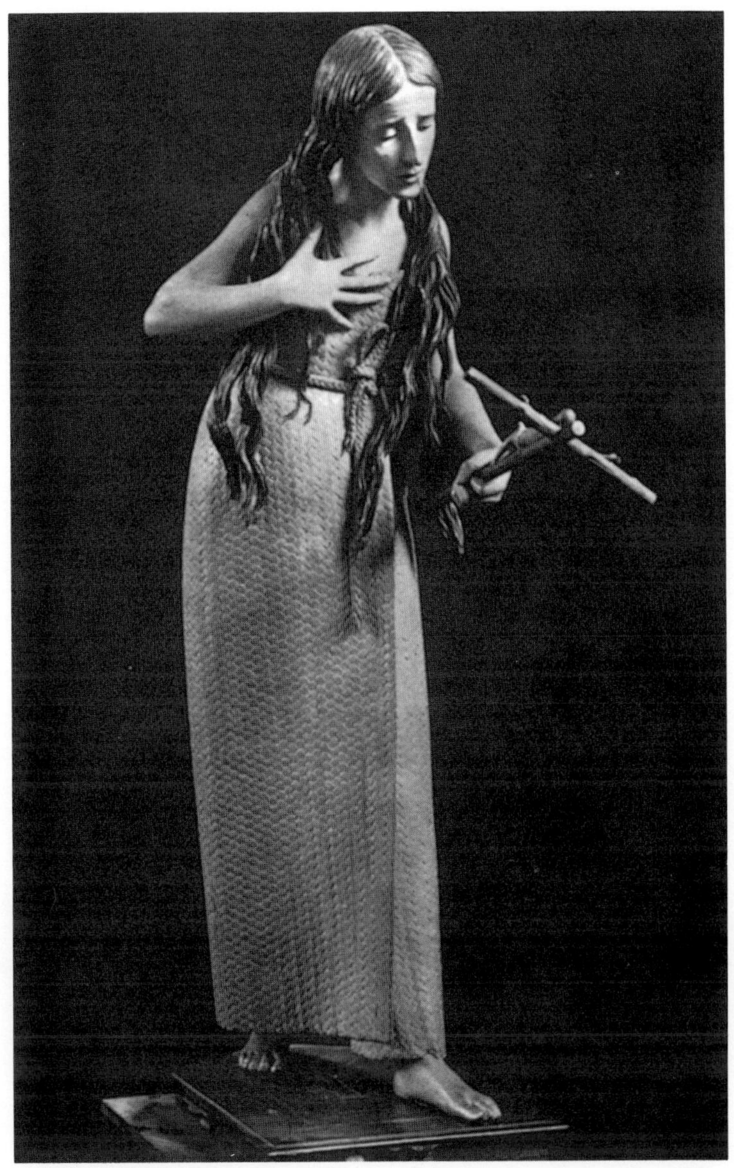

109b. Pedro de Mena, The Penitent Magdalen

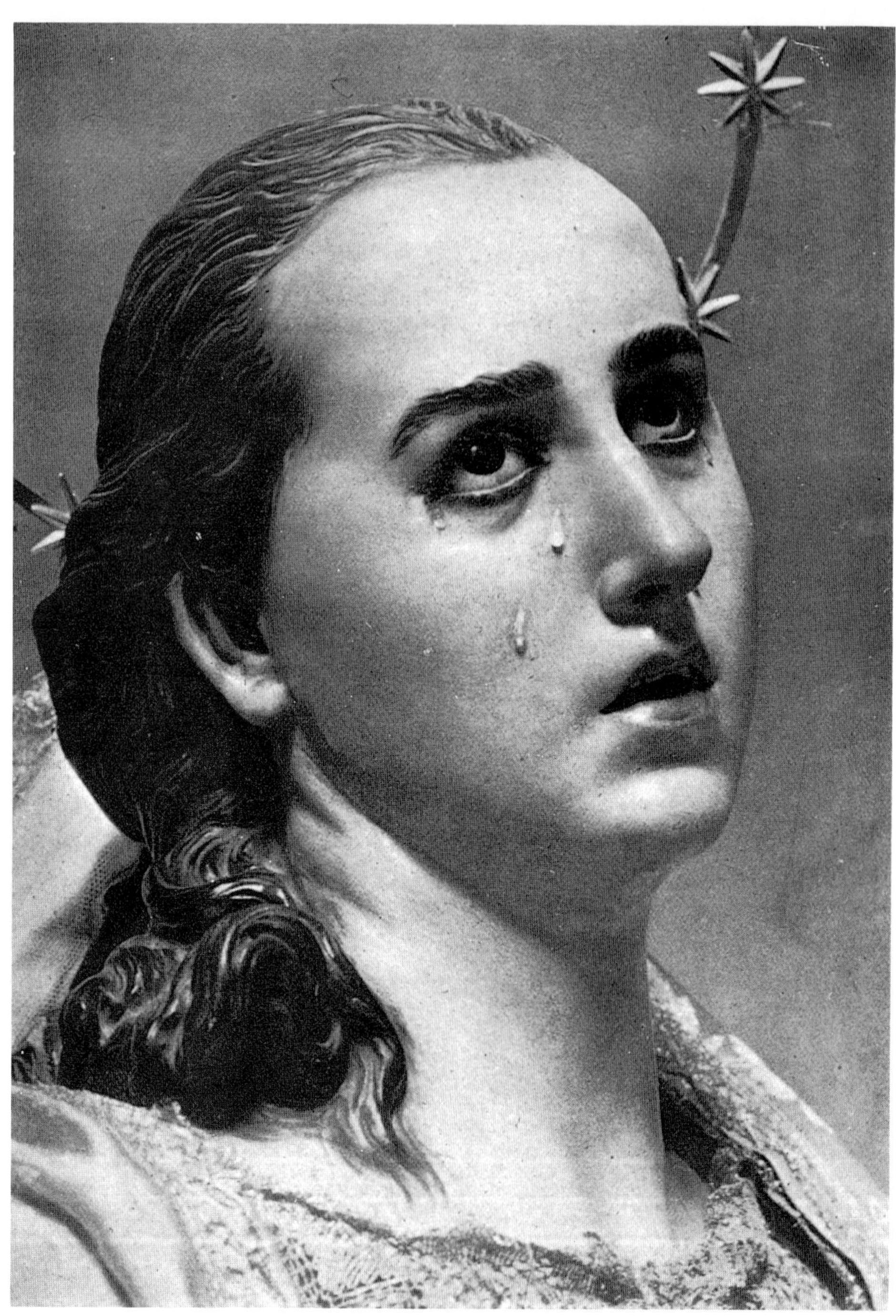

110a. Francisco Salzillo Alcaraz, Dolorosa, detail

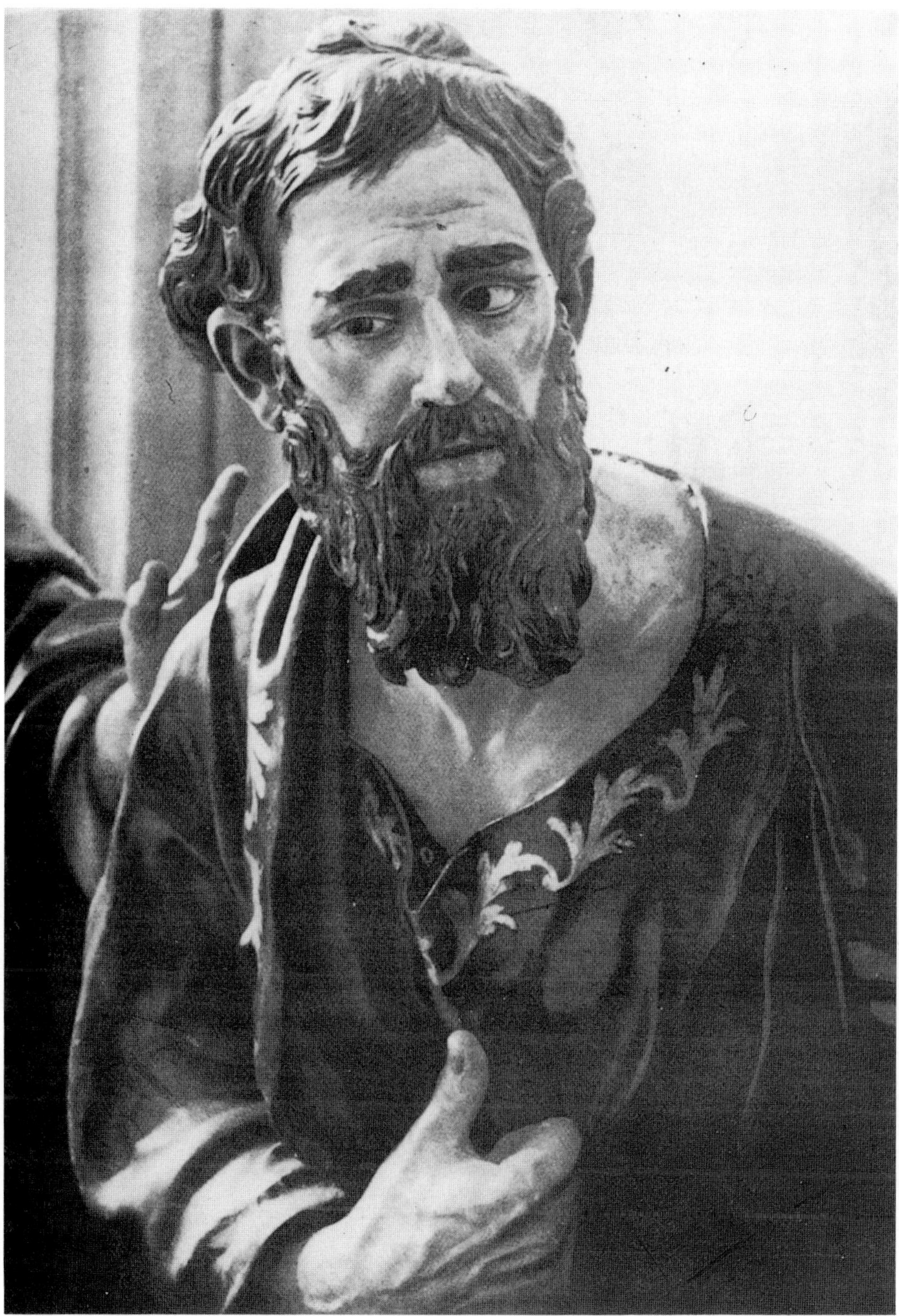

110b. Francisco Salzillo Alcaraz, Judas, detail

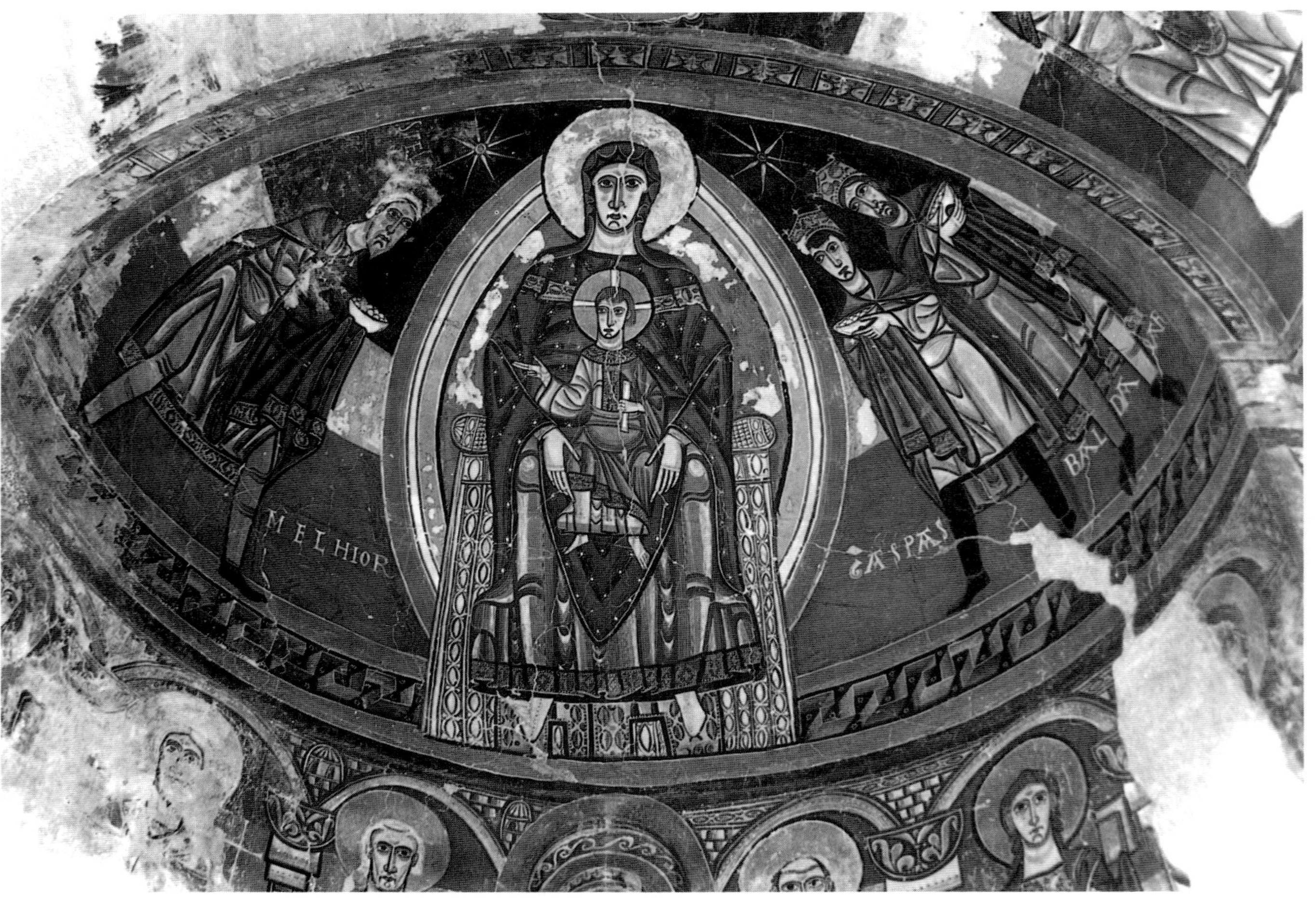


111. Seated Virgin, Sta. María de Tahull

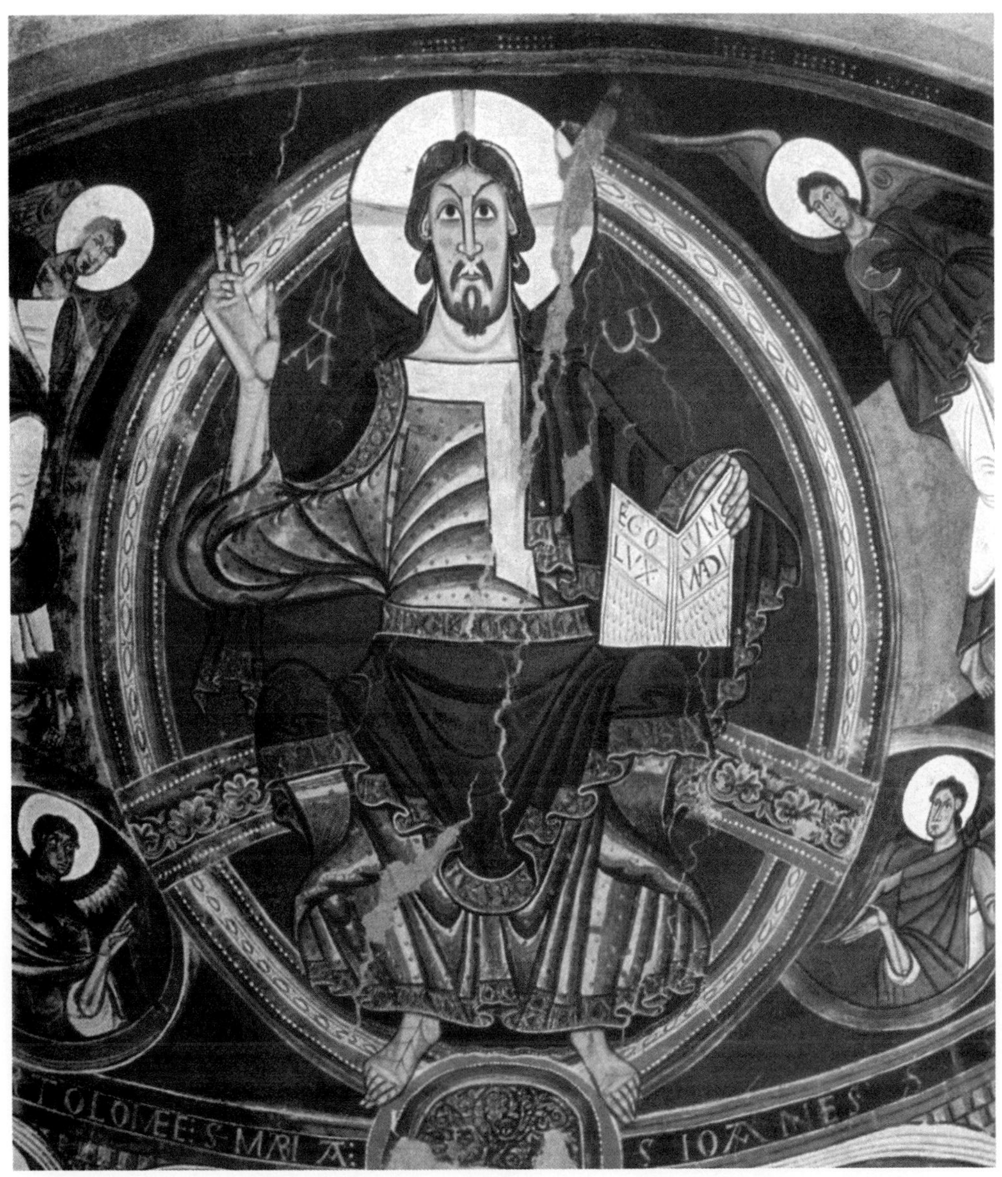

112. Pantocrator, San Clemente de Tahull (detail)

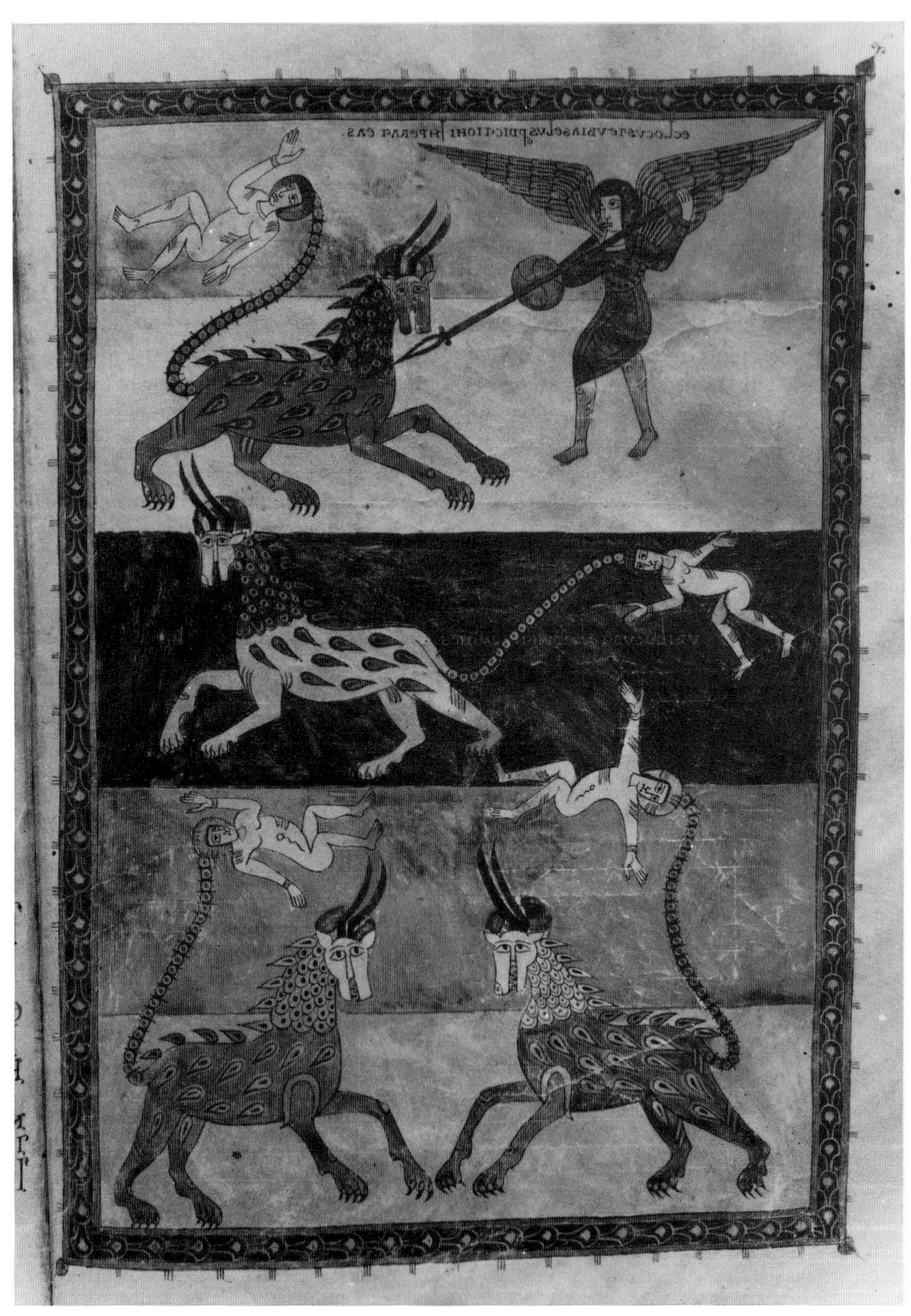

113. Page of Beatus Apocalypse, Gerona Cathedral

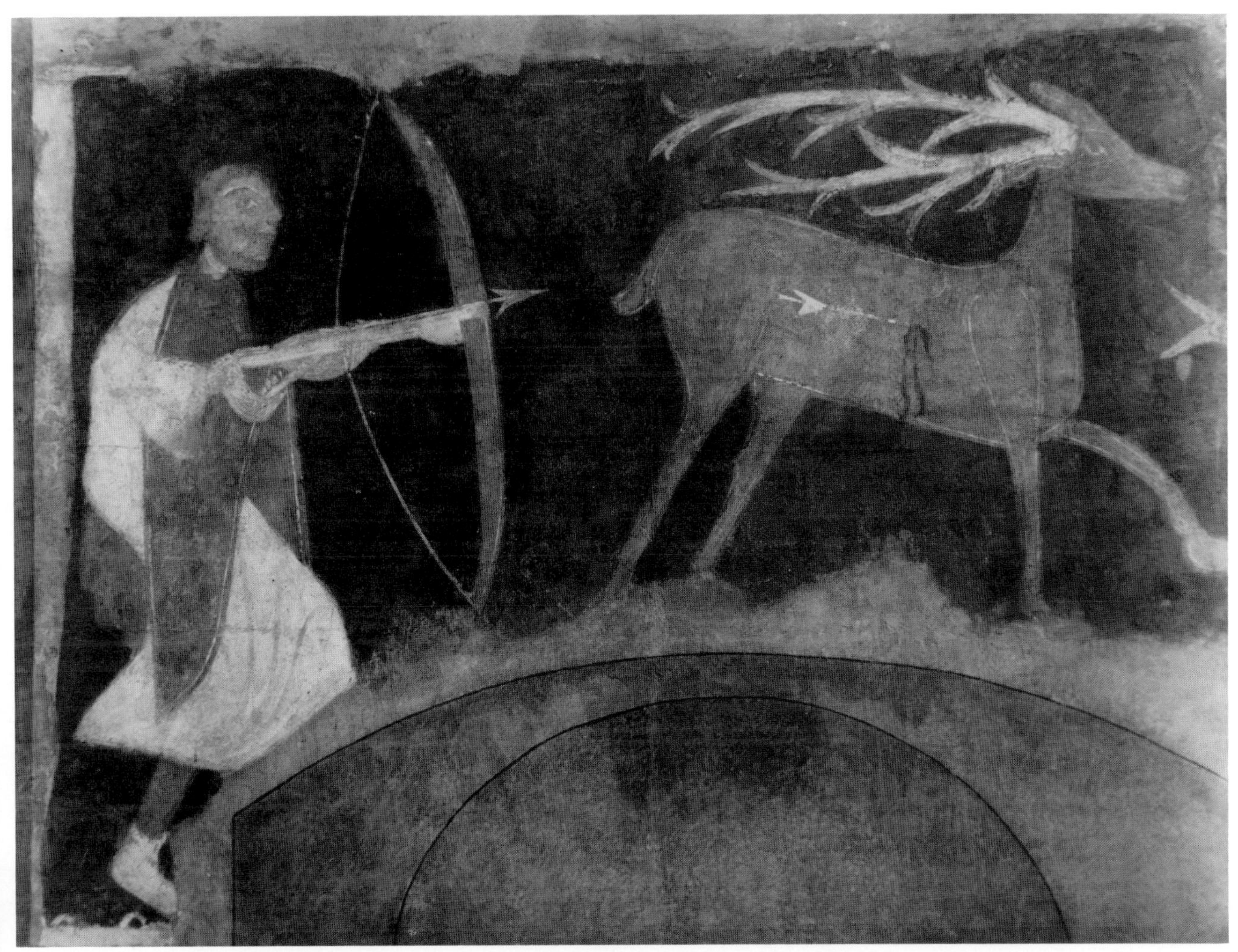

114. Deer pursued, ''Hunting scene,'' detail, mural, San Baudelio de Berlanga (Soria)

Enigmatic indeed is the hunting scene with the graceful inoffensive deer pursued by evil-looking men (*Plate 114*), a sinful, evil action redeemed in another scene where man's action becomes that of self-protection, self-shielding from a now evil beast (*Plate 115*) and the latter's hieratic, and heraldic, apotheosis as a chosen symbol of this psychomachic metamorphosis of evil into good (*Plate 116*).

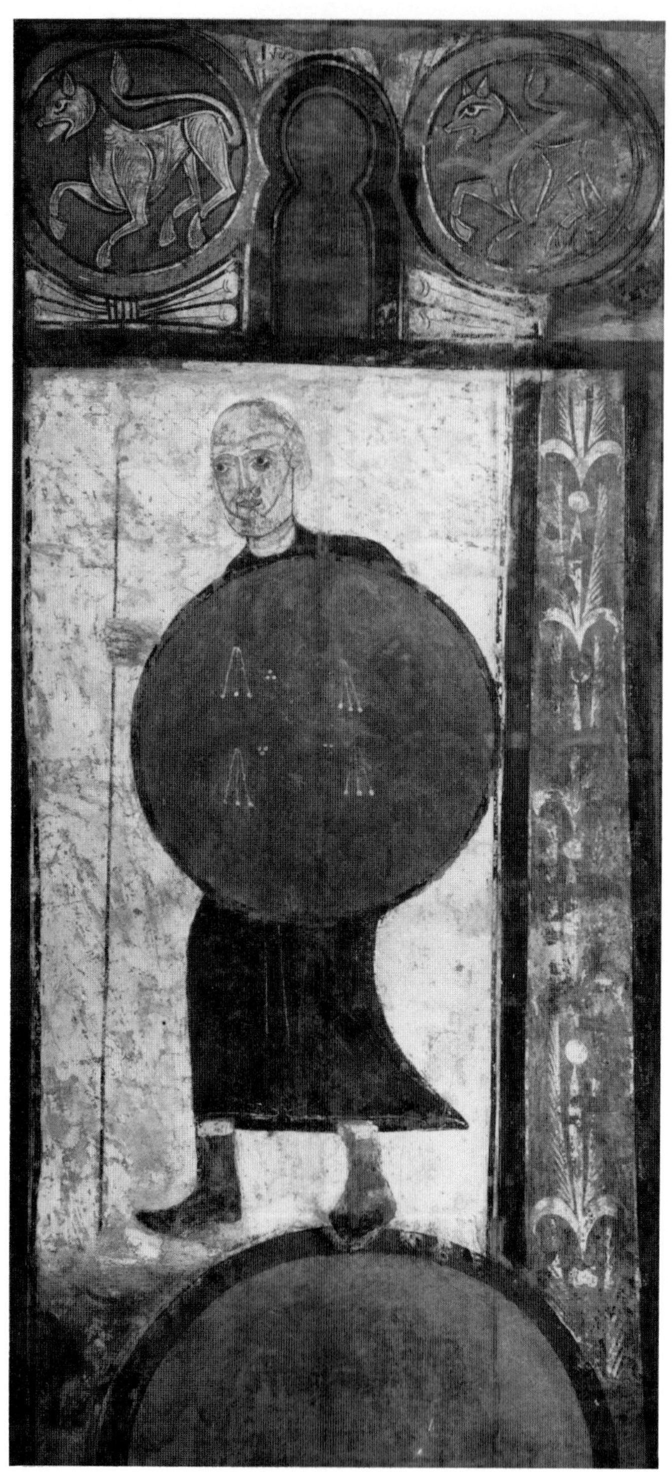

115. Man shielding himself from beast, "Hunting scene," detail, San Baudelio de Berlanga

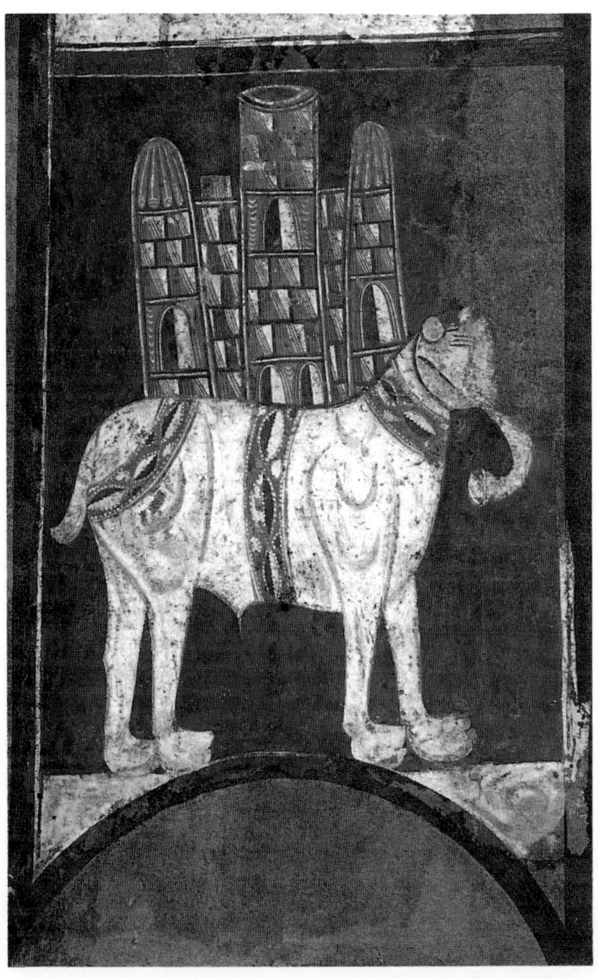

116. Elephant and castle, "Hunting scene," detail, San Baudelio de Berlanga

The painted vaults of San Isidoro, religious in subject matter, usually the most praised of all Romanesque Spanish paintings, are frankly un-Spanish in their mainly Italian accents, rounded, secure, at once suave and energetic in the rhythmic serenity and naturalness, the ease, of the famous "Pastoral Scene" (*Plate 117*), the playful dancing elegance of the Virgin's folds in "The Annunciation," all connections, not adhesion (*Plate 118*); the Italo-Byzantine plastic fleshy consistency and decorative "accompaniment" of the Pantocrator's mandorla, "classical" also the color harmonies there, the blending of blues, browns and greys, with no Tahull accents, no Tahull surprises!

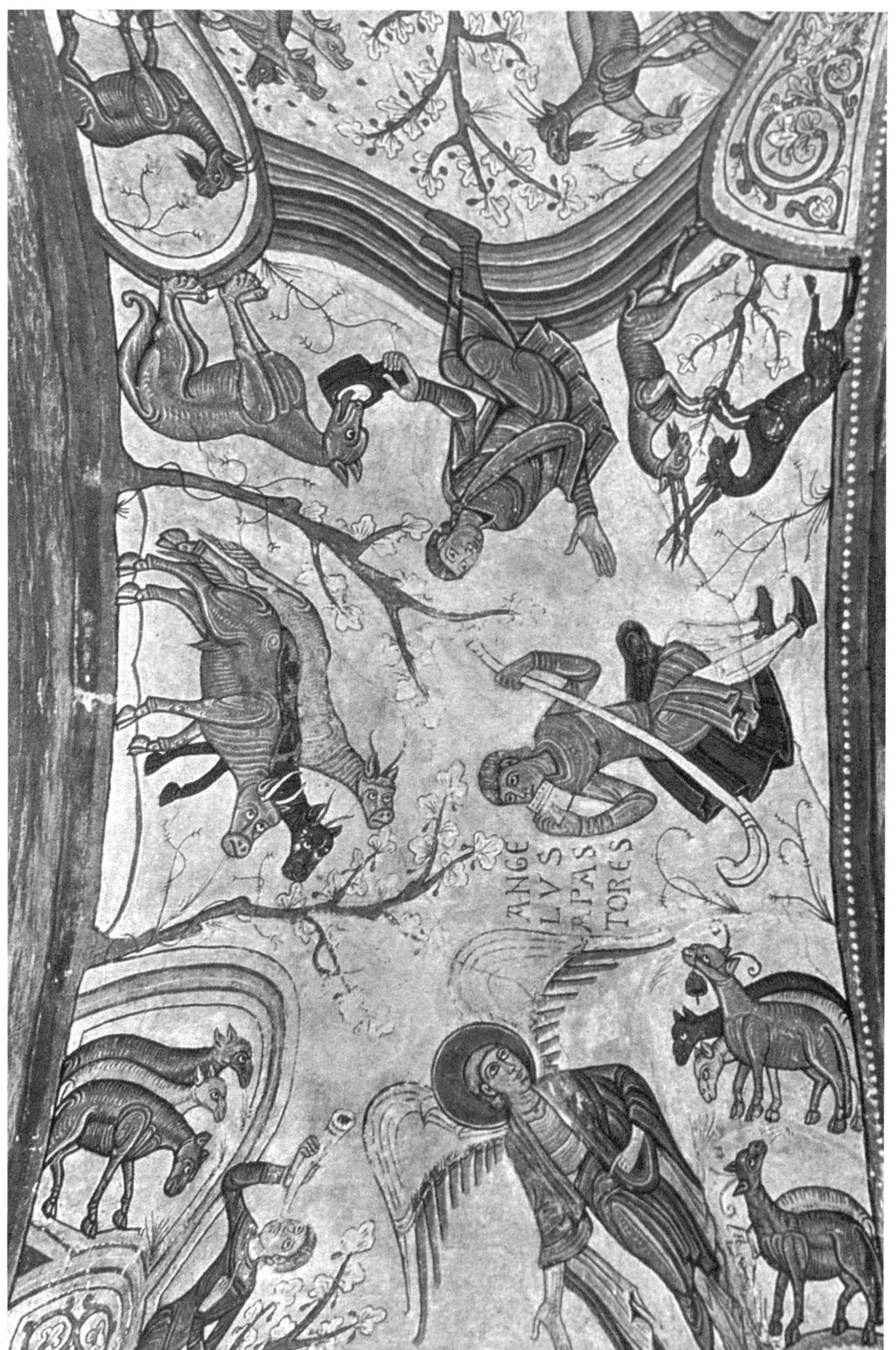


117. "Pastoral Scene," mural painting, San Isidoro, León

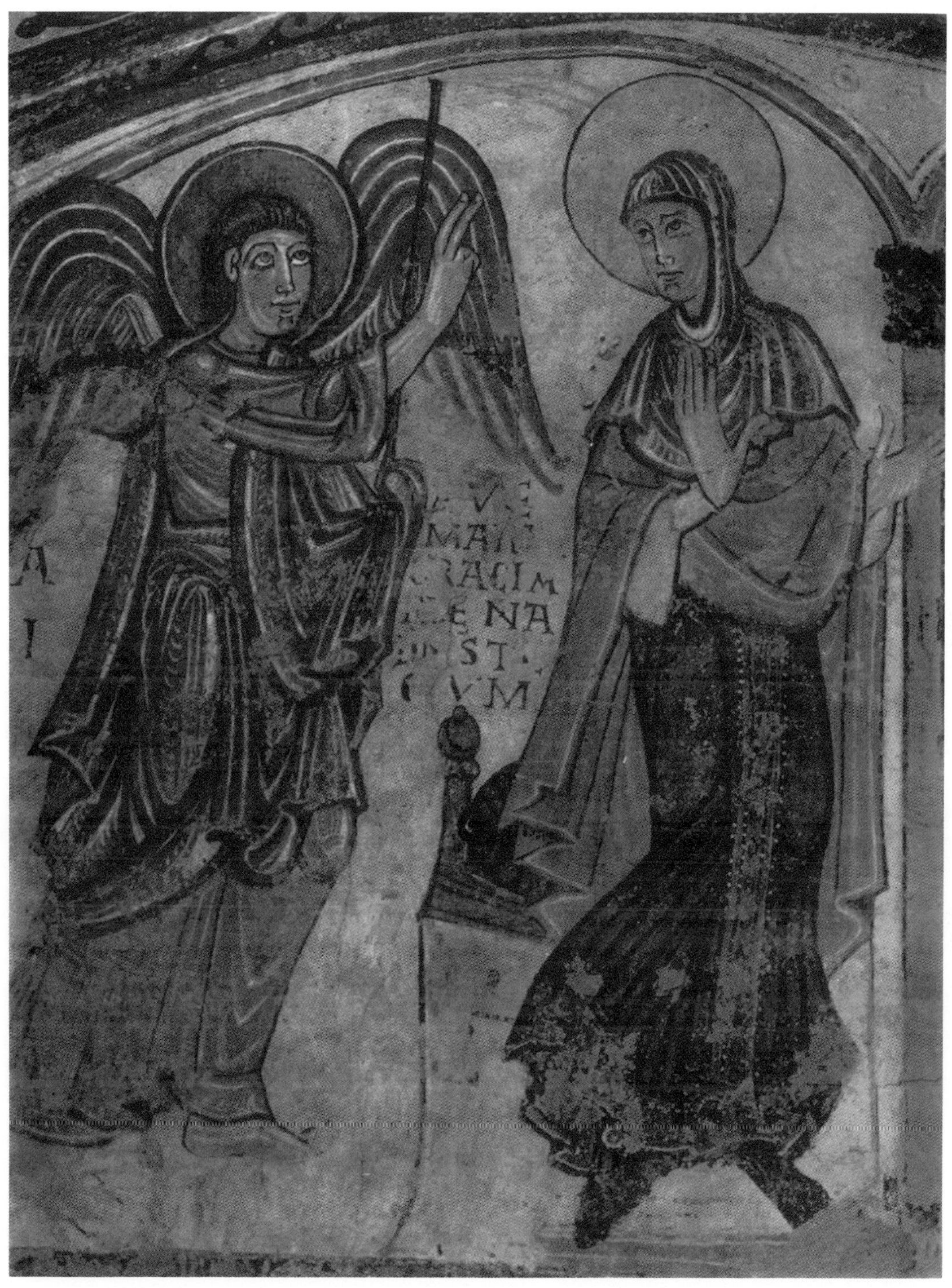

118. Virgin of the Annunciation, mural painting, detail, San Isidoro, León

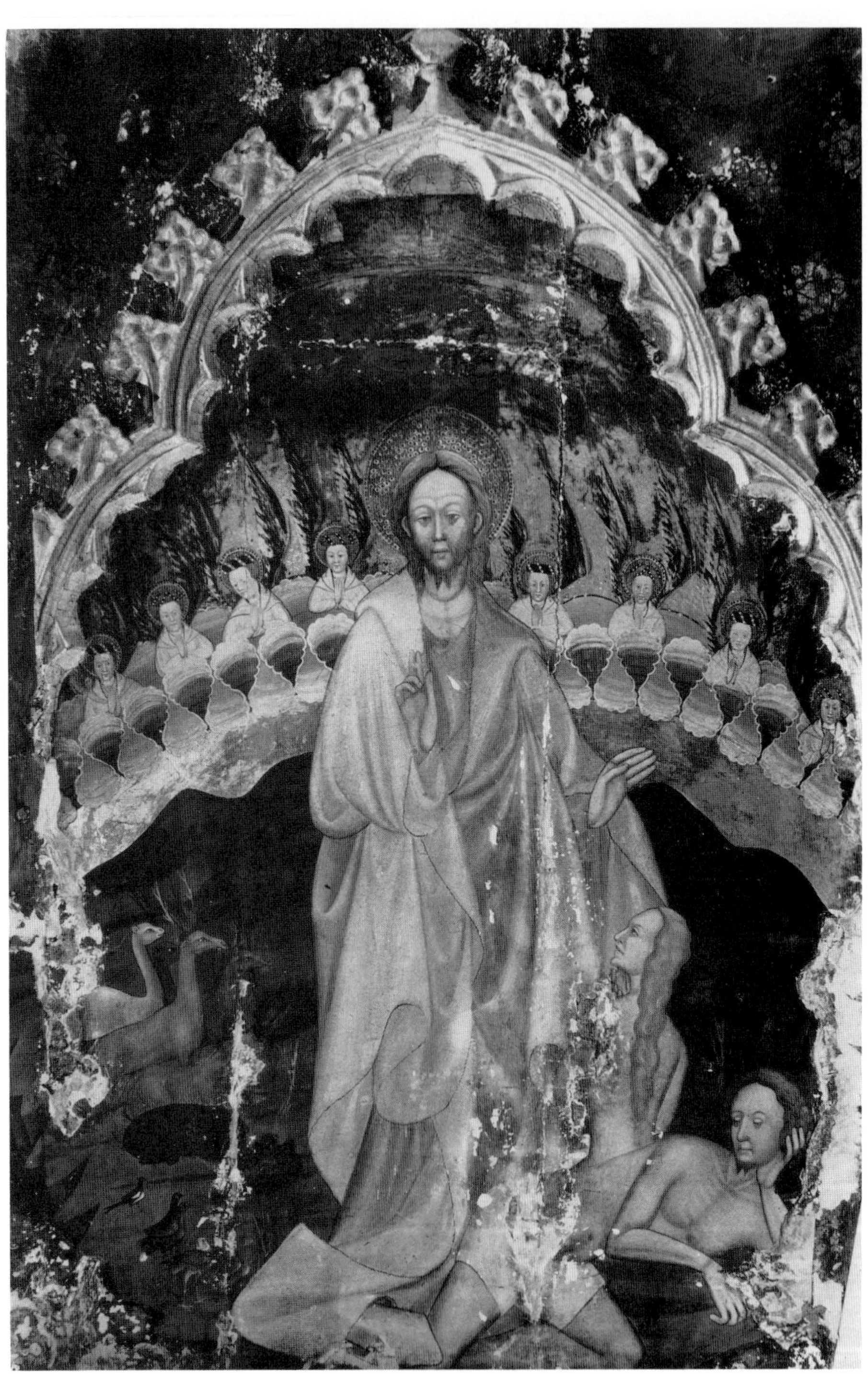

119a. Ramón de Mur, The Creation of Man and Woman

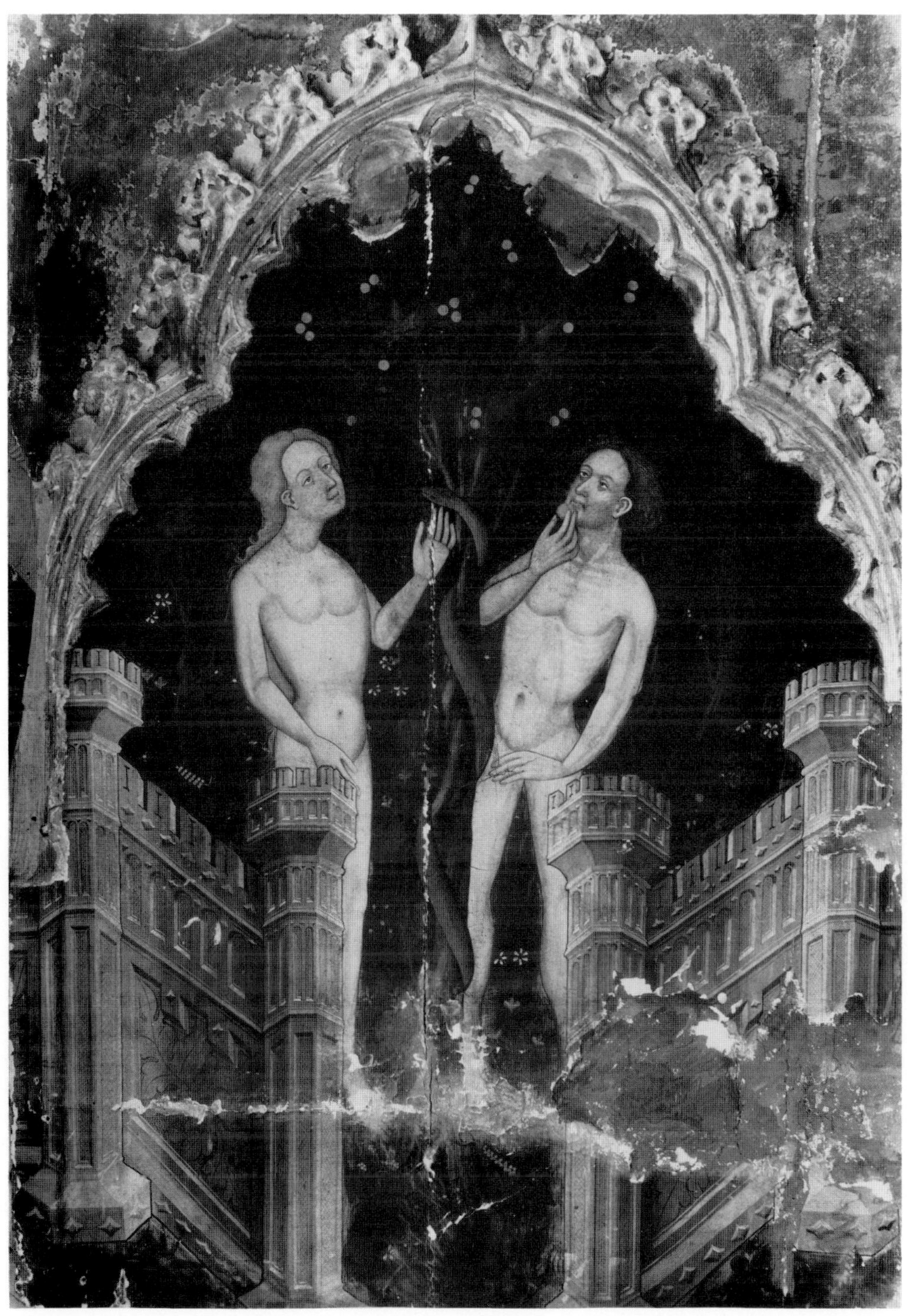

119b. Ramón de Mur, Original Sin, with Adam and Eve

*

It was then, in musing over the destiny of Iberia's aesthetic decision, that I became puzzled—and still am, even today—by the obvious distinction between the "classical"—so Hellenic!—"purity" and "stability" of Catalan medieval architecture and the "mobility," the Romanesque *Baroqueness* of Catalan medieval painting. Would it not be—so I thought (puzzled, but not interrogating)—because of the primacy of numerical-musical "classical" proportionality, belonging both to the very thought-structure of Antiquity and to the inner structure, the "nature," of the "abstract" art of architecture itself, and because the fluidity, the drama of interlacing—the Baroqueness—of forms and contents, in the historical Romanesque as well as in the historical Baroque, belong also to the the fluid, free "nature" of the art of painting itself?

But what was still more puzzling to me—an admiring puzzlement I must say—was the historical continuity, the persistence of Catalonia's aesthetic will throughout the entire so-called medieval era. The fully evolved Catalan Gothic architecture remained always essentially "classical," while Catalan painting remained "Romanesque-Baroque". In spite of the impact, first of the French Gothic anti-Romanesque "classical" wave, then of the wave of the Italian *trecento's* humanism, the art of the "ornament-monster" continued to reveal itself in such works as the altar pieces of a Mur, or a Martorell (*Plates 119a&b*); or, still later (with the incoming Franco-Flemish fifteenth-century innovations), in the art of the Catalan-Valencian master, Luis Dalmáu. On the surface totally, if provincially, Van Eyckian, without, though, any of Van Eyck's luminist subtlety, compactness, breadth and complexity, the famous triptych by Dalmáu, the "Retablo dels Consellers" (*Plate 120*)[89] is still, in reality, a magnificent Romanesque "significant ornament." The enthroned Virgin holding the Child, her figure abruptly receding to the background, is optically diminished in size, yet "secretly" magnified, emphasized, in significance: the throne, whose stepped platform-"ornament," enlarged abnormally, dominates tactilely—intentionally—from its foreground, the entire space of the composition, and the Virgin herself become one compound being (a Franco-Flemish version of Santa María of Tahull's theme), one new, unexpected being, giving to the narrated

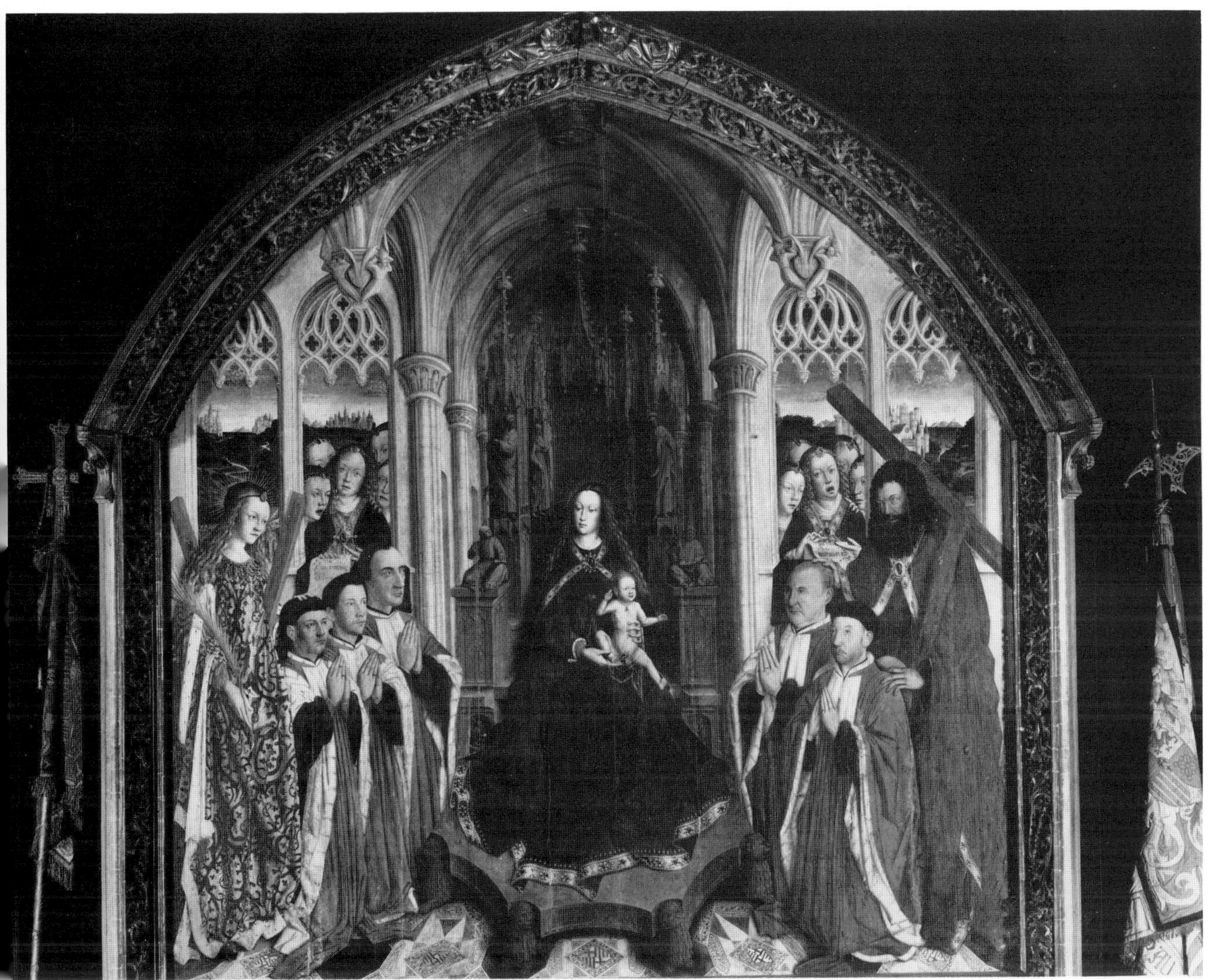

120. Luis Dalmáu, Retablo of the Councillors, Museum of Catalan Art, Barcelona

subject of the work a new, unexpected, different sub-subject: the meaning at once lyrical and epic-cosmic in aspiration, of a Presence.

My own interrogation made useless in the world where I was now, I could feel free to wonder (and to wander) as much as I wished. How surprising also, perhaps revealing—who knows?—to watch at the opposite, western shore of the Peninsula, in Portugal, the birth of a masterwork, contemporary with Dalmáu's and equally Flemish-inspired, yet fundamentally so opposite in spirit:

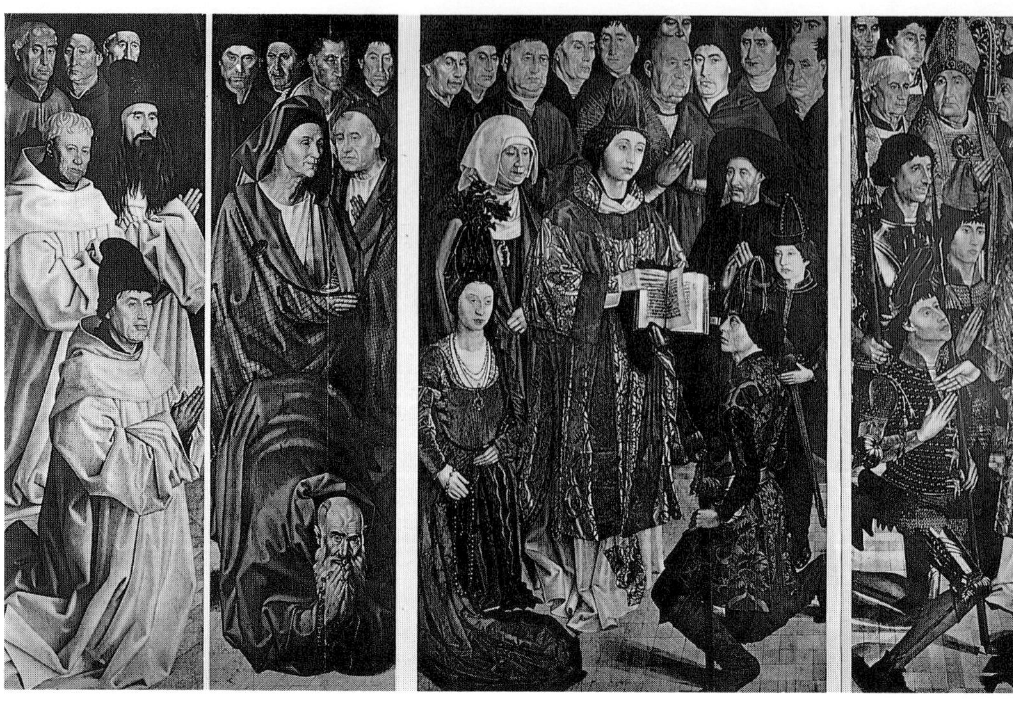

121. Master of the St. Vincent Panels (Nuno Gonçalves?

the polyptych of São Vicente (1460–70) by Nuno Gonçalves (*Plate 121*).[90] Whether Van Eyckian or not in its stylistic externalia, this exceptional pictorial monument is simply a negation of both the Spanish-Catalan and the Flemish or North European "Romanesque" credo of continuity and spatial depth-certainty. Narration and space in Gonçalves come to us, upon us, with all the closeness and immediacy, almost frightening, of faith-doubt: such is the unsurpassed Iberic *verismo* of his portraiture—witness of reality's wonder, flesh and wound (illusion of reality? reality of illusion? [*Plate 122*]).[91]

How precisely or factually is this work related—and it seemed to me then it was—to, say, the "Pieta of Avignon" in the Louvre (*Plate 123*) or to those, later, of Bermejo and, still later, of Zurbarán (*Plate 124*). I wondered . . .

And the puzzle continued its intriguing demands on me: why in the geographical and cultural zone of "Catalan" aesthetic decision was there such continuity of the "Romanesque" tradition? Why was it so rhythmically or periodically interrupted in the

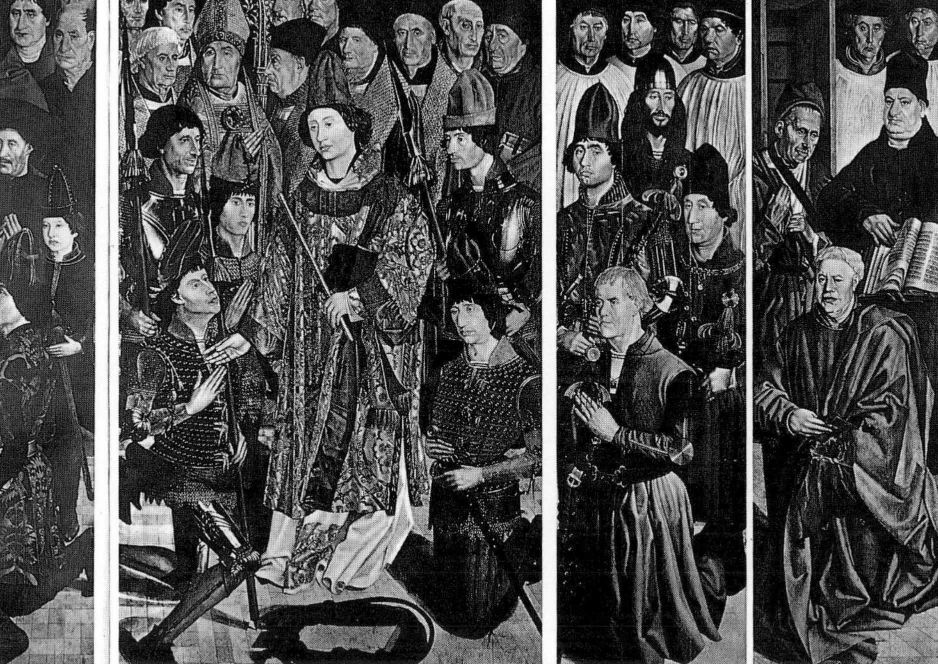

ão Vicente polyptych, Museu Nacional de Arte Antiga, Lisbon

rest of the Peninsula's art? And why each time the interruption was terminated (or interrupted in its turn) did a revival of the "Romanesque" universe of discourse take place there, with an accrued energy whose intensity and passion made each revival an unprecedented historical creation?

Without interrogating, I continued to wonder and wander.

I saw it was after a period of Iberia's apprenticeship to the "classical" Gothic—French, of course—and her masterly absorption of it, that a revival of the art of the Romanesque "ornament-monster" took place in Spain proper and in Portugal—a revival closely related (hence the ease and rapidity of acceptance) to the similar revival in the arts of trans-Iberian Europe, brought to the Peninsula by Northern artists, the de Colonias, the Guases, the de Egases, the de Siloes, at the time, in Spain, of Isabel and Ferdinand's Castilian-Aragonese Catholic Kingdom, and, in Portugal, during the early and most creative era of the Avizes, the reign of Dom Manuel.

A new visual idiom was introduced, so rich in modes and

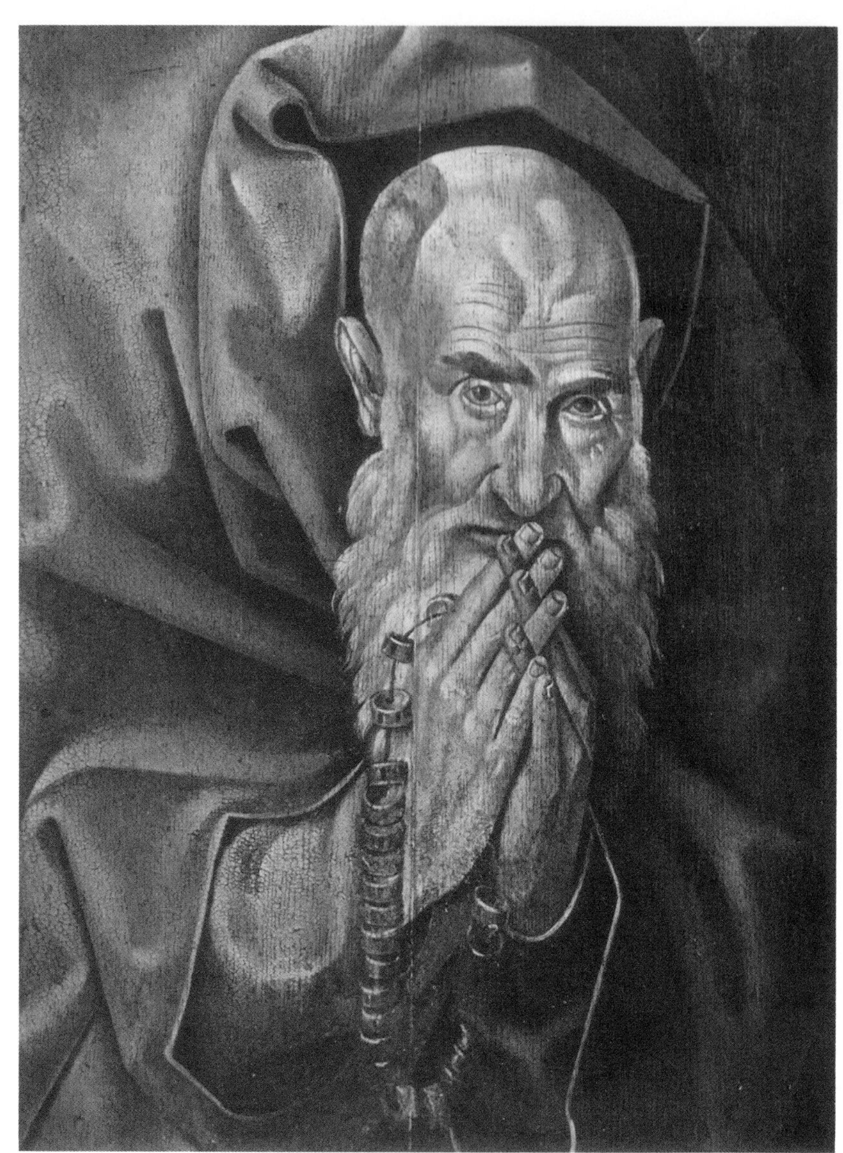

122. Master of the St. Vincent Panels (Nuno Gonçalves?) São Vicente polyptych, detail

moods, the idiom of the late flamboyant Gothic, French, Flemish, German, English. The swarming, tense world of the ancient ''barbarians''' personal ornament came back again! I saw *retablos* and the *retablo*-like façades of palaces, churches, learned colleges of the so-called Isabellan era toward the end of the fifteenth century, and those of the so-called Cisneros era and style—the ''plateresque,''

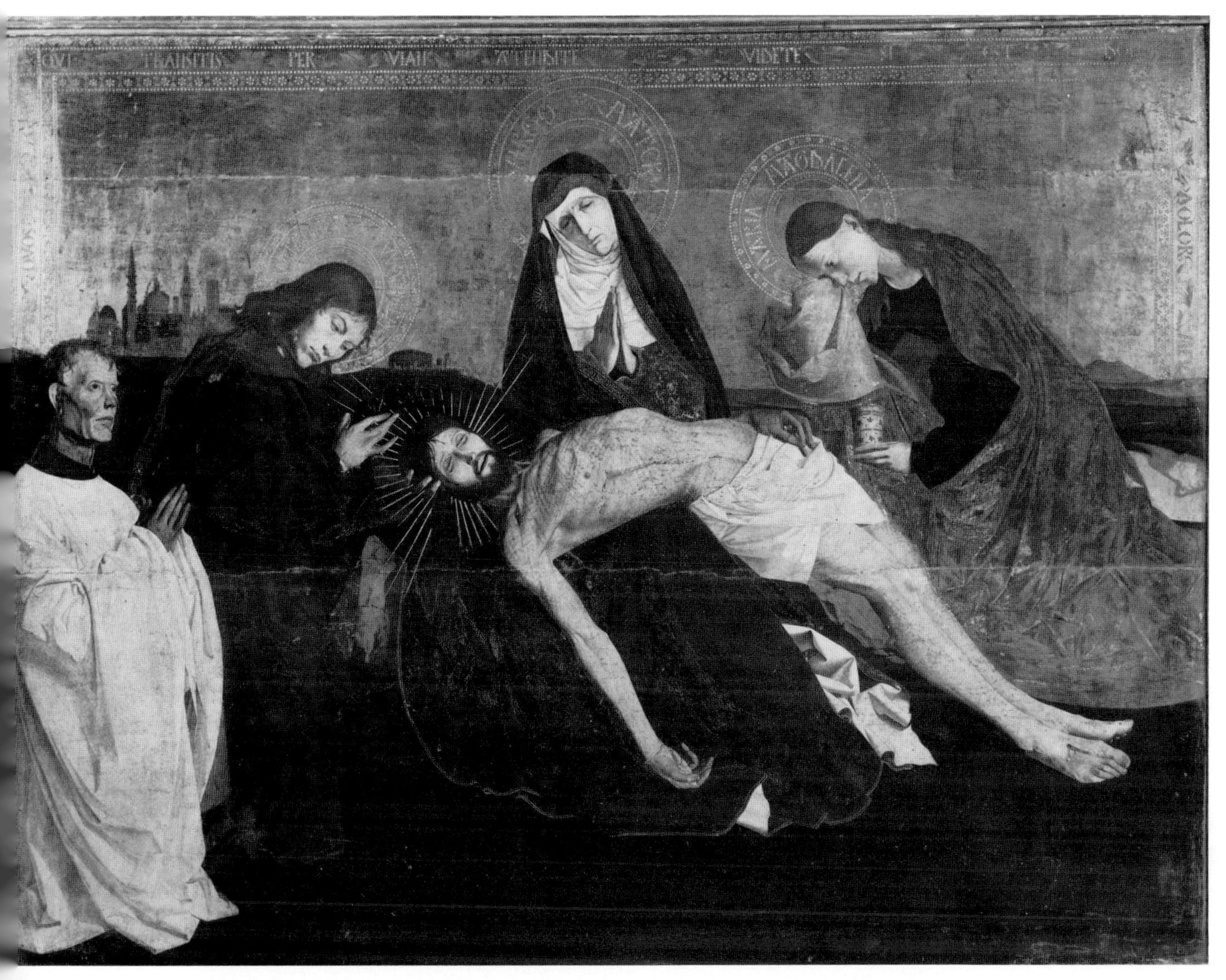

123. Enguerrand Quarton, "The Pieta of Avignon"

superficially so Italian already—of the first half of the sixteenth century: giant toys or jewels, deep caves hewn out of earth, fire and air, discovered by children left to be alone there, to hide and to delight in them and be sheltered by them (*Plates 125a&b* and *see Plate 29*)! And contemporary, or almost, with this art, the Manueline of Portugal, very Iberian indeed in its loyalty to heraldic-interlacing (Celto-Iberic, Visigothic, Moslem) origins (*Plate 126*).

But there was something else, and new, that I saw there: the Lusitanian nostalgia—*saudades*—of great waters, the unending, tempting, conquering and conquered waters of the ocean—of the oceans!—that Portugal had to face always, in her body, soul and mind; the great waters that led Portugal's naval ambitions and genius to the encounter with the marvels of India's thought in art: the Gupta, Cāḷukya or Pallava palaces and temples and their walls, often silent for the eye, plain, unadorned, and then suddenly awakened to the polyrhythmic, fleshy opulence of their giant windows, giant doorways, jewels of fertility's dreams (*Plates 127a,b&c*)! All this *Manuelino.* But first the waters again and again, the great waters themselves, this secret charm and greatness of the ocean itself, heavy-light, weighty-flexible, opaque-translucid: heavy gold upon light blue (=water!) of Portugal's late Baroque church interiors (*Plate 128*), and before that in Manuel's era (early sixteenth century), the tense and fluid, brutal, subtle, space-and-time-embracing ocean-"ornament," the mariner's rope!—soul, body, and symbol of navigation, of Portugal's being on-and-in ocean. Ocean's, São Jeronymos' vertiginous columns=ropes (*Plate 129*) falling, falling down and not, as pillars do, reaching up to the equally vertiginous vaults!

*

An era of, perhaps, the greatest and most original Peninsular creativity and invention it was! Yet, how promptly it was swallowed up (oh, but after what a gigantic struggle of the late Gothic against the Renaissance invader—the *epos* of this struggle told and chanted in the exalted stony elevations and intricacies of the immense naves of Spain's last cathedrals: the new cathedral of Salamanca, the cathedrals of Segovia, of Plasencia, of Seville, Granada, Malaga (*Plate 130!*), swallowed up by the thundering wave of Italy's late and imperious Renaissance (*Plate 131*)! And it was only after this brief but temporarily decisive triumph of the foe of the "Romanesque" that the revival of the latter, incommensurably intensified, the "Romanesque" of the Spanish and Portuguese Baroque of the seventeenth and eighteenth centuries, asserted itself again, this time violently: in Spain proper in the so-called Churri-

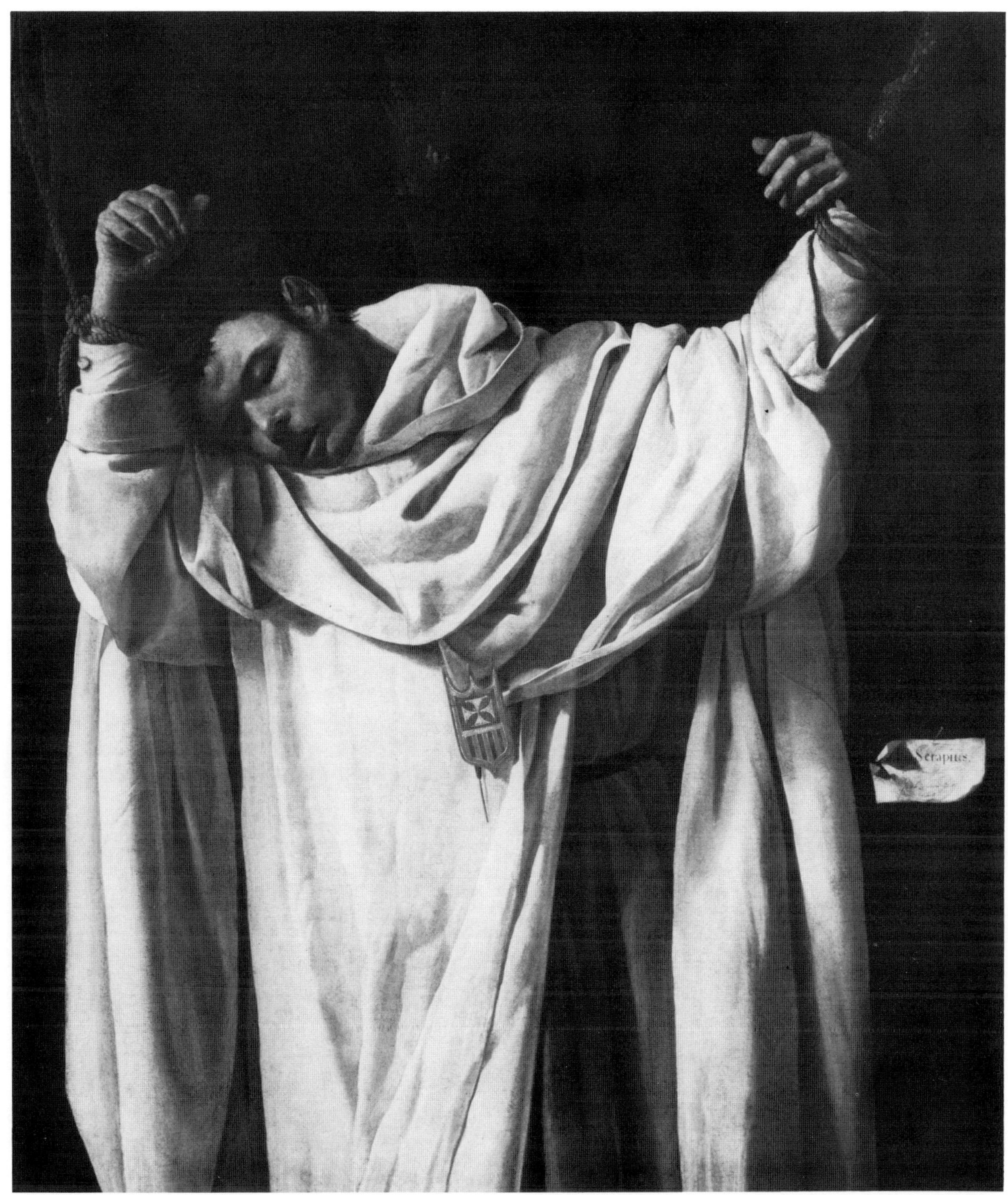


124. Zurbarán, St. Serapion

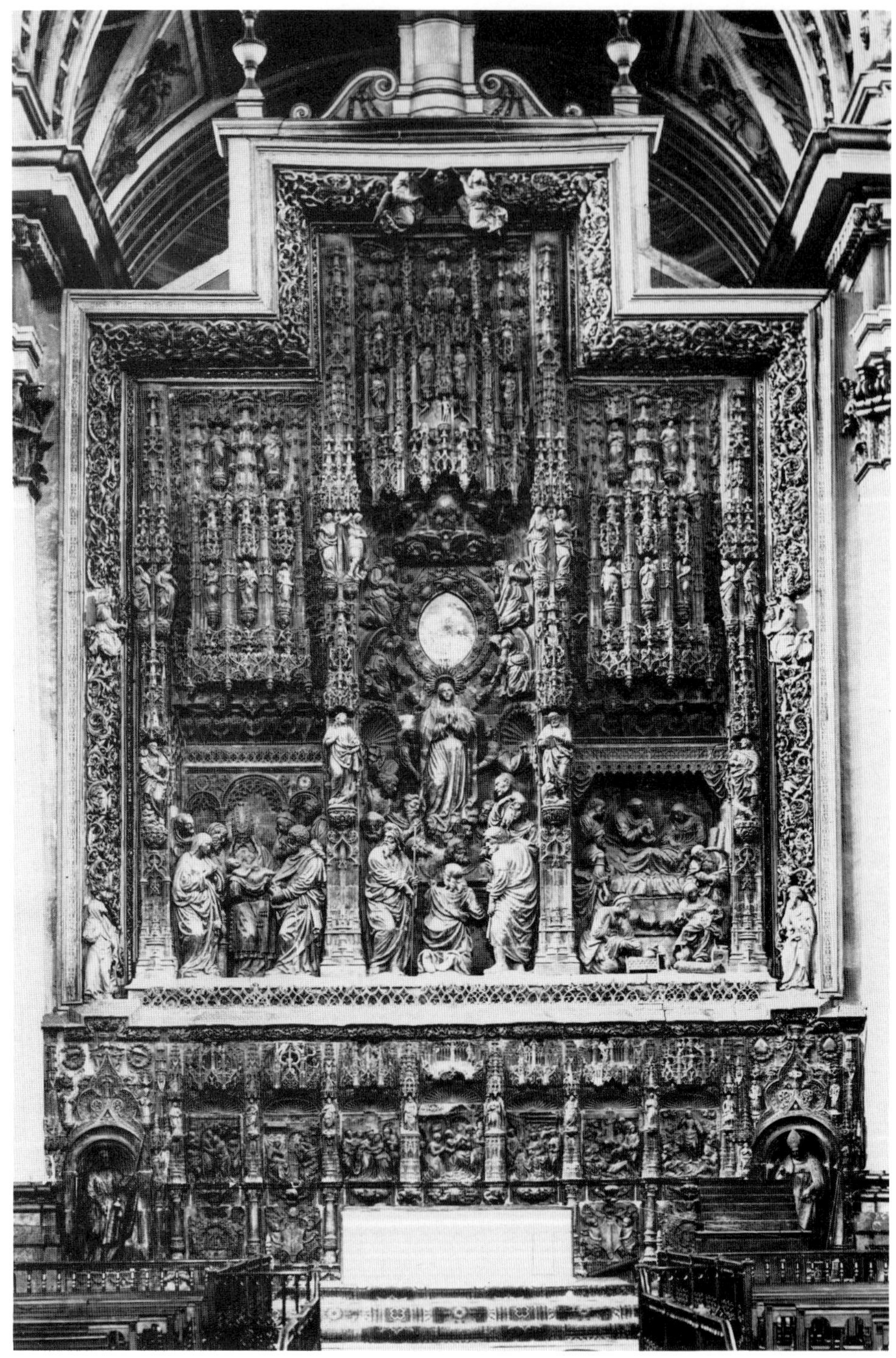

125a. Damián Forment, high altar, Cathedral of Nuestra Señora del Pilar, Saragossa

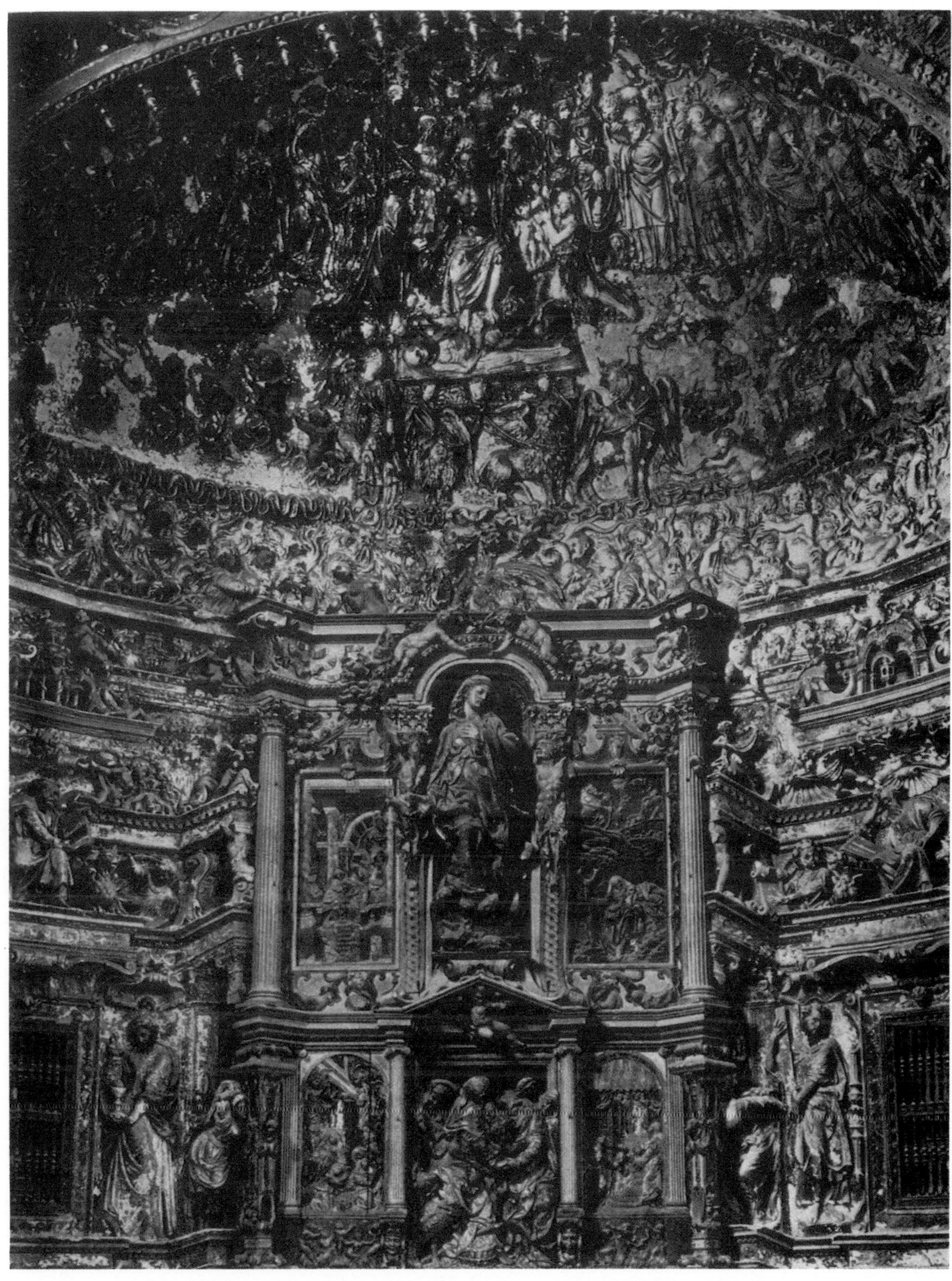

125b. The Benavente Chapel, church of Sta. María at Medina de Rioseco, near Valladolid

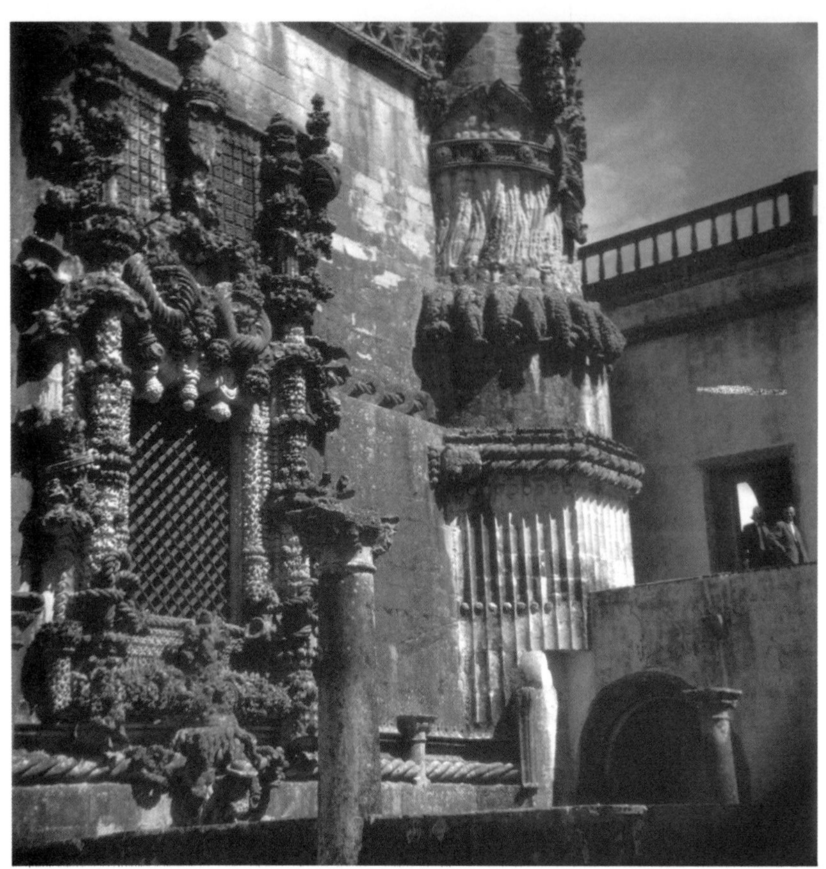

126. Window, façade of the church of the Order of Christ, Tomar, Portugal

gueresque art, not so much the creation of the famous brothers Churriguera, José Benito and Joaquin, whose style was rather restrained, but whose reputation came, mistakenly, to overshadow that of other Spanish personal, ''Baroque'' inventions, the creation of all the exalted freedom-drunk *''locos''* of Baroque Spain, of Portugal and of their dominions (*fatuos delirantes,* ''delirious fools'' or crazy ones, as they were called by the early nineteenth-century neo-classical critic E. Llaguno): a Pedro de Ribera (*circa* 1683–1742) and his portal of the Hospicio de San Fernando in Madrid, a Leonardo Figueroa (*circa* 1650–1750) and his work on the Palacio de Santelmo in Seville; the façade of the Palace of the Marqués de dos Aguas in Valencia, remodeled 1740–44 by Hipolito Rovira Brocandell, Luis Domingo and Ignatio Vergara (*Plate 132*).

But in its total absorption of the so-called rococo international vocabulary and the ''Spanishness'' of its own visual syntax, excel-

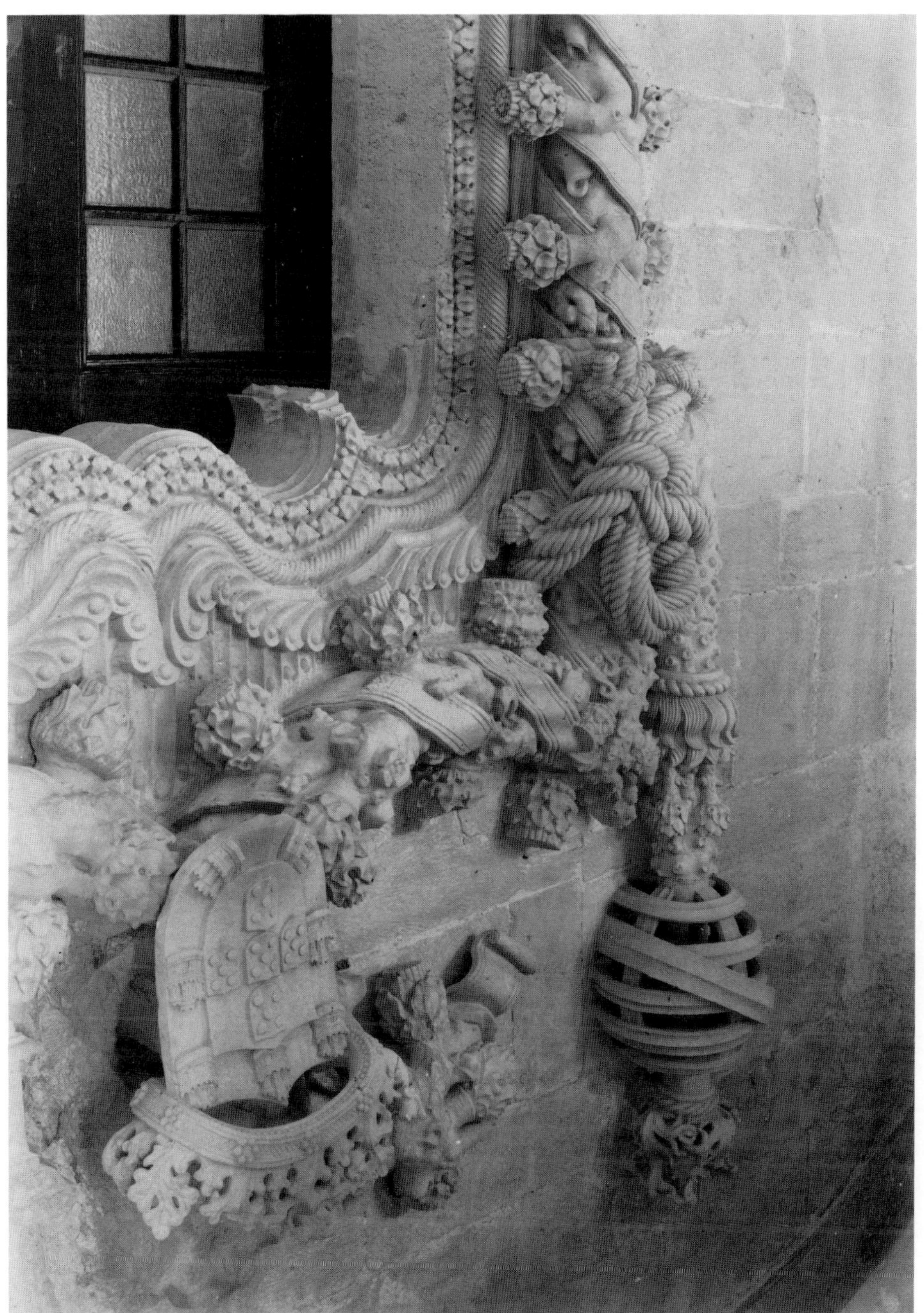

127a. Detail of a side window, chapter house of the Order of Christ, Tomar, Portugal

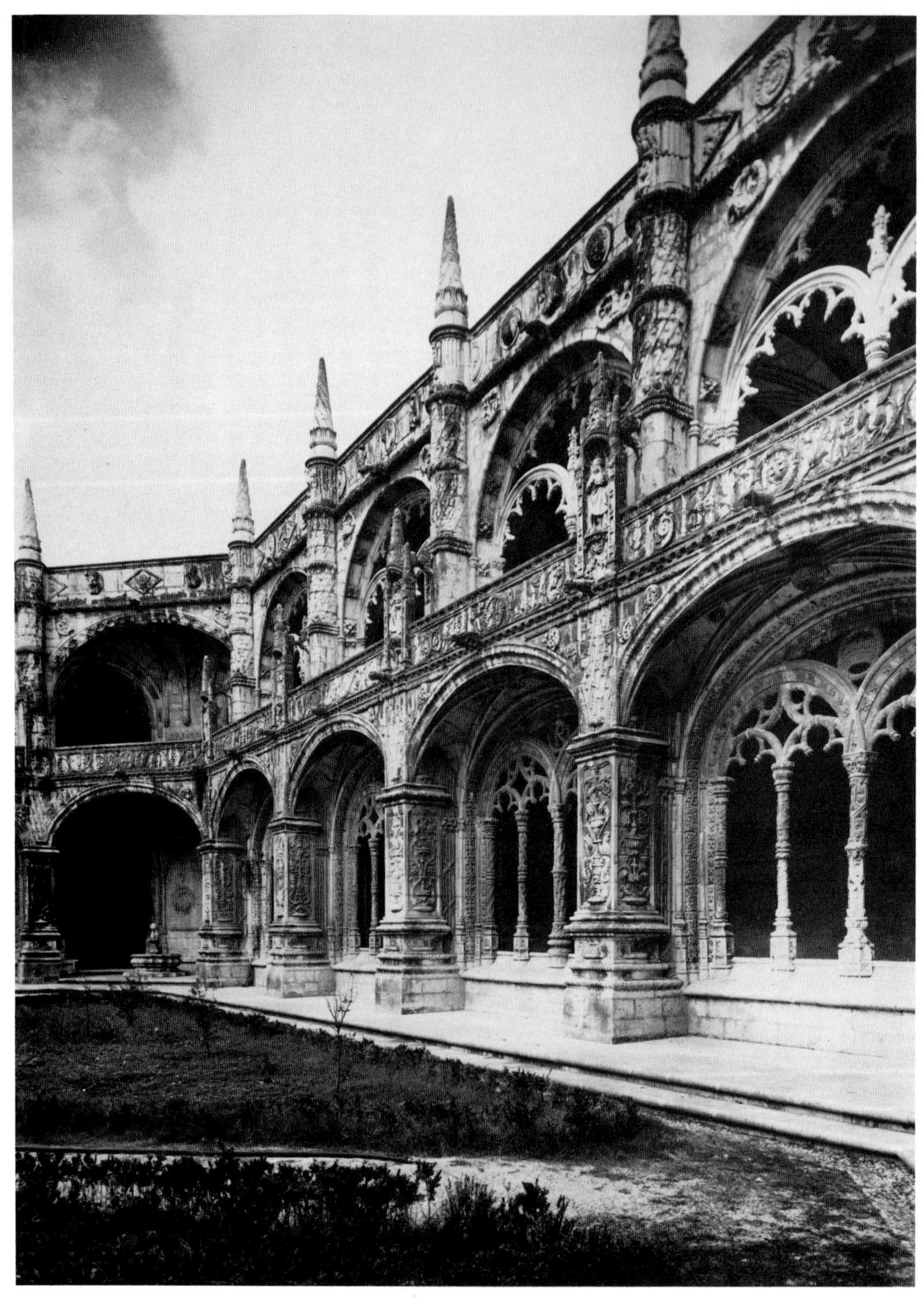

127b. Cloister, Convent of the Jeronymos, Belém, Portugal

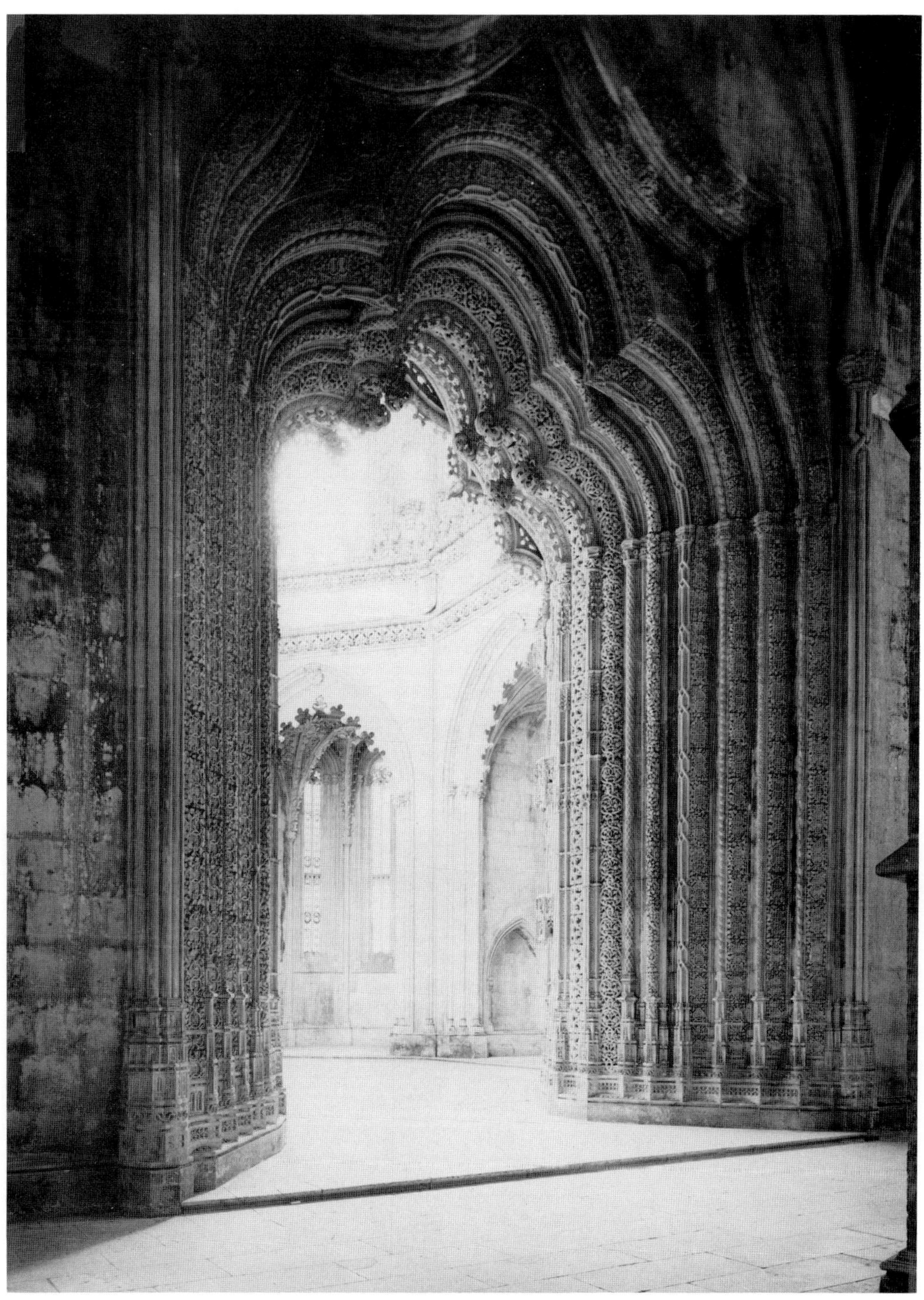

127c. Portal, ''Unfinished Chapels,'' Monastery of Batalha, Portugal

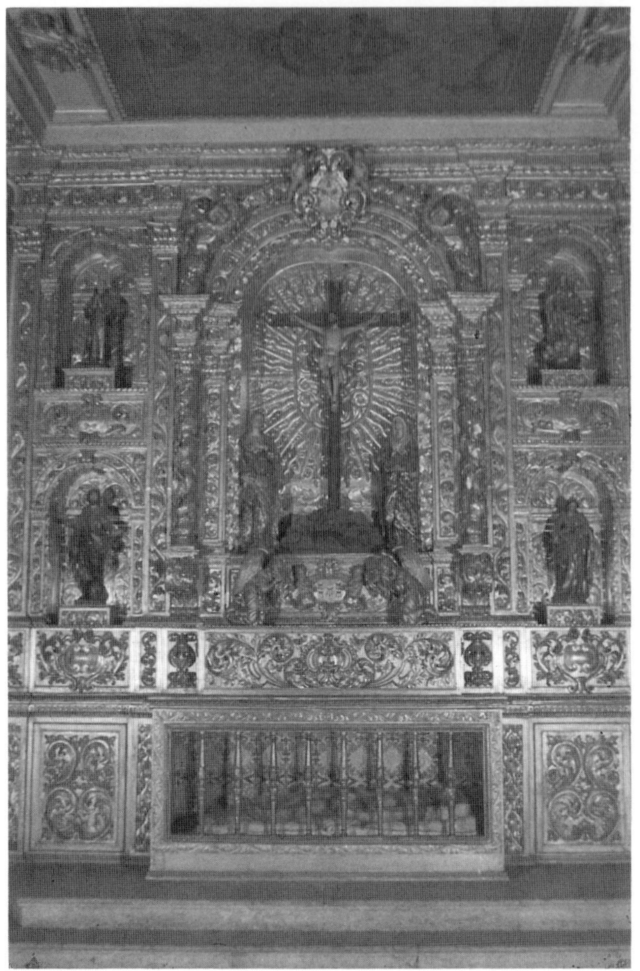

128. Altar, church of Madre de Deus, Lisbon

ling all other Spanish ''Romanesque''-Baroque testimonials in *locura* (craze), this creation of the most *loco* of all *locos delirantes*, Narciso Tomé's *Transparente* in Toledo's Gothic cathedral (*Plate 133*)—''a sacramental chapel without walls, made of light and inscribed by theatrical artifice upon the space of a Gothic ambulatory,''[92] a translucid architectural (sculptural-pictorial rather) attire covering the pious intimacy of the cathedral's *camarin;*[93] an ''ornament-monster'' born of light, in light, the light of Spanish earth, Spanish air, Spanish fire; ''an ingenious conception that clings to the old Gothic stones . . . like exuberant vegetation that attaches itself to some ruins without disturbing their beauty.''[94]

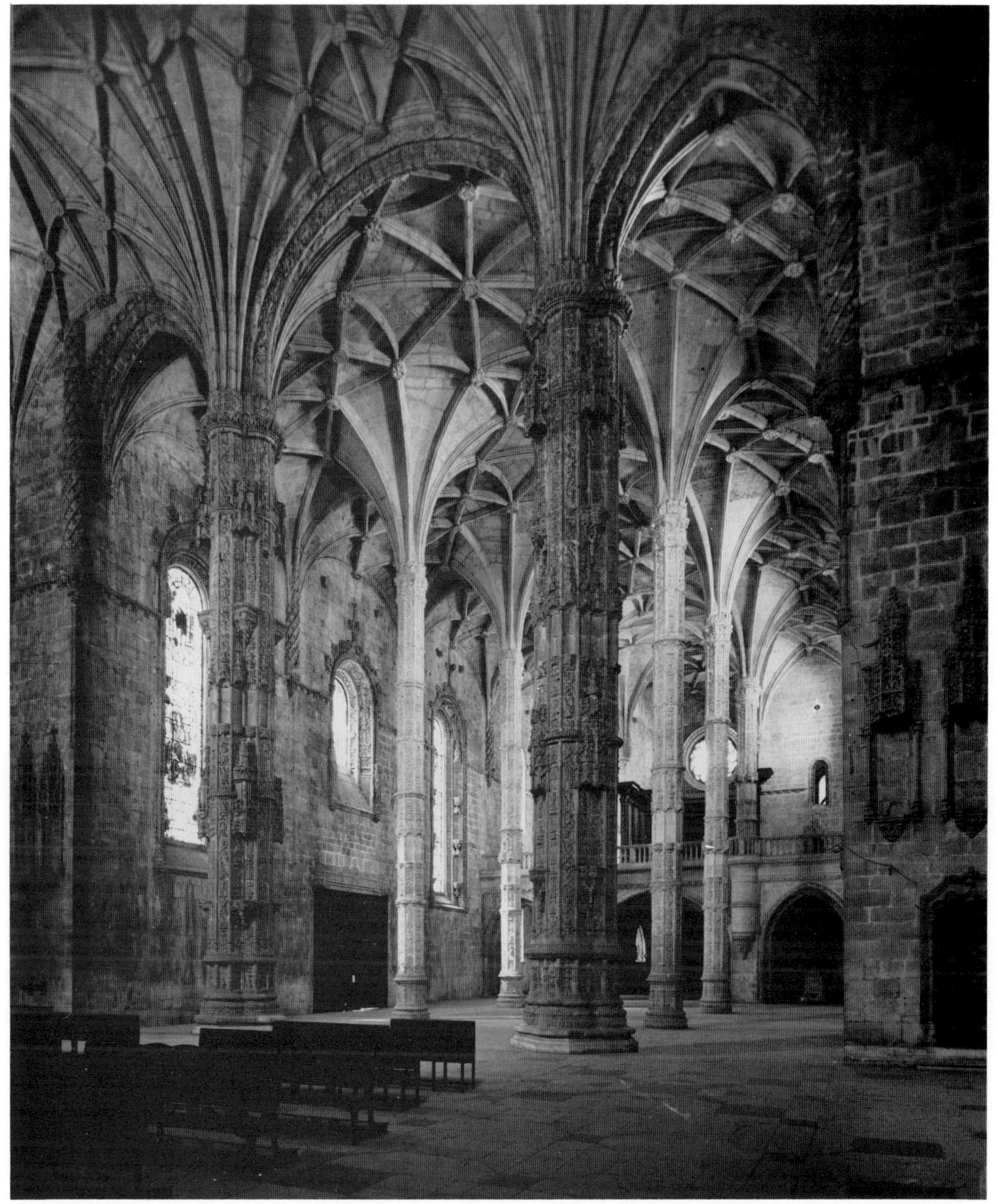

129. Columns and vaults, church of the Convent of the Jeronymos, Belém, Portugal

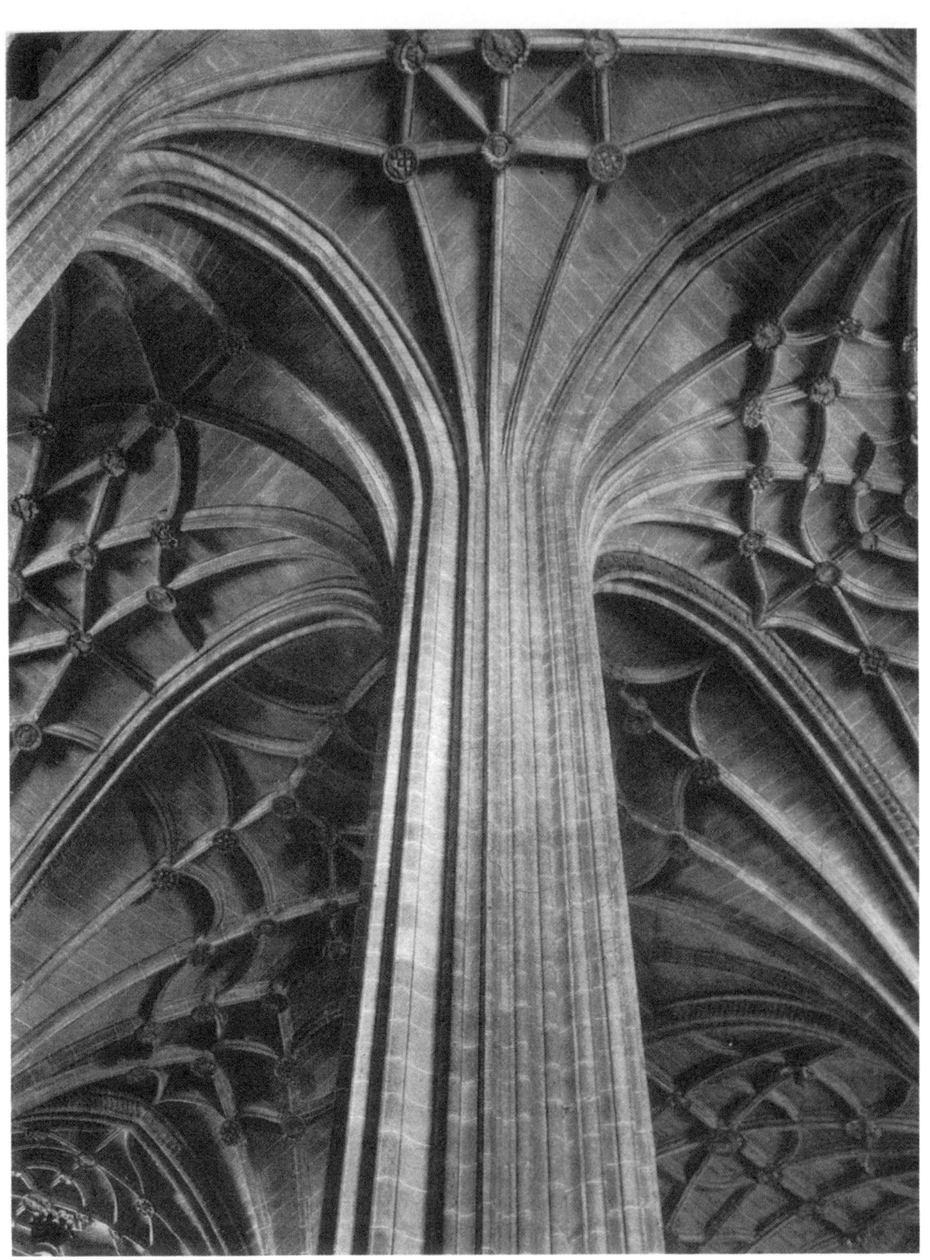

130. Detail, pillars and vaults, New Cathedral of Plasencia

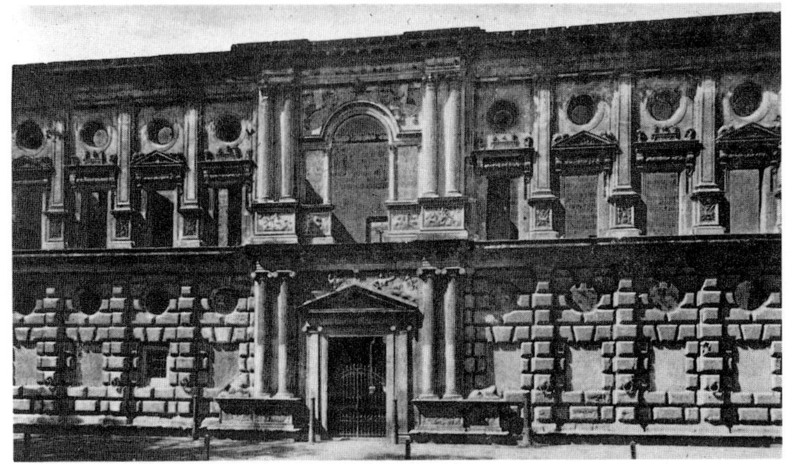

131. South façade, Palace of Charles V in the Alhambra

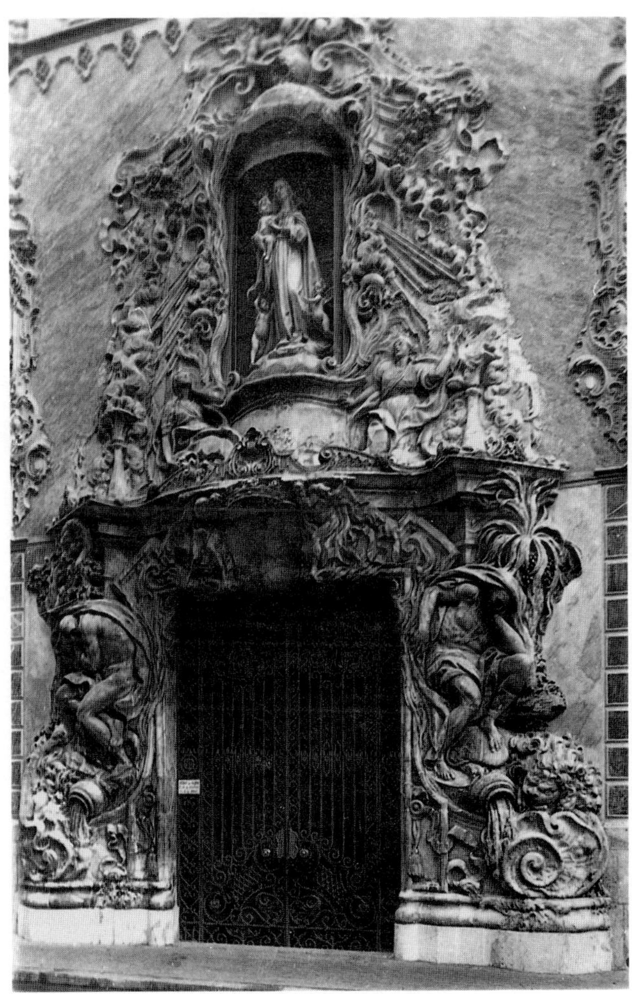

132. Portal, façade of the Palace of the Marqués de dos Aguas, Valencia

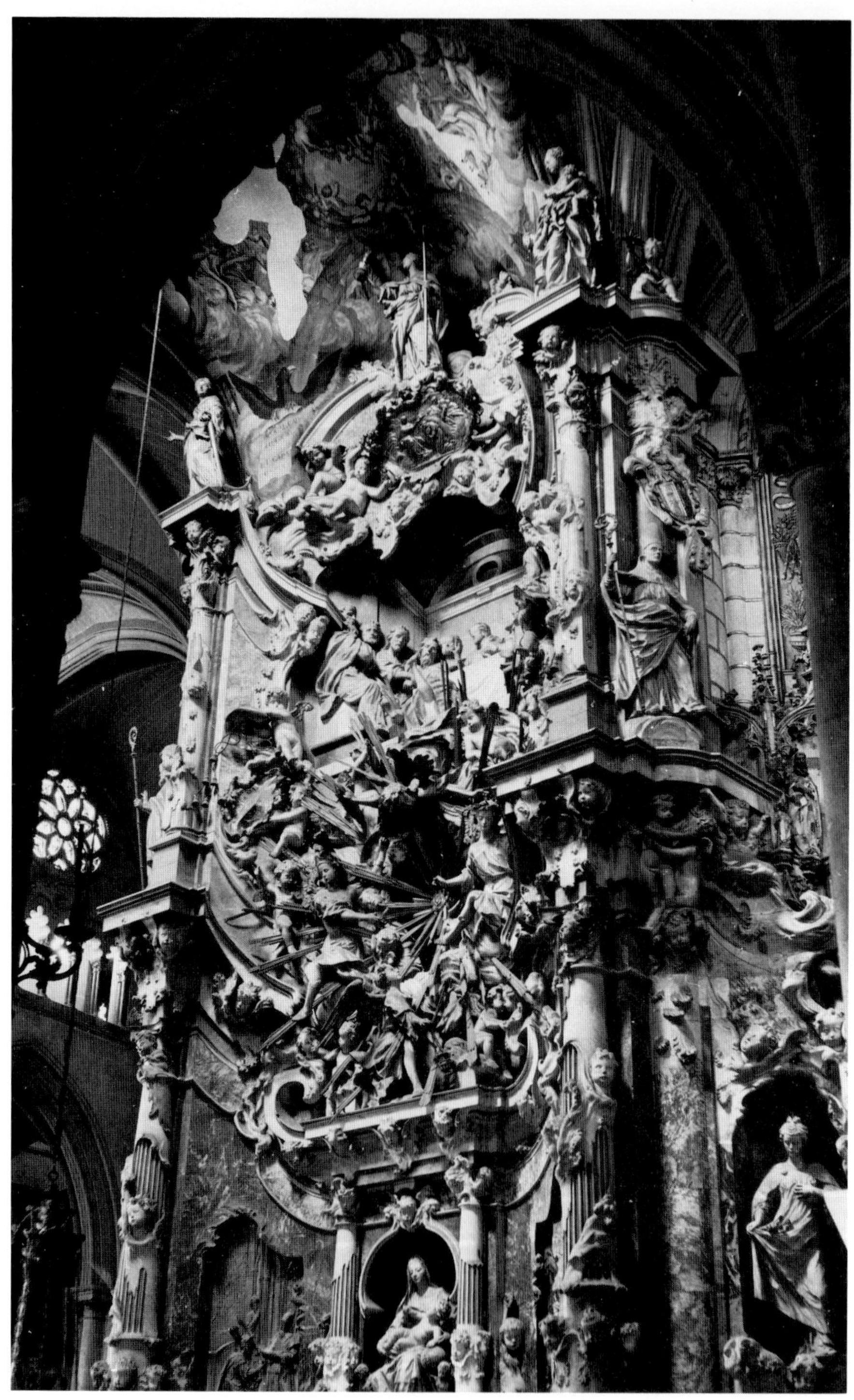

133. "Transparente," Cathedral, Toledo

*

*''Allah is Great! I bear witness that there is no God but God. I bear witness that Muhammad is His Prophet. Come to prayer. Come to salvation. Allah is Great. There is no God but Allah!''*

The muezzin's call to prayer, the *adhān,* melodious, nostalgic, convincing—Islam's call for unity, absolute, sovereign over all dissent, over all the multiples in it, had been heard for centuries along the valleys and plateaux of Iberia, between the shores of the Mediterranean and the Atlantic.

The immense span of this message and of its impact, covering initially almost the whole of the peninsula, started slowly, slowly its tidal retreat southward, the bloody, alternating successes and failures of the Reconquista never stopping the constant flow of Islamic cultural gifts into the bloodstream of Christian Iberia. And when, after the momentous and decisive Spanish thirteenth century, the victory at Las Navas de Tolosa, which opened the gates to the fertile opulence of al-Andalūs; the victorious prowesses of the Catalan Jaume I that gave to the Catalan-Aragonese crown Moslem Valencia and the Balearics; and those that made the Reconquista final for Portugal—when Christian Spain could see the Moslem rule reduced to the small albeit splendid Nasrid kingdom of Granada; and finally, when even this last remnant of Moslem might had been annihilated by the rising might of the Catholic Kings—then, and then only, the passion and the intense persistence of Moslem ''Spanishness,'' laid bare now, could bring its indigenous fruit: the *mudejarismo* of the post-Reconquista's visual thought.[95]

''All was silence here: I, Spain and Spanish art. Nothing else.''

Much has been said for and against the importance, if not the primacy, of *mudejarismo*'s role and impact in Spain—*mudejarismo* not, certainly, in its external-mechanical, factual sense only (such or such Islamic technical or stylistic detail applied or added to a particular ruling Western Christian style, Romanesque, Gothic, Isabellan-plateresque, or Baroque), but in the structural sense of a global—Islamic—attitude.

I saw how those who gave weight to the importance of this attitude for Spain were in the right. Indeed, the great puzzle of

Spanish art, its being at once so unique and so much the West's, ceased to be a puzzle to me. *Passion* as a *quantitative* category, as a quantitative *persistence of emotion's intensity* was precisely this uniqueness, and passion was precisely also Islam's greatest gift to Spain.

And I saw, more and clearly, this:

Islam's gift to Spain was the gift of a quantitatively enhanced, added quality that was at once Islamic proper and universal (thus the West's also).

It was universal because it revealed in its innermost structure the dichotomy of any culture and any individual, the braiding of the Apocalyptic and the Psychomachic or, transferred into the visual, the braiding of two motions, two vehicles of emotion, motion-''stability,'' mnemonic, mediate, expected and fulfilled, and motion-''mobility,'' immediate, sudden, at once continuous and rigid.

It was Islamic proper, unique, because, based as it was on the same triple psycho-historical foundation as the West's, that of classical Antiquity, of the most ancient Near East, and of the ''barbaric'' steppes, it developed, nevertheless, its own artistic—*Islamic*—vocabulary; it did so not only because of the divergence in combining those three elements, but mainly because of the ''barbaric'' inheritance itself, essentially the same, yet different in its native, localized idiom, from the West's: not Celtic-Germanic predominantly, but Central-Asiatic, Scytho-Turkic predominantly (*Plate 134*). (Medieval Islam, as a world religion, culture and polity, occupied at one time an area that extended from North Africa, Arabia, the middle East and the Indus valley, through Iran to the Caspian regions; and from Iberia to the farthest confines of Central Asia.)

It was this quantitative addition to all the qualities of Spain's visual thinking—not a triple but a quadruple foundation!—that gave to Spain its character of uniqueness, the passion, the intensity of its Glance, and at the same time allowed it to remain the mirror—an intensifying, magnifying mirror—of the West.

*

''Islam is the life of work and duty, with rest in between''—so I read once, I don't remember where, in a Moslem author. Rest, total, blissful rest; the bliss of rest: Paradise in Islam. The gardens

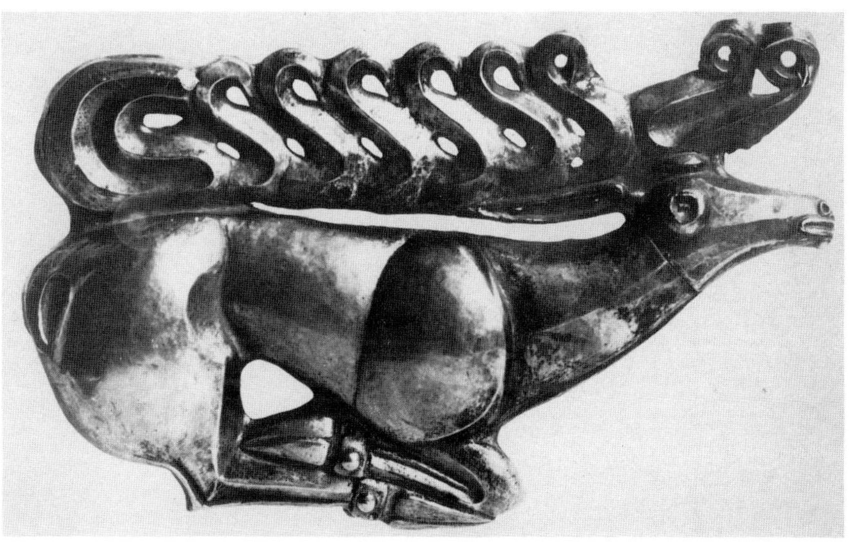

134. Detail of girdle clasp, Scythian, 5th c. B.C.

of Paradise, you know: the gardens of Islam's heart, mind and body. Bliss, Paradise, and its reflection on earth: Islamic Art. And Bliss in Islam, whether ''orthodox'' Sunni or dissenting, as Shī'ah[96], or un-Shī'ah fettered, as Sūfī, is always the bliss of intimacy that is Islam's ''happiness of whole creation''[97]: the intimacy and bliss of Islam's unity of Being and Oneness. The intimacy and bliss of its creed, a totally sufficient, all-certainty-and-faith embracing creed, the *Shahāda: la ilāha illa 'llah, Muhammadan Rasūla'llāh*—''there is no god but God and Muhammad is the Apostle of God.''

Islam: the intimacy of bliss in the Unity of Oneness and of Being: in the God-given prophetic Law, the Sharī'a; in the *umma, the Ummat as-Islām,* the community of the believers and the individual believer himself: solitude-solidarity fulfilled on all levels of earthly existence under Islam. Solitude-solidarity fulfilled under the bliss of ''obedience to the will of God,'' a sovereign and proud obedience without any ruling of imposed humility in it, with only the ruling of unavoidable, inescapable, necessary and austere reason: there is no other presence than the Presence—how then could anything or anybody be outside it and still remain a being, an existence, a *presence?* Impossible. The true, the beautiful, the good work-and-duty of the believer cannot be but to make the world one *Ummat al-Islām,* the true and beautiful and good Rest—Paradise. And its reflection on earth: Islamic art. The art of embellishing the ''place of prostration,'' the Mosque. The blissful rest within

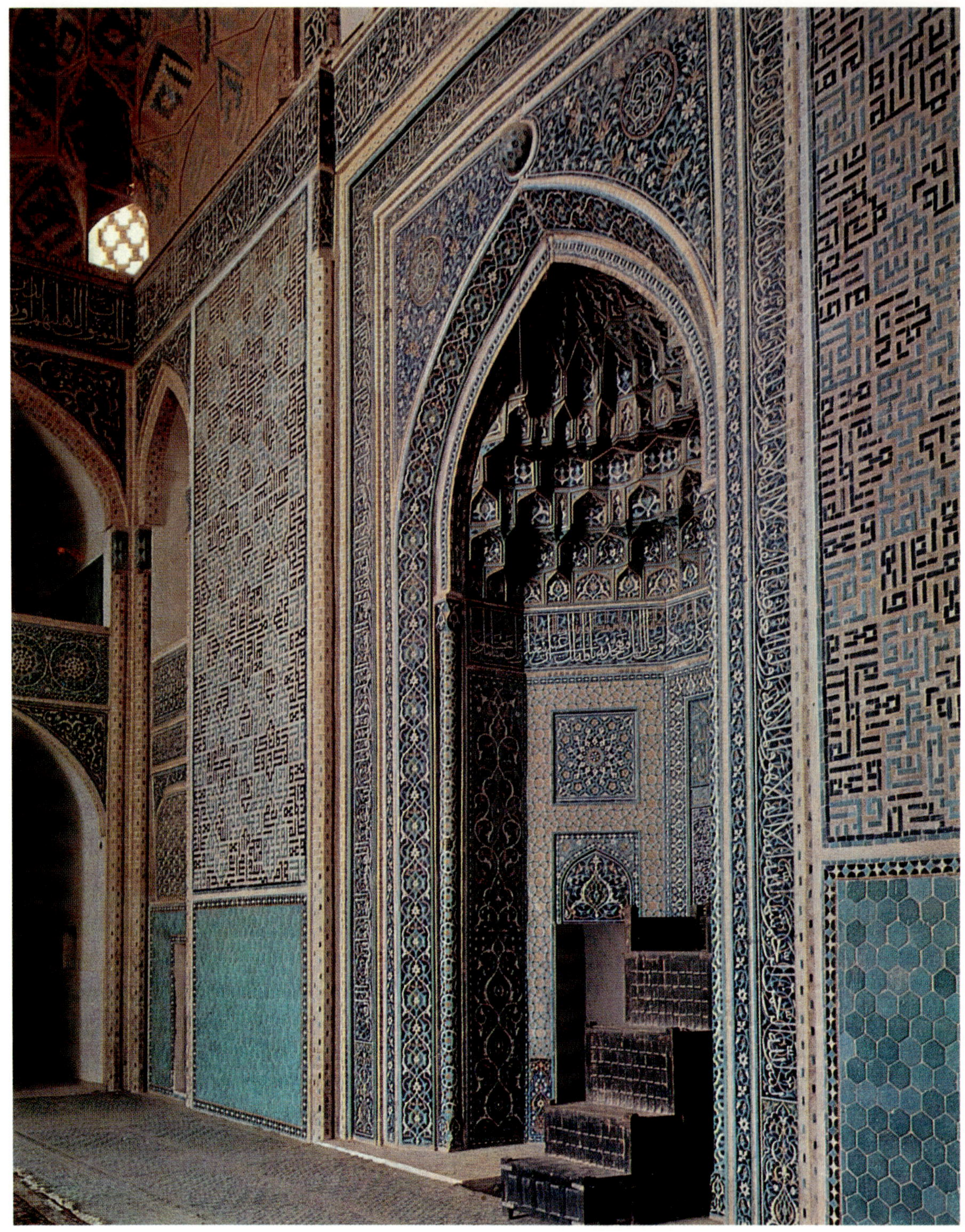

135. Mihrab, Masjid-i-Jami, Yazd, Iran

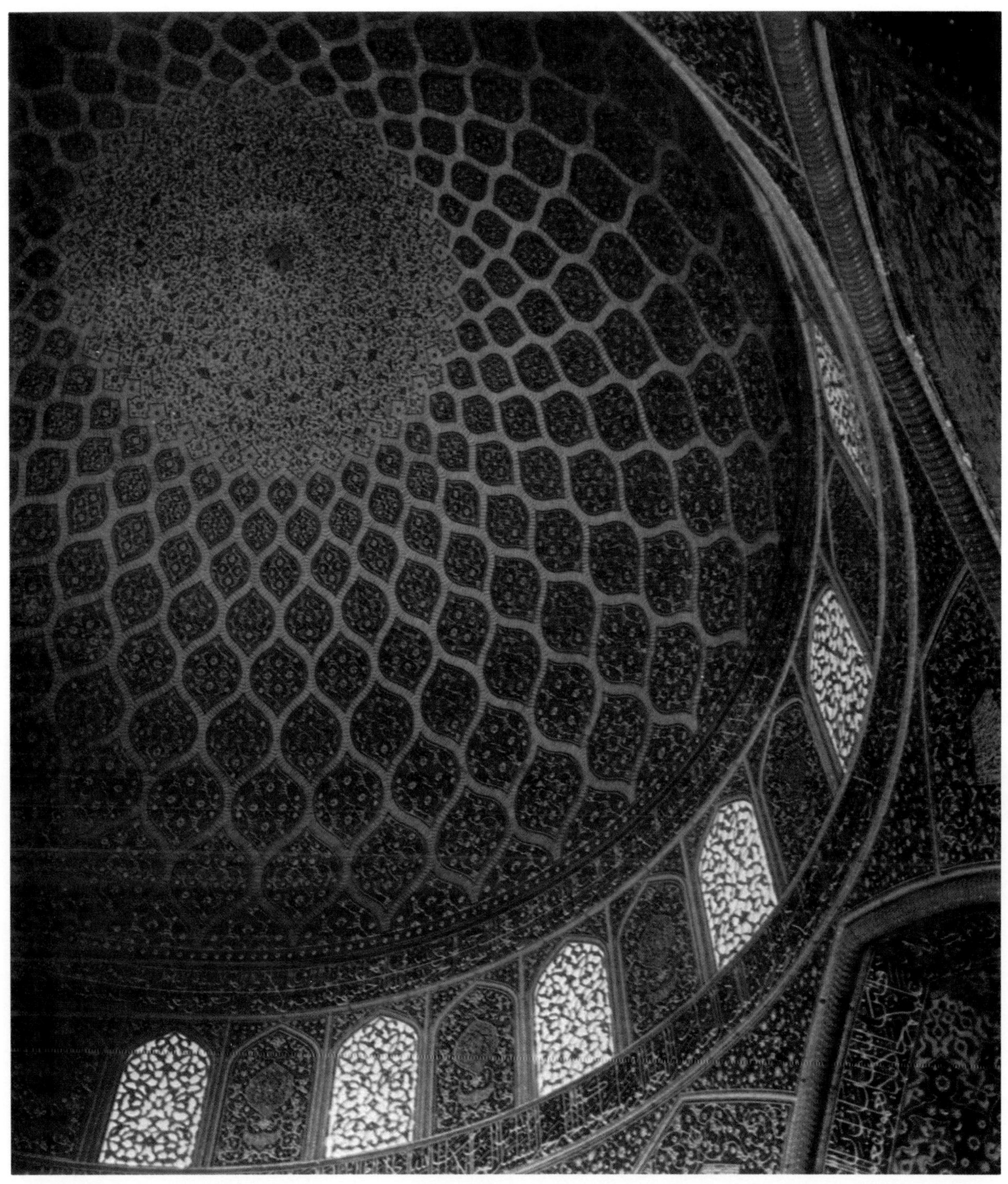

136. Interior of dome, Masjid-i-Shayk Lutf Allah, Isfahan, detail

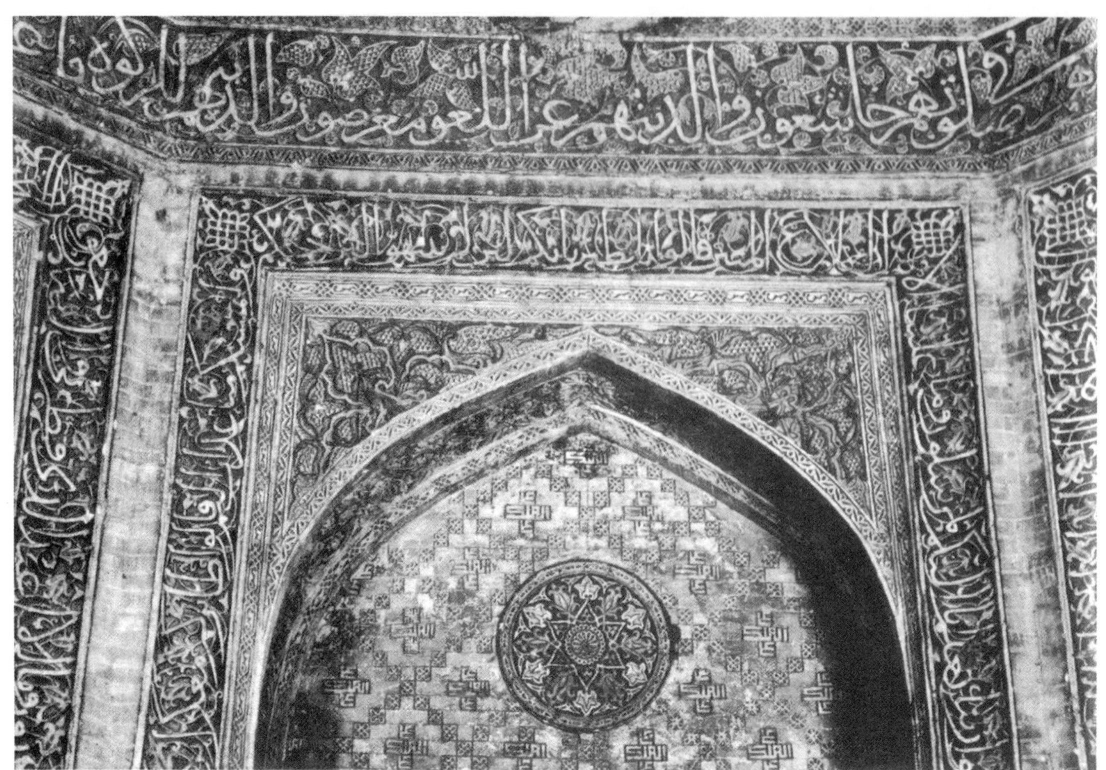

137. Architectural inscription, niche, tomb-tower of Imad-ad-din, Qumm, Iran

the presence and intimacy of their oneness—I and *Shahāda-umma-sharī'a*—one within the silent lustre, the shimmer of a *mihrab*[98] (*Plate 135*) within the exalted blue-green-red-white of an Iranian mosque (*Plate 136*) or within the sensuous discovery of the "pure" abstract in the intimacy and bliss of the Islamic textile world.

*

The pride of Islam in being "obedience to the will of God" is pride in His Word, His written Word, the "Precious Book," the Koran—its sacredness, its script, so exalted as to overflow the limits of exclusive domains of the Koran and become the glorious, varied script of Islamic poetry and speculative thought, the wonderful Arabic-Iranian calligraphy.

Here: the monumental architectural inscriptions (*Plate 137*) or the pages of the Koran and of the poets. And the living animated letter becomes, in the arts of Islam, the hypostasis of the living, animated figure itself, the human figure inhibited, but not pro-

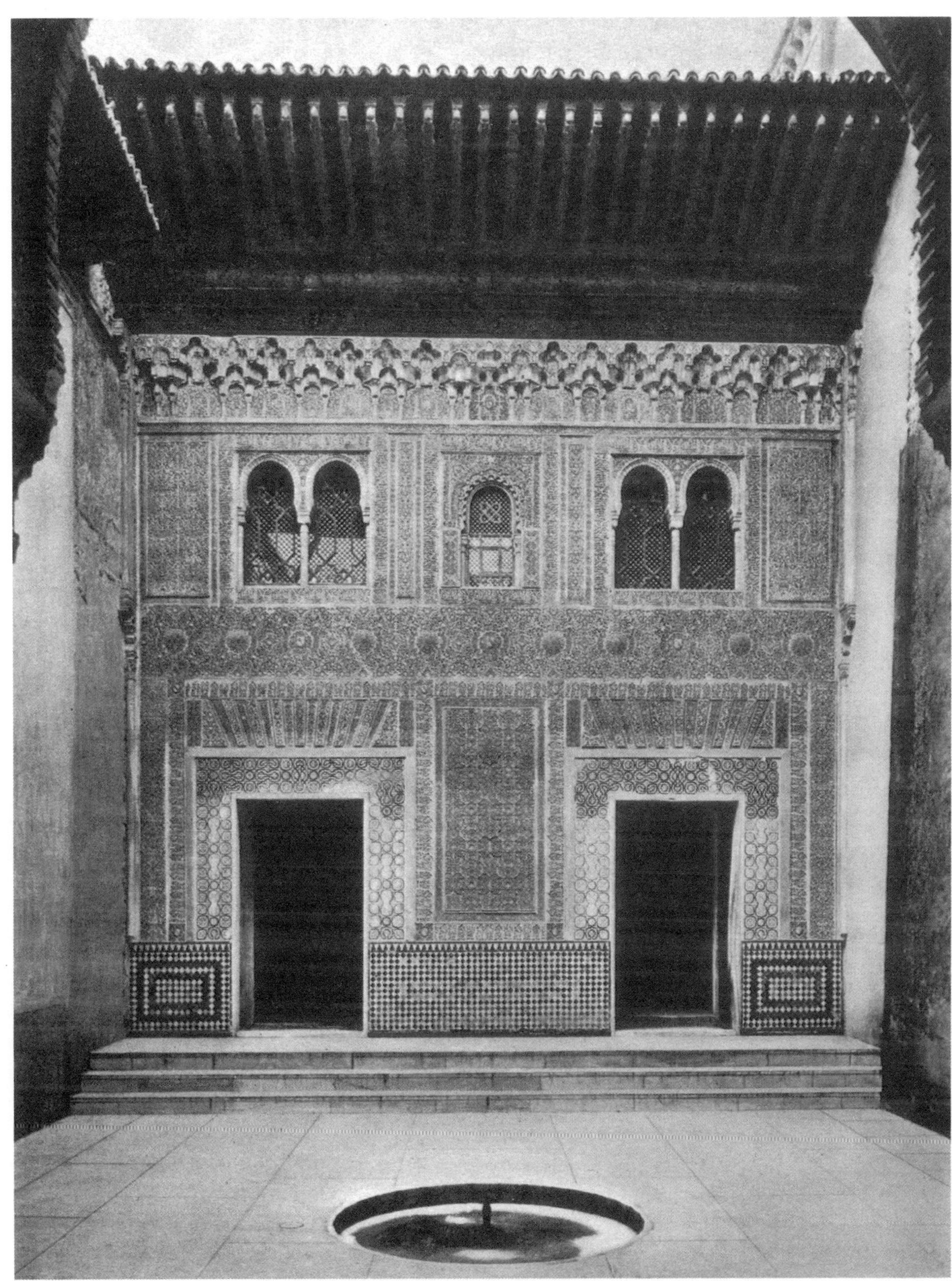

138. Façade of Comares Hall, the Alhambra

hibited canonically, only relegated to the secular world of sensuous-abstract demands and joys. The ancient (already ''post-split'') alliance of the magician and the chieftain-dancer, the lordly alliance of the verbal and military elite, is supreme in Islam. The artist-artisan is subservient to it. But, just because of it, once the guiding dictates of the verbal—the narrative subject and its intention—were fulfilled and obeyed, the visual-manual, the artist-artisan's will, was left free and alone, on the ''what-of-the-how'' level, to plunge into the bliss of its origins: the bliss of being ''pure,'' or totally loyal to these origins, that is, of being at once duality, as all origins are, as all reality is, and of being oneness.

And that is how Islamic art, its historical being, became a new *''dramatis persona''* kin to the others in my chronicle's intrigue.

*

I evoke the Alhambra first. The Alhambra's façade and entrance to the fourteenth-century great Hall of Comares (*Plate 138*): all the musical-mathematical—Pythagorian—proportionality, the bliss of the sensuous-abstract fullness of a Doric temple, of a Catalan cloister or of a Brunelleschian interior is equated here with the classical ''stability'' and ''purity'' of this Nasrid masterpiece! And at the same time all the bliss of being the ''mobile'' no-beginning-no-end continuity, the ''barbaric''-Romanesque, Isabellan ornament-block, the significant, freedom-to-choose telling ''ornament-monster,'' is equated here with the endless, ''mobile'' interlacing on the ceiling of the same royal hall or on the cupolas-and-walls of two of the Alhambra's other grand interiors, the fourteenth-century Hall of the Two Sisters and the Hall of the Abencerrages (*Plates 139a&b*).

It is from there on that, in a visual-oratorial gesture of testifying, a rapid panorama of Islamic monuments-events, West and East, unfolded itself before me, a dual current—a braid—distinct in each of its constituents (how similar in this to what Spain had already given me!): the one a current of structurally ''purest'' ''classicism,'' from the Córdoba mosque's *mihrab* (tenth century) (*Plate 140*)—a marvel of perfect, thus equated, geometrical forms, the very marvel of a classical Greek head (*Plate 141*)—to other ''Hellenic'' marvels of Islamic builders (Islam's bliss of final one-

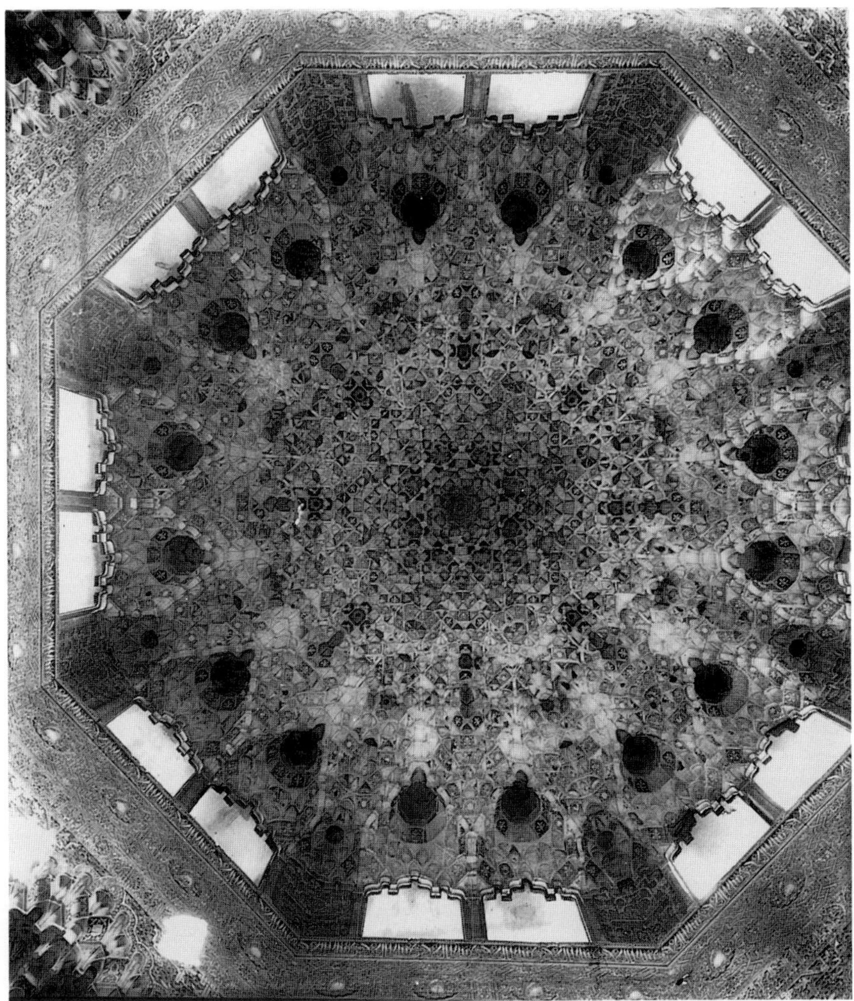

139a. Ceiling-cupola, Hall of the Two Sisters, the Alhambra

ness-unity giving them their own idiom), the Moroccan Kutubiya (eleventh century) or the Ibn Tulun mosque's *sahn* (court) in Cairo (ninth century), and farther and farther East, the harmonic and austere design of Bukhara's Samanid Tomb (tenth century [*Plate 142*]), or the grand Turabek Khanum mausoleum in Urgench (fourteenth century [*Plate 143*]); the ardent coolness of perhaps the most astonishing monument in the Islamic East, the tomb-tower Gunbad-i-Qabus (eleventh century [*Plate 144*]) and, unsurpassed in architectonic unity and engineering self-reliance, the mausoleum of Oljeitu Khudabenda (early fourteenth century) in Sultaniya, the North dome chamber in Isfahan's Masjid-i-Jami (late eleventh cen-

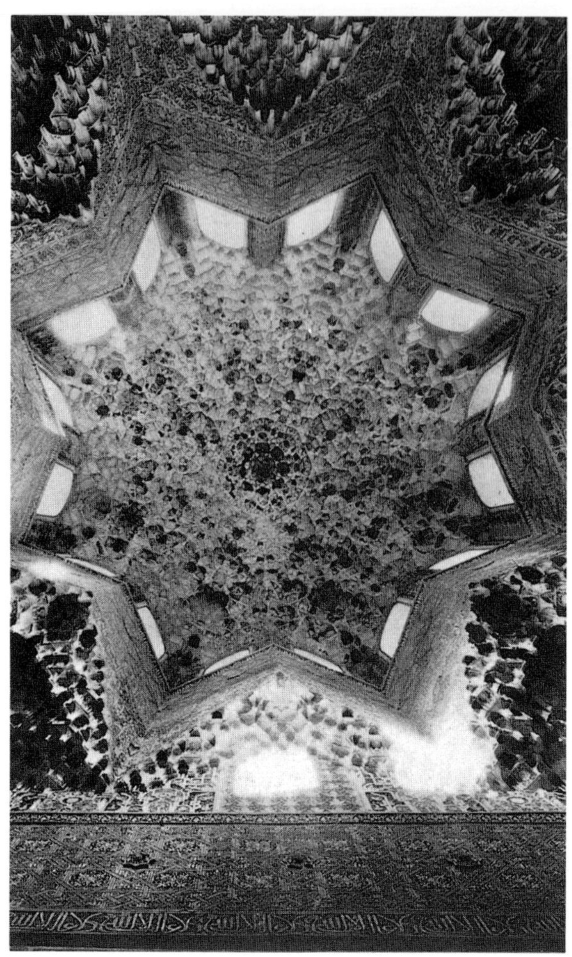

139b. Ceiling-cupola, Hall of the Abencerrages, the Alhambra

tury [*Plate 145*]), or the lofty and pointed blessedness of Iranian *ivans* (*Plates 146a&b*).

Opposite all this, and blended with it, the other current of no-beginning-no-end continuity and interlacing, Islam's intimacy of bliss in it; from the Alhambra's ceilings-and-walls, or the Cordoba mosque's inner domes and self-multiplied arches to the ''illegible'' intricacies—the linear and chromatic, architectonic, intricacies of motion—of the domes, the *ivans,* the minarets, mausolea and *mihrabs* in Iran and elsewhere (*Plates 147a&b*).

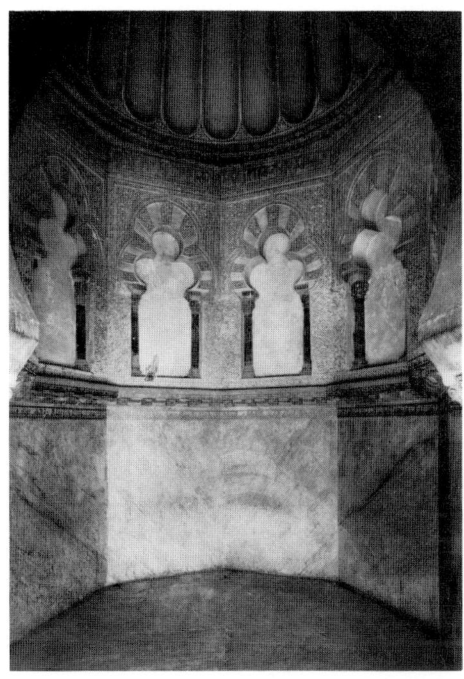

140. Mihrab, Great Mosque, Cordoba

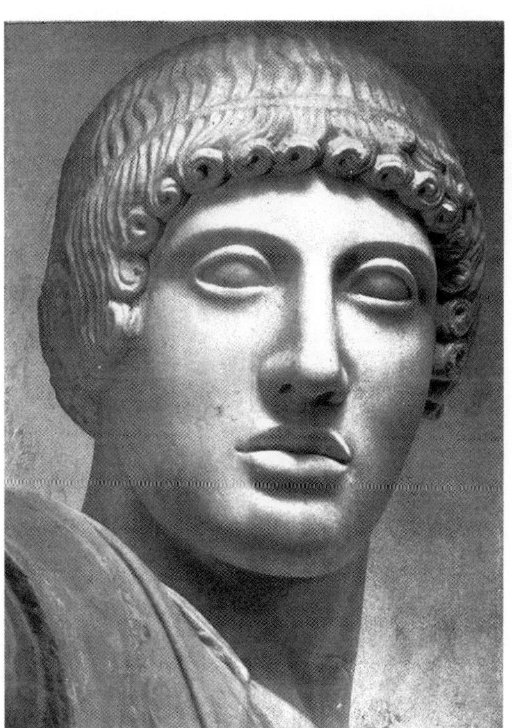

141. Head of Apollo, Temple of Zeus, Olympia

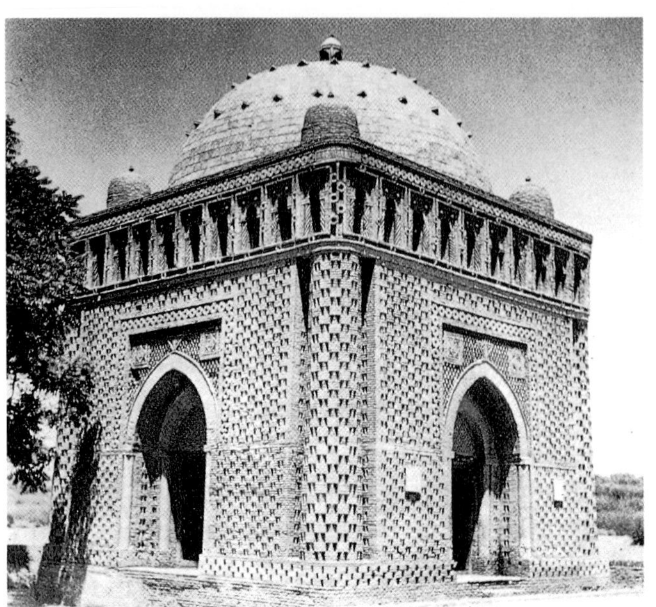

142. The Tomb of the Samanids, Bukhara

*

This is what Islamic man gave or added to what in Iberia had already been given or added there by the Atlantic and Mediterranean man. And that is why I said Islam's gift to Spain was the gift of a *quantitatively* enhanced—added—quality that was at once Islamic proper and universal: the gift of persistent intensity, of passion.

That is also how it is, because of the structural affinities, in depth, of the visual thinking in Islam and in the Christian West—the element of psychomachic "mobility" being the most inventive and the most typical in both of them—and because of the reinforcement of this element in Spanish art by the impact or apport of the Islamic gift, that Spain rather than being "orientalized" or "Islamicized" became the faithful, indeed the strongly intensified reflection—a magnifying mirror—of Western man.

*

And now, I wish to tell you about my last visitation in the world where I found myself, my meeting with El Escorial, the last *dramatis persona* of my History-and-Mind's Intrigue. I was prepared

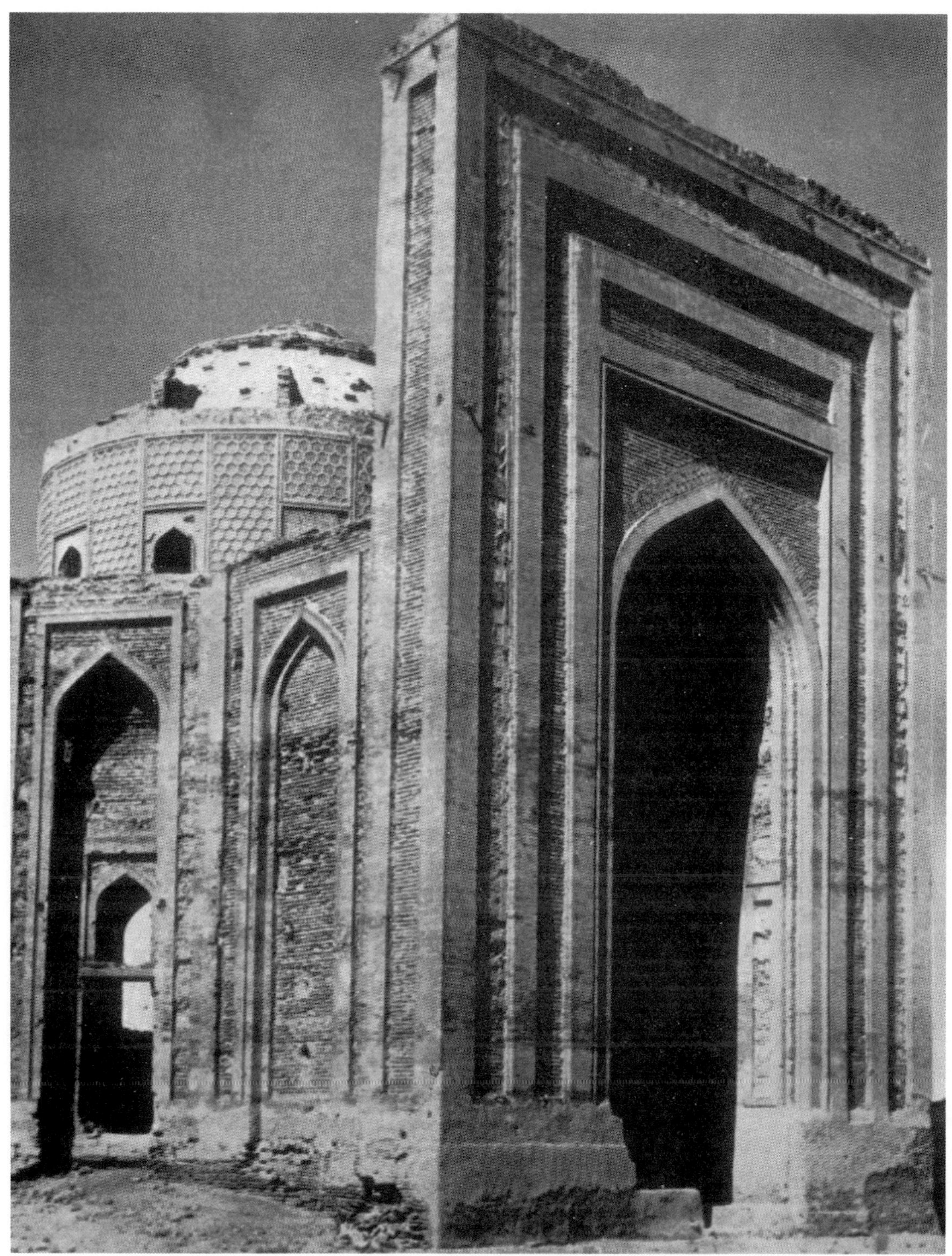

143. Turabek Khanum mausoleum, Urgench

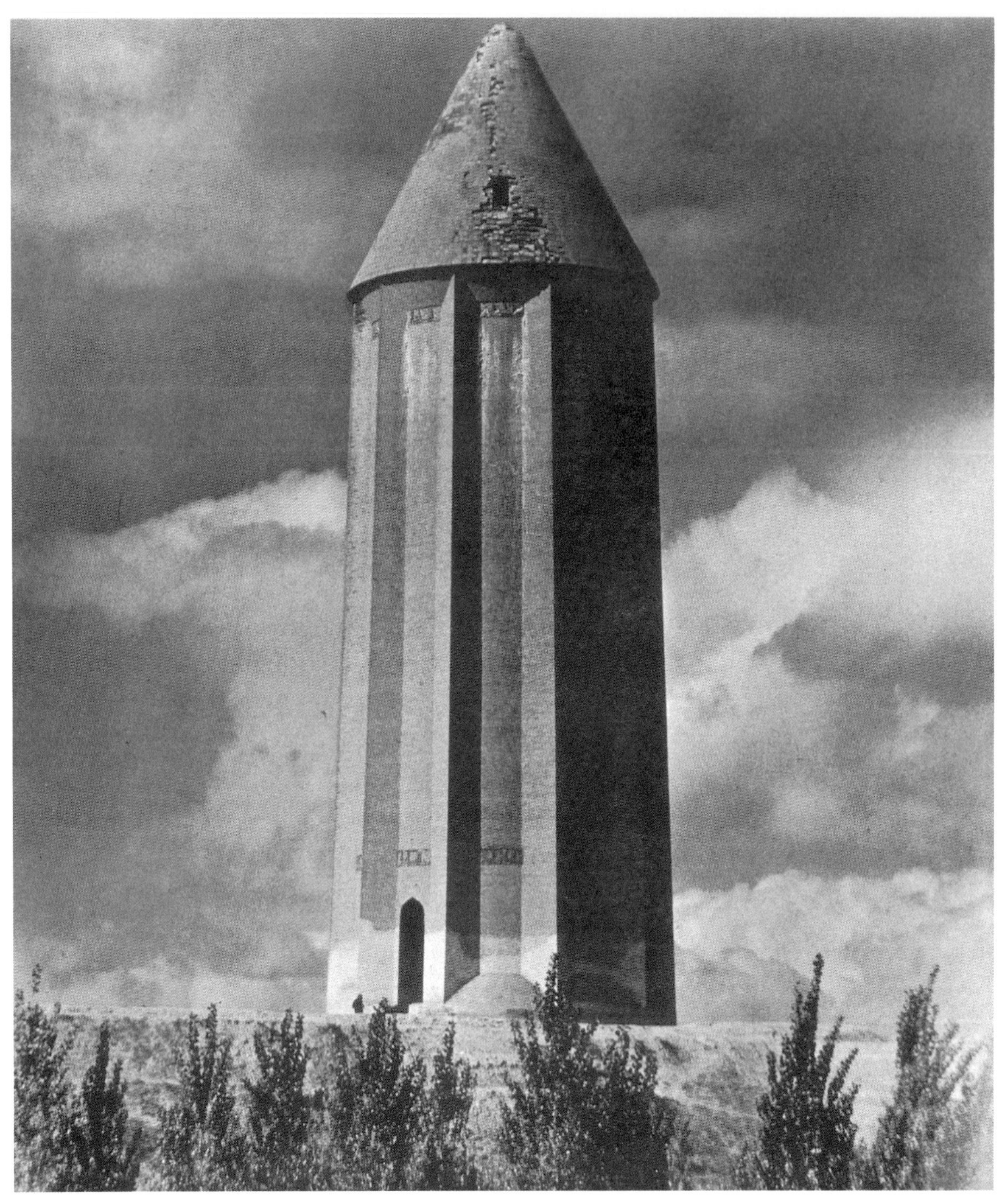

144. Tomb-tower, Gunbad-i-Qabus, Iran

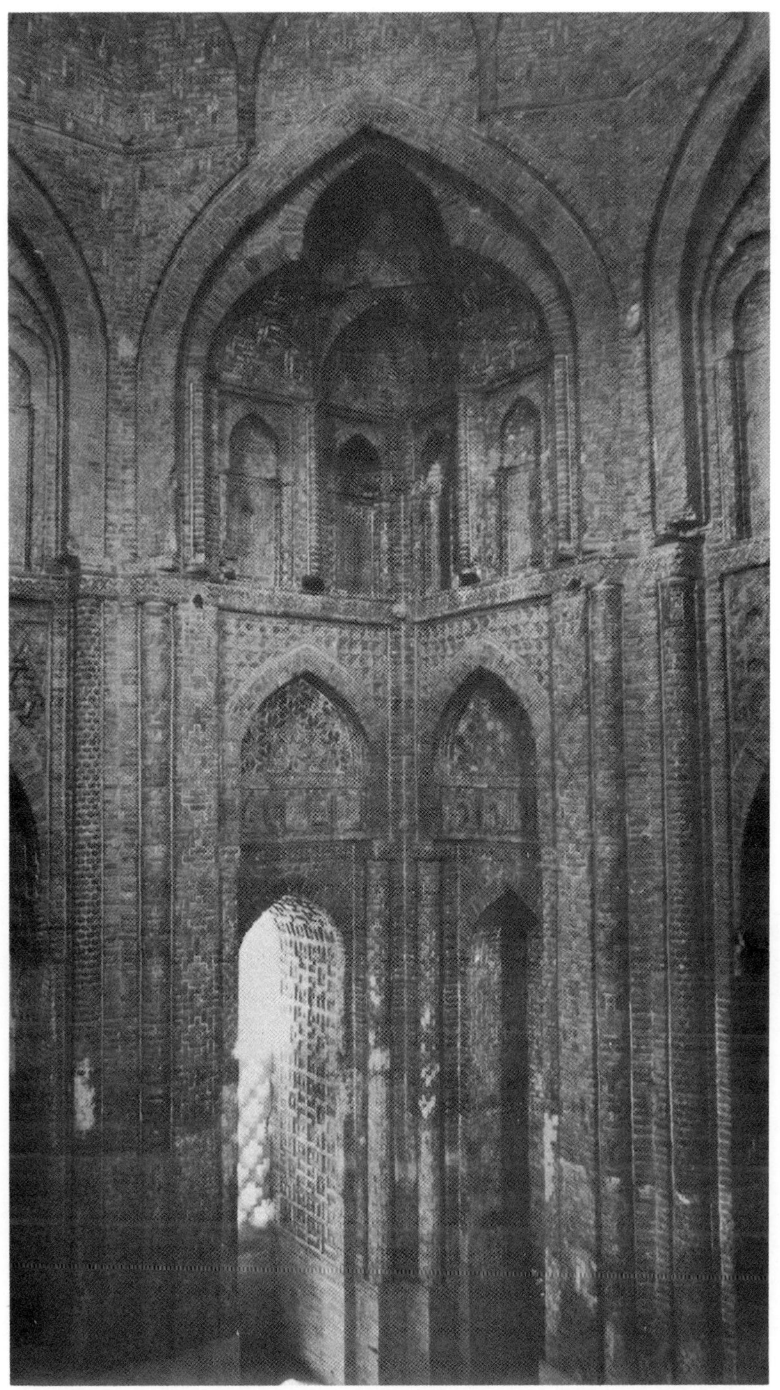

145. North dome chamber, west corner of interior, Masjid-i-Jami, Isfahan

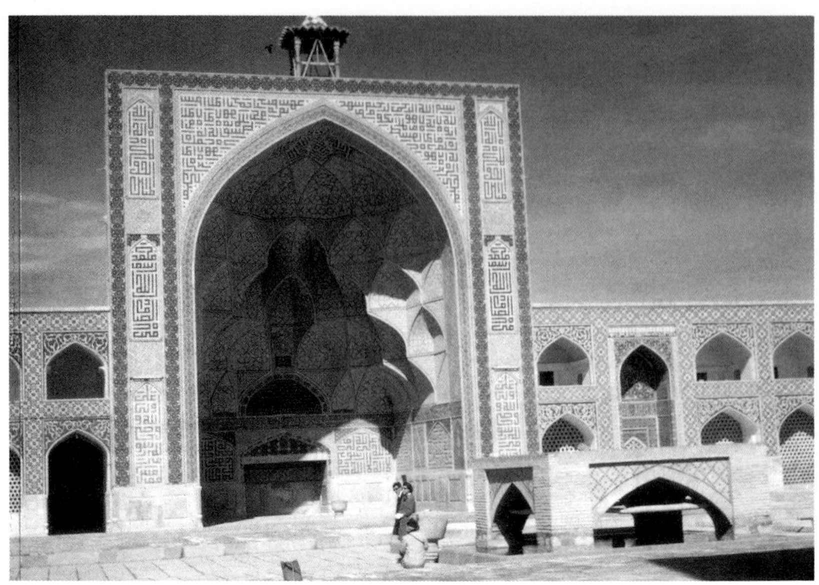

146a. Northwest *ivan,* Masjid-i-Jami, Isfahan

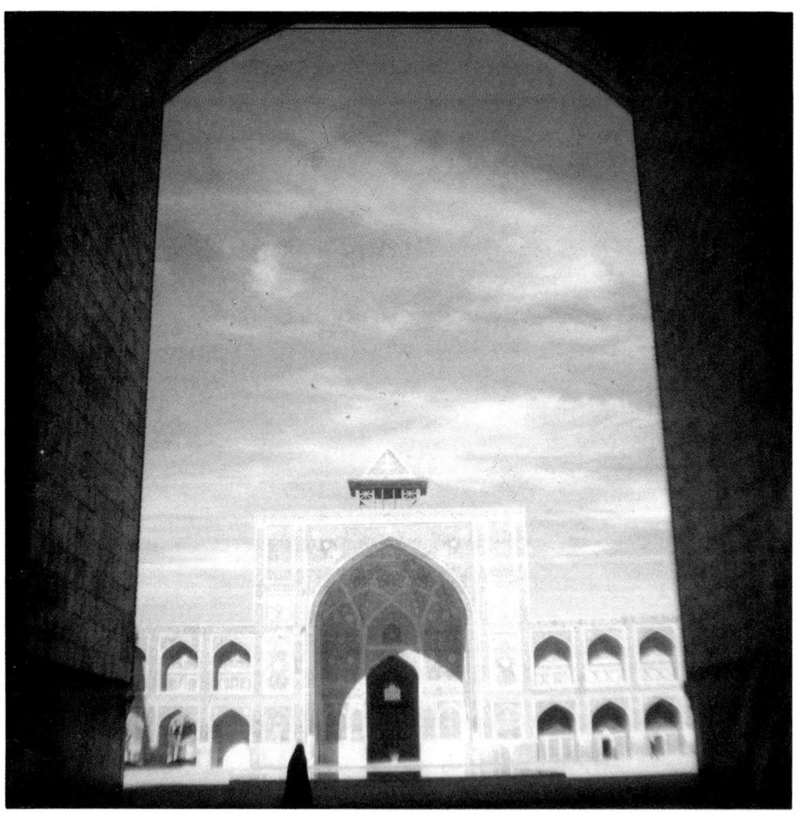

146b. Northwest *ivan,* Masjid-i-Shah, Isfahan

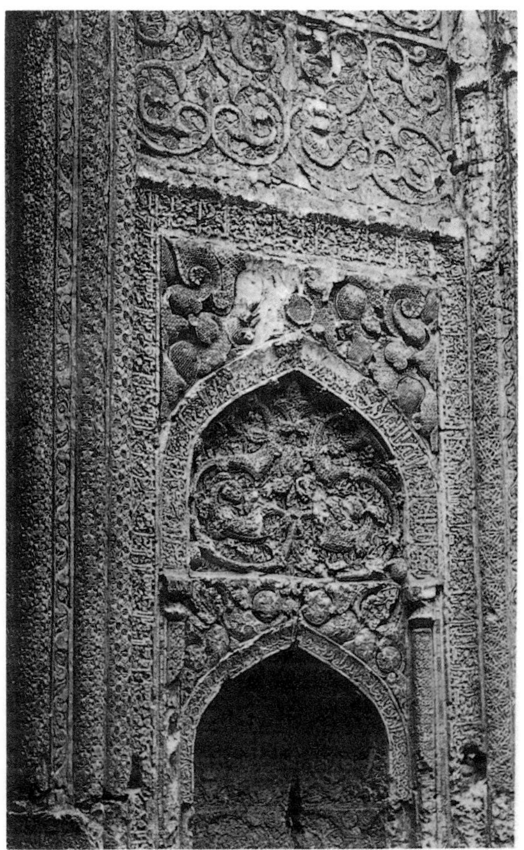

147a. Mihrab, the Alaviyan, Hamadan, Iran

for the meeting—was expecting it. From the numerous written records, testimonies and communications I could learn, much in advance, a lot about this astonishing monument of the late sixteenth-century post-Trentine West—the West's magnifying mirror: a granitic mausoleum-monastery-palace (*Plate 148*) ordered by Philip II of Spain to be erected—in total isolation then—behind a slag-heap (*escorial,* hence Escorial) facing on one side the Castilian rudeness, the healthy, frugal, protecting rudeness of the Guadarrama peaks, on the other, the Castilian gentleness, healthy, smiling, expanding, of green valleys.

And I knew then already that in the initial planning and the tenacious—passionate—surveillance of its long and laborious erection (from 1563 to 1584) by the king and his two chief architects, the famous Juan de Toledo and (after the latter's death in 1567, perhaps even before), his assistant and successor Juan de Herrera (1530–1597), there was much more than the realization of the vow

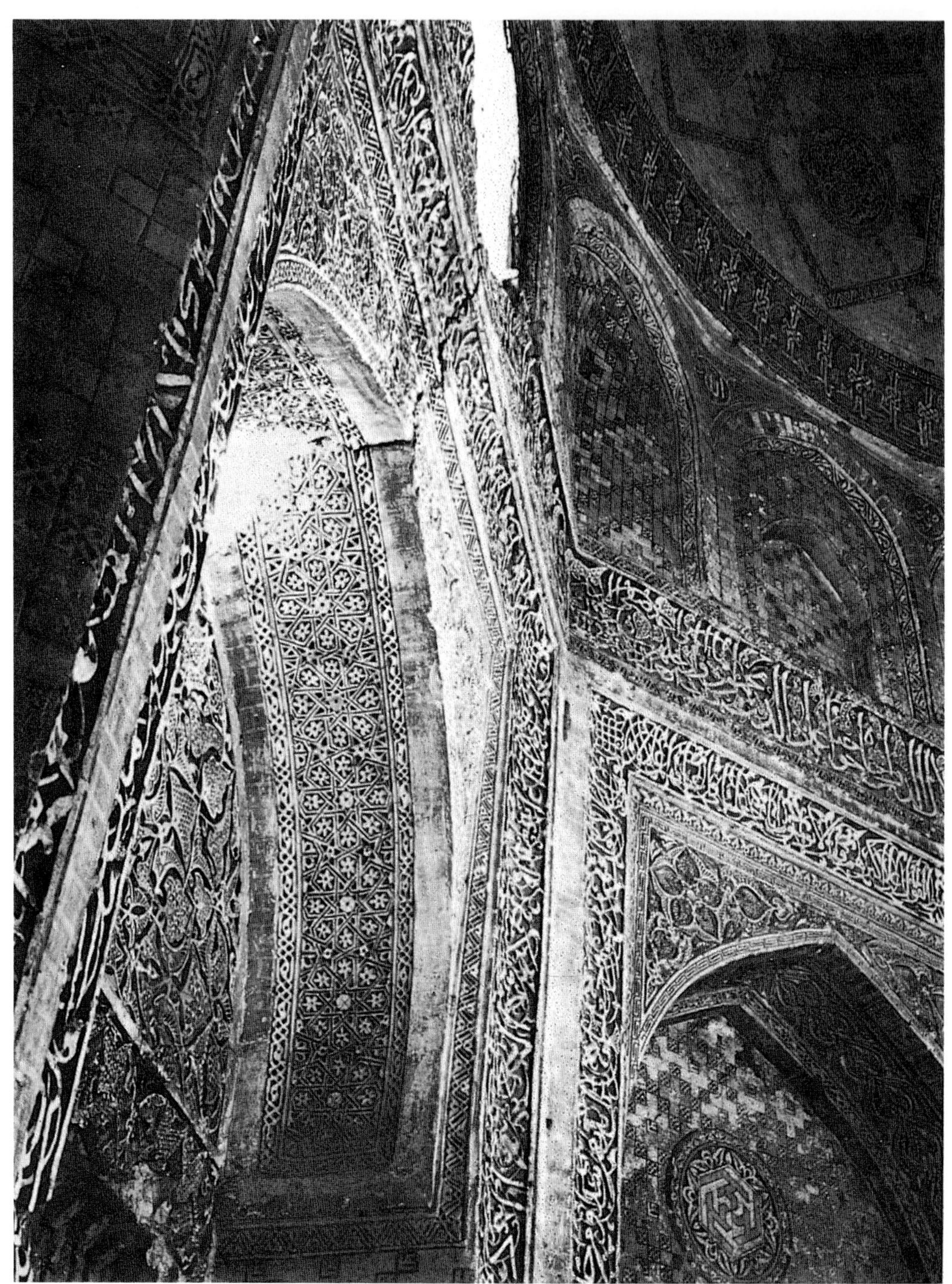

147b. Tomb-tower, Imad-ad-din, Qumm, Iran

made by the king (then still a prince) after the battle of St. Quentin, fought and won St. Laurence's day, to build at home a great sanctuary dedicated to the martyr-saint, whose emblem of martyrdom,

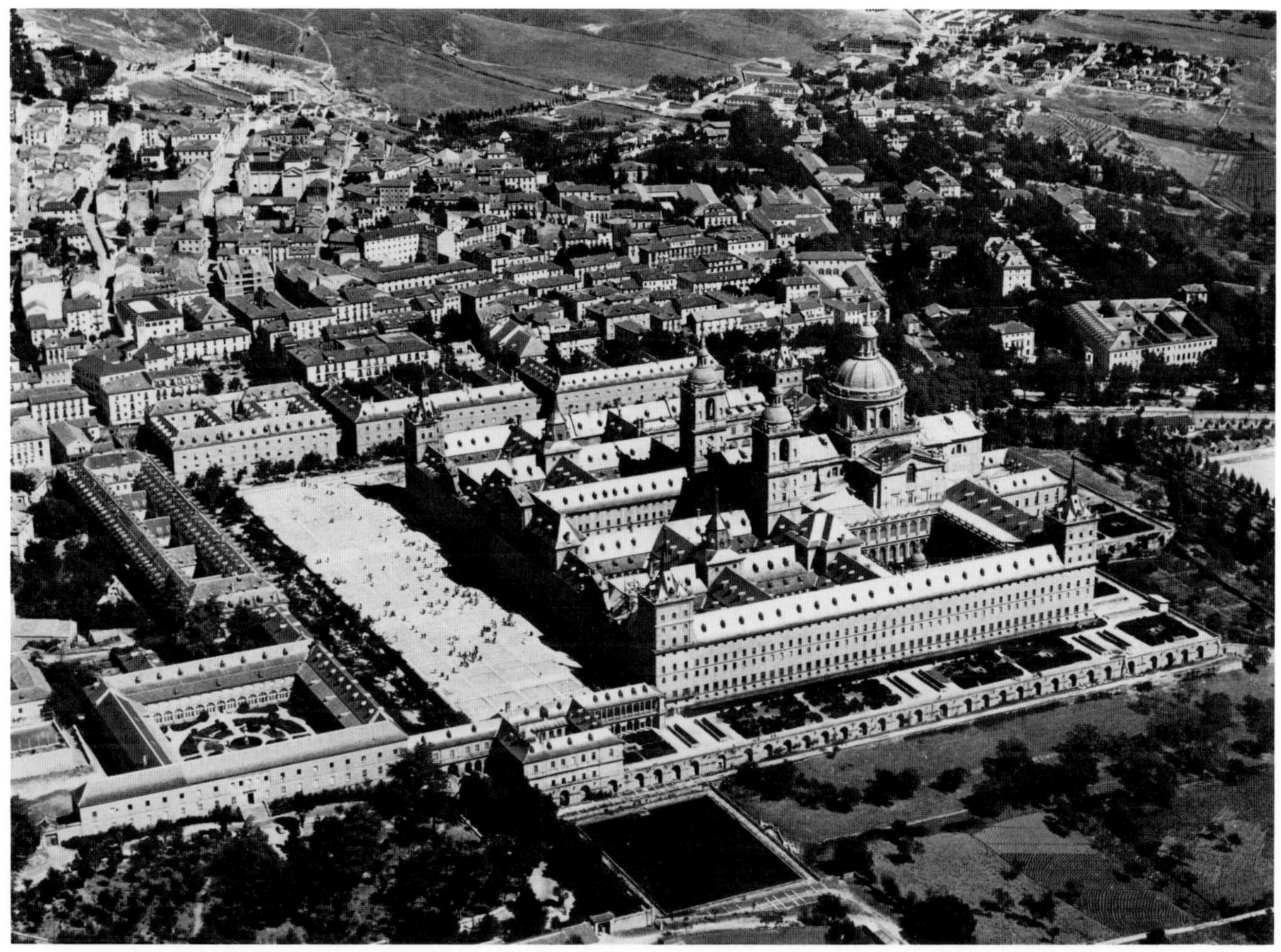

148. The Escorial, aerial view

the grill, had to be reproduced in the ground-plan of El Escorial; more even than the power-dream of a sensuous, frail, imperious and tormented monarch (the lips and the pallor of Felipe's face in Titian's portrait!) to create for his anxieties a shelter, both imperial and intimate, a shelter for the corpses of his royal parents and his relatives, a shelter for solemn prayers—monks, monks, and monks living close to the *pudridero,* praying day and night for the still possible half-salvation of the sinful rulers; shelter for himself, for his own watchful, retired contemplation and his fright perhaps (the serious and tidy modesty of Felipe's habitations in El Escorial!); more also than the king's and his architects'—indeed, of the entire, hermetically oriented, Renaissance's daydream to *reproduce* (not as a *vera imago,* of course, but as a symbolic resemblance) in a building-model, the perfection, God's perfection itself, of Solomon's Temple in Jerusalem, as described in Ezekiel's prophecy;[99] more, thus, than the wish and ambition to make of El Escorial both the final and unique—Spanish—repository of all the laws of divine, inexorable proportions, which from God's unicity to the plurality of His cosmos and thence to man's mind and body had descended once upon a unique time, to be embodied in the musical-numerical occult harmonies of Jerusalem's temple-paradigm.

Years before my visitation I had already sensed what this "much more" could be when, student of things Spanish, I happened to read what the venerable and still authoritative historian of Spain, the old, grand Menéndez y Pelayo had to say about El Escorial's final creator, the architect-mathematician, Juan de Herrera: "A mind both vigorous and synthetic, Herrera delights in lofty speculations, not about aesthetics, but about philosophy and mathematics, at times invading the domain of metaphysics.

"He was an ardent partisan of Ramon Lull's *Ars Magna,* of which he made a very original application in his *Discurso de la Figura Cúbica,* a treatise discovered and copied in Mallorca by Jovellanos [1744–1811], now kept in my private library.

"In this extraordinary treatise Juan de Herrera, with obvious originality in his treatment of details, proposes to simplify and make accessible the combinatory logic of Lull making use of only one [geometrical] figure, the cube."[100]

Herrera's metaphysics of the cube! Its embodiment in stone, El Escorial! Puerile this? Greatly intrigued, I confess, I went to the sources themselves: the *Ars Magna* of Ramon Lull,[101] the Catalan-Mallorcan thinker and poet (born in Mallorca 1232, died 1316, victim—legend came to insist—of his impetuous apostolic zeal),[102] and Juan de Herrera's *Discurso de la Figura Cúbica.*[103]

And there I could see again the living presence of the Braid in man and the world, presence invisible, yet, where I was, fully revealed, and there could receive, also, the last glance of passion and interrogation Spain had to give me.

And I saw this braiding so tight and so delicate that nothing else, or less, than the untouched integrity—the stony flesh and presence of the whole of El Escorial, as I saw and understood it later—could reveal it. (That is why nothing of Herrera's other architectural achievements, left unfinished by him, completed and changed by others—bereft thus of their integrity—could be Herrera's any more, not even the traces of what was left of his ''purest'' creation, the ''cubic'' cathedral of Valladolid.)

*

Time and again, intrigued and suspicious at once, I would try to penetrate further and further into the intricacies of Lull's medieval, rational-mystical and encyclopaedic—''all-knowable-to-be-known''—vision, as well as into Herrera's reasons, his readiness, to accept them. And each time in front of the basic asset of Lull's philosophical conviction and structuring (so uncritically established a priori, so puerile as they appeared to me then, at first, yet accepted, just as they stood, by his late-Renaissance admirer-mathematician, Juan de Herrera), Lull's doctrine of Divine Dignities, Father-Creator's attributes whose vestigial resemblances (the *semblances* of Lull), to be found in each creature, were the cause of all beings to be—each time, I would come out from my plunge with the same feeling of fatigue and irritation. Brought up in the world of intellectual watchfulness and caution, not only of thinking about thinking—this exclusive gift of Hellas to the West!—but of thinking about thinking about thinking itself—how could one accept this medieval and basic doctrine of static Absolutes—God's Dignities, or, in their cliché abbreviations, God's Attributes or Principles (sixteen in Lull's classification during the earlier phase of his life activity, reduced to nine in the second or final phase)? Yet, on this unconvincing foundation Lull could erect, for those who would follow him, a most convincing super-structure of ''algebraic logic,'' as it was sometimes called, and of metaphysical certainty.

But my curiosity very soon got the better of my rejection. In Lull, I saw it clearly, the nine absolute Principles, absolute as far as pertaining to the Creator, relative as far as pertaining to the Creature, were all, for ''necessary reasons,'' interconnected not only among themselves (reason and the ''*natura*'' being interlaced also in their turn) *but with the act or action of interconnection itself.* They form thus an all-catching net of a totally intelligible science or art of the *combinatory,* the very *Ars Magna* of Lull, the science and the art of Lull's purposeful, unending Being of Growth. Such, his beloved all-encompassing figures of the Tree of Science and, parallel to these figures, interchangeable with them, the superstructure of all his graphs-schemata, geometric-numeric-alphabetic, which, sprouting from an initial, perfect triangular configuration:

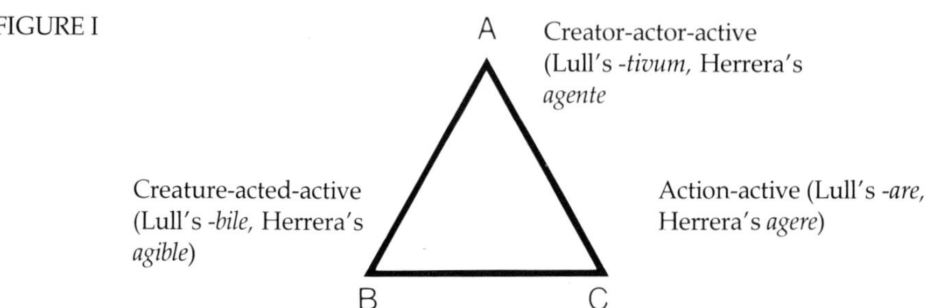


FIGURE I

[*Ed: Lull's* tivum, bile, are: *these are suffixes, as in* (*from* bonitas) bonificabile, bonificativum, bonificare.]

evolved "naturally," because interchangeably (echo of Greek reversibility—the proportionality of all unsurpassable, perfect, thus inter-equated, shapes), into a compound—square-triangle-circle-figure, the *square* of four *elements,* earth, water, air, fire and their qualities; the *triangle* of all existences; the *circle* of all perfections; thence into the interconnected succession of final diagrams and back to the plenitude of God's Dignities (*Plates 149a,b*).[104]

FIGURE II

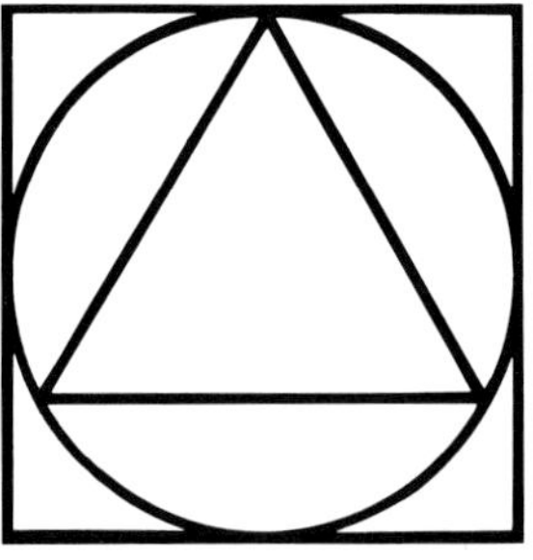

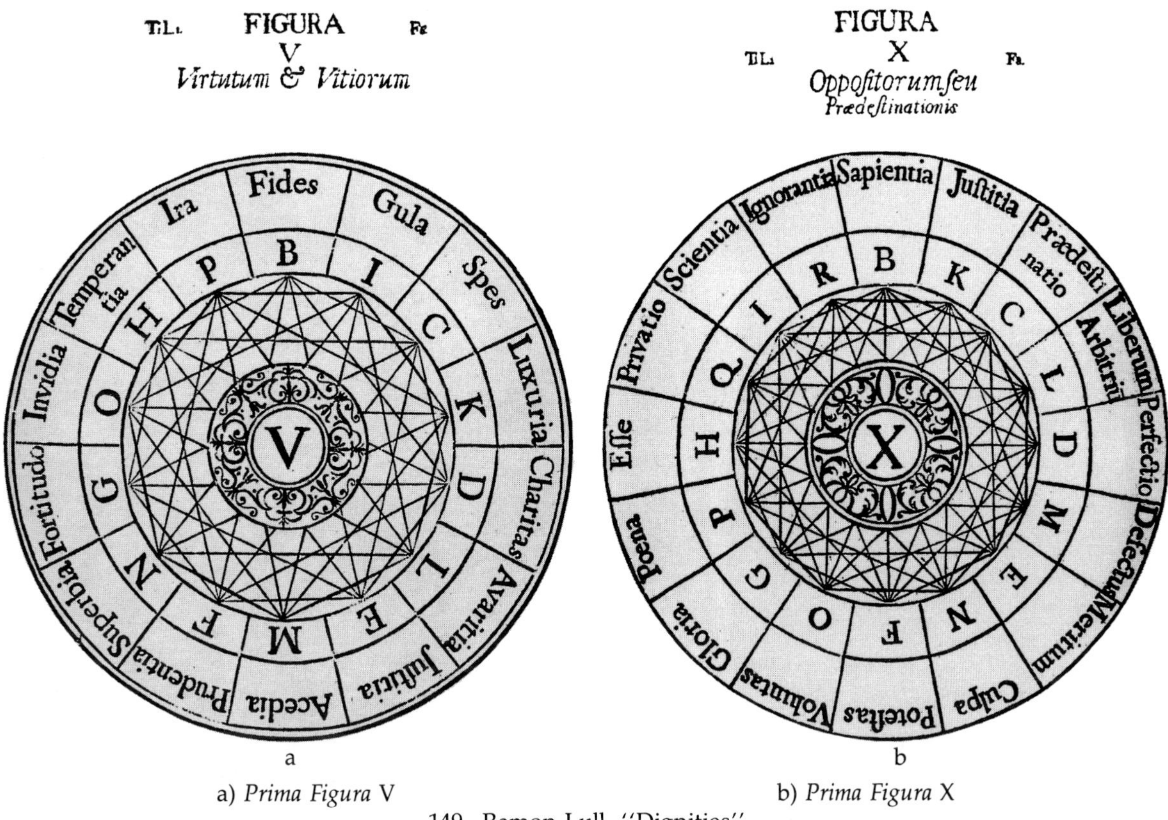


a) *Prima Figura* V
b) *Prima Figura* X

149. Ramon Lull, ''Dignities''

And then, one day, the still deeper intention of Lull, unspoken and underlying the unitive one, became clear to me. For Lull, the proof of the Absolute, of God, of His Dignities—the absolute necessity in reason's ''natural,'' inherent, mirroring of them—was in the very proving, indeed, in the very process of proving the Absolute's real presence. The absolute Being—of all beginnings and all ends—was to be found, reached, in the very Becoming—with no beginnings and no ends—of the Absolute. And for Lull, I saw, the structure, at once logical, mathematical and ''natural,'' of this Being = Becoming was the very structure of his own *method* in convincing and proving, the method, Lull's *par excellence* (added to other medieval logical-Aristotelian ways of persuasion), called *per aequiparantiam,* the way of reversibility.

For Lull, all of God's absolute Principles—*bondad; grandeza; duración; potestad; sabiduría; instinto; voluntad o apetito; virtud; verdad; y gloria o suavidad, y deleitación* (in Herrera's words), each signified by a letter, B = *bondad,* G = *grandeza,* etc.[105]—in their descent through Definitions and through Rules to the Creature, and in their simultaneous ascent to their common source of Being=Becoming, all are interchangeable, reversible; Goodness is Grandeur is Glory, is Suavity is Virtue and Will and Delectation. Exactly: the signifying fullness of each of the mathematical-moral-metaphysical diagrams, the fullness of a point-sphere, of a line, a surface, a solid, all are interchangeable, as is their apparent transcendentality, so that to none of Lull's *ars combinatoria's* geometrical-numerical schemas, to none of his numerical-alphabetic signs, distributed along or within the frames of his *''figures''* or his *''cámeras''* (each often colored accordingly) could or should the term ''symbolic'' be applied. They are significations, not symbolizations. They are not substitutions, not transfers, but mutual transformations and correspondences, not things (*res*) of mind, but beings of mind (*personae:* being=becoming)—finite participants, each in the uncessant, unfinite in-and-e-volvement of the Wheel (*Aeternitas*).

Lull's is the universe of certainty, because of continuity, of movement uninterrupted and expected in it, without the anxieties of faith-doubt, the discontinuity of a sudden, unforeseen, rigid motion-mobility.

Seen from historical heights, in widest possible detail-levelling perspective of facts-bunched-together, of global attitudes, this world of Ramon Lull is the Indic world: ancient India's ''selling-for-less'' trade's result,[106] the inclusion of the unknown number *X* or *Y* in the plethoric, incessant production of known numbers and their fearless equation therein as participants, all of them, in the turning of the Wheel, is also Lull's speculative result and Lull's equations, his ''algebraic logic,'' his *per aequiparantiam* multi-relational way and act of convincing and ''proving.'' Whether Lull's final vision of God's Dignities could be traced factually to the Islamic Sūfīs, and thence to India itself (Ibn Arabi's, the Murcian thinker-mystic's [1164–1240] *Hadras,* God's Perfections, as Miguel Asín Palacios advanced it) or simply, as the majority of Lullian students would have it, to the medieval West's Anselmian-Augustinian tradition, this doctrine covers a sub-level of psychological certainty similar to what India in her own sub-level's multiple structurations, Hindu-Upanishadic, pan-Buddhist, or Jain, has been revealing to us more openly.

Basically this:

That nothing exists beyond the compound. This is how Reality exists—and Reality does exist. It exists not as any finite and ultimate unit or even unity, but as unit-compound. Reality is compoundness. Existence is compoundness *ab initio. And compoundness cannot but be comprehension of compoundness:* nothing can be comprehended but what is already compound. The reality of existence outside and inside us, the reality of this very compoundness, is co-extensive, co-existent with the reality of the comprehension of this. Not mind's stuff, but mind-stuff itself. For Mind is of Flesh; Flesh is of Mind (and levitation is a natural, and not a super-natural event). Mind-stuff: incessant mutual transformation and correspondence; the compound of function, structure, content and relation.

And so it is in Lull. The Absolute is dissolved there, as it were, in the undifferentiated, ''unimpeded interdiffusion of particulars.''[107] The most complicated and complex figural results of Lull's ''combinatory Art''—the schemata made of intersecting, interconnected and interconnecting lines, circles, triangles, etc., are the West's ''mandalas''[108]—their structure-meaning, structure-essence, being that of India, in spite of all the differences of their respective ''abstract'' idioms and their means of persuasion. For, after all, India's centuries-and-centuries-long maturation could achieve or arrive at, in her sacred psycho-cosmic diagrams= compounds, a crystal clear reduction of their semantic complexity to the simplest, ''purest'' (most loyal-to-the-origins) expression of her speculative thought. Such is the Hindu supreme mandala, the Śrī-Yantra, a dynamic diagram (*Plate 150*), its outer square frame enclosing a series of concentric circles and lotus-petal circles—the whole representing the cosmos, the temple, the center of the heart of the devotee, seat of all action, all at once—whose inner central space is filled by nine interlacing triangles, interpenetrating each other, four triangles pointed upward—the *vahni* triangles, fire, male, quietude, Śiva—and five pointed downward, *yoni,* female energy, Śakti.[109] The four *vahni* triangles form pairs with four of the Sakti triangles: the remaining innermost Śakti triangle forms a pair with the invisible drop=*bindu* (the expected triangle to be visualized by force of concentration only as a vanishing dot or

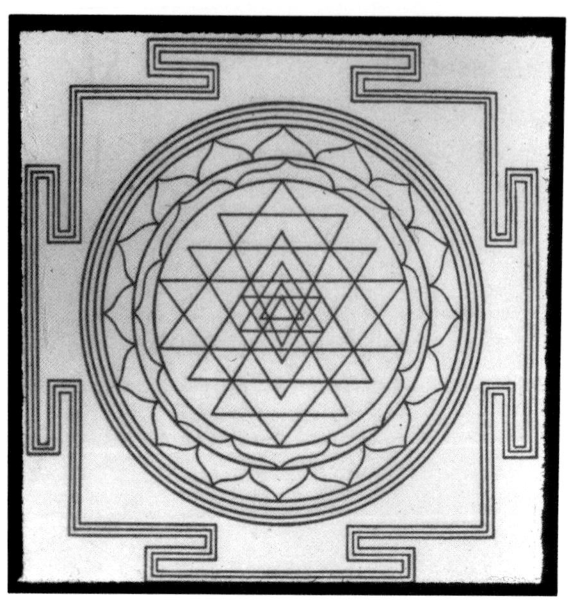

150. *Śrī-Yantra,* instrument of Hindu worship

point, as a drop=*bindu*), amidst the interplay of all the triangles: "the power-point, the invisible, elusive center from which the whole picture expands. This innermost triangle represents the primeval Śakti, creative . . . energy, in union with . . . Śiva or pure, quiescent Brahman-principle, the *Bindu.* The other four pairs of interpenetrating triangles represent the creative activity of the male-female polarity of cosmic energy on successive stages of . . . evolution. Thus the . . . diagram . . . represents Life universal and individual as the incessant interaction of cooperating opposites, producing everything by an unending dynamism."[110]

India at large: a universe of certainty, of continuity, of motion expected, rounded, "mnemonic" and convincing-satisfying, without the anxiety of faith-doubt in it (though faith-doubt is present, invisible, hidden within the Braid), without the sudden discontinuity of a motion immediate, the "mobile rigidity" of the Witness in it (present, though, invisible, temporarily hidden within the Braid).

Such is Lull's also. In depth. From the downward roots-pointed graphics of his *per-aequiparantiam* method of *atrobar veritat* ("meeting the truth") to the upward, Dignities-pointed branches of his Tree of Science, whose structure-and-content was the very structure-and-content of this method itself, namely the three personae-essences of the basal Triangle, the creator-actor, the creature-actor, the action-actor (Lull's-*tivum,-bile,-are*) Lull's comprehension = compoundness of Being-Becoming's three-unity, the doctrine of Trinity itself, so abhorred by Muslims and Jews alike, and for whose defense and proof Lull's entire life was given—from this to that, Lull's universe was the universe of certainty and continuity.

This is how, in subtle braiding and its ''silence and secrecy'' Lull understood St. Anselm's *credo ut intelligam* (''I believe in order to understand'').

And this is also how Lull's certainty and energy have fascinated so many of the best minds of the Renaissance and post-Renaissance (repelling many others, of course), from the influential fifteenth century Ramón de Sabunde—through whom admiration for the *Ars Magna* was inherited by Montaigne and later by Pascal—to Cardinal Cisneros, Nicolas de Cusa, Juan Luis Vileta, Giordano Bruno, and many others down to Leibnitz. So great was the charm of the unitive content of the combinatory art, as well as Lull's literary way of philosophical communication, his ''uninterrupted confession,'' made *coram populo,*[111] that even those who rejected Lull's method and proof, like Gerson or the famous fifteenth century Spaniard, Fernando de Córdoba, or Francis Bacon, or Descartes, could not resist the attraction of his ''universal science'' of interconnectedness.

*

The Renaissance and post-Renaissance man had inherited two great historical legacies, absorbed them and enriched them immensely in expansion, meaning and vigor: the Lullian—essentially Western medieval—and the ancient Hellenic and Near Eastern, essentially Eastern medieval, Byzantine.

The Western medieval legacy, Pythagorean, Neo-Platonic, late Antiquity's legacy of metaphysical certainty:

That what is true of the harmonic and combinatory proportionality in abstractions, numbers, shapes, must also be true of the combinatory proportions in the human mind, the human *anima,* the human body, and certainly should be true of any structure made or created by human skill—architecture, music, poetry, sculpture, painting, even economy or government.

And braided with this legacy, its opposite—the legacy of metaphysical faith-doubt:

That the destiny of man's salvation and man's creativity on earth is in the *must* of an unattainable, transcendental will of the Father-Creator, His will to make all that is His creation and creature converge towards, into, His centered totality. Such, transferred now to the world of human action and thought, is the centralized, totalitarian will in Renaissance man himself. In still narrower transfer into the visual-manual, his will to make all optical directions converge towards, into, their centered "vanishing point."

In painting this means, of course, to make the orthogons of the new linear perspective converge towards, into, their centered "vanishing point," initially a simple "carpenter's device"[112] (for the Renaissance was the "victory day" of my Fable's artisan-artist), from whose pragmatic premises sprang all the new laws of projective, analytical space structurings in mathematics and the arts (starting with the great Italian visual thinkers: Brunelleschi, Alberti, Peruzzi, Bramante, Serlio, da Vinci, Vignola, Palladio, Lomazzo).

In architecture, it means the will to make all the architectonic harmonies of building converge—the must!—towards, into, their centered "vanishing point," the cupola; in music, as well as in painting's color structuring, the chromatic and tonal three-dimensionality as it were, the convergence—the must!—of all the inherent over-and-under-tones towards, into, their centered "vanishing point," the apex-tone of a triadic chord, the apex-tonality of a chromatic compound (painting and music in sixteenth-century Venice).

In political thought it was the will to make all the social-political orthogons converge towards, into their "vanishing point," the centralized, unchallengeable authority of an enlightened, personal rule; and in the world of economy this same *must* of Father-Creator's infinity substituted by man's finite fragment-will and fragment-reason—to make all human needs, aspirations and rights converge towards, into, the now transcendental, "sacred," centered "vanishing point": self-sufficient, self-reproducing capital.

*

The Renaissance man, in his didactically oriented will to transfer the problems of critical inquiry from the domain of the ''sacral'' to that of the secular (without losing, though, anything of his religious medieval ardor—quite the contrary) shed a new light upon that very will and that very inquiry: this was precisely the birth of the West's modern epistemology—not only the rebirth of ancient Greek ''thinking about thinking,'' but the birth of modern man's thinking about thinking about thinking itself. Under this new light the Renaissance man could make visible, clearly, totally, centrally, for the first time in the history of my Intrigue, the presence in him of both opposites and of their braiding.

*

Juan de Herrera, Spaniard, man of the late Renaissance, was professionally familiar with the writings of most of the Italian, Vitruvius-oriented Renaissance thinkers-theorists (the contents of his personal library testify to it);[113] Alberti, Peruzzi, Serlio, Vignola were translated into Spanish during the sixteenth century.

Herrera's central theme in his *Discurso de la Figura Cúbica* is, in its external descriptive and demonstrative content and procedure, typical of both medieval and Renaissance thinking in its emphasis on the implications both mathematical and practical of perfect geometrical shapes and their harmonic relations. But (and here my surprise in plunging into Herrera's real intention was equalled only by that of my plunge into Lull's) in Herrera's treatment of his subject, the mathematical-metaphysical meaning of the perfect geometrical figure, the cube—optically so simple, mathematically so complex in its geometric and arithmetic genesis and its structure-meaning[114]—becomes the finite and final shape, inexorable in the plenitude of its perfection, to which infinity, its unseizable totality, is reduced; infinity as conceived by Renaissance and medieval man alike in his theo-anthropological (as Lullian philosophy has sometimes been called) vision of himself and his destiny, of the cosmos and its destiny.

For this idea, so peculiarly Spanish in its boldness, passion and explicitness, Herrera is avowedly indebted to Ramon Lull and his *Ars Magna.* Yet, in spite of undeniable external similarities (accepted by all those who have studied this subject), underlying the communicated meditation one finds a contrast: in Lull the global attitude of correspondence between the finite and the infinite; in Herrera the attitude of substitution by the finite for the infinite.

Throughout the *Discurso de la Figura Cúbica,* Herrera speaks of himself as a loyal, thorough Lullist,[115] the interpreter of Lull's most intimate thought, a thought penetrated through and through with the medieval certainty of micro-macrocosmic correspondence and interconnection, ultimately the *psychomachic* ''leaning on one's own self''—one's own freed decisions. And yet, in scrutinizing Herrera's text attentively, one discovers that Juan de Herrera, true Renaissance man that he was, and a typical Spaniard in his intense loyalty to the origins of his inner choice, tinctured this Lullian certainty with an opposite, very Renaissance tonality of attitude—that of substitution, ultimately the *apocalyptic* ''leaning on something outside oneself'' and one's own decisions.

Lull's voice was that of assuredness; Herrera's was not. His speech is the speech of faith-doubt, of anxiety. Of mystery, as Lull's never was.

''But the Lord in whom is all plenitude of knowledge''—thus starts the *Discurso*—''opens at times the understanding of those who know little and makes them speak of certain things which when understood deeply and meditatively, and not superficially, as is sometimes the case, reveal in themselves, although they may appear small, great and sudden mysteries and secrets difficult to penetrate . . . and among those things I shall mention the cubic figure, which is the root and foundation of Lullian Art.''[116] And later on ''. . . and the *Are* [*agente*=agent=actor in Herrera's own definition] together with the *Tivum* [*agible*=acted upon] and the *Bile* [*agere*=the action itself, the acting] form the cube of total plenitude, the total plenitude of being and acting . . . thus, there is in the cube a trine relation [the very roots of the Holy Trinity's intelligibility] which is Raimundo's *Tivum,* . . . *Bile* and *Are,* these being of the essence and nature of the same cube that has the total plenitude and total complement of all the plenitudinal differences, neither less, nor more.''

And ''Thus we have defined the cube both as a discrete quantity [the cube as numerical-arithmetical entity] and as a continuous quantity [the cube as geometrical entity]. From here on we shall endeavor to prove that the cube exists in all things, *in the natural as natural, in the moral as moral* [italics mine: moral cube!] . . . and that it is contained besides in each of the nine principles, absolute and relative, of Raimundo and in whatever other principles might exist outside [*fuera*] of those . . . '' *Fuera*—''outside''—could never have been Lull's here!

Herrera's Glance is Spain's Glance of metaphysical interrogation. He needs the repetition of the very sound *cubo.* ''*Cubo! Cubo!*'' the anxiety of his faith-doubt is there in his obsession and the tone of this very sound repeated by him. He says ''the cube of being,'' the ''cube of time,'' ''cubic penetration and its plenitude.'' He says and repeats: '' . . . the total plenitude of mixture and operations consists in all of them being cubically full,'' and he invents and uses the verb ''cubicar.''

*

And this is why I said my visitation of El Escorial was prepared, expected.

In this ''most enormous mass of stone that exists in the world,''[117]—''mouse-grey, coarse as kitchen salt''[118]—I saw the granitic incarnation of the cube. I saw only the cube. The poison of identification with an idea—threshold of man's insanity—was in me: Isolde's philtre of love meant to be of death.

El Escorial was for me the monument-paradigm of the universal-human braiding in man of the Apocalyptic and Psychomachic, here, in this Spanish Renaissance building, the Apocalyptic being to the fore. I saw only the cube: the substitution for total infinity by the finity of its fragment, the cube. It became indifferent or almost so to watch the factual denial of this in the variety of other shapes there (*Plate 151*)—the Eros, the Desire of the cube was in all of them: the Eros-cube in the acute triangle of the horizontal skyscraper piercing the triangular narrow sky there (*Plate 152*); the desire-cube in the perfect circularity of the magnificent dome of the church; the cube-desire in the earthly, ''normal'' cube of the Patio de los Reyes. (*Plate 153*)

And Juan de Herrera was the true creator of this. Had the immensely elongated west front of El Escorial's granitic mass been left as Juan de Toledo had planned it, its architectonic, quietly combined harmonies would have been enhanced by the lordly dome visible from outside of the great basilica dominating the lowered

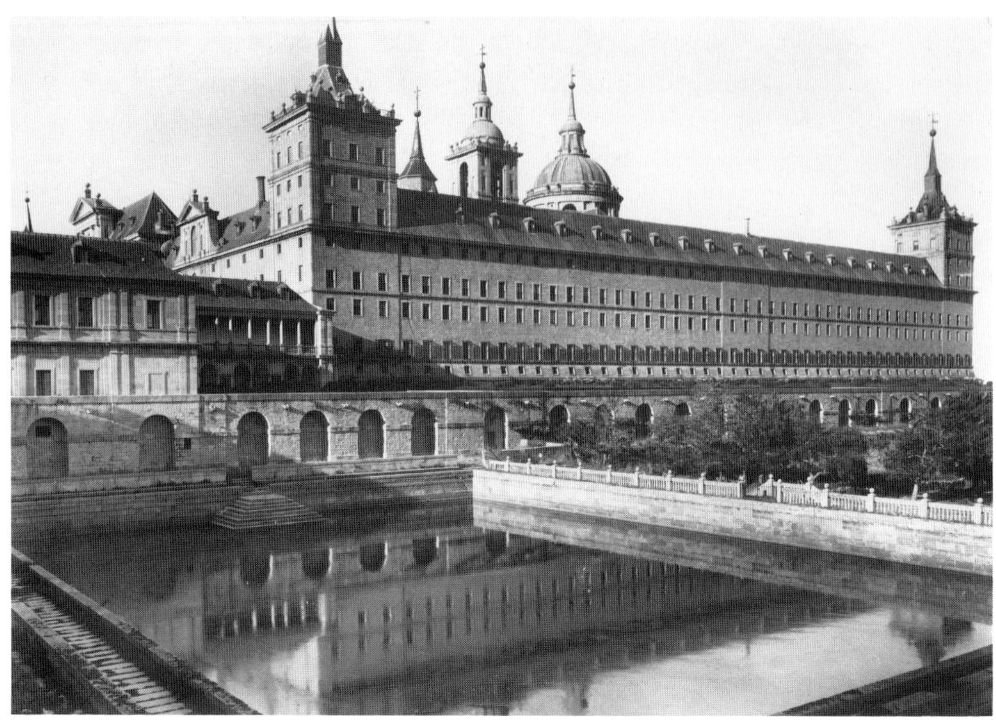

151. The Escorial, monastery, south façade

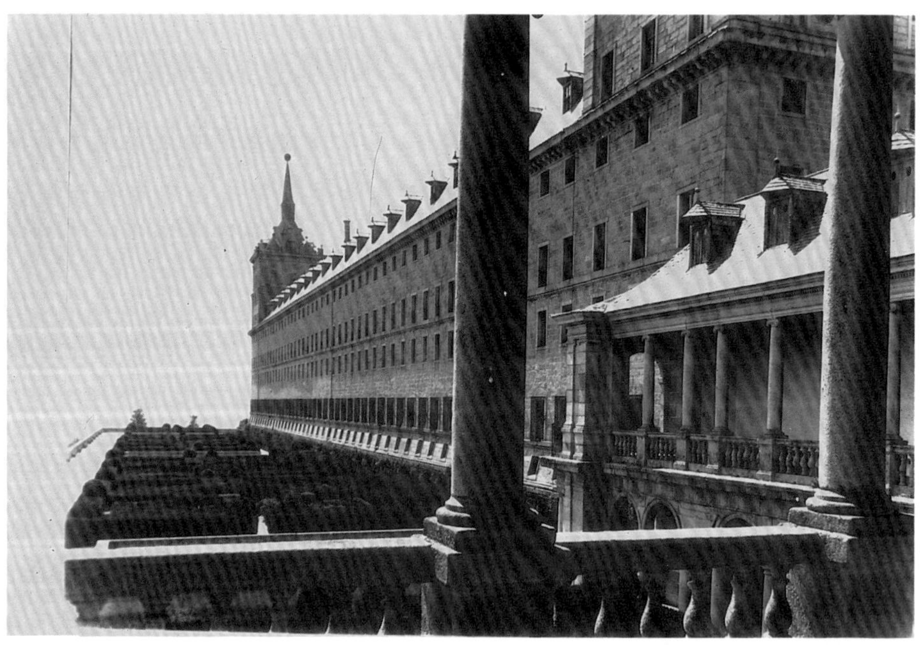

152. The Escorial, monastery, south façade, detail

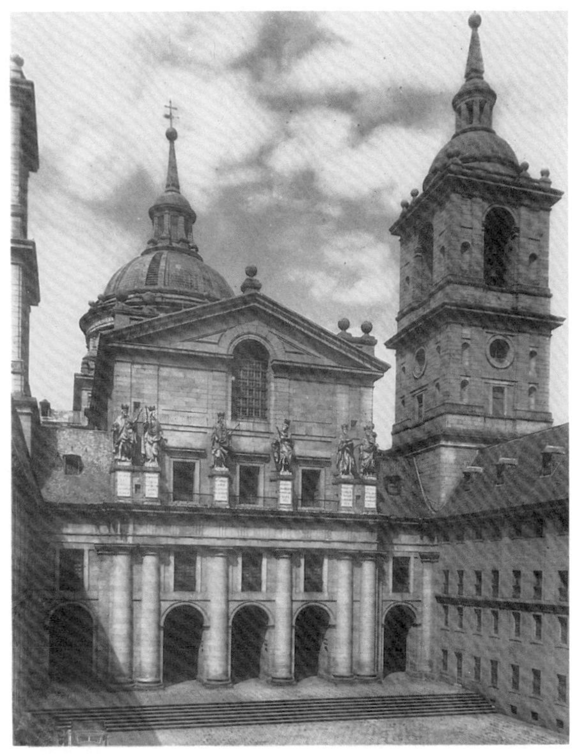

153. The Escorial, Patio of the Kings

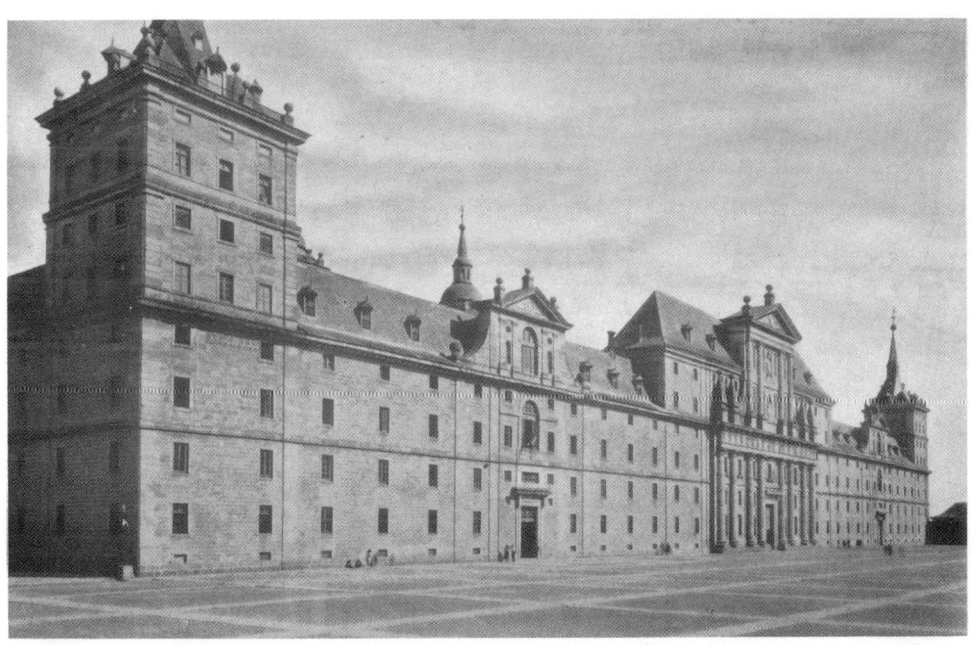

154. The Escorial, monastery, west (main) façade

walls, and then all this picturesque and balanced ensemble could have been admired simply as a compounded exemplar of the best Italian late Renaissance achievements and inventions. But the new design of this front by Herrera (*Plate 154*) totally changed it. Probably for the practical reason of accommodating an augmented number of Jeronymite monks there (reason, however, not necessarily to be final for a skillful architect in the choice of his final decision), the front's wall was heightened by Herrera, hiding from the outside view the majestic Bramante-Michelangelesque dome, and, at the same time, by reducing the number (twelve) of Juan de Toledo's towers to six, opening to this view the immense monotony ("spirit is monotonous" somebody said once) of an unadorned front whose "ardent coolness" makes it unique in the world at large, unique in Spain also. Unique. And no learned references to Italian model buildings of fame could be brought in here with any gain: the appropriate "coolness" of Filarete's Hospital in Milan or the simplicity, both exalted and studious, of Vignola's creations. El Escorial is unique. And Spanish. Spanish as Machuca's vigorous Roman-Renaissance masterpiece, the palace of Charles V in the Alhambra (*see Plate 131*) is not, not entirely; or Vásquez' or Covarrubias' or Villalpando's creations. Spanish as only, at the extreme opposite of El Escorial's place in the history of Spain's architecture, two earlier marvels of Spanish sixteenth century architecture appeared to me at that hour of my love-visitation: the architectural "ornament-monster" of the *cimborio* in the Cathedral of Burgos (by Juan de Vallejo, 1543–68 [*Plate 155*]), and the *rotonda*—the ambulatory's cylindrical chevet—of Granada's Cathedral (*circa* 1552), Diego de Siloe's unrivaled masterpiece (*Plate 156*). And nothing short of the direct visual experiencing of it can reveal the meaning of what is told there: Herrera-Lull's *"en lo natural como natural, en lo moral como moral"* of the "interdiffusion of all particulars" (and not only of the "total cube") prophesied in the "Romanesque"-Islamic glance of the starry *cimborio,* in the sculptured, vertical ascension and descent of the *rotonda's* voids and solids, lights and shadows—arches, pillars, windows, in fluid, elastic ascent and descent of Lullian correspondences and interpenetrations.

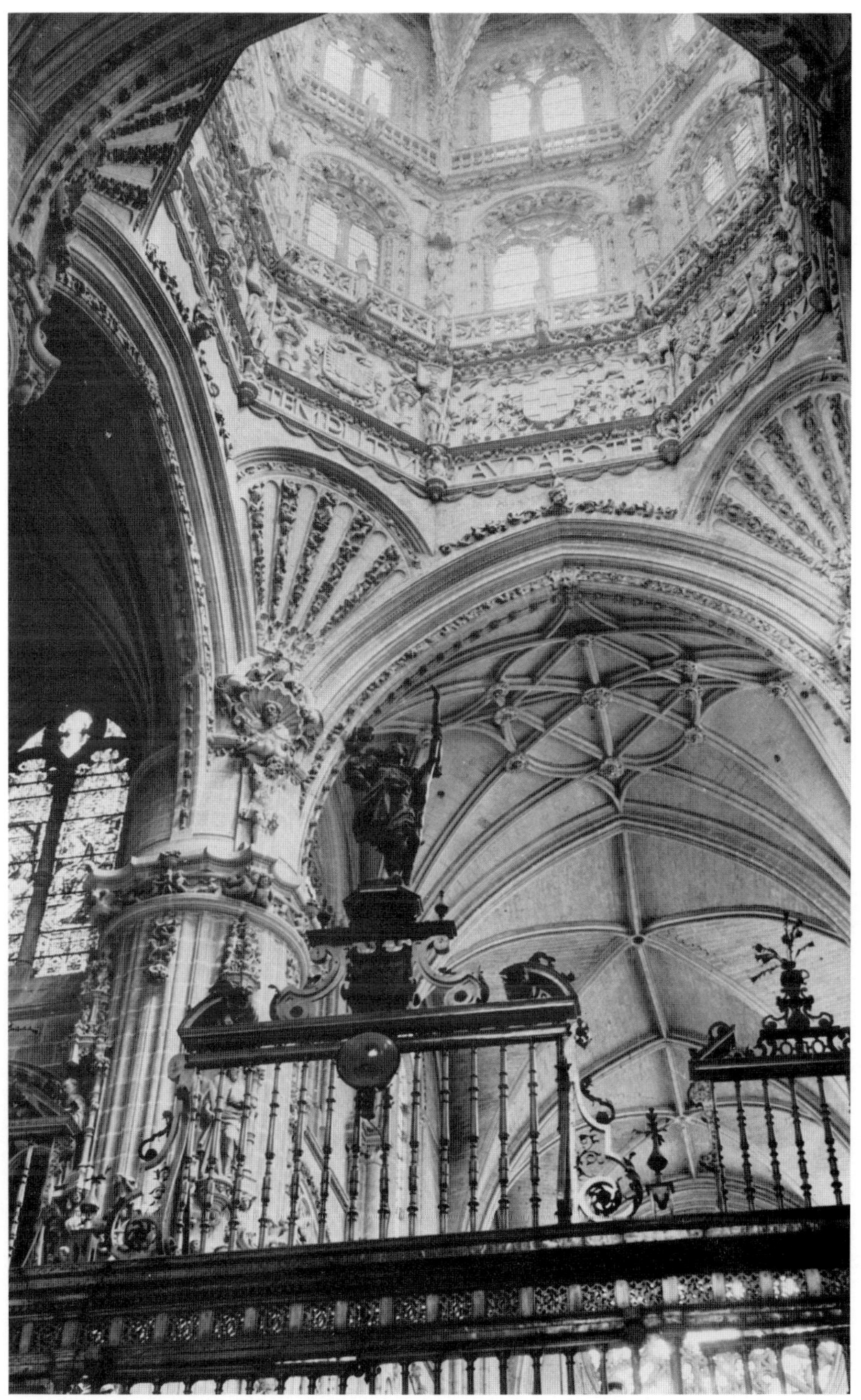

155. *Cimborio,* Burgos Cathedral

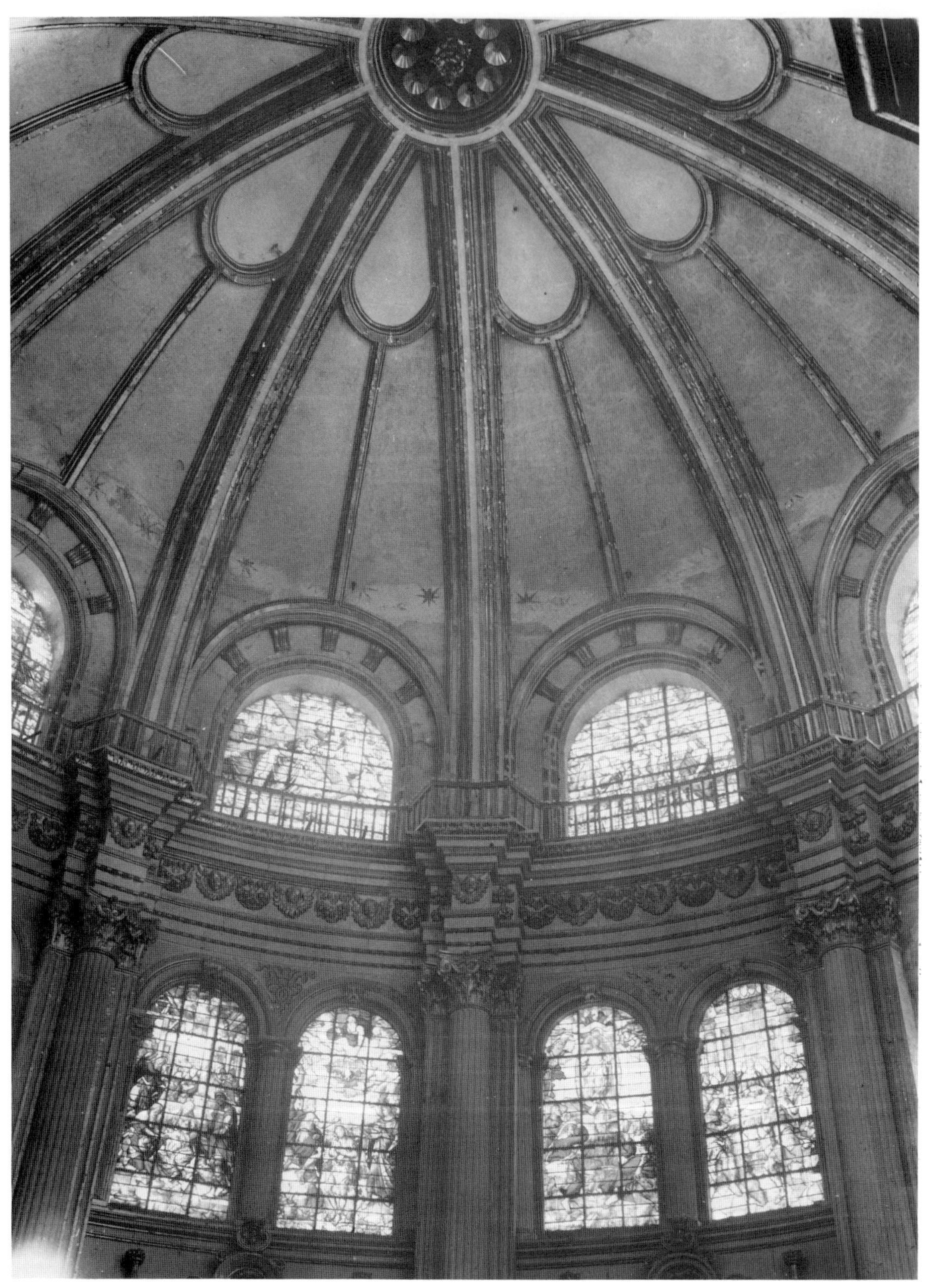

156. Chevet, detail, Granada Cathedral

*

Again and again I returned to El Escorial, the love-death poison in me. I knew it was not right. I was not right. But it was true. I was true. For in the world where I was now and where the Braid was invisible although present, I could see the Braid again.

And I had the feeling then and now—El Escorial visited and revisited—that the passage I knew, and had thought closed, leading from the world of *Tendresse,* the world of the Ancestor and his Children, all present but invisible to me, to the world of Pandora's evils, where *Tendresse* was dead, but the Children alive and visible, shall be open to me.

And so, when I . . .

## *Interrupted. Epilogue.*

Léo Bronstein was never able to finish even the sentence which was meant to usher his narration to its *finale.*

And I, these many years his friend, amanuensis, editor, and literary executor, am left with the duty of putting together and in due order all the parts of the manuscript with their corresponding illustrative material, and of trying to make it ready, if possible, for publication.

For I am certain that, in spite of its abrupt interruption, the manuscript—the "chronicle" as such—was finished. And I know also from our last conversations that what had to follow there at the end of the story, his future monk's, Pimen's, return to the world of Pandora's evil gifts, was planned by him to be the subject of another, a future tale.

What he wished to say, to reiterate emphatically, as if anew, in the last part—the epilogue—of his manuscript was this: That, because of the ubiquity of man's dual being-becoming—the "Intrigue," as he called it, in man's history, in man's mind, in man's "laws of nature"—the fable-chronicle of a bygone age was to be, in his earnest intention, the fable-actuality of his own age.

For he called our twentieth century, now at its perspective-revealing decline, the century of confrontation, the most open and boldest confrontation in man's planetary history, of the ''Apocalyptic'' and ''Psychomachic'' in man's totalitarian, the else's, *must* choice on all levels of his existence, and man's *freed*, the self's, pluralistic-relativist choice on all levels of his existence.

A most dangerous, a catastrophe-inviting confrontation, to be sure, but also, and because of that, the most open, revealing, thus enlightened and decisive confrontation. That is why he called his century the century of historically enlightened and ''permitted'' choice. And he meant choosingly, the confrontation and the choice in Western Christian man, par excellence—this great, struggling villain of man's history, and his great and struggling conscience-crisis in my friend's story. I said choosingly because, as he had perceived it, it has been Christian Western man's historical destiny to see himself, to look at his own image-reflection in the magnifying mirror of his past, and to learn there about the meaning of his struggles—his personal crises—and the why of his final choice or victory, the final, future victory of the Psychomachic man.

Now, it is here precisely that I felt something went wrong with my reconstruction. I felt uneasy. For the notion of victory, the very word victory he had to use sometimes himself, was, I knew, detested by my friend: victory was for him never the opposite of defeat. For success was not the opposite of failure. If success, I remember his telling me once, is the accomplishment of a goal known and open, failure could also be an accomplishment of a goal, but of a goal still hidden, unknown, *to be discovered* and far off.

And yet throughout the entire Chronicle it was shown how the triumph—the success—of Western man was to be foreseen: as the triumph—the success—of the Psychomachic and not of the Apocalyptic, present there also and always. How could this be denied now, or even changed? It could not.

It could. For, I believe, recalling what, in his loyalty to the autobiographic origin or beginning of his ''fable-chronicle,'' my friend thought should be included and explained, as an autobiographic episode at its end—I believe that he decided, he the participant in his Chronicle's intrigue, to face and to complete the epic choice of Western man with his own, personal, lyrical choice—Montaigne's *"Que sçais-je?"*

*"Que sçais-je?"*—I must say it myself here. For certainly it was in challenge to the respectability inherent in his own *must*-choice of historical "proof" that he chose for himself to be the witness of his own Fable's freedom or free choice, and to become—was it irony's revenge or despair? mysterious, hidden success of an obvious failure? Montaigne's *"Que sçais-je?"*—the obscure, obedient, resigned, and so obsolete figure of an old Muscovite-Byzantine monk-chronicler, monk-witness? Was there any connection, I ask myself here, as the reader himself would ask, between this personal decision and the return to the world of Pandora's evils—the world of dead *Tendresse?*

I cannot know. And why, one would continue asking, the choice of Pushkin's monk Pimen? Was it my friend's nostalgia of his early youth's love for a great native poet? Was it also, foreigner in a noisy world, as he was all his adult life, the nostalgia of an unattainable, because so quiet and meditative, old age, now that he was old himself—the image of an old monk "very old now, writing at the edge of night's and day's light in his silent cell, loving its stillness and the silenced memories of what lives in it?" Or was it also the nostalgia and the premonition of a close-by death? *"Córdoba./Lejana y sola/ . . . ¡Ay que la muerte me espera antes de llegar a Córdoba!"*

I don't know.

And I leave his manuscript as it is, interrupted, its subject defined in and by its title: *Romantic Homage to Greece and Spain*—the two lands that made his wanderings lovable. His Fable—my old friend's fable. Their Art—their living art.

# Notes

## Part I

1. William Butler Yeats, ''A Prayer for Old Age,'' *The Collected Poems of W. B. Yeats* (London: Macmillan, 1955), p. 326.
2. Federico Garcia Lorca, ''Cancíon de jinete,'' *The Penguin Book of Spanish Verse,* J. M. Cohen, ed., revised ed. (Harmondsworth, Middlesex, Penguin Books, Ltd., 1960), p. 382, where the following ''plain prose'' translation appears:

   *The Rider's Song*

   *Cordoba. Far-away and lonely.*
   *Small black horse and great moon, and olives in my saddle-bag.*
   *Although I know the roads, I shall never reach Cordoba.*
   *Over the plain, through the wind, small black horse, red moon.*
   *Death is staring at me from the towers of Cordoba.*
   *Oh how long the road is! Oh how brave is my little horse!*
   *Alas that death is expecting me before I reach Cordoba!*
   *Cordoba. Far-away and lonely.*
3. ''The dull mind rises to truth by means of material things.'' *Trans.* the editors.
4. San Juan de Bohí. The paintings, executed *ca.* 1123, were transferred with great skill and delicacy to Barcelona's famous Museum of Catalan Art.
5. Josep Gudiol Ricart says: ''These figures could not represent Nebuchadnezzar and Daniel because both of them have halos. We believe that the personages who complete the scene of the *Jongleurs* are the four Hebrew youths in the act of refusing to worship the statue.'' *Trans.* Léo Bronstein, from Josep Pijoán with the collaboration of Josep Gudiol Ricart, *Les Pintures Murals Romaniques de Catalunya* (Barcelona: Alpha, 1948), p. 95. (*Monumenta Cataloniae,* materials pera la història de l'art a Catalunya, vol. IV).
6. François-Noël Babeuf, called ''Gracchus'' (1760–97).
7. Babeuf's paper, *L'Éclaireur du peu-*

*ple: ou, Le Défenseur de 24 millions d'opprimés,* was a great sensation in 1796 in Paris, then in full crisis.

8. *Trans.* the editors, from Maurice Merleau-Ponty, *La Structure du Comportement* (Paris: Presses Universitaires de France, 1942), p. 247. The original reads as follows: ''Il nous a semblé que matière, vie, esprit ne pouvaient être définis comme trois ordres de réalité ou trois sortes d'être, mais comme trois plans de significations ou trois formes d'unité.''
9. ''Stabilisatrice'' in Charles Picard's definition of Crete's Great Goddess and her openness to all cults. Charles Picard, *Les Origines du Polythéisme Hellénique: l'Art Créto-Mycènien* (Paris: Laurens, 1930) and *Les Religions Préhélleniques* (Paris: Presses Universitaires de France, 1948), *passim.*
10. Now in the museum at Delphi. The four sides of the frieze supposedly represent the *Judgement of Paris* on the west; on the east, the epic battle before Troy—''. . . a sort of synthesis of the Iliad. The assembled gods, on the left half of the frieze . . . looking . . . from the summit of Olympus, at . . . the battle. . . on earth (right half).'' Pierre de la Coste-Messelière, *The Treasures of Delphi* (Paris: Éditions du Chêne, 1945), p. 25; on the south, a scene of abduction, perhaps Pelops and Hippodamia or perhaps the daughters of Leucippus; and, on the north, the combat of gods and Titans. This last scene directly overlooked the sacred way to the great temple of Delphi, thus iconographically it should stand as the central or crucial theme of the ensemble.
11. Jean Charbonneaux and Pierre Devambez, ''L'Art Egéen Préhellenique: La Crète et Mycène'' in *Histoire générale de l'art,* preface by Émile Mâle (Paris: Flammarion, 1950–51), I, p. 107.
12. Frontons and metopes, Temple of Zeus, Olympia.
13. The *Jijimuge* doctrine of the Kegon School of Buddhism in Japan. *See* Christmas Humphreys, *Buddhism* (Harmondsworth: Penguin Books, 1956), p. 151.
14. In the Cassirer school's definition.
15. The term is used here in a sense at once more intimate and psychologically larger and more complete than in Prudentius' literal sense of virtue-versus-vice.
16. Léo Bronstein, *Five Variations on the Theme of Japanese Painting* (Freeport, Me.: The Bond Wheelwright Co. for Brandeis University, 1969), p. 3.
17. (Santa Maria del Pí in Catalan, Santa María del Pino in Castilian. The author often uses the Catalan names of churches, places, etc., in Catalonia; Castilian equivalents appear in the glossary.)

    The façade of Santa Maria del Pí is in all probability of the first half of the 14th c. The church itself, a beautiful single-naved structure, was begun a little before 1322, the covering with the vaults, in the second half of the 14th c.
18. Louis Courajod, *Leçons Professés à l'École du Louvre* (Paris: A. Picard

et Fils, 1899), I, pp. 29–34, 135, 186, *passim.*

19. Juan Contreras y López de Ayala, marqués de Lozoya, *Historia del Arte Hispanico* (Barcelona: Salvat Editores, 1931–49), I, p. 287. *Trans.* Léo Bronstein.

    The original reads as follows: ''Es paquenita, pues con grueso de paredes no tiene mas de cuerenta piès de largo y la mitad de ancho; mas en este poquito hay tan linda proporción y correspondencia, que qualquier artifece de los mas primos de agora tendria bien que considerar y alabar.''

20. The old Catalan domain of the Counts of Rousillon is now part of the French department of the Pyrénées-Orientales; Elne is near Perpignan, its capital.

21. The first stone of the church was laid in 1329; the vaults were built from 1363 or 1366 to 1378. The façade was erected in the second quarter of the 14th c. Through the centuries, seismic disturbances and fires, especially the fires of 1378, of 1414, and of 1936, greatly endangered the structure. In 1428 the great rose window fell down and was promptly replaced. *See* Juan Ainaud, José Gudiol, and F. P. Verrié, *La Ciudad de Barcelona* (Madrid: Consejo Superior de Investigaciones Cientificas, Instituto Diego Velázquez, 1947), I, pp. 118–21. (Catálogo monumental de España.)

22. *Lonjas* (sing. *lonja*) in Castilian, an edifice where men of the same profession as well as merchants dealing with the same articles met and made their transactions.

23. The Sant Iu façade (San Ivo in Castilian) antedates, in style as in time, that of Santa Maria del Pí. It is considered to be the latter's prototype (as well as that of several other Catalan churches of the first half of the 14th c.). Spanish art historians emphasize also the Romanesque elements there. *See* Juan Ainaud, José Gudiol, and F. P. Verrié, *op. cit.*, p. 49. For Santa Maria del Pí, pp. 109–10.

24. Yevgeny Yevtushenko, ''Flowers and Bullets,'' *trans.* The New York Times, *New York Times* (May 19, 1970), p. 7.

25. The church has no triforium.

26. Maurice Merleau-Ponty, *The Primacy of Perception and Other Essays,* ed. and with an introduction by James M. Edie (Evanston, Il.: Northwestern University Press, 1964) pp. 52–54.

27. *See* Siegfried Giedion, *Mechanization Takes Command* (New York: Oxford University Press, 1948), pp. 15–16.

28. All these quotations are to be found in Alfred Korzybski, *Science and Sanity,* 2d ed. (Lancaster, Pa.: The International Non-Aristotelian Library Pub. Co., 1941), p. 53 (Eddington); p. 223 (Poincaré); pp. 7, 371 (Whitehead); p. 247 (Bell); p. 66 (Einstein).

29. *Trans.* the editors, from Maurice Merleau-Ponty, *La Structure du Comportement, op. cit.*, p. 247. The original reads as follows: ''En accédant à la connaissance vraie, en dépassant la dialectique du vivant ou de l'être social et de son milieu circonscrit, en devenant le sujet

pur qui connaît objectivement le monde, l'homme réalise à la limite la conscience absolue au regard de laquelle le corps, l'existence individuelle, ne sont plus que des objets, la mort dépourvue de sens. . . . les rapports de l'âme et du corps, obscurs tant qu'on traite par abstraction le corps comme un fragment de matière, s'éclaircissent quand on voit en lui le porteur d'une dialectique. Puisque le monde physique et l'organisme ne peuvent être pensés que comme des objets de conscience ou des significations, le problème des rapports de la conscience et de ses "conditions" physiques ou organiques n'existerait qu'au niveau d'une pensée confuse qui s'attache à des abstractions, il disparaîtrait dans le domaine de la verité où seul subsiste à titre originel le rapport du sujet epistémologique et de son objet. Ce serait là le seul thème légitime de la réflexion philosophique."

30. *See* Plate Note 41.

31. Léo Bronstein, *Five Variations . . .*, op. cit., pp. 117–25.

32. From the Japanese Noh play *Nishikigi, trans.* Ernest Fenollosa and Ezra Pound, in: *'Noh': or Accomplishment* (London: Macmillan & Co. Ltd., 1916), p. 132.

33. Paul-Henri Michel, in *La Fresque Romane* (Paris: Pierre Tisné, 1961), p. 68, speaks of these figures as saints.

34. Léo Bronstein, *op. cit.*, pp. 182–87, with slight changes introduced by the author.

35. Léo Bronstein, *ibid.*, pp. 243–46, *passim,* with slight changes introduced by the author.

36. *See Fresques Romanes des Églises de France,* ed., and with an introduction by Paul-Henri Michel (Paris: Éditions du Chêne, 1949), p. 27. In Michel's view it is the figure of Anger, in mine, of Lust.

37. Tavant, Indre-et-Loire. The crypt of the church, dedicated to St. Nicholas, was probably decorated in the last quarter of the 11th c. or the beginning of the 12th.

38. It is significant that Paul-Henri Michel has this to say about the artist's (several artists'?) rendering of the battles of good and evil at Tavant: "The painter gives more importance to the struggle than to triumph. Nowhere do we find Vice meekly prostrate and crushed beneath the feet of the Enemy, though mortally wounded [Vice] always remains upright, whether as Lion beneath the sword of David or fiery Devil overcome by warrior or Lust. . . . All the figures at Tavant are as though consumed by fierce living flame." Paul-Henri Michel, *The Frescoes of Tavant,* Introduction. (New York: Studio Publication, 1944), p. 9.

39. *See* Hans Swarzenski, "Unknown Bible pictures by H. de Brailes," *The Journal of the Walters Art Gallery* (Baltimore), I, 1938, p. 58, fig. 2. On page 65, Swarzenski says: "The style of the miniatures indicates the second quarter of the thirteenth century."

40. Léo Bronstein, *Five Variations . . . op. cit.*, pp. 1–2.

41. In the Boston Museum of Fine Arts and the National Museum, Rome.

42. Indeed, the two ''thrones'' are perhaps the most controversial objects of art historians' recent scrutiny, controversial in their iconography, and, as far as the ''Boston throne'' is concerned, of most conjectural authenticity. For many historians (and for their ''proofs'') it is a 19th c. falsification (von Gerkan, Cellini, Becatti, Baroni, Alsher); for many others it is authentic, but does not belong to the same monument, and is not even Greek, but rather Roman (Bastet, Bielefeld, Jucker, Ashmole, Moebius). What is curious here is the variety of their interpretations and the frequent suggestion by them of an esoteric, or a mystery cult's, iconography, an allegory of the triumph of an ''initiated'' soul over an ''uninitiated'' (H. Goldman); an allegory of Death, the ''Ludovisi throne'' representing Birth (Johnson). A good and succinct résumé of the entire problem is given in Giovanni Becatti, ''Trono di Boston'' and Enrico Paribeni, ''Trono Ludovisi,'' *Enciclopedia dell' Arte Antica, Classica e Orientale* (Rome: Instituto della Enciclopedia Italiana, 1958–66), VII, pp. 1018–22.

43. Or differently worded: ''The Son of God was crucified: I am not ashamed—because it is shameful. The Son of God died: it is immediately credible—because it is silly. He was buried, and rose again: it is certain—because it is impossible.'' *Tertullian's Treatise on the Incarnation,* ed., trans., and with an introduction and commentary by Ernest Evans (London: S.P.C.K., 1956), p. 19.

44. Grégoire Palamas, ''Défense des Saints Hésychastes,'' ed., trans., and with an introduction and critical notes by Jean Meyendorff, in *Spicilegium Sacrum Lovaniense* (Louvain, 1959), II, *passim.*

45. *See* Ludewijk Herman Grondijs, ''La mort du Christ et le rit du Zéon,'' *Byzantion* XXIII (1953) pp. 257–59.

46. Steven Runciman, *Byzantine Civilization* (London: E. Arnold and Co., 1933), 229–30.

47. I refer to the fatal blow of the Seljuk victory at Manzikert in 1071, to the successful attacks on mainland Greece by the Norman, Roger II, and to the subsequent economic disasters of the 11th and 12th centuries: the loss of supremacy in international trade, the loss of the supremacy of the imperial silk industry, transferred to Sicily, now Norman, and to south Italy.

48. Steven Runciman, *op. cit.,* p. 204.

49. Think of the ''legal rights'' of revolution that the Patriarch Nicholas Mysticus in the 10th c. was not afraid to voice, discussed by Steven Runciman, *op. cit.,* p. 62, or of Patriarch Photius' 9th c. revival of the old idea of a double and sacred domain of *regnum* and *sacerdotium,* the famous Dyarchy, the divine Grace reaching symmetrically the one and the other, discussed in André Grabar, *L'Iconoclasme Byzantin* (Paris: Collège de France, 1957), p. 225.

50. The cry of Juan Ramón Jiménez' poetry.

51. Georgio de Santillana and Hertha von Dechend, *Hamlet's Mill* (Boston: Gambit, 1969), *passim.*

52. ''The Annunciation,'' Novgorod School according to N. P. Kondakov, *The Russian Icon* (Prague: Seminarium Kondakovianum, 1928), Plate XLV.

53. From the Dioscuri House in Pompeii. *See* Paul Herrmann, *Denkmäler der Malerei des Altertums* (Munich: F. Bruckmann,1904–34), Plate 130 and Mabel M. Gabriel, *Masters of Campanian Painting* (New York: H. Rittner and Co., 1962), p. 34.

54. Kariye Djami, the old church of Chora monastery, several times restored, finally and splendidly rebuilt and redecorated by the illustrious Grand Logothete, Theodoros Metochites (*ca.* 1269–1332), covered with mosaics and frescoes in 1320–1721 and dedicated to both Christ and the Virgin, Christ, ''the Chora [dwelling place or land] of the living,'' as the inscription on one of Christ's images tells us, and the Virgin, the Theotokos, ''the Chora of the uncontainable.'' *See* Paul A. Underwood, *The Kariye Djami* (New York: Pantheon, 1966), I, p. 27 and *passim.*

55. For the ''daring'' backgrounds, their complex spatial schemes, etc., *see* Tania Velmans, ''Le rôle du décor architectural et la représentation de l'êspace dans la peinture des Paléologues,'' *Cahiers archéologiques,* 14 (1964), pp. 183–216.

56. How far and in what sense the secular and ''pagan'' accent given to this work and to others close to the iconoclast era was the effect of the lavish promotion of secular-pagan elements in the palatial arts of the iconoclast emperors is still veiled behind scholarly conjectures and the absence of adequate monuments.

57. Folds in all medieval figural arts, West and East, already belong to the beyond-of-man, that is, to still cryptic ''landscape.''

58. The Akathistos Hymn, the most celebrated hymn of the Byzantine Church, probably dates from the 6th c. or even earlier.

## Part II

59. Léo Bronstein, *Lutte et Réconcilation* (Paris: Félix Alcan, 1927), pp. 140–50.

60. Hesychasm, far from being simply, as it is so often defined, a sect of mystics that originated in the 14th c. among the monks of Mt. Athos and was accepted and institutionalized by the Eastern Orthodox Church as its essential belief (decision of the Councils of 1341, 1351) in the midst of Byzantium's most acute socio-political and religious crisis (*see* Fiodor Ivanovich Uspenskii, *Istoria Vizantiikoi Imperii* (Moscow/Leningrad: Academy of Sciences USSR, 1948) III, pp. 708–20), was the result of centuries-long development and of strife between the two opposite camps of Byzantine ''spirituality'': the humanistic-progressive and the patristic-monkish, ultra-''conservative.''

The Hesychast movement of

the middle of the 14th c. was the culmination of this struggle, its last outburst, led by equally eloquent and belligerent representatives: in the one camp, the learned Aristotelian scholar and humanist, Barlaam, a Calabrian Greek, protégé and friend of Petrarch in Italy and, when in Greece, protégé of the "humanist" Emperor Andronicas; and, in the other, Gregory Palamas, the famous learned Athonite monk, who later, victorious, was made archbishop of the rebellious city of Thessaloniki.

The Hesychast doctrine, or, which is the same, the Hesychast method of prayer, the "Prayer of the Heart" or the "Prayer of Jesus," consists, in the words of one of the most attentive modern interpreters of Hesychasm—Jacques Albert Cuttat, *The Encounter of Religions, trans.* Pierre de Fontnouvelle with Evis McGrew (New York: Desclée, 1960), p. 87: ". . . essentially in making the intelligence descend into the heart, in order to introduce the name of Jesus therein, by means of the repeated invocation, timed to follow the respiratory rhythm, of a formula containing his Name." And further—pages 92–93— ". . . the Hesychast method aims precisely at changing this connection [between the bodily modalities of consciousness, the spiritual modalities and their transcending principle] or inner continuity from a potentiality into an actuality, starting in particular with the two vital functions of breathing and action of the heart, whose interdependence was well known, even in Antiquity. The relationship between the inhaled or inspired 'breath' and the Spirit (Pneuma, the 'divine Breath') is then much more than a metaphor; it constitutes a real, 'analogical' correspondence, making of the former the providential vehicle of the latter. The same 'vertical' connection links the heart, physical center and 'sun' of the body, to the intellect (*noûs*), spiritual center and light of the soul, and by the same token to God, the increate Light, metaphysical Center and Heart of the universe, to use the words of Gregory Palamas, Maximus the Confessor, and Clement of Alexandria. According to Saint Gregory of Nyssa, the heart, 'image of image' (i.e., image of the *noûs*, God's mirror in man), becomes 'God's abode' to the extent that man lives 'in the physical heart but not physically.' . . .

"It is not the least of Hesychasm's merits," says in conclusion the same author—page 153—"forcefully to have recalled the dignity of the body as temple of the Holy Spirit and as 'epitome' of the universe . . . "

61. As far as this "yogic" technique of the Hesychasts is concerned, Jean Meyendorff says: ". . . as we see, we have to do not with a more or less esoteric clan [the Hesychasts], focused on the bodily practices of the 'Prayer of Jesus,' but with a movement which brought together in its ranks the most vital

personalities of Byzantine Christianity. That Palamas presents Theoleptus and Athanasius as masters of these bodily practices without their having themselves mentioned them in their writings, proves the wide currency of these practices and at the same time the secondary valuation the spiritual masters attached to them.'' Grégoire Palamas, ''Défense des Saints Hésychastes,'' ed., trans., and with an introduction and critical notes, by Jean Meyendorff, in *Spicilegium Sacrum Lovaniense,* (Louvain, 1959), I, pp. XL-XLI.

''And why'' says Palamas himself (*ibid.*, I, p. 190) ''have I spoken only of the kinship which will then be established between the body and the intellectual nature? St. Maximus says in effect: 'The soul becomes God in participating in divine grace, after having itself halted all activity of the mind and of the senses, as well as the natural energies of the body; for the body is made divine at the same time as the soul, participating in deification in the manner appropriate to it: God alone then appears in the soul and in the body. . . .' . . . but then, O miracle, it is God who will look [make visible to Himself] not only by the soul which is within us, but also by the body. That is why we shall then distinctly see [in Hesychia], by our bodily organs themselves, the divine and inaccessible light. . . . Have you understood now that the light which illuminated the apostles on Mount Tabor was not perceptible in the proper sense of the word?'' And Palamas quotes from Psalm 60:8: ''*La loi de Dieu est au milieu de mon ventre*'' (in the French version used by Meyendorff). *Ibid.*, I, p. 96. (The King James version: ''. . . O my God . . . thy law is within my heart.'') Other passages, *trans.* the editors.

The originals of the first two passages quoted above are as follows: '' . . . *il ne s'agit pas, comme on le voit, d'un clan plus ou moins ésotérique* [the Hesychasts] *et concentré sur les pratiques corporelles de la prière de Jésus, mais d'un mouvement qui réunit dans ses rangs les personnalités les plus vivantes de la chrétienté Byzantine. Que Palamas nous présente Théolepte et Athanase comme des maîtres de ces pratiques corporelles sans qu'eux-mêmes les aient mentionnées dans leurs oeuvres, prouve à la fois la large diffusion de ces pratiques et la valeur secondaire que les maîtres spirituels leur accordaient.*''

And: ''*Et pourquoi ai-je seulement parlé de la parenté qui s'établira alors entre le corps et la nature intellectuelle? Saint Maxime dit en effet: 'L'âme devient Dieu en participant à la grâce divine, après avoir elle-même arreté toute activité de l'esprit et des sens, aussi bien que les énergies naturelles du corps; car le corps est divinisé en même temps qu'elle, en participant à la déification de la façon qui lui convient: Dieu seul apparaît alors dans l'âme et dans le corps . . .' . . . mais alors, ô miracle, c'est Dieu qui regardera [se fera visible à lui-même] non seulement par l'âme qui est en nous, mais aussi par notre corps. Voilà pourquoi, nous verrons alors distinctement* [in Hesychia], *par nos organes corporels mêmes, la lumière divine et inaccessible. . . . As-tu compris maintenant que la lumière qui illumine les apôtres sur le Thabor n'était pas sensible, au sens propre du terme?''*

62. *See* Edgar de Bruyne, *Études d'Esthétique Médiévale* (Brugge: ''De Tempel,'' 1946), III, *passim.*

63. Edgar de Bruyne, *ibid.*, III, p. 20.

64. All this still, of course, speculatively conceived, though helped in some experimental tentatives of medieval scholars by the daring ''positivist'' achievements, newly introduced to the West, of Islamic thinkers, in particular, the most influential psycho-physiology of light of Alhazen (Ibn al-Haytham, translated about 1200).

65. *Ca.* 1355–1452. *See* Milton V. Anastos, ''Plethon's Calendar and Liturgy,'' *Dumbarton Oaks Papers* (1948), No. 4.

66. The editors were unable to identify the version of the Bible quoted. They believe this verse was translated by Léo Bronstein. The King James version reads: ''But we preach Christ crucified, unto the Jews a stumbling-block and unto the Greeks foolishness.''

67. That St. Benedict's Rule might have been modeled on the slightly earlier Regula Magistri (510–25) does not change the problem *here*, the problem-as-attitude. *See* Michael Paulin Blecker, ''Roman Law and Consilium in the Regula Magistri and the Rule of St. Benedict,'' *Speculum* (1972) XLVII, No. I.

68. André Grabar, *Martyrium: Recherches sur le Culte des Reliques et l'Art Chrétien Antique* (Paris: Collège de France, 1943–46), pp. 28–29.

69. André Grabar, *ibid., passim.*

70. André Grabar, *L'Iconoclasme Byzantin, op. cit.*, p. 32. [see also note 49 above]

71. Robert Byron and David Talbot Rice, *The Birth of Western Painting* (New York: Alfred A. Knopf, 1931), p. 48.

72. Ludewijk Herman Grondijs, ''La mort du Christ et le Rit du Zéon,'' *op. cit.*, pp. 257–59.

73. André Grabar, *L'Iconoclasme Byzantin, op. cit.*, pp. 79, 136.

74. Described in Paul A. Underwood, *The Kariye Djami, op. cit.*, III, pp. 192–219.

75. *Ibid.*, p. 192.

76. The fidelity to early Christian humanism of the Roman mosaicists who participated in the creation of this 9th c. masterpiece added, surely, its charm to the charm of the humanism of their teachers, the skilled Greek iconodule monks-artists who took refuge from the iconoclast storm at home in the then so hospitable Italy.

77. The story is told near the end of the novel by Yambo Ouologuem, *Bound to Violence, trans.* from the French by Ralph Manheim. (New York: Harcourt Brace Jovanovich, Inc. 1971), quoted in Christopher Lehmann-Haupt, ''Books of the Times,'' *The New York Times* (March 5, 1971), p. 33.

78. James Taylor, ''Hey Mister That's Me Up on the Jukebox'' (New York: Blackwood Music, Inc., Country Road Music, Inc., 1971), quoted in Susan Braudy, ''James

Taylor, the New Troubadour," *The New York Times Magazine* (Feb. 21, 1971), p. 28.

79. Joni Mitchell, "Both Sides Now" (Los Angeles: Siquomb Pub. Corp., 1967), quoted in Susan Braudy, *ibid.*, p. 90.

80. A line in the Japanese Noh play *Funa Benkei.*

81. So similar to, surely derived from other, North African in particular, *laudae.* The *lauda* in question is the so-called *de Optium,* that of an important citizen of Tarragona. *See Ars Hispaniae, op. cit.*, II, p. 221.

82. *See* H. V. Livermore, *A History of Spain,* (New York: Grove Press, 1960), pp. 21–50.

83. As in the story "Lazarus" in Leonid Andreyev, *When the King Loses His Head and Other Stories, trans.* Archibald J. Wolfe (New York: International Book Publishing Co., 1920).

84. Léo Bronstein, *Fragments of Life, Metaphysics and Art* (New York: The Bond Wheelwright Co., 1953), p. 133.

85. Enrique Lafuente Ferrari, *Goya. The frescoes in San Antonio de la Florida in Madrid, trans.* Stuart Gilbert (Geneva, New York: A. Skira, 1955), p. 30.

86. Enrique Lafuente Ferrari, *ibid.*, p. 28.

87. Mozarab, from the Arabic *musta'rib,* a Christian who lived in districts under Spanish Moslem rule.

88. The authenticity of the Kabūs-Nameh is dubious, yet the "Islamic" quality of it is very striking.

89. Painted *ca.* 1445 for the chapel in Barcelona's city hall. Saints Eulalia and Andrew presenting five town councillors to the Virgin. Now in the Museum of Catalan Art, Barcelona.

90. *See* João Couto, *Nuno Gonçalves, O poliptico de São Vicente* (Lisbon: Estudios Cor, 1954). (Ed.: Now controversial, the attribution of the panels to Nuno Gonçalves is still accepted by most authorities.)

91. The polyptych as assembled since 1940 (the original arrangement is unknown) consists of six oak panels, two larger ones, one of which gives us the portrait of the famous Infante, Prince Henry the Navigator, and that, probably, of Dom Alfonso V, both kneeling before the central figure of the young St. Vincent. The polyptych contains sixty figures belonging to all strata of society, from the king, his family and court, to the bishop and his canons, the friars, knights, burghers (a physician and chronicler), fishermen, and even a beggar. The fishermen's panel, so called because of the three fishermen there, wrapped in a net, contains in its foreground the astonishing figure of an old man with a rosary "depicted in an unusually daring manner." João Couto, *ibid.*, p. 11.

92. George Kubler and Martin Soria, *Art and Architecture in Spain and Portugal and their American Dominions 1500 to 1800* (Harmondsworth: Penguin Books, 1959), p. 40. For detailed description of the *Transparente, see Ars Hispaniae,* XIV, pp. 186–87 and George Kubler and Martin Soria, *ibid.*, pp. 40, 159. For the "Spanishness" of its structure

and expressiveness and, above all, for the essential difference, in spite of the many architectonic similarities between this exalted creation of Spanish Baroque genius and *locura,* and the even more exalted example of Italo-Germanic rococo *''locura,''* the altar and nave of the abbey church in Weltenburg near Regensburg, 1717–21, by Cosmas Damian Asam, *see* Oskar Hagen, *Patterns and Principles of Spanish Art* (Madison, Wisconsin: The University of Wisconsin Press, 1943), pp. 72–73.

93. An elevated and withdrawn holy of holies built behind the main altar, unknown elsewhere in Europe.

94. *Trans.* Léo Bronstein from Juan Contreras y Lópes de Ayala, marqués de Lozoya, quoted in *Ars Hispaniae, op. cit.,* XVII, p. 75.

95. *Mudejar,* from *mudajjan,* ''submitted tributary . . . who remains where he is,'' a Moslem vassal of the Christians, who is allowed to preserve his religion and his ways of life. The term *mudejar* is not to be found in any documents of the 13th c. in Spain. It is mentioned often in the 14th c. and later. *Trans.* Léo Bronstein from Leopoldo Torres Balbás in *Ars Hispaniae, op. cit.,* IV, p. 237, *q.v.*

96. Shī'ah, the general name for a large group of very different Moslem sects, of which the common starting point is the recognition of Ali as the legitimate Caliph after the death of the Prophet. *See Encyclopedia of Islam.*

97. Ibn Rushd (Averroës to the West) quoted in Erwin I. J. Rosenthal, *Political Thought in Medieval Islam* (Cambridge, Mass.: Cambridge University Press, 1958) p. 183.

98. *Mihrab:* a niche in the end wall of a mosque, marking the prescribed direction of prayer.

99. For a detailed account of this problem, *see* R. C. Taylor, ''El Padre Villalpando (1552–1608) y sus Ideas Estéticas,'' *Annals and Bulletin of the Royal Academy of San Fernando* (second semester, 1952), and René Taylor, ''Architecture and Magic: Considerations on the *Idea* of the Escorial,'' in Douglas Fraser, Howard Hibbard and Milton J. Lewine, eds., *Essays in the History of Architecture presented to Rudolf Wittkower* (London: Phaidon Press Ltd., 1967), I, pp. 81–109.

100. *Trans.* Léo Bronstein from Marcelino Menéndez y Pelayo, *Historia de las Ideas Estéticas en España* (Madrid: Consejo Superior de Investigaciones Científicas, 1974), I, pp. 850–51. The original is as follows: ''Espíritu vigoroso y sintético, complacíase Herrera en altas especulaciones, no de estética, sino de filosofía matemática, invadiendo a veces el terreno de la Metafísica. Fué ardiente partidario del *Arte Magna* de Raimundo Lulio, de la cual hizo muy original aplicación en su *Discurso sobre la figura cúbica,* descubierto y copiado por Jovellanos en Mallorca, y conservado hoy en mi biblioteca [a manuscript lost since then]. En este peregrino tratado, Juan de Herrera, con evidente originalidad en los pormenores, intenta simplificar y hacer accesibles las combinaciones de la lógica luliana valiéndose de una sola figura, el cubo. . . . ''

101. A general title given to and comprising all the numerous variants of Lull's ''Art'', from his earliest ''Art Abreujada d'Atrobar Veritat'' and ''Art Demostrativa'' of the 1270s and 1280s, the ''Ars Inventiva'' and the ''Art Amativa'' of the 1290s, up to the variants, most rigorous and comprehensive, the ''Arbre de Ciencia'' (1295), the ''Logica Nova'' (1303), the ''Liber de Ascensu et Descensu Intellectus'' (1304), and, crowning all his previous efforts, the ''Ars Generalis et Ultima'' (1305–08). *See Obres Essencials de Ramon Llull* (Barcelona: Editorial Selecta, 1957, 1960), I and II.

    Perhaps the most comprehensive and concise biographical account of Lull's missionary and literary activity is to be found in P. M. Batllori, *Ramon Llull en el Món del Seu Temps* (Barcelona: Rafael Dalman, 1960).

    Editor's note: And *see* Anthony Bonner's magisterial two-volume *Selected Works of Ramon Llull,* in English (Princeton University Press, 1985), published after Léo Bronstein's death.

102. A revived and strengthened zeal, and typical of that century—very Franciscan—to conquer the ''infidel'' by arms of persuasion rather than by armed attack. Ramon Lull's entire life, after his ''illumination'' at the Mount of Randa in his ''golden island'' of Mallorca, was an uninterrupted, stubborn (irritating to many of his contemporaries) dedication to this purpose: for example, his insistence on the necessity of opening special schools where the languages of the ''infidel'' could be learned, his daring and dangerous preaching to the ''infidel,'' the Moors of Tunisia, in their own land, and his death—his martyrdom?—there. *See* P. M. Batllori, *ibid,* in Catalan, and, in English, Edgar Allison Peers, *Ramon Lull* (London: Society for Promoting Christian Knowledge, 1929).

    Editor's note: But *see* Anthony Bonner, *op. cit.,* according to which the circumstances of Lull's death remain unknown.

103. *Juan de Herrera, Arquitecto Constructor del Monasterio de El Escorial. Discurso de la Figura Cubica* (subtitle *Tratado del Cuerpo Cúbico, conforme a los principios y opiniones del ''Arte'' de Raimundo Lulio/ hecho por Juan de Herrera/ Arquitecto y aposentador mayor del Rey don Felipe II*), ed., with a prologue by Julio Rey Pastor (Madrid: Editorial Plutarco, 1935), from one of the two Escorial mss.

104. Many a thoughtful and earnest mind in the past and in recent times has attempted to penetrate and explicate—who knows how successfully?—the meaning, the impact, and the function of these configurations. Though too concise, the most lucid among the older résumés would be that of Herrera in his *Discurso.* Among the modern: I. Borras, *Sistema Cientifico Luliano. Esposicion y Critica* (Palma: 1916); S. Bove, *El Sistema Cientifico Luliano, Ars Magna* (Barcelona: 1908); Antonio Reyes, *El Racionalismo Averroista y el Razonamiento Luliano* (Madrid: 1935);

R.D F. Pring-Mill, *El Microcosmos Lul•lia* (Palma: 1961); Enrique de Antón, ''La Actualidad de Raimundo Lulio,'' *Revista de Filosofía del Instituto Luis Vives, XVII,* No. 64 (Madrid: 1953); Tomás Carreras y Artau and Joaquín Carreras y Artau, *Historia de la filosofía española; filosofía cristiana de los Siglos XIII al XV* (Madrid, Real academia de ciencias exactas, físicas y naturales: 1939–43) I, on Ramon Lull, pp. 233–531, and II on Lullism; Joaquin Carreras y Artau, ''El Lul•lism de Juan de Herrera, L'Arquitecte de L'Escorial'' in *Miscel-lania Puig i Cadafalch* (Barcelona: Societat Catalana d'Estudis Històrics, 1951), I, pp. 41–60; and especially Joaquín Xirau, *Vida y Obra de Ramón Lull, Filosofía y Mística* (Mexico: Editorial ''Orion,'' 1946).

Editor's note: Had Léo Bronstein lived to see Anthony Bonner's *Selected Works of Ramon Llull, op. cit.,* he would surely have given it a prominent place in this list.

105. Herrera's *Discurso,* Julio Rey Pastor, ed., *op. cit.,* p, 29.

106. *Ibid. See* pp. 32–33.

107. *See* text page 30, Footnote 13.

108. ''MANDALA. A ritual or magic circle. In Tibet, a diagram used in invocations,meditation and temple services. . . . '' *A Buddhist Students' Manual,* Christmas Humphreys, ed. (London: The Buddhist Society, 1956), p. 156.

109. Henry R. Zimmer, ''Śri-Yantra and Śiva-Trimūrti'', *The Review of Religion* (New York: Columbia University Press, November 1943), pp. 9–10.

110. *Ibid.,* p. 10.

111. Tomás Carreras y Artau and Joaquín Carreras y Artau, *op. cit.,* I, p. 234.

112. *See* William M. Ivins, Jr., *Art and Geometry* (Cambridge, Mass.: Harvard University Press, 1946), pp. 87–88.

113. *See* Francisco Javier Sanchez Cantón, *La Librería de Juan de Herrera* (Madrid: Consejo Superior de Investigaciones Científicas Instituto Diego Velázquez, 1941).

114. In the first part of his treatise Herrera gives a lucid Euclidian-Lullian demonstration of this genesis and structure; the second part he devotes to their metaphysical implications.

115. Indeed, he was a convinced Lullist all his life. It was probably one of the reasons for the predilection of the King—a Lullist himself—for Herrera, at that time a still obscure architect and mathematician. Philip's Lullism was probably inherited by him from the cultural tradition of the Spanish court prevailing since the days of the Catholic Monarchs and Cardinal Cisneros' activity. In I582, from Lisbon, Philip II ordered the opening in Madrid of the Academy of Mathematics under the direction of Juan de Herrera, who was also appointed head of the Academy's Department of Lullian Studies. Herrera's private library included more than a hundred works of Lull in manuscripts and books, in Catalan, Latin and Arabic.

116. This and the following quotations from Herrera's *Discurso* are found in Julio Rey Pastor, *op. cit.*, pp. 26 ff., *trans.* Léo Bronstein. The Spanish texts appear below:

''Pero el Señor, en quien está toda la plenitud de sabiduría''—thus starts the *Discurso*—''abre a veces los entendimientos de los que poco saben, y les hace decir algunas cosas, que penetradas y rumiadas bien y no a sobre peine como algunas veces se suele hacer, se hallan en ellas, aunque en sí parescen pocas, grandes y subidos misterios y secretos difíciles de calar . . . y entre ellas entiendo ser una la figura cúbica, raíz y fundamento de la dicha Arte luliana.''
'' . . . y el Are [*agente* in Herrera's own definition] juntamente con el *Tivum* [*agible*] y con el Bile [*agere*] son el cubo o plenitud total de ser y obrar . . . y entonces hay en el cubo relación ternal, que es el Tivum, Bile y Are de Raimundo, los cuales son de la esencia y natura del mismo cubo, en el cual hay plenitud y cumplimiento total de diferencias plenitudinales, sin falta ni sobra. . . .

''Hemos ido declarando el cubo así en la cuantidad discreta [the cube as a numerical-arithmetical entity] como en la cuantidad continua [cube as a geometric entity] y de aquí adelante se procurará probar cómo en todas las cosas está el cubo, en lo natural como natural, en lo moral como moral [moral cube!] . . . y que está, trosí, en cada uno de los 9 principios absolutos y relatos de Raimundo y otros cualquier principios que fuera de estos pudieren dar. . . .
'' . . . la plenitud total de la mixtión y operación consiste en estar todos cúbicamente llenos. . . . ''

117. Marcelino Menéndez y Pelayo, *op. cit.*, *trans.* Léo Bronŝtein.

118. Théophile Gautier quoted in George Kubler and Martin Soria, *op. cit.*, p. 13.

# *Notes on Illustrations*

half 5th c. B.C., Olympia Museum. Upper part, except for head of bull, cast from original now in the Louvre.

20. Praxiteles, Apollo with Lizard, *ca.* 350–325 B.C. Roman copy, bronze statuette now in Villa Albani, Rome. The lost original was listed with the bronze works of Praxiteles. 33

21. "Vénus Accroupie." Marble copy, Roman imperial period. Original Greek bronze, probably late 3rd c. B.C. Now in the Louvre. 33

22. Head of a girl, school of Praxiteles, 4th c. B.C. The "Bartlett" head, Museum of Fine Arts, Boston. 35

23. Head of Lapith woman, western pediment, Temple of Zeus, Olympia, 1st half 5th c. B.C. Now in Olympia Museum. 36

24. Hittite Thunder God seated on lion pedestal. Basalt, H. ca. 63 in. (*ca.* 161 cm.), from Carchemish, 1050–850 B.C. Statue of god now destroyed. Lion pedestal in Museum of Archaeology, Ankara; one lion's head in British Museum, London. 40

25. Mycerinus and Queen. Egyptian, from Giza, Dynasty IV, 2599–2571 B.C., slate schist, H. 54½ in. Now in Museum of Fine Arts, Boston. 41

26. Façade, Santa Maria del Pí, Barcelona. *See* Footnote 17. 44

27a. Façade, Notre-Dame-la-Grande, Poitiers. The original church was rebuilt at the end of the 11th c. and remodelled in the 15th and 16th. 45

27b. Detail of façade, Cathedral of St. Pierre, Angoulême. Built 1105–28; restored 1630–54, the cathedral was rebuilt in 1866. Despite the modern addition of turrets and pediment, the form and sculptures of the façade retain their Romanesque features. 46

28. Façade, Cathedral of St. Pierre, Angoulême. *See* Note 27b. 47

48. Horsemen, the Parthenon frieze, *ca.* 440–38 B.C. Now in the British Museum, London. 84

49. Personification of Lust, fresco, 12th c., in the crypt, Saint-Nicolas, Tavant (Indre-et-Loire). 87

50. Scenes from the life of Moses, detail: the crossing of the Red Sea. Fresco, *ca.* 1100, vault of the nave, Saint-Savin-sur-Gartempe (Vienne). 89

51. W. DeBrailes, Bible illustrations, 13th c., England. Now in The Walters Art Gallery, Baltimore.
    a) The Red Sea overwhelms Pharaoh and his army, folio 11. 89
    b) The Flood, folio 3. 90
    c) Lot and his family leaving Sodom, folio 4. 91

52a. Kiss of Judas, fresco, 12th c., St. Martin de Vic, Nohant-Vicq, central France. 92

52b. The Visitation, fresco, 12th c., St. Martin de Vic, Nohant-Vicq, central France. 92

53. Giotto, Kiss of Judas, *ca.* 1305, Scrovegni chapel, Padua. 93

54. Eros holding scale, center of three-sided relief, ''Boston Throne,'' marble, *ca.* 460 B.C., Greece, now in Museum of Fine Arts, Boston. 96

55. Aphrodite, center of three-sided relief, ''Ludovisi Throne,'' marble, second quarter 5th c. B.C., now in Museo Nazionale, Rome. 97

56a. *Kouros* with lyre, side of ''Boston Throne.'' *See* Note 54. 99

56b. *Kore* with flute, side of ''Ludovisi Throne.'' *See* Note 55. 99

56c. Young woman, side of ''Ludovisi Throne.'' *See* Note 55. 101

56d. Old woman, ''Boston Throne.'' *See* Note 54. 101

57. Gaudí, detail of towers, Sagrada Familia church, Barcelona. The church (begun 1884, and, after 102

87a. Francisco José de Goya y Lucientes, 1746–1828, Dog in Sand, painting, late work from the Finca del Sordo. Now in the Prado, Madrid. 164

87b. Francisco José de Goya y Lucientes, 3rd of May (1808), painted 1814, the Prado, Madrid. 165

88a. Juan de Valdés Leal, 1622–90, Friar Fernández Yáñez de Figueroa, or, de Caceres, detail, *ca.* 1656–57. [Formerly identified as Apparition of the Virgin of Guadalupe to Friar Gonzalo de Illescas. *See* Duncan Theobald Kinkead's *Juan de Valdés Leal (1622–1690) His Life and Work,* Garland Publishing, Inc., New York and London, 1978, for evidence that Fr. Gonzalo did not have a vision of the Virgin of Guadalupe but that she appears in the painting because Fr. Fernández was the founder of the Hieronymite monastery at Guadalupe.] From the monastery of San Jerónimo de Buenivista outside of Seville, now in the Museo de Bellas Artes, Seville. 168

88b. Juan de Valdés Leal and workshop, Saint Ignatius receiving the bull for the founding of the Jesuit Order from Pope Paul III, detail, *ca.* 1675. Museo de Bellas Artes, Seville. 170

89. Francisco José de Goya y Lucientes, 1746–1828, Last Communion of San José de Calasanz, painted 1819, church of San Antonio Abad, Madrid. 171

90. Goya, Last Communion, detail. *See* Note 89. 172

91. Saint Peter and Saint Paul, detail of Apostolado, stone, last quarter 12th c., Camara Santa, Oviedo Cathedral. 173

92. St. John, wood, fragment in sacristy, 2nd quarter 12th c., ex-Cathedral of Roda de Isábena, Huesca. 174

93. Altar angel, detail, stone, 12th c., San Martin de Mondoñedo (Lugo). 174

94. "Doncel of Sigüenza," detail, tomb of Martín Vázquez de Arce, last quarter 15th c., in chapel of Santa Catalina, Cathedral of Sigüenza. 175

105. Gregorio Hernández (or Fernández), 1556–1636, Saint Francis Xavier, detail, polychrome wood sculpture, 1613, church of San Miguel, Valladolid. 190

106. Manuel Pereira of Portugal, d.1667, Saint Bruno, detail, 1635 or soon after, polychrome wood, from the chapel of St. Bruno in the Cartuja de Miraflores, near Burgos. Philip IV said of this figure ''he does not speak, but only because he is a Carthusian monk.'' 190

107. Juan Martínez Montañés, 1568–1649, Saint Bruno, *ca.* 1627, polychrome wood, from the Cartuja de las Cuevas. Now in Museo de Bellas Artes, Seville. 191

108. Alonso Cano, 1601–67, unfinished bust of Adam, one of Cano's last works, polychrome oak, Cathedral of Granada. 191

109a. Pedro de Mena y Medrano, 1628–93, Saint Francis of Assisi, polychrome wood, detail, *ca.* 1663. Treasury of the Cathedral of Toledo. 192

109b. Pedro de Mena y Medrano, The Penitent Magdalen, polychrome wood, 1664. National Museum of Sculpture, Valladolid. 193

110a. Francisco Salzillo Alcaraz (sometimes called Zarcillo), 1707–83, Dolorosa, detail of a *paso* (a group of figures carried in the Holy Week procession), polychrome wood, 1755–56, from the Ermita de Jesús, Murcia. Now in Murcia's Museo Salzillo. 194

110b. Francisco Salzillo Alcaraz, Judas Iscariot, detail from The Last Supper, *paso,* polychrome wood, 1763, from the Ermita de Jesús, Murcia. Now in Murcia's Museo Salzillo. 195

111. Seated Virgin, mural painting, 12th c., apse, Santa María de Tahull (in Catalan, Santa Maria de Taüll). Now in Museum of Catalan Art, Barcelona. 196

112. Pantocrator, mural painting, 12th c., apse, San Clemente de Tahull (in Catalan, Sant Climent de Taüll). Now in Museum of Catalan Art, Barcelona. 197

# *Credits*

We gratefully thank the following sources of our illustrations:

Ampliaciones y Reproduciones, MAS, Barcelona:
Plates 1, 4, 10, 26, 29b, 31, 32, 34a, 34b, 35, 36, 37, 38, 39a, 39b, 40, 57, 87a, 87b, 88a, 88b, 89, 90, 94, 95, 96, 99, 100, 101, 102, 104a, 104b, 105, 106, 107, 108, 109a, 109b, 110a, 110b, 111, 112, 113, 114, 116, 117, 118, 119a, 119b, 120, 125a, 125b, 130, 131, 132, 133, 138,139a, 139b, 140, 151, 152, 153, 154, 155, 156.

Alinari/Art Resource, New York:
Plates 2, 20, 53, 74, 75, 77a, 86a, 86b.

Giraudon/Art Resource, New York:
Plates 3, 7, 27a.

SCALA/Art Resource, New York:
Plates 60a, 71b, 97a, 97b.

Bibliothèque Nationale, Paris:
Plate 5.

Courtesy Annika Barbarigos:
Plates 6, 8, 14b, 15a, 15b, 16, 67a, 67b, 67c, 67d, 70, 71a, 72a, 72b, 78b, 79, 80, 81, 82.

Georges de Miré, from Pierre de la Coste-Messelière, *The Treasures of Delphi,* Editions du Chêne, Paris, 1945:
Plates 9a, 9b, 11, 12, 13.

Max Hirmer, courtesy Hirmer Verlag, Munich:
Plates 14a, 17a, 17b, 17c, 17d, 18, 24, 48, 66.

Walter Hege, courtesy Deutscher Kunstverlag G.m.b.H., Berlin:
Plates 19, 23, 141.

Courtesy Columbia University Press, New York:
Plates 21, 150.

Museum of Fine Arts, Boston:
Plates 22, 25, 54, 56a, 56d, 103a.

© Arch. Photo SPADEM, Paris/VAGA, New York:
Plates 27b, 28, 44b, 44c, 52a, 52b.

Friedrich Rahlves, courtesy Éditions Arthaud, Paris:
Plate 29a.

Elizabeth Römmelt, Munich:
Plate 30.

Enric Grass, courtesy Xavier Grass, Grass Scientific Editions, Barcelona:
Plate 33a.

Courtesy B.T. Batsford, Ltd., London:
Plate 33b.

Metropolitan Museum of Art, New York, Rogers Fund, 1947:
Plates 41, 42, 43.

Arthur Kingsley Porter, courtesy Hacker Art Books, New York:
Plates 44a, 91, 92, 93.

Courtesy Societé Française du Livre, Paris:
Plate 45.

Archives Éditions Arthaud, Paris:
Plate 46.

Courtesy Oriental Institute, University of Chicago Press:
Plate 47.

Éditions Albert Skira, S.A., Geneva:
Plates 49, 50, 63, 69, 73.

Courtesy Walters Art Gallery, Baltimore:
Plate 51.

Soprintendenza Archaeologica di Roma, Rome:
Plates 55, 56b, 56c.

Courtesy Amiens Municipal Library:
Plate 58.

From N.P. Kondakov, *The Russian Icon,* Seminarium Kondakovianum, Prague, 1928, Plate XLV:
Plate 59.

National Gallery, London:
Plate 60b.

© SPADEM, Paris/VAGA, New York:
Plates 61, 98.

From Shichi Tajima, *Masterpieces Selected from the Fine Arts of the Far East,* The Shimba-Shoin Press, Tokyo, 1910, vol. 8, Plate XXX:
Plate 62.

Courtesy F. Bruckmann, Munich:
Plate 64.

Dumbarton Oaks Center for Byzantine Studies, Washington, D.C.:
Plates 65, 83, 84, 85.

Courtesy Vatican Library, Vatican City:
Plate 68.

Courtesy Pericles Papachatsidakis, Athens:
Plates 76a, 76b, 78a.

Courtesy University of Chicago Press:
Plate 77b.

The Norton Simon Foundation, F.72.6.P., Pasadena:
Plate 103b.

Courtesy The Prado, Madrid:
Plate 115.

Courtesy Phaidon Press, London:
Plates 121, 122.

Cliché des Museés Nationaux, Paris:
Plate 123.

Courtesy Wadsworth Atheneum, Hartford, The Ella Gallup Sumner & Mary Catlin Sumner Fund:
Plate 124.

Eleanor L. Wolff:
Plates 126, 146a, 146b.

Courtesy Academia Nacional de Belas-Artes, Lisbon:
Plates 127a, 127b, 127c, 129.

Courtesy Portuguese Tourist Board, New York:
Plate 128.

Collection of the author:
Plate 134.

Kermani:
Plate 135.

Hans C. Seherr-Thoss:
Plate 136.

Arthur Upham Pope:
Plates 137, 144, 145, 147a, 147b.

Courtesy Derek Hill:
Plates 142, 143.

Courtesy Trabájos Aereos Fotogrametricos, S.L. (TAF):
Plate 148.

Courtesy Minerva G.m.b.H., Frankfurt/Main:
Plates 149a, 149b.

We thank the following for adding to the above credits their courteous consent to use photos of works in their possession:

Museum of Catalan Art:
Plates 1, 4, 111, 112, 120.

Republic of Greece, Ministry of Culture and Sciences:
Plates 8, 15a, 15b, 17c, 17d, 18, courtesy National Archaeological Museum, Athens.
Plates 14b, 16, courtesy Acropolis Museum, Athens.
Plate 17a, courtesy Heraklion Museum, Crete.
Plates 19, 23, 141, courtesy Olympia Museum, Olympia.

Valentine de France (for her late father, Georges de Miré):
Plates 9a, 9b, 11, 12, 13.

The Glyptothek, Munich:
Plate 14a.

Prähistorische Staatssammlung, Munich:
Plate 30.

Musée Rolin, Autun:
Plate 44c.

Trustees of The British Museum:
Plate 48.

Museo Nazionale Romano, Rome:
Plates 55, 56b, 56c.

Tate Gallery, London:
Plate 61.

Art, Prints and Photographs Division, The New York Public Library, Astor, Lenox and Tilden Foundations:
Plate 62.

Vatican Library, Vatican City:
Plate 63.

Byzantine Museum, Athens:
Plates 72a, 72b.

The Prado, Madrid:
Plates 87a, 87b, 114, 116.

Museo de Bellas Artes, Seville, and The Ministry of Culture, Madrid:
Plates 88a, 88b, 107.

Museu Nacional Arqueologic, Tarragona:
Plate 95.

National Archaeological Museum, Madrid:
Plate 96.

Picasso Museum, Barcelona:
Plate 98.

Norton Simon Museum of Art at Pasadena:
Plate 103b.

National Museum of Sculpture, Valladolid, and The Ministry of Culture, Madrid:
Plates 104a, 104b, 109b.

Editora Nacional, and Museo Salzillo, Murcia, and The Ministry of Culture, Madrid:
Plates 110a, 110b.

Episcopal Museum, Vich:
Plates 119a, 119b.

Museu Nacional de Arte Antiga, Lisbon:
Plates 121, 122.

The Louvre:
Plate 123.

The Hermitage Museum, St. Petersburg:
Plate 134.

Courtesy Jay Gluck:
Plates 135, 136, 137, 144, 145, 147a, 147b.

Patrimonio Nacional, Madrid:
Plates 151, 152, 153, 154.